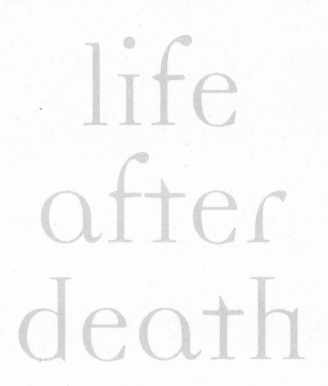

life
after
death

life after death

eighteen years on death row

DAMIEN ECHOLS

First published in the United States of America in 2012 by Blue Rider Press, an imprint of the Penguin Group Inc.

First published in Great Britain in 2013 by Atlantic Books, an imprint of Atlantic Books Ltd.

10 9 8 7 6 5 4 3 2 1

A CIP catalogue record for this book is available from the British Library.

Trade paperback ISBN: 978 1 78239 122 7

OME paperback ISBN: 978 1 78239 211 8

E-book ISBN: 978 1 78239 123 4

Printed in Great Britain by TJ International Ltd, Padstow, Cornwall

Atlantic Books
An Imprint of Atlantic Books Ltd
Ormond House
26–27 Boswell Street
London
WC1N 3JZ

www.atlantic-books.co.uk

for Lorri

Silently I sit by
Watching men pace their cells
Like leopards

Biting their nails
With furrowed brows
The scene speaks for itself

—Damien Echols,
Varner Super Maximum
Security Unit,
Grady, Arkansas

What you're about to read is the result of many things I've written in the past twenty years, including parts of a short memoir self-published in 2005. I was sent to Death Row in 1994, and almost immediately I began keeping a journal. I didn't date most of my writings, it was simply too painful to look at days, months, years slipping past, the reality outside just beyond my reach. Many of the journals I kept are gone, stolen or destroyed when guards raided the barracks—anything personal or creative is a prime target in a shakedown. I've included as much as I could of what remained, and I hope the subject or context of these entries is helpful in placing some of them. Others don't need a time stamp. The conditions I have described in the prison system—the sadness, horror, and sheer absurdity that I've seen many human beings subjected to—will not have changed by the time you hold this book in your hands.

life
after
death

Saint Raymond Nonnatus, never was it known that anyone who implored your help or sought your intercession was left unaided. To you I come, before you I stand. Despise not my petitions, but in your mercy hear and answer me."

Saint Raymond Nonnatus is one of my patron saints. I would be willing to bet that most people have no idea that he is the patron saint of those who have been falsely accused. I like to think that means I have a special place in his heart, because you can't get much more falsely accused than I have been. So me and old Raymond have struck a bargain. If he helps me out of this situation, then I will travel to all the world's biggest cathedrals and leave roses and chocolate at the feet of every one of his statues that I can find. You didn't know saints liked chocolate? Well then, that's one thing you've already learned, and we're just getting started!

I have three patron saints in all. You may be wondering who the other two are, and how a foul-mouthed sinner such as myself was blessed with not one but three saints to watch over him. My second patron saint is Saint Dismas. He's the patron saint of prisoners. So far he's done his job and watched over me. I've got no complaints there. So, what deal do Saint Dismas and I have? Just that I do my part by going to Mass every week in the prison chapel, unless I have a damn good reason not to.

My third patron saint is one I've had reason to talk with many times in my life. Saint Jude, patron saint of desperate situations. I'd say being on Death Row for something I didn't do is pretty desperate. And what does Saint Jude get? He just likes to watch and see what ridiculous predicament I find myself in next.

If I start to believe that the things I write cannot stand on their own merit, then I will lay down my pen. I'm often plagued by thoughts that people will think of me only as either someone on Death Row or someone who used to be on Death Row. I grow dissatisfied when I think of people reading my words out of a morbid sense of curiosity. I want people to read what I write because it means something to them—either it makes them laugh, or it makes them remember things they've forgotten and that once meant something to them, or it simply touches them in some way. I don't want to be an oddity, a freak, or a curiosity. I don't want to be the car wreck that people slow down to gawk at.

If someone begins reading because they want to see life from a perspective different from their own, then I would be content. If someone reads because they want to know what life looks like from where I stand, then I will be happy. It's the ghouls that make me feel ill and uneasy—the ones who care nothing for me, but interest themselves only in things like people who are on Death Row. Those people give off the air of circling vultures, and there's something unhealthy about them. They wallow in depression and their lives tend to follow a downward trend. Their spirits seem mostly dead, like larvae festering on summer-day roadkill. I want nothing to do with that energy. I want to create something of lasting beauty, not a grotesque freak show exhibit.

Writing these stories is also a catharsis for me. It's a purge. How could a man be subjected to the things I have been and not be haunted? You can't send a man to Vietnam and not expect him to have flashbacks, can you? This is the only means I have of clearing the trauma out of my psyche. There are no hundred-dollar-an-hour therapy sessions available for me. I have no need of Freud and his Oedipal theories; just give me a pen and paper.

I've witnessed things in this place that have made me laugh and things that have made me cry. The environment I live in is so warped that incidents that would become legends in the outside world are forgotten the next day. Things that would show up in newspaper headlines in the outside world are given no more than a passing glance behind these filthy walls. When I first arrived at the Tucker Maximum Security Unit located in Tucker, Arkansas, in 1994, it blew my mind. After being locked down for more than ten years, I've become "penitentiary old," and the sights no longer impress me as much. To add the preface of "penitentiary" to another word redefines it. "Penitentiary old" can mean anyone thirty or older. "Penitentiary rich" means a man who has a hundred dollars or more. In the outside world a thirty-year-old man with a hundred dollars

3

would be considered neither old nor rich—but in here it's a whole 'nother story.

The night I arrived on Death Row I was placed in a cell between the two most hateful old bastards on the face of the earth. One was named Jonas, the other was Albert. Both were in their late fifties and had seen better days physically. Jonas had one leg, Albert had one eye. Both were morbidly obese and had voices that sounded like they had been eating out of an ashtray. These two men hated each other beyond words, each wishing death upon the other.

I hadn't been here very long when the guy who sweeps the floor stopped to hand me a note. He was looking at me in a very odd way, as if he were going to say something but then changed his mind. I understood his behavior once I opened the note and began reading. It was signed "Lisa," and it detailed all the ways in which "she" would make me a wonderful girlfriend, including "her" sexual repertoire. This puzzled me, as I was incarcerated in an all-male facility and had seen no one who looked like they would answer to the name of Lisa. There was a small line at the bottom of the page that read, "P.S. Please send me a cigarette." I tossed the note in front of Albert's cell and said, "Read this and tell me if you know who it is." After less than a minute I heard a vicious explosion of cursing and swearing before Albert announced, "This is from that old whore, Jonas. That punk will do anything for a cigarette." Thus Lisa turned out to be an obese fifty-six-year-old man with one leg. I shuddered with revulsion.

It proved true that Jonas would indeed do anything for ciga-

4

rettes. He was absolutely broke, with no family or friends to send him money, so he had no choice but to perform tricks in order to feed his habits. He was severely deranged, and I believe he also liked the masochism it involved. For example, he once drank a sixteen-ounce bottle of urine for a single, hand-rolled cigarette. I'd be hard-pressed to say who suffered more—Jonas, or the people who had to listen to him gagging and retching as it went down. Another time he stood in the shower and inserted a chair leg into his anus as the entire barracks looked on. His reward was one cigarette. These weren't even name-brand cigarettes, but generic, hand-rolled tobacco that cost about a penny each.

As I've hinted, Jonas was none too stable in the psychological department. This is a man whose false teeth were painted fluorescent shades of pink and purple, and who crushed up the lead in colored pencils in order to make eye shadow. The one foot he had left was ragged and disgusting, with nails that looked like corn chips. One of his favorite activities was to simulate oral sex with a hot sauce bottle. He once sold his leg (the prosthetic one) to another inmate, then told the guards that the inmate had taken it from him by force. The inmate got revenge by putting rat poison in Jonas's coffee. The guards figured out something was wrong when Jonas was found vomiting blood. He was the single most reviled man on Death Row, hated and shunned by every other inmate. A veritable prince of the correctional system. You don't encounter many gentlemen in here, but Jonas stood out even in this environment.

I do not wish to leave you with the impression that Albert was a gem, either. He was constantly scheming and scamming. He once wrote a letter to a talk show host, claiming that he would reveal where he had hidden other bodies if the host would pay him a thousand dollars. Being that he had already been sentenced to death in both Arkansas and Mississippi, he had nothing to lose. When he was finally executed, he left me his false teeth as a memento. He left someone else his glass eye.

For all the insanity that takes place inside the prison, it's still nothing compared with the things you see and hear in the yard. In 2003, all Arkansas Death Row inmates were moved to a new "Super Maximum Security" prison in Grady, Arkansas. There really is no yard here. You're taken, shackled of course, from your cell and walked through a narrow corridor. It leads to the "outside," where without once actually setting foot outside the prison walls, you're locked inside a tiny, filthy concrete stall, much like a miniature grain silo. There is one panel of mesh wire about two feet from the top of one wall that lets in the daylight, and you can tell the outdoors is beyond, but you can't actually see any of it. There's no interaction with other prisoners, and you're afraid to breathe too deeply for fear of catching a disease of some sort. I went out there one morning, and in my stall alone there were three dead and decaying pigeons, and more feces than you can shake a stick at. The smell reminds me of the lion house at the Memphis Zoo, which I would visit as a child. When you first enter you have to fight against your gag reflex. It's a filthy business, trying to get some exercise.

Before we moved here we had a real yard. You were actually outside, in the sun and air. You could walk around and talk to other people, and there were a couple of basketball hoops. Men sat around playing checkers, chess, dominoes, or doing push-ups. A few would huddle in corners smoking joints they bought from the guards.

I'd been there less than two weeks when one day on the yard my attention was drawn to another prisoner who had been dubbed "Cathead." This unsavory character had gained the name because that's exactly what he looked like. If you were to catch an old, stray tomcat and shave all the fur off its head you would be looking at the spitting image of this fellow. Cathead was sitting on the ground, soaking up the sun and chewing a blade of grass that dangled from the corner of his mouth. He was staring off into space as if absorbed in profound thought. I had been walking laps around the yard and taking in the scenery. As I passed Cathead for the millionth time he looked up at me (actually it was more like he was seeing some other place, but his head turned in my direction) and he asked, "You know how you keep five people from raping you?" I was caught off guard, as this was not a question I had ever much considered, or thought I'd ever be called upon to answer. I looked at this odd creature, waiting for the punch line to what I was hoping was a joke. He soon answered his own question: "Just tighten your ass cheeks and start biting." I was horrified. He was dead serious, and seemed to think he was passing on a bit of incredibly well-thought-out wisdom. The only things going through my mind were *What kind of hell have I been sent to? Is this what passes for conversation here?* I quickly went back to walking laps and left Cathead to his ponderings.

Prison is a freak show. Barnum and Bailey have no idea what they're missing out on. I will be your master of ceremonies on a guided tour of this small corner of hell. Prepare to be dazzled and baffled. If the hand is truly quicker than the eye, you'll never know what hit you. I know I didn't.

One

My name is Damien Echols, although it wasn't always. At birth I was different in both name and essence. On December 11, 1974, when I came into the world, I was named Michael Hutchison at the insistence of my father, Joe Hutchison. My mother, Pam, had a different name in mind, but my father would hear none of it. They argued about it for years afterward.

The hospital where I was born still stands in the small run-down town of West Memphis, Arkansas. It's the same hospital where my maternal grandmother, Francis Gosa, died twenty years later. As a child I was jealous of my sister, Michelle, who was lucky enough to be born, two years after me, across the bridge in Memphis, Tennessee. In my youth Memphis always felt like home to me. When we crossed the bridge into Tennessee I had the sensation of being where I belonged and thought it only right that I should have been the one born there. After all, my sister didn't even care where she was born.

My mother and grandmother were both fascinated by the fact that after I had been delivered and the doctor had discharged my mother from the hospital, I was placed in a Christmas stocking for the short journey home. They kept the stocking for years, and I had to hear the story often. I found out later that hospitals all over the country do the same thing for every baby born in the month of December, but this fact seemed to be lost on my mother, and it marked the beginning of a lifetime of denial. After saving the stocking as if it were a valuable family heirloom for seventeen years, it was unceremoniously left behind in a move that was less than well planned.

Other than the stocking I had only one memento saved from childhood—a pillow. My grandmother gave it to me the day I left the hospital, and I slept on it until I was seventeen years old, when it was left behind in the same ill-fated move. I could never sleep without that pillow as a child, as it was my security blanket. By the end it was nothing more than a ball of stuffing housed in a pillowcase that was rapidly disintegrating.

Being born in the winter made me a child of the winter. I was truly happy only when the days were short, the nights were long, and my teeth were chattering. I love the winter. Every year I long for it, look forward to it, even though I always feel as if it's turning me inside out. The beauty and loneliness of it hurts my heart and carries with it all the memories of every winter before. Even now, after having been locked in a cell for years, at the coming of winter I can still close my eyes and feel myself walking the streets as everyone else lies in bed asleep. I remember how the ice sounded as it cracked in the trees every time the wind blew. The air could be so cold that it scoured my throat with each breath, but I would not want to go indoors and miss the magick of it. I have two definitions for the word "magick." The first is knowing that I can effect change through my own will, even behind these bars; and the other meaning is more experiential—seeing beauty for a moment in the midst of the mundane. For a split second, I realize completely and absolutely that the season of winter is sentient, that there is an intelligence behind it. There's a tremendous amount of emotional pain that comes with the magick of winter, but I still mourn when the season ends, like I'm losing my best friend.

The first true memories I have of my life are of being with my grandmother Francis, whom I called Nanny. Her husband, Slim Gosa, had died about a year before. I recall him vaguely: he drove a Jeep, and I remember him being very nice to me. He died the day after my birthday. Nanny wasn't my biological grandmother; Slim had had an affair with a Native American woman, who gave birth to my mother. My grandmother, unable to have her own children, raised my mother as her own. My parents, sister, and I had been living in different places in the Delta region—the corner where Arkansas, Tennessee, and Mississippi meet. After my sister was born, my mother felt she couldn't take care of two children. So Nanny and I lived in a small mobile home trailer in Senatobia, Mississippi. I remember the purple and white trailer sitting on top of a hill covered with pine trees. We had two large black dogs named Smokey and Bear, which we had raised from puppies. One of my earliest memories was of hearing the dogs barking and lunging against their chains like madmen as Nanny stood in the backyard with a pistol, shooting at a poisonous snake. She didn't stop shooting, even as the snake slithered its way under the huge propane tank in the backyard. Only in hindsight, years later, did I realize she would have blown us all straight to hell if she had hit the tank. At the time I was so young that I viewed the entire scene with nothing but extreme curiosity. It was the first time I had ever seen a snake, and it was combined with the additional spectacle of my grandmother charging out the back door, blazing away like a gunslinger.

My grandmother worked as a cashier at a truck stop, so during the day she left me at a day care center. I can remember it only because it was horrific. I remember being dropped off so early in the morning that it was still dark, and being led to a room in which other children were sleeping on cots. I was given a cot and told that I should take a nap until *Captain Kangaroo* (my favorite television show) came on. The problem was that I could not, under any circumstances, go to sleep without my pillow and security blanket. I began to scream and cry at the top of my lungs, tears running down my face. It awakened and frightened every other child in the dark room, so that within a few seconds everyone was crying and screaming while frantic day care workers ran from cot to cot in an attempt to find out what was wrong. By the time they got everyone quiet and dried all the tears it was time for *Captain Kangaroo* and I was quickly absorbed into the epic saga of Mr. Green Jeans and a puppet moose that lived life in perpetual fear of being pelted with a storm of Ping-Pong balls. After that day, my grandmother never forgot to send my pillow with me.

She would recite the same rhyme every night as she tucked me into bed. She'd say, "Good night, sleep tight, don't let the bedbugs bite." I had no idea what a bedbug was, but it seemed pretty obvious from the rhyme that they were capable of inflicting pain. As she closed the door and left me in total darkness, all I could think about were those nocturnal monster insects. I never formed a definite mental image of what they looked like, and somehow that vagueness only made the fear worse. The closest I could come to picturing them was something like stinkbugs with shifty eyes and an evil grin. No matter how tired I was when she tucked me in, the mention of those bugs would wake me up like a dose of smelling salts.

There was something else Nanny used to say that made my hair stand on end. Late at night we would be watching television with all of the lights in the house turned off. The only illumination was the flickering blue glow of the TV screen. She would turn to me and say, "What sound does a scarecrow make?" My eyes would bulge like Halloween caricatures as she looked at me grimly and said, "Hoo! Hoo!" I had no idea what it meant, or why a scarecrow would make the sound of an owl, but for the rest of my life I would never think of one without the other. Later in life those images began to feel like home to me and they brought me comfort. They became symbols of the purest kind of magick, and reminded me of a time when I was safe and loved. There's something about it that can never be put into words, but the sight of a scarecrow now makes my heart swell. It makes me want to cry. The memory of those jovial October scarecrows on southerners' front porches takes me to some other place. Now the scarecrow symbolizes a kind of purity.

Every so often, sitting here in solitary confinement, I need to become something else. I need to transform myself and gain a new perspective on reality. When I do, everything must change—

emotions, reactions, body, consciousness, and energy patterns. I turned to Zen out of desperation. I had been through hell, traumatized, and sent to Death Row for a crime I did not commit. My anger and outrage were eating me alive. Hatred was growing in my heart because of the way I was being treated on a daily basis. The cleaner you are, the more light that can shine through you. Clear out all the bad, and the current will float through like light through a windowpane. It's a process I have pushed myself through many times. Each day that I wake up means that I'm one day closer to new life. I can feel the years of accumulated programming and trauma melting away from my body, leaving behind a long-remembered cleanness. I usually have at least a vague idea of what I hope to accomplish or experience—create an art project, explore other realms of consciousness—but this time I'm blindly flowing to wherever the current carries me. I feel younger than I have in the past decade, and memories I had long forgotten are now once again within touching distance.

In the movies it's always the other prisoners you have to watch out for. In real life, it's the guards and the administration. They go out of their way to make your life harder and more stressful than it already is, as if being on Death Row were not enough. They can send a man to prison for writing bad checks and then torment him there until he becomes a violent offender. I didn't want these people to be able to change me, to touch me inside and turn me as rotten and stagnant as they were. I tried out just about every spiritual practice and meditative exercise that might help me to stay sane over the years.

I've lost count of how many executions have taken place during my time served. It's somewhere between twenty-five and thirty, I believe. Some of those men I knew well and was close to. Others, I couldn't stand the sight of. Still, I wasn't happy to see any of them go the way they did.

Many people rallied to Ju San's cause, begging the state to spare his life, but in the end it did no good. He had committed such a heinous crime. Frankie Parker had been a brutal heroin addict who killed his former in-laws and held his ex-wife hostage in an Arkansas police station. Over the years he had become Ju San, an ordained Rinzai Zen Buddhist priest with many friends and supporters. On the night of his execution in 1996, shortly after he was pronounced dead, his teacher and spiritual adviser was allowed to walk down Death Row and greet the convicts. It was the first time that a spiritual adviser had been permitted to speak to inmates after an execution. He told us what Frankie's last word was, what he ate for a last meal, and he described his execution to us.

I had been watching the news coverage of Ju San's death when someone stepped in front of my door. I turned to see a little old bald man in a black robe and sandals, clutching a strand of prayer beads. He had these wild white eyebrows that were so out of control they looked like small horns. He practically had handlebar mustaches above his eyes. He seemed intense and concentrated as he introduced himself. A lot of Protestant preachers come through Death Row, but they all seem to think themselves better than us. You could tell it by the way most of them didn't even bother to shake hands. Kobutsu wasn't like that at all. He made direct, unwavering eye contact and seemed to be genuinely pleased to meet me. It had been his personal mission to do everything he could to help Ju San, and he was pretty torn up over the execution. Before he left, he said I should feel free to write to him at any time. I took him up on that offer.

He and I began corresponding, and I eventually asked him to become my teacher. He accepted. Kobutsu is a paradox: a Zen monk who chain-smokes, tells near-pornographic jokes, and always has an appreciative leer for the female anatomy. He's a holy man, carnival barker, anarchist, artist, friend, and asshole all rolled up in one robe. I immediately took a shine to him.

Kobutsu would send me books about the old Zen masters, different Buddhist practices, and small cards to make shrines out of. He returned not long after Ju San's execution to perform a refuge ceremony for another Death Row inmate, and I was allowed to participate in the ceremony. Refuge is the Buddhist equivalent of baptism. It's like declaring your intention to follow this path, so that the world witnesses it. It was a beautiful ceremony that stirred something in my heart.

Under Kobutsu's tutelage, I began sitting zazen meditation on a daily basis. Zazen meditation entails sitting quietly, focusing on nothing but your breath, moving in and out. At first it was agony to have to sit still and stare at the floor for fifteen minutes. Over time I became more accustomed to it, and managed to increase my sitting time to twenty minutes a day. I put away all reading material except for Zen texts and meditation manuals. I'd read nothing else for the next three years.

About six months after the other prisoner's refuge ceremony,

Kobutsu returned to perform it for me. The magick this ritual held within it increased my determination to practice tenfold. I started every day with a smile on my face, and not even the guards got to me. I think it was a little unsettling to them to strip-search a man who smiled at you through the whole ordeal.

Kobutsu and I continued to correspond through letters and also talked on the phone. His conversations were a mixture of encouragement, instruction, nasty jokes, and bizarre tales of his latest adventures. Through constant daily practice, my life was definitely improving. I even constructed a small shrine of paper Buddhas in my cell to give me inspiration. I was now sitting zazen meditation for two hours a day and still pushing myself. I'd not yet had that elusive enlightenment experience that I'd heard so much about, and I desperately wanted it.

One year after my refuge ceremony, Kobutsu decided it was time for my Jukai ceremony. Jukai is lay ordination, where one begins to take vows. It's also where you are renamed, to symbolize taking on a new life and shedding the old one. Only the teacher decides when you are ready to receive Jukai.

My ceremony would be performed by Shodo Harada Roshi, one of the greatest living Zen masters on earth. He was the abbot of a beautiful temple in Japan, and would fly to Arkansas for this occasion. I anticipated the event for weeks beforehand, so much that I had trouble sleeping at night. The morning of the big event I was up before dawn, shaving my head and preparing to meet the master.

Kobutsu was first in line through the door. I could see the light reflecting off his freshly shaved pink head. I also noticed he had abandoned his usual Japanese sandals in favor of a pair of high-top Converse tennis shoes. It was odd to see a pair of sneakers protruding from under the hem of a monk's robe. Behind him walked Harada Roshi. He wore the same style robe as Kobutsu, only it was in pristine condition. Kobutsu tended to have the occasional mustard stain on his, and didn't seem to mind one bit.

Harada Roshi was small and thin, but had a very commanding presence. Despite his warm smile, there was something about him that was very formal in an almost military sort of way. I believe the first word that came to mind when I saw him was "discipline." He seemed disciplined beyond anything a human could achieve, and it greatly inspired me. To this day I still strive to have as much discipline about myself as Harada Roshi. Beneath his warmth and friendliness was a will of solid steel.

We were all led into a tiny room that served as Death Row's chapel. Harada Roshi talked about the difference between Japan and America, about his temple back home, and about how few Asians came to learn at the old temple now; it was mostly Americans who wanted to learn. His voice was low, raspy, and rapid-fire. Japanese isn't usually described as a beautiful language, but I was entranced by it. I dearly wished I could make such poetic, elegant-sounding words come from my own mouth.

Harada Roshi set up a small altar to perform the ceremony. The altar cloth was white silk, and on it was a small Buddha statue, a canvas covered with calligraphy, and an incense burner. We all dropped a pinch of the exotic-smelling incense into the burner as an offering, and then opened our sutra books to begin the proper chants. Kobutsu had to help me turn the pages of my book because the guards made me wear chains on my hands and feet. During the course of the ceremony I was given the name Koson. I loved that name and all it symbolized, and scribbled it everywhere. I was also presented with my rakusu.

A rakusu is made of black cloth, and is suspended from your neck. It covers your hara, which is the energy center about two finger-widths below your belly button. It has two black cloth straps and a wooden ring/buckle. It's sewn in a pattern that looks like a rice paddy would if viewed from the air. It represents the Buddha's robe. This is the only part of my robe the administration would allow me to keep inside the prison. On the inside, Harada Roshi had painted beautiful calligraphy characters that said, "Great effort, without fail, brings great light." It was my most prized possession until the day years later when the prison guards took it from me.

The canvas on the altar was also given to me. Its calligraphy translates to "Moonbeams pierce to the bottom of the pools, yet in the water not a trace remains." I proudly put it on display in my cell.

I ventured into the realm of Zen to gain a handle on my negative emotional states, which I had learned to control to a great extent, but I now approached my practice in a much more aggressive manner. Much like a weight lifter, I continued to pile it on. On weekends I was now sitting zazen meditation for five hours a day. My prayer beads were always in my hand as I constantly chanted mantras. I practiced hatha yoga for at least an hour a day. I became a vegetarian. Still, I did not have a breakthrough Kensho experience. Kensho is a moment in which you see reality with crystal-clear vision, what a lot of people refer to as "enlightenment." I didn't voice my thoughts out loud, but I was beginning to harbor strong suspicions that Kensho was nothing more than a myth.

A teacher of Tibetan Buddhism started coming to the prison once a week to instruct anyone interested. I attended these sessions, which were specifically tailored to be of use to those on Death Row. One practice I and another inmate were taught is called Phowa. It consists of pushing your energy out through the top of your head at the moment of death. It still did not bring about that life-changing moment I was in search of.

Two

My memory really starts to come together and form a narrative once I started school. I can still remember every teacher I ever had, from kindergarten through high school.

My parents, sister, and I moved into an apartment complex called Mayfair in 1979, as far as I recall. We had an upstairs apartment in a long line of identical doors. When I went out to play, I could find my way back home only by peeking in every window until I saw familiar furnishings. My grandmother also moved into an apartment in the complex, one row behind us. This was the year I started kindergarten, and I remember it well.

Mayfair was located in a run-down section of West Memphis, Arkansas, although not nearly as run-down as it would later become. We were in the worst school district in the city, and on the first day I saw that I was one of only two white kids in the entire class. The other was my best friend, Tommy, who also lived in Mayfair. Our teacher was a skinny black woman named Donaldson, and I'd be hard-pressed to find a more hateful adult. She wasn't as bad to the girls, but seemed to harbor an intense hatred for all male children. I honestly don't know how she ever became a teacher, as she seemed to spend all her time racking her brain to come up with new and innovative forms of punishment.

I was very quiet at this age, almost to the point of being invisible. I managed to avoid her wrath most of the time, but twice she noticed me. Once, for a reason I never understood, a girl told her that I had my eyes open during nap time. Every day after lunch we were to pull out our mats, lie on the floor, and sleep for half an hour while the teacher left us alone. No one knew where she went or why. For her it was not enough that we lay still, she wanted us to sleep, and expected us to do so on command. She would appoint one person to be the class snitch while she was gone, and whoever she chose got to sit at the teacher's desk like a god and look out over everyone else sprawled facedown on the floor. The chosen person was always a girl—never a boy.

So one day after lunch I was on the floor as usual, breathing dust and hoping for no spiders. The teacher came back half an hour later and asked the girl at her desk for the daily report—who had and had not been sleeping. The girl pointed straight at me and said, "His eyes were open."

I had not stirred from my mat or made a sound, yet this teacher made me stand before the class as she hit my hands with a ruler. It hurt my hands, true enough, and then there was the shame of having this done in front of the entire class, but the most frightening and traumatic part was the vengeance and hatred with which she carried it out. She was wild and furious, gritting her teeth and grunting with each smack of the accursed ruler. The one other time she noticed me I can't remember what, if anything, I had done wrong.

I do remember the punishment, though, and this time I was not alone. Once again I had to stand before the entire class, this time along with two other boys, and hold a stack of books over my head for half an hour. All three of us stood with our arms straight up in the air, shaking with effort as we held a stack of books aloft. During the entire punishment she howled at us in a rage, saying things like "You're going to learn that I'm not playing a game with you!"

So much for kindergarten.

A couple of strange incidents occurred during this period of my life, both of which I remember vividly, but neither of which I can explain. The first happened while I was still living in the Mayfair apartments.

One evening as dusk approached, my mother told me not to leave the walkway right in front of our apartment door. Being the undisciplined heathen that I was, I beat a hasty departure the moment she was out of sight. I ran around to the very back of the complex, where a huge mound of sand was located, and proceeded to dig a hole with my bare hands. This was one of my favorite activities, in which I invested a huge amount of time as a child. I would get out of bed in the morning, have a bowl of cereal for breakfast, lick the spoon clean, and carry it outside with me. I spent the day digging, nonstop. The front yard looked like a nightmare, and my mother would always step out on the front porch and screech, "Boy, you fill in them holes 'fore somebody breaks an ankle."

I looked up from my digging that evening only to realize it had become completely dark. I could see the streetlights on in the distance, and the night was deathly silent. No crickets chirping, people talking, or cars driving by. Nothing but the silence that comes once the movie is over and the screen goes blank. Knowing that I was now officially in trouble, I dusted myself off and started to make my way back to our apartment.

As I walked home I had to pass a place where two sections of the building came together to form a corner. The last time I had noticed this corner the apartment there was empty. Now it was dark, but the front door was open.

The inside of the apartment was as void of illumination as some sort of vacuum. Standing in the doorway, propped against the frame with his arms folded across his chest, was a man in black pants and no shirt. He had black shoulder-length hair and wore a shit-eating grin. His eyes followed my progress as I passed, until I stood right in front of him. "Where you goin', boy?" he asked in a way that said he was amused, but didn't really expect an answer. I said nothing, just stood looking up at him. "Your mamma's looking for you. You know you're going to get a whipping."

After a moment I continued on my way. When I encountered my mother, she had a switch in one hand and a cigarette in the other. I did indeed receive a whipping.

I didn't think about this incident again until a day or so before I was arrested and put on trial for murder. I was eighteen years old, and the cops had been harassing me nonstop for weeks. My mother asked me one day after lunch, "Why don't you take your shirt off and go in the backyard so I can take pictures? That way, if the cops beat you we'll have some before-and-after photos." Nodding my head, I made a trip to the bathroom, where I took my shirt off. When I looked in the mirror over the sink, it hit me that I looked exactly like the man I'd seen all those years before in the dark apartment.

When I was seven or eight, I saw a man shot in the head. We had moved recently to a two-family house in Memphis. One summer afternoon we left the front door open so a breeze could blow through the house. I was standing right at the threshold looking out at my father, who was standing in the front yard. His hands were in his pockets and he was staring at the ground but not really seeing it. I'd been watching him for a good amount of time and he'd never blinked even once. In his mind he was a million miles away, doing who-knows-what. He did this quite often, but it was different this time. Like an omen.

We heard a small, distant-sounding popping noise, nothing like the gunfire on television. My father later said he first thought it was a car backfiring on the next block. We both looked up at the same time to see a man crossing the street, coming toward us. His hands were holding his head and he was covered in blood.

My father turned toward me and started barking like a Marine drill instructor—"Go! Go! Go! Move your ass!" I retreated into the house with my father right behind me. No sooner had he closed and locked the door than the man hit it running full force. There was a tremendous impact, then nothing. All was quiet. My father stood looking at the door while my mother ran into the room with a scared but questioning look on her face. When he told her what had happened, they stood around trying to figure out what to do next.

We didn't have a phone, so it was decided that my mother would run out the back door and over to the neighbors' house where she would ask to use theirs. The only problem was that the neighbors wouldn't answer the door. My mother stood on the porch hammering and yelling, "We need help! Please let me use your phone!" It was all to no avail, as the neighbors refused to respond. After the cops arrived, the neighbors said it was because they thought my mother had shot my father and was trying to get in to them.

In the meantime, the man smeared blood everywhere. By the time the cops showed up with an ambulance, the man had collapsed on our steps. There were bloody handprints all over the front door and all over our white station wagon. The ambulance drove away with the man in the back while the cops questioned my mom and dad. My paternal grandmother and grandfather, Doris and Ed Hutchison, arrived to take my sister and me away for the night, and tried to keep us from seeing as much of the mess as possible.

My young mind bounced back from the incident without a mark on it. The next day I was able to go back to playing childhood games with all the other kids. There was zero lasting trauma. However, if I were to undergo the exact same experience at my present age I would need counseling for the rest of my life. The nightmares would rob me of precious sleep, and my nerves would be frazzled.

I can't pinpoint exactly when I began to lose my flexibility, my ability to bounce back from an unsettling incident; I can only look back and see that it's gone. Going on trial for a crime I didn't commit screwed me up a bit, no doubt. But I survived it intact, more or less. Don't get me wrong—my heart, soul, body, and mind all have scars that will never properly heal. Still, I survived. I'm not so sure I could do that if the whole thing had happened to me later in life. I believe it would have been entirely possible for me to drop dead of shock and trauma right in the courtroom.

If I hadn't been sent to prison at such a young age there's no way I could ever have adapted to it. Prison is bad enough, but it's a million times worse when you know you did nothing to be here for. That fact magnifies and amplifies the shock and trauma. As it is, I grew up in this place. Perhaps that's what robbed me of my inner flexibility.

I no longer approach each situation in life with an open heart, ready to learn. Instead I come like a wary old man scared of being knocked on his ass again. An old man knows that at his age those bruises don't heal as quickly as they used to. I used to learn as a youth because I was curious. I didn't necessarily even think about learning; it was more like being one of those baby animals you see on the nature shows. They almost learn by accident, just from being wide-eyed and playful. Now I hoard knowledge out of fear. I figure the more I know, the more I'll be able to control a situation and keep from getting hurt again.

I hate it. I hate the signs and symptoms of age I see more and more in myself as each day passes. I'm now the same age that Hank Williams was when he died. Our situations and circumstances made us both old before our time. Don't think me cynical, though. I believe it to be wholly reversible. I believe love can fix damn near anything. Love and iced tea. I just need larger doses of both than I can get in here. Perhaps soon someone will correct this injustice and rescue me from this nightmare. Until then I have no choice but to struggle on as I have been. "Saint Raymond Nonnatus, hear my prayer . . ."

Three

The year, the idea of a year, has become paper-thin. I can almost reach out and tear a hole through it with my fingernail. December is coming. I can feel it waking up. It brings me a haunted place to rest my head and a clearer vision of all I see. The whole world seems to be putting on its holiday trim, and every day that passes is another mile traveled through the ice-cold desert.

When I was in second grade, a friend of Nanny's decided to rent the tiny three-room brick building in her backyard to my family, because her Social Security check wasn't quite enough for her to survive on. In hindsight it strikes me as incredibly odd that someone would have had such a structure in the backyard of a small suburban home. It was more like a bomb shelter.

Someone had wired the place for electricity, and the water worked well enough, but there was no heat. Sometimes it would get so cold in there that the toilet would have ice in it. To keep from freezing to death my mother would turn the oven on as high as it would go and leave the door open. We had a small cat who would hop up onto the oven door and make herself at home by curling into a ball and sleeping.

After a while my mother and father managed to borrow a small portable heater. My mother would stand my sister and me in front of it as we dressed for school in the morning, so that we wouldn't shiver ourselves to pieces. One day as we were getting dressed, my sister backed into the heater. You could hear her shrieking all down the street, a loud, wordless wail of pain. I can still see my mother on her knees, clutching my sister and rocking back and forth as they both sobbed. After things calmed down my mother examined my sister, and nothing looked to be seriously wrong, so we were sent off to school.

As we walked back home that afternoon, the back of my sister's shirt and pants were soaking wet. The parts of her that had touched the heater had blistered during the day, and all the blisters had broken open. When my mother saw it, she started crying again. That year was one of the poorest my family ever lived through.

There was much excitement one day about a week before Christmas when three older men in suits showed up at our door carrying boxes and bags of food. I think they were either Shriners or Masons, but I can't remember. I do remember my mother hugging them all and thanking them over and over while my sister and I ran around their legs like hungry cats, anxious to see what treats were in those sacks. My mother was crying uncontrollably and kept hugging the men. They didn't say much, just told her she was welcome and left as quickly as they came. This was our Christmas dinner. We received gifts from such groups more than once. Most often it was the Salvation Army.

My father was deeply ashamed for having to accept a handout. That's something that gets drilled into the heads of white males in the South from the moment they can speak—never accept anything that you haven't earned for yourself. Having to accept the handout deeply wounded my father in some way that pushed him close to the edge of an emotional cliff. I wasn't old enough to really understand it; I just knew that my dad was acting strange, and that he was chewing his nails so viciously that sometimes it looked like he was going to put his whole hand in his mouth. Now I know it's because a man who accepted a handout wasn't really seen as being much of a man—especially by the man himself. Any man with two working arms and legs who signed up on welfare wasn't seen very differently from a thief, a liar, or a rapist.

In the end I think that's part of what caused my parents' marriage to begin falling apart. The stress of poverty. I usually think of these things around Christmastime. Probably because there was a bag of hard candy in the sacks of food the men brought us, and my grandmother always called it "Christmas candy."

As I grew older I learned to be ashamed of being poor, too. It became humiliating, something I'd do everything I could to hide from the rest of the world. I developed an overwhelming sense of being excluded from everything. Everywhere you look you see people with things that you do not have, and it has a profound mental effect. That's mostly during the teenage years.

Later still, I developed a fierce sense of pride at having come from such situations and circumstances. I look at the people who have done horrible things to me, who have lied about me, abused me, and tried to take my life, and I know they would never have been able to rise above the things that I have. They would have died inside.

I've talked to some of the other guys on Death Row about our lives as children, and they laugh at my poor childhood. I laugh along with them. One guy will say he was poor because he grew up in the projects, and I become outraged. "Poor? You had water! You had heat! You were wearing shoes that cost a hundred dollars! That's not poor! Let me tell you what we had. . . ." Everyone snickers when they hear that certain areas of the trailer park were considered to be where the "rich people" lived. Now that I can look back on it all, it's funny to me, too. I didn't always see the humor in it, though. It's no laughing matter when you have to fight with the roaches to see who gets the cornflakes.

Now I believe my parents just weren't meant to be together. Perhaps they weren't meant to be with anyone, as my father has now been married and divorced several times, and my mother follows closely behind in her number of failed relationships. The trouble between them began when I was in second grade.

Nanny had gotten remarried to a respectable man named Ivan Haynes. He's the one I always remember as being my grandfather on my mother's side of the family. He could be a real asshole sometimes. I could always expect to hear his amused chuckle anytime he witnessed my pain and misfortune. Upon hearing tales of my childhood, some people have speculated that perhaps he didn't like me so much. I don't believe that. There was much love between him and me; he was just doing what comes naturally to members of my family. Laughing and teasing others helps take your mind off your own troubles.

I remember one sunny afternoon when I was about seven years old, and Ivan was sitting on our front porch in a lawn chair, drinking a can of beer. I saw him drink only once or twice a year, and he never consumed anything stronger than Budweiser. For some reason he always dumped a couple spoons of salt into the can before he drank it. He once gave me a tiny sip from his can, and I could taste nothing but salt.

I was playing out in the front yard wearing nothing but a pair of shorts. I was open for attack. "Hey, boy," Ivan called out, blinking like a cat in the sunshine. "Bring me that board over there." He pointed to a piece of plywood lying across the road.

I picked it up unsuspectingly and started to make my way back to the front porch. When the pain came, it seemed to inflame every part of my body at once. I began to shriek and flail about wildly. The pain was so intense that it short-circuited my logic. I spun in circles, slapping myself and stomping my feet, giving voice to one unending scream. The board had been sitting atop a nest of fire ants. This wasn't the first time I'd been bitten, nor would it be the last, although it was the worst and most painful.

What was my grandfather doing while I was going into a frenzy? Sipping his beer and watching me in a half-interested way. My mother came running out of the house and grabbed me up. She already knew what the problem was, and she carried me in to the bathtub to pour cold water over me. As we crossed the porch and passed my grandfather, I heard him chuckle.

I heard that maddening chuckle again after one of his trips to an auction, which he loved. He would go through people's garbage, show up bright and early at every garage sale listed in the local paper, and bid on ungodly amounts of junk at auctions all over the state. He took this rubbish and fixed it up, then sold it at his booth in the flea market.

One day he came home with a box of odds and ends that contained a pair of swim fins, or swimming flippers. They weren't pliant and flexible the way professional-quality fins are. These were as hard as bricks, like petrified frog feet. They would have broken before they bent. My grandfather tossed them to me and said, "Put 'em on and try 'em out."

I carried them out into the backyard, where a four-foot-deep pool had sat for a couple of years. It had never been drained or cleaned since its initial setup, so the water was dark green and disturbing. Odd-looking bugs skimmed along the surface, looking for someone to bite. I did not relish the thought of having to splash about in that muck.

I sat on the rickety ladder and attached the flippers tightly to my feet. Standing on the ladder, I launched myself out into the middle of the pool and began kicking. My efforts were futile, and I quickly found myself thrashing around on the bottom. I began to wonder if perhaps these flippers were made for imaginary swimming and not intended for actual water wear. Whatever the case, I thought, *To hell with this,* and decided to get out. The problem was that I couldn't stand up. The rock-hard plastic flippers made it impossible for me to get my feet under me. Frantic, I managed to get my head above the water one time for what I believed to be my final gasp of air. What sight did I behold as I was drowning? My grandfather, hands on hips, chuckling. Next to him stood my sister, also giggling, as she squinted against the sun. My terror evaporated in the face of the rage that swept through my small body, and I managed to get a hand on the ladder and pull myself up.

For a few moments I could do nothing but cough, sputter, and try to expel the water from my nose, which was making the inside of my head burn like fire. When I could speak, I snatched off the flippers and began to shriek in outrage, putting the finger of accusation on them both. "Stupid! You're both stupid! I'm telling Mom!" I shot into the house like a scalded cat, my grandfather shouting after me, "Don't you drip that water on the rug!"

I found my mother inside folding clothes. In a rush I spit out the entire sordid story, my bare foot stomping in fury. After hearing that my sister and grandfather had stood by laughing as I nearly drowned, she simply continued to fold clothes. Brow furrowed, she lit a cigarette and expelled a stream of noxious gray smoke into the air before suggesting, "Don't put the flippers back on, then." I was dumbfounded and my feelings were hurt. I had expected to be fussed over. Instead, no one took my trauma seriously.

Sometimes my grandfather would pass on bits of strange and highly suspect information to me, often involving the nature of feet. He had lots of time to think on these mysteries, as he spent most of his days sitting quietly in the flea market, waiting for someone to come and offer him a deal on some of his wares. He once obtained several large boxes of socks, which he proceeded to put on display. I hated those socks. There was nothing even remotely interesting about them. I strolled through the flea market inspecting all the other booths, which always held strange and fantastical devices. When you came to my grandfather's booth there was nothing but a bunch of boring socks.

I was eating my usual summertime lunch of a peanut butter and banana sandwich, and washing it down with a Scramble soda, when I started to suspect that all white people were as disdainful of those socks as I was. Every white person who approached the booth seemed to show no interest in the socks, and would almost turn their nose up if my grandfather attempted to draw their attention to his discount hosiery. I also noticed that almost every black person who happened past would buy at least one pair, sometimes several. This struck me as highly peculiar.

"How come only black people are buying the socks?" I asked Ivan in between bites of sandwich. He eyed me over the rim of his cup as he took a sip of coffee. "Because they don't want their feet to get cold," he answered eventually. There seemed to be some deep mystery to me here. Was there some special reason they were being protective of their feet? Did white people not care if their feet got cold? I know that I myself was opposed to cold feet, yet I had no desire to purchase flea market socks.

"Why?" I blurted in frustration. "Why don't they want their feet to get cold?" He looked at me as if I had gone insane, frowned, and shook his head before answering with "Because if their feet get cold they die." This was a stunning revelation. Now I was getting to the bottom of this thing. I was amazed, and wondered why no one had bothered to teach me this fact of life in school. I had one last question. "Will white people die if their feet get cold?" He chuckled, turned his back to me, and went about the business of trying to draw more customers. This conversation stuck with me for many years. I even told a guy on Death Row about it, and it became a running joke. When he was getting ready to go out into the yard on cold winter mornings, I'd yell over and remind him, "Make sure you've got your socks on. You know what happens when your feet get cold." He'd laugh and say, "You and your old racist granddaddy ain't going to trick me."

There was one other incident in my youth that involved my grandfather and socks. For some reason I couldn't sleep without socks on. It just didn't feel right. I would put on my pajama bottoms and tuck them into my socks. The socks had to be pulled up almost to my knees so that it looked like a bizarre superhero's costume. The problem was that I often didn't change the socks for three or four days at a time. I would howl in outrage if anyone caught me and forcibly pulled them off.

This changed when my grandfather told me that sleeping with my socks on could cause my feet to burst open, because they weren't getting any air. In my head I saw my toes exploding like kernels of popcorn. It actually caused me to have bad dreams, all of which contained bursting feet. He was always telling me something crazy, and seeming to believe it himself. I now tell my sister's children bizarre tales, which they swear by. At least I can say I'm not sending them into a den of fire ants. Ivan was a nice man, in a nice house, in a nice neighborhood. There's not a hell of a lot more to say about him, other than that I grew to love him over time and cried like a baby when he died a few years later.

After the wedding Nanny moved from her apartment to Ivan's house, which was in the nicer, middle-class section of West Memphis. They hadn't been living together long when we moved in with them. By "we," I mean me, my parents, and my sister. It was supposed to be a short-term arrangement while my father found us another place. We had hopped from place to place, and for roughly two years we lived in six states before finally crashing to a halt with my grandparents.

My mother and father slept on the bed in the guest room while my sister and I slept on the floor next to them. I remember my father's strong arms picking me up off the floor on more than one occasion when he had been awakened by the sound of me gasping for breath, having an asthma attack. He'd carry me to the emergency room, which I despised because I knew many needles awaited my arrival. Now I actually look back on those days with a warm feeling in my heart, and I miss them. Times were simpler then.

I once asked my father how fish get into a previously empty pond, and he told me in all sincerity that they ride the rain. He believed that when water was evaporated from a lake, the fish were evaporated with it. Somehow the fish survived the process, and when it began to rain, the fish came back down with the water. There was no question in his mind about the truthfulness of the statement. Of course he also believed that you would die if you were to toss your hat onto a bed. When I asked him why fish didn't rain down *everywhere*, he said they sometimes did. He told me that once when he was a kid he saw fish flapping on the highway after a rainstorm. He refused to eat them because it would bring bad luck. He was uneasy just talking about it.

After we had been there for a few months my mother and father began to fight, though I still to this day do not know what they fought about. Perhaps it was the usual strain of being broke and on hard times. Whatever the reason, my father moved out and into a motel.

They tried to work through it at first, seeing each other a couple of times a week and maintaining a relationship, sort of like dating. My father would come pick us all up on weekends and take us out to eat, or to a drive-in movie to watch the latest horror release and fill up on hot dogs and popcorn. We always watched horror movies. As a child I remember sitting up into the early hours of the morning watching horror movies with my father. I still watch horror movies and read horror novels because they remind me of "home." Nostalgia, you could say.

At any rate, it didn't work. I knew things between my parents were finished when I was walking home from a friend's house one day and saw my father's car in the driveway. As I approached I saw that the driver's-side door was open and my father was sitting on the seat. One leg was on the ground, the other was in the car, and his face was hidden behind his hands as he cried so hard that his entire body was shaking. At first I thought he may have been laughing, until I looked up at my mother. She was standing outside the car next to him, with bloodshot eyes. When I got within arm's length, my father grabbed me and held me while he continued to cry. It scared the hell out of me, and I had no idea what to do.

My mother gave me a saccharine-sweet explanation of how my father wasn't going to be living with us anymore, but that he'd still come by to see my sister and me on weekends. And he did for a while. He'd come get us and take us to visit my aunt or grandparents on his side of the family. It all came to an end soon enough, though.

Four

It wasn't long before my mother met someone else. I would have been in third grade at the time. His name was Jack Echols and he was twenty years older than my mother, though you wouldn't guess it by looking at her. A steady diet of greasy fried food, cigarettes, no exercise, and a dead-end life had all come together to give my mother the look of years she didn't yet own by the age of twenty-five or so when they were married. I've never encountered a single person in my life who had anything good to say about Jack. He was a hateful bastard who only grew worse with age.

After breaking up with my father, my mother started going to a Protestant church not far from our house. This is where she met Jack, who had been attending services there for an eternity, or at least since Jesus, the carpenter, built the place with his very own hands.

I can still close my eyes and see the first time I noticed him. Church had just come to an end, and I rushed out into the parking lot to play a quick game of tag with all the other little heathens when I looked up to see Jack walking out the front door with his arm around my mom. My mind snapped to attention like a dog's ears standing up at a strange sound. It interested me only for a moment; then I went back to what I was doing. I felt a great deal of resentment toward her, and I clearly recall one day when she found me crying and asked me what was wrong.

I told her that I wanted to live with my father, to which she responded, "Well, he doesn't want you to." I knew he had never said any such thing, but it still hurt to hear it. She couldn't imagine the depth to which such a remark wounded me; she informed me that she had already told my father that she would soon be getting remarried, and I had better start getting used to the idea. At any rate, the moment she said that, I felt as if there were no comfort to be found anywhere in the world. I felt so cold inside, and there was nowhere to turn. By the look on her face I could tell she took pleasure in informing me of this. It wasn't a happy or gleeful expression—it seemed more defiant than anything. I felt like Jekyll and Hyde— part of me still wanted to seek some sort of comfort from her, for her to tell me that everything was going to be okay. The other part wanted to say things that would go straight to her heart and hurt her the way I was hurting.

At home I used to walk through emotional wastelands where the lines on craggy faces were so deep that the wind whistled through them. People fell in and out of my life, but it was the *places* that really mattered. Even now I can feel them tugging at my sleeve and spinning around in my head. All the old stories have it wrong, because it's not the ghost that haunts the house; it's the house that haunts the ghost. I feel lost out here, and everything reminds me that I'm not quite real. In the end it's always home that damns us.

My days have somehow become as rich and twisted as the kudzu vines that grew around my grandmother's house back home. It's almost too much to take, and my heart is on the verge of breaking. I'm overwhelmed with things I can't even articulate. I'm haunted by the way overhanging leaves used to cast reflections on asphalt puddles. I want to go home. Never have I wanted anything so badly. Ghosts are using my head for a neon disco, and I want to go home. My heart is a haunted house that I cannot leave behind. Everything here vibrates slower than mud, and no one has a soul.

Time spoils quickly in here, and it smells like rotten meat. Every day adds a little more weight, barely noticeable at first, but eventually it will crush you to death. In this place your life can be measured by how long you can keep fighting. The ghouls can sense it if you have any life behind your eyes, and they move in to extinguish it. The guards, the prisoners, the administration—the energy spirals downward forever, creating a hellish staircase that leads nowhere. The most frightening part is how they're all too thick to realize what they're doing. They seem to believe that if they keep digging in the same hole, they'll eventually reach heaven.

My exhaustion is beyond bone-deep. It has seeped into my soul, and every day it robs me of a little more of what I once was. Of what I was meant to be. There is no rest here, and there is no life. When I try to look ahead the light seems a little farther away each day. There is despair on my breath and no savior in sight. They say it's death only if you accept it, but more and more these days I'm feeling like I don't have a choice. I keep saying to myself, "I will not stop. I will not stop." If for no other reason than that I will it to be so. If everything else fails, I will keep moving ahead on willpower alone. There has to be some magick in something, somewhere.

I caught a glimpse of my shadow today. It's usually so hard to see because it always hides behind me. It's so much easier to see everyone else's.

My mother and Jack never did go out on dates more than a handful of times, and it seemed that most of their conversations took place in that cursed parking lot. After church my grandmother would arrive to pick us up, being smart enough to avoid the place herself. My mother, sister, and I would all get in the car, then Jack would come dragging out at the end of the herd and cut a path straight to us. My mother would roll down her window and he would stand there talking to her until every other car had left the lot and our brains were cooking in our heads from the heat of the brutal summer sun. Years later when I heard the teachings on purgatory, that's what I imagined it to be like—not quite hell, but bad enough to make you curse the bastard hanging on to the window and forcing you to grow old in this desolate place.

Jack was bald on top, but he practiced the art of the comb-over. He had a ring of hair that grew around his ears, and he would comb it over the top of his head, which was as bald as an egg. Most of his teeth were missing, and the few he had left were yellow and crooked like old tombstones. His skin had been cooked to the texture of leather by the sun, and his stomach was bloated with ulcers. I wondered what appealed to my mother about such a creature, but the answer is quite simple. Jack Echols was the very first man to pay attention to my mother after my father left, and that's all it took. She was striving for attention, and he gave it to her.

Jack had forced us to start attending services at a place called The Church of God. It was a real freak show where people spoke in tongues and rolled around on the floor screaming when they "had the spirit." The minister was a morbidly obese man whom you could hear breathing from across the room.

Twice every Sunday, once in the morning and once at night, he would preach about how the end of the world was at hand. Before leaving he always got out a bottle of olive oil and asked if anyone had any infirmities that needed to be healed. Anyone who stepped forward would have olive oil smeared on their face before being shoved to the ground amid a flurry of shouting while a horde of rabid believers waved their hands in the air and howled at the ceiling.

This made quite an impression on my young, fourth-grade mind, and I gave quite a bit of thought to all the miracles I could perform if only I had that bottle of magick oil. My sister went up to be "healed" many times, because she had been very hard of hearing since she was a baby and always had to have some sort of tubes inserted into her ears. She never fell on the floor quivering, and never could hear any better.

My mother's wedding to Jack was nice enough as far as white-trash shindigs go. The wedding ceremony was in an old church that stood next to the highway. Our family came, Jack's family came, and any observer could point out who belonged on each side. Jack had six kids, the oldest of whom was only a year or two younger than my mother. He had four sons and two daughters, all older than me, ages seventeen to about twenty-four. His daughter Sharon and son Barney lived with us at this time. There was no music, no flowers, and not much of a reception afterward. My mother wore a blue gauzy dress and Jack was in his shirtsleeves. He didn't even put on a tie. The ceremony was incredibly short, and after Jack slipped the minister ten dollars for his trouble, everyone climbed back into their cars.

Jack was pretty bad at this point, but not nearly as bad as he would later become. He forced us to go to this church three times a week, giving us no choice in the matter. He was one of the most hateful people I've ever encountered, yet he was always in church. Now I know this is nothing unusual, that it's more the rule than the exception, but back then I couldn't comprehend it. He stood guard every night as he made my sister and me kneel down next to the bed and pray. We had a small dog, a Chihuahua named Pepper, and I once saw him punch the dog with a closed fist because she dared to hop up on the bed while he was praying.

After making us go to this ghoul's wasteland of a church for several months, he announced that we would be moving into the church itself. The place we moved to almost defies description, because it was neither house nor apartment. The back rooms of the church had been converted into a bedroom, bathroom, kitchen, and living room, so that it could be rented out to bring in more money for the church. It wasn't bad, really. Only the kitchen and bathroom had windows, so the rest of the place was dark and cool like a cave. At least we had more room than in the apartment, and I was in a new school closer to where I considered home to be.

Jack only ever committed two acts of undisguised violence against me, and both were around this point in time. The first happened in the kitchen one Saturday morning. I was sitting at the table looking over my sticker collection, which I had recently become a fanatic about. I coveted stickers more than anything else on earth and had quite the little album of them. My mother was cooking, and Jack stood blocking the doorway. I got up and tried to squeeze past him, with the intention of going to watch cartoons. I could feel the rage in him as he shoved me across the kitchen and into the refrigerator door, where the handle gouged my back. I lost my balance and fell to the floor.

When I started to cry, my mother looked up with no real sense of urgency and asked, "Why did you do that?"

He bellowed, "He has to learn he can't bully his way around here!"

I had no idea what he was talking about, which only served to scare me. It's frightening to be punished when you have no idea what you've done wrong.

The second act of violence was a "spanking." I can't remember what it concerned, but I had been arguing and pleading with my mother, attempting to get her to change her mind about something she had forbidden me to do or have. I can no longer remember what the argument was about, but I remember Jack's reaction as though it were yesterday. He grabbed me and slammed me down on the bed with such force that I bounced off and landed on the floor. He slung me back onto the bed and began hitting me with rage. The most frightening part was the way he went into a frenzy, cursing (this is the only time I ever heard him curse) and turning blood-red.

My mother did nothing. As long as he continued to feed her the attention she desperately craved, she didn't care what atrocities he performed. Before, I had merely disliked him. Now the seed of hatred bloomed.

I said these were the only undisguised acts of violence, because he did so many other things—pinched me until I turned purple with bruises, bent my fingers backward, jerked on my arms, and twisted my ankles—but all of these activities were only "playing" with me. If he managed to make me cry, which was less and less often as time went by, his excuse was that he was trying to "toughen me up." The only thing that grew tough was my heart. Perhaps he was reminded of my father when he looked at me, and resented me for it. I never knew what caused his behavior, and now I no longer care. Over time I became crafty and learned to avoid him altogether.

I allowed Jack to legally adopt me because my mother explained to me that if I did, my father wouldn't be punished for being unable to pay child support. If my sister and I were adopted, then he would be free of this monetary obligation. My mother was gung ho about it because she wanted us to be seen as one big happy family, and she wanted to erase any and all traces of my father. She even made us call Jack "Dad." When I protested that I did not wish to give him such a title, my mother went into a veritable rage. I finally gave in and did as she demanded because the stress and the pressure wore me down. It's a form of torture to have to sit at the dinner table while no one speaks and an aura of anger hangs over everything like a cloud. They wouldn't even look at me. It's impossible even to eat in such circumstances, and a child can't bear such psychological pressures. I relented, though I felt a sense of betrayal by my mother that I've never gotten over, and every time I had to say "Dad" it was ashes in my mouth.

My mother denied later that they treated me like this. She has a very convenient way of forgetting and rearranging the past to fit whatever view she currently wishes to promote, much like the history changers in George Orwell's *1984*. She now knows very little about me, but makes up stories so as to seem closer to me than she truly is. It gains her more attention.

The only thing that could soothe and calm me during this era was music. That's continued to be true throughout my life. My mother would put my sister and me to bed and turn on the radio to sing us to sleep. There was something very comforting about being in a dark, cold room with Prince, Tina Turner, Cyndi Lauper, or Madonna playing quietly. I didn't have to think about anything— the music took me away from myself and I got lost in it. I needed it like a drug. I felt disconnected and alone, and I realized around this time that things would never get better. It got so bad that I would pretend to be sick at school just so I could come home and lie in bed listening to music. It was like being adrift on the ocean at night. I still have trouble falling asleep without music now.

Our next house, right outside the city limits of Marion, Arkansas, was beyond a shadow of a doubt the worst place I ever lived, and it ushered me into the most miserable period of my life. Jack obtained this prime piece of real estate for the price of thirty dollars a month, and still he paid too much. This was an honest-to-God shack, made of old clapboard that would have collapsed in a strong wind; it was built on an old Indian burial mound. The entire house consisted of four rooms covered with an aluminum roof. There was no running water or electricity to speak of, no heat or air conditioner, and half of the front porch had caved in on itself. Looking at it you would believe that such structures were inhabited only in third-world countries.

During the summer you felt that you were being cooked in your skin. The sun beating down on that metal roof made the place so hot that you'd literally think you were going to lose your mind and go stark raving mad. At night I would lie in bed sweating and being eaten alive by mosquitoes.

The winter wasn't much better, as the only source of heat was a small wood-burning stove, which filled the house with more smoke than heat. Our eyes always burned and our clothes always smelled of soot. My feet got so cold that I wanted to cry. No one could stay awake all night to constantly feed wood into the stove, so the fire was guaranteed to go out right when the temperature reached its coldest point. In the morning, the temperature in the house was only slightly higher than the freezing air outside. The house always gave me the creeps, and I despised it with a passion. When we decided (were forced) to move there, it was literally filled with knee-high garbage. Trash, sticks, broken tractor parts—it was all one big ocean of garbage, and the rats swam through it, delighted with their lot in life. There were no flushing toilets, and our drinking water came from a well that the crop dusters regularly sprayed with pesticide. It was fucking misery. I remember times when my entire family had to bathe in the same water. My stepfather would drag a big steel tub into the kitchen while my mother boiled pots of water to fill it up. There's nothing like marinating in a lukewarm pool of other people's filth to make you feel clean.

The shack was situated on top of a raised platform of earth in the middle of several miles of field that was used for farming. It was a stereotypical sharecropper's shanty. Someone probably thought that putting it on the isolated lump of higher ground would keep the rains from washing it away during a flood. That seemed to work, but there were still times when we had to use a fishing boat to reach dry land (the highway, which ran alongside the property) if the nearby swamp overflowed. It turned the only road to town into a small lake so that cars couldn't get in or out.

We had fourteen large dogs that lived underneath the house. We didn't mean to have that many originally; they just kept breeding. People who have never known the hunger of being dirt poor always ask why we didn't have the dogs spayed or neutered. As if the money to do that was just lying around, waiting on us to pick it up. We couldn't afford a trip to the doctor ourselves, much less for the dogs. More often than not, we had trouble scraping the rent together. The farmer who owned the house didn't mind if we were a little late with the payment, because he knew we'd eventually come up with it, even if we had to cash in aluminum cans to do so.

Strange things were always hovering at the periphery of my family life, but none so much as during our years in that house. There was just a bad feeling around the place. The house felt malevolent. I could never escape the feeling that the entire place wished me ill. It was the sort of place where, if you lived long enough, a doctor would eventually inform you that your insides were black with cancer and you had only days left to live. It was unpleasant in every regard, and the entire house had the aura of the inside of a body bag. It always felt dark, even on the sunniest summer days. There were odd drawings left on the walls by whoever had lived there before us—things like a grandfather clock with a single eye where the face should have been. They looked like the sorts of things an insane person with a great degree of artistic talent would have created. We painted over most of them, but ran out of paint before we got to the clock. It was worse at night, when you could feel it staring at the back of your head.

That place was never quiet at night. I would lie in bed listening as the dogs dragged strange things to and fro beneath the floor. Inside the house was as dark as an oil slick, so you couldn't *see* anything moving in the room but you could *sense* it. It was the same sort of sensation you would experience if a closet door were to swing silently open behind your back. Later I learned a term to describe that sensation—air displacement. What I was sensing was air being displaced by something moving from one spot to another. Sometimes late at night I would be overwhelmed with the feeling that someone was standing by the bed, leaning over me, so close they could have brushed their lips across mine if they'd so desired. The breath would pass from its lips to my lips like the taste of something unmentionable. It wasn't like a ghost or anything; it was just a feeling the house itself radiated, like an aura. My eyes would bulge and strain like an animal's, fiercely trying to penetrate the darkness.

Eventually we were told to move, and the house was torn down. The suburbs around Marion were expanding, and people who lived in the houses that cost a quarter of a million dollars did not want a tin-roof shack standing on a bone hill in their line of sight. Something like that tends to lower the property values.

Before the shack was torn down, it drew someone else's attention. All of us used to go to the bank with my stepfather on Friday afternoon to cash his paycheck, especially in the summer. It was the rare few minutes when we could sit inside an air-conditioned building. We probably didn't smell very nice, because we were sweating twenty-four hours a day. We poured into the bank like a carload of Vikings and tried not to mess anything up.

Every week I would walk around the bank looking at things I'd examined a hundred times before. There wasn't much else to do. I was taken aback when we walked in one week to see an art display in the lobby. It consisted of a folding wall, almost like a room divider, and it held about twenty paintings. A laminated sheet of paper attached to the display informed the reader that the paintings had been produced by the art class at the local high school. I moved down the line, examining each piece in turn. Most were nothing to write home about. A few were outright bizarre and even a little scary. When I reached the end of the line I stopped dead in my tracks and held my breath. I was witnessing something both miraculous and cruel. Someone, some high school kid, had painted our house. Here it was displayed to the world in all its squalor. It had been rendered in perfect detail. One side of the porch was dilapidated and had caved in on itself. There were wild roses growing over all the ruins. The flesh prickled along my spine and I looked around, as if perhaps the artist were standing nearby and watching to see my reaction. There were no customers in the bank except us. The teller didn't even glance in my direction.

I stood in the bank staring at this painting of our house with its collapsing front porch, surrounded by cotton fields, when my mother walked up behind me and asked, "Is that our house?" Her brow furrowed in concentration before exclaiming to herself in a low voice, "Oh, wow." When my stepfather came over to see what we were looking at, she said, "Look, it's our house." He put on his glasses and leaned forward to study it intently. Finally he said, "Maybe. It might be some other house, though."

I knew my stepfather wasn't the brightest guy in the world, but this was pushing it even for him. I pointed out the details, elaborating. "Look. Half the porch done fell in. It's ours." He dug his heels in, stubbornly. "That don't mean nothin'. The porch fell in on other houses, too." I knew better than to try to argue with him. When you proved he was wrong he'd just make your life miserable for the next week.

I wish I had that painting now. I'd keep it locked away somewhere, and take it out every year or so, just to remind myself where I came from. I'd show it to my wife and son, and try to tell them how hard life was out there, and the effect it had on me. That never works, though. I learned a long time ago that you have to experience something for yourself or you never really comprehend it.

Looking back, the worst part about the shack wasn't the poverty, the heat, the cold, or even the humiliation of living in such circumstances; it was the absolute and utter loneliness. For many years in that old house, I didn't have a friend in the world to keep me company. It was far out in the middle of nowhere, surrounded by nothing but fields. No kids or neighbors to even speak to you. I was so lonely that I thought even death was preferable. If not for my small battery-powered radio, perhaps I would have died inside.

Years later, I read a book by Nick Cave called *And the Ass Saw the Angel*. It struck me because of how close he comes to catching the feel of life in that lonely shack. None of the more well-known southern writers like Carson McCullers or Flannery O'Connor have done it for me. It's like they may have witnessed life, but never lived it. Nick Cave comes damn close, though. More so than anyone else.

Books helped me to survive out there. The only places close enough to walk to were the courthouse and the library. I had no interest in reading anything but horror at this age, so I read the few tattered paperbacks housed there numerous times. I read Stephen King and Dean Koontz novels more times than Billy Graham read his Bible. They kept me company on many a long and maddening summer day.

Later I discovered the ultimate horror—the Inquisition. The

first time I stumbled across this atrocity was in a book by some demented adult that was titled something like *The Children's Book of Devils and Fiends*. It was filled with tales (and woodcuts) of witches having orgies, standing in line to kiss the devil's arse, eating children, and cursing people so that they went into convulsions. The book didn't explain that all these things were nothing more than the fevered dreams and insane concoctions of religious zealots that the educated world now knows them to be. It put them forth as being true, much as they were originally published during the Inquisition itself. Then there was the additional horror of people being tortured and burned at the stake simply because someone accused them of being witches. It explained how they were strangled, burned, cut, drowned, and dismembered in an effort to make them confess to flying on broomsticks to attend secret meetings.

It's not possible to overstate the impact all this had on my young mind. I would lie in bed at night scared to move, while my imagination conjured up horrific images. I had already had scenes of hell and damnation drilled into my head by Jack and his wonderful church-folk friends, and these new discoveries did nothing to ease my terror. If I would have known then that in just a few short years I would be subjected to the same kind of witch hunt, that I would have some of the same accusations made against me, and that the same merciless zealots would imprison me and sentence me to death, then my heart probably would have burst of fright right on the spot. Who would have thought you could see the future by reading a book about the past?

I was miserable and under tremendous pressure, believing I

would burn in hell for all eternity because I couldn't stop myself from thinking bad things about people—not to mention the fact that I was entering puberty and knew with absolute certainty that my uncontrollable lust was earning me a one-way trip to the Lake of Fire. I had recently discovered masturbation and applied myself to the act with the utmost diligence. I couldn't seem to stop myself, and afterward would pray to God, begging his forgiveness. I had no idea that it was normal to have such urges, for no one ever explained such things to me.

There was a nonstop war going on inside me—I wanted to be "good," but couldn't quite seem to manage it. My sexual appetite was insatiable, and as a typical adolescent, I thought most people were morons. I was on my way to the devil's playground, all right. It all seems so ridiculous now, but back then it was the most deadly serious thing in the world.

Oddly enough, that same children's book was where I first encountered Aleister Crowley. Now I know it was all propaganda, but at that young age I was amazed that someone could be so brazenly hedonistic and "sinful." I've read much about this man and his life's work over the years, and it's incredible how people have misunderstood him. One of my favorite examples is his "How to Succeed / How to Suck Eggs" wordplay. It comes from chapter sixty-nine (wordplay: get it?), in which he talks about sexual practices; anyone not reading closely won't pick up on the "suck seed" reference. His words have been misconstrued, twisted, taken out of context, and misunderstood continuously. If you don't know the key with which to decipher him, then you'll never understand what you're reading. Others don't even want to understand, and would rather use his name or image to sway and scare the ignorant, just as the prosecutor did during my trial.

Our financial situation continued its steadily downward spiral, and the tension continued to build. We started trying to grow our own food, and it was hot, backbreaking labor. We had no irrigation system, not even a hose and running water, so we had to haul water by the bucketful to our "garden." Everything was done manually. Some days you'd go up one row of cucumbers or potatoes and down another with hoe in hand, busting up the dry, cracked ground. Other days you'd spend hours hunched over, pulling weeds from between plants with bare hands. That task was especially hazardous, as you had to constantly be on the lookout for poisonous snakes, bumblebees, and wasps. If you let the monotony of the task lull your mind into a stupor you'd often receive a nasty surprise. After all the hard work, only about half the food would be edible. The bugs and animals would have gotten some of it, while other areas couldn't be saved from rot.

The only thing we didn't have to do ourselves was crop-dusting. Our house was in the middle of the field the plane flew back and forth over, and it gave us a healthy dose of poison every time it passed overhead. If you didn't run for cover when you heard him coming, you'd get dusted, too. During that time, I inhaled enough pesticides to put a small country out of action. My mom's and Jack's advice? "Don't look up at the plane, and try not to breathe deeply until he gets a little ways past." I developed allergies so bad that my mother had to start giving me injections at home. She had no bedside manner and wielded that syringe in an entirely unpleasant way.

You had to be certain you had all the food out of the garden by the end of summer or there was a chance the fire would destroy it. Every year after the final harvest, farmers would ride through the fields surrounding our house and set them ablaze with instruments that looked like flamethrowers. This was so all the burned and left-over vegetation would fertilize the ground for the next year's crop. I don't know what prevented the house from burning, because the flames would come to a halt only a few feet away. If the wind changed direction you would nearly suffocate on thick, black smoke.

The house did nearly burn to the ground one time because the wood-burning stove started a fire in the ceiling. The fire department had to come and spray the place down. Unfortunately, the trucks arrived in time to put it out. As I watched, I desperately prayed that the entire shack would burn so I'd never have to see it again. It survived with little damage.

Jack was a roofer by trade, and he started taking small jobs on the side, repairing residential homes to bring in a little extra cash. I started going with him, learning the process. I was only about thirteen, so mostly what I did was clean up the area when he was finished, and he'd give me a few dollars.

Perhaps up until this point I've painted a completely unsympathetic portrait of Jack. He wasn't an absolute monster any more than anyone else is. He was just a man, both good and bad. I believe he did care about both my sister and me, in his own way. He could be generous. He would stop to help every single person whose car was broken down on the side of the road, and he always gave hitchhikers a ride. He was also more tolerant of any form of self-expression I chose than any other parent would have been. I was free to dress however I pleased and listen to whatever music I liked. He had no problem with things like me wearing earrings, and I heard him tell my mother more than once, "He's just trying to find himself."

My mother was also a more complicated character than she may seem. She always made certain we had enough to eat (even though it was usually junk food), she always went to Open House Night at school to meet my teachers, and she made sure we got Easter baskets with chocolate rabbits. She tried to take care of us when we were sick, although sometimes her idea of taking care was to sit next to the bed as I struggled with bronchitis and keep watch while smoking generic cigarettes.

I'm now at a point in my life where I look back on both of them with mingled feeling of love, disgust, affection, resentment, and sometimes hatred. There's too much betrayal to ever be completely forgiven. I am not like my mother, who may argue with you one day and go back to life as usual the next. The best I can do is say that their good deeds may have softened the blow of the bad ones.

Five

Being in prison and having a case as well-known as mine puts me in an odd position. In a way, complete strangers come to feel that they know me just because they've watched me on television or read about me. It takes away their inhibitions when they approach me. I don't mind it at all; it keeps my days interesting. Sometimes it provokes a great deal of thought, and sometimes it leaves me flabbergasted.

The letters I receive from people come from a variety of mental and emotional planes. I see the entire spectrum of human life. I'm like a bartender without a bar; people just tell me their stories. Some of them just want to get something off their chests, as if they just need to tell *someone*. Others look at me as some sort of oracle, and ask me questions about major life decisions. People going through divorces, people losing their children, people considering abortions—they all write and tell me their personal business. Others write and ask me about mine. I've even met a few of them in prison.

Years ago I was often visited by a religious couple. They were devoutly Pentecostal and much older than I was, though with almost no life experience. They had never been out of Arkansas or ever associated with people who were outside their own walk of life. They didn't really know what to make of me but kept returning. I must admit that I enjoyed shocking them. In some ways they were as alien to me as I was to them.

More often than not they would bring the conversation around to sex. They truly had no idea that people practiced any sort of sex other than intercourse in a missionary position. When I informed them that there were indeed other positions, and that it could even be done orally, they looked like they were about to go into shock. They couldn't comprehend it and eventually delivered the verdict that only extreme deviants would conceive of or engage in such acts. They stated that there was no way that a normal person could enjoy such a thing, although they seemed to enjoy discussing it.

Hate mail is the term used to describe the letters from people who haven't actually stopped to learn the facts of my case and never get past their initial knee-jerk reaction. As a matter of fact I could count the non-supportive letters I've received on one hand, whereas I could build a small mountain out of the letters I've received from people expressing support and wanting to know how they can help.

Most people who spew hatred aren't very intelligent or motivated. They tend to be lazy, and if for some reason they are coaxed into picking up a pen, their messages are mostly incoherent and largely illiterate. Their spelling and sentence structure tends to be atrocious, so it's hard to take offense at anything they'd say even when they do write. After all, if they're not motivated or intelligent enough to re-search the simple spelling of a word in a dictionary, then you know they certainly aren't going to take the time to research the case. Still, all in all, hateful people just don't seem to like writing, I guess. Either that or there simply aren't many people in the world who wish me anything but good fortune.

There is one odd thing that happens every now and then, though. I think of it as a drive-by preaching. Occasionally I'll receive a plain white envelope in the mail, with no return address. This alone makes the item suspect, because people usually want me to write back, so a return address is prominently displayed. When I get one of these anonymous missives I lay it aside to be inspected after I finish with the rest of the day's mail.

When I get around to opening it, it's always the same thing: a load of religious tracts and pamphlets. There's no letter, no message, just a bunch of John 3:16s and Turn or Burns. I always get the feeling these things are sent in the same spirit with which the perpetrator would fling a flaming bag of dog shit at my front door. I picture an overweight housewife with dishwater-colored hair licking the envelope with a look of smug satisfaction on her face. It seems that the messages printed on these greasy, creased pieces of paper must have gone right over the sender's head. Perhaps it's just me, but I don't think Jesus' words were meant to be tied to a brick and chunked through your neighbor's window at midnight. Anytime you drop a picture of Christ in the mailbox while muttering a self-righteous "This'll teach 'em," something has gone terribly wrong.

Preachers visit Death Row all the time, including Baptist ministers who try to convince us that death is preferable to life. Some go so far as to tell us that we should even drop our appeals and voluntarily allow the state to kill us. When someone is executed, these vultures make comments like "He's in a better place now." Somehow I doubt that even they themselves believe this. I think they'd be pretty quick to seek medical attention if they had a problem. They say the Bible tells them that death is more wonderful than life. I've read it, and I see a different picture. If death is so great, then why did Jesus raise the dead? Why did he call Lazarus back to life? That in itself causes me to believe there must be something wholly unpleasant about that particular condition. They know it, too. They just get high on watching people die. It's the only thing left for them to get off on.

I cannot explain it, the way everything in my soul shrieks and gibbers for some sort of closure. How do you make someone understand what it means or how it feels to be torn in half? Not many people know this desperate need to be put back together again. I have been split like the atom, and the effect on my psyche was just as powerful. Part of me is missing, even if it can't be seen with the naked eye. A coin is not complete without both heads *and* tails.

All of the negativity and unsavory characters in this environment only serve to make the exceptions shine all the more brightly. It causes you to appreciate kindness and consideration even more. When those with an inner beauty make their way into this hellish reality it shines forth like a beacon, and we denizens swarm to it like bugs to a zapper. In a very real way we're starving to death, and these bright spots in the darkness are the only thing that can fill the hole.

On an average day there is nothing kind, generous, caring, or sensitive within these walls. The energy directed at you is hatred, rage, disgust, stupidity, ignorance, and brutality. It affects you in mind, body, and soul, much like a physical beating. The pressure is relentless and unending. Soon you walk with your shoulders slumped and your head down, like a beast that's used to being kicked. You never make eye contact, and you constantly cringe mentally. That's encouraged and enforced every day. The prison staff does not look at you as human, and they go out of their way to let you know it. The message that you are inferior and worthless is hammered in at every conceivable turn.

Take, for example, the way in which we are fed. On more than one occasion I have found insects such as grasshoppers and crickets that were boiled in my broccoli or greens. That's because after it was picked no one even bothered to wash it. If the meat is starting to go bad, just smother it in generic barbeque sauce to cover the taste. Often the food is mixed together in inedible combinations, due to lack of care—pickled beets dumped in the applesauce, or a soggy roll floating in the boiled squash. The fat- and gristle-laden meat is never fully cooked, while vegetables are boiled to the point of disintegration. The only time a decent meal is prepared by the kitchen is when a tour or inspection is sent through by some outside agency. This happens a handful of times every year.

Every inmate in prison is assigned an account that family and friends can deposit money into, which inmates use for basic necessities. Everything in prison must be paid for. Most of the food I eat is bought with donations from supporters and friends. That alone enables me to avoid a great deal of the prison fare. Most aren't so fortunate.

It used to be that the greatest time for prisoners was Christmas.

This was because many local churches, both Protestant and Catholic, along with the Buddhist center, the ACLU, and many independent donors, would spend their time and money putting together what were commonly called "Christmas sacks." These sacks contained fresh fruit (Christmas is the only time of year you get it), candy, homemade cookies, pairs of socks, a couple of stamped envelopes, and various other goodies. (In prison these snacks are called "zoo-zoos" and "wham-whams.") People would talk about these sacks, anticipating them, for many weeks ahead of time. There was excitement in the air. This was the only thing that made Christmas different from any other day. Until the year that the prison administration decided they would no longer allow the volunteers to do this. They would not be allowed in to sing Christmas carols or donate fresh food. We would receive nothing, and Christmas would be just another day, unless you count the perceptible stench of depression in the air as a difference. No one knows why this tradition was suddenly banned, other than that our overseers arrogantly declared "because I say so." No one explains themselves to inferior creatures.

One of the people who helped put together the Christmas sacks every year was a lady named Anna. She was from the local Buddhist center, and she visited the prison once a week to hold an hour-long meditation session. She told stories, gave teachings, and taught the inmates all sorts of Tibetan meditation practices. The number of people who could fit into the small room to attend her classes was extremely limited, so afterward she would walk from cell to cell, talking to anyone who wanted to chat or discuss a problem. She gave blessings and recited prayers, never turning anyone away. The inmates all behaved as if she were the Dalai Lama himself. You would know when she had arrived because word would spread like wildfire down the halls and through the barracks—"Anna's here! Anna's here!" Buddhists, Christians, Muslims—she welcomed all. She cut through the darkness like a spotlight, and for that reason the guards hated her. They did everything within their power to keep her out, but nothing worked. She would stand patiently outside the door for hours at a time until they finally had no choice but to let her in.

Sadly enough, failing health has put a severe cramp in her lifestyle, so we no longer get to see her. I believe part of the problem was that she spread herself so thin. No matter how valiant the effort, a single person cannot lift all this darkness. So many needed her that there just wasn't enough of her to go around. She would have had to live here twenty-four hours a day and give up sleeping in order to talk to everyone. One candle cannot illuminate the entire universe, and not many people are interested in the job.

One other person the guards couldn't seem to dissuade, no matter how much effort they put into the enterprise, was a priest of the Roman Catholic Church named Father Charles. He was unlike any priest I've ever known, before or since.

Father Charles always arrived at the prison, as he did everywhere else, on his motorcycle. He loved that thing and rode it everywhere. It's odd to see a man in a priest's collar sitting atop such a machine, and sometimes the mind finds it difficult to accept such a sight until it grows accustomed.

The first thing you noticed about Father Charles's appearance was a bald head. His skull was shaved as slick as Kojak's or

Mr. Clean's, and the light reflected off it as he crossed the barracks. Framing his mouth and chin was a Fu Manchu mustache and goatee, which seemed to be a perfect complement to the bald head. The only thing about his appearance that was traditional was his black suit and white collar.

It wasn't only his appearance that deviated from the norm, as he had all sorts of interesting quirks and habits, one of which was that he brewed and bottled his own beer in his garage. After much practice he believed he'd stumbled upon the perfect recipe, and was quite proud of it. Also in his garage was a giant pet boa constrictor, which he confided to me he'd once watched swallow a chicken whole. He said this with awe in his voice, as if amazed by the intricacies of God's creatures. In his spare time he played violin and was accomplished enough to tackle the works of Paganini.

Father Charles was one of the most gentle and intelligent people I've ever had the privilege of knowing. His eyes were alight with life, and even the non-Catholics on Death Row loved and wanted to talk to him. He was a very enlightened individual, and often told me to think of God more like "the Force" in the *Star Wars* movies. I don't believe his approach was always popular with the bishop, but it appealed to me.

Over the years I had gradually drifted away from the Catholic Church, because the experiences I'd been through had left me bitter. I blamed Christianity in general as being a huge part of the reason I was sitting on Death Row for a crime I didn't commit. It was Christians who had labeled me "satanic" and condemned me to death. It was hard for me to get past that, so I sought a new home in Zen

Buddhism to help me deal with the anger and resentment. More than likely it saved my life, by preventing all the negativity from eating me alive. Some Christians would have frowned on my interest in Buddhism. Father Charles did not. He thought it was great.

It was Father Charles who lured me back into attending Mass in the small prison chapel as a complement to my Buddhist training. It's the beauty of the Catholic Church that has always caused me to fall in love with it. It still does. I later learned that I wasn't the only one to embrace both practices. Jesuit priests at certain churches have started teaching Buddhist meditation techniques to their congregations as a valid approach to dealing with life situations. Interestingly enough, I had wanted nothing more than to become a Jesuit priest in my youth. It was the whole celibacy thing I couldn't handle.

Unfortunately, Father Charles was eventually transferred to another parish. He didn't want to leave, and we didn't want him to, but the decision was in someone else's hands. Now, years later, people on Death Row still write to him, and he to them. People respect him and the advice that he gives. No one since has been capable of taking his place.

I have the shape of a dead man on the wall of my cell. It was left behind by the last occupant. He stood against the wall and traced around himself with a pencil, then shaded it in. It looks like a very faint shadow, and it's barely noticeable until you see it. It took me nearly a week to notice it for the first time, but once you see it you can't un-see it. I find myself lying on my bunk and looking at it several times a day. It just seems to draw the eyes like a magnet. God only knows what possessed him to do such a thing, but I can't bring myself to wash it off. Since they executed him, it's the only trace of him left. He's been in his grave almost five years now, yet his shadow still lingers. He was no one and nothing. All that remains of him is a handful of old rape charges and a man-shaped pencil sketch. Perhaps it's just superstition, but I can't help but feel that erasing it would be like erasing the fact that he ever existed. That may not be such a bad thing, all things considered, but I won't be the one to do it.

At one point I entertained thoughts that perhaps the living inmates weren't the only ones trapped on Death Row. After all, if places really are haunted, then wouldn't Death Row be the perfect stomping ground? At some time or another it's crossed the mind of everyone here. Some make jokes about it, like whistling to yourself as you pass the cemetery. Others don't like to speak about it at all, and it can be a touchy subject. Who wants to think about the fact that you're sleeping on the mattress that three or four executed men also claimed as their resting place? Imagine looking into the mirror every day and wondering how many dead men had looked at their own reflections in it. When anything odd happens, some men blame whoever was executed last.

Once for a period of several months at Tucker Max, I had the privilege of having an entire floor of the Death Row barracks to myself. Recent executions had opened up cells on the first two floors, so the guards thought it a good idea to move people from the third floor down to the first and second, to fill the empty slots. They were hoping to be able to get out of walking up to the third floor alto-gether. The problem was that they were one short, so I was the only one to be left up there with another seventeen empty cells.

There were a lot of benefits to the situation, so I didn't complain. For one thing, I had a television all to myself. No arguing about what to watch. I also had my own phone, and no longer had to wait for anyone else to get off it. There was no one above me to stomp on the floor and annoy me, and no one next to me. I could sit in medi-tation for as long as I liked without fear of interruption. I was up high enough in the air that I could look out of my slit of a window and see a field of horses. I used to watch them playing for hours at a time. Even better than the horses was the field itself, especially when it snowed during the winter. Looking at that snowy field and a ring of leafless, gray trees made my heart ache like you can't believe. Nothing makes me wail with heartache and homesickness more than the winter. Sometimes the cold wind feels like it's blowing right through a hole in my chest. It hurts, folks. It hurts like hell and re-minds me of how long I've been here.

I did have a tiny cellmate for a short time—a little white-haired, blue-eyed kitten. I don't believe she was even old enough to be away from her mother yet, as you could cradle her in the palm of one hand. I've absolutely no idea where she originally came from or where she eventually went, but she was being passed around so the guards wouldn't find her. When it was time for her to be passed on she'd be placed in a stocking cap and sent down the line.

The kitty didn't seem to want to do anything but sleep. The problem was that she was much like a fussy baby and wanted to be held as she slept. She would lie on your chest, curled into a small white ball, and sleep forever. The moment you put her down, the tiny blue eyes would pop open and she would begin to give voice to her outrage. Tiny but high-pitched meows could soon be heard from a considerable distance. It was amazing that such a minuscule creature could be heard from so far away. Perhaps it was the fact that the sound was so alien to the environment. No amount of talk would console her. "Shhh! Hush, you little monster, or they shall discover our plot." She paid no heed to my warnings.

Her only other fault was that a steady diet of tuna and milk caused her to leave long, brown kitty puddles on the floor. She knew herself to be the queen of Death Row and had no doubt that it was my honor and privilege to clean up after her. Once my tour of duty came to an end she went on to her next residence and I never saw her again.

The kitten wasn't the only pet to ever be kept on Death Row. The most common are mice and rats, but I've also seen spiders, a couple snakes, and even a bird. The mice and rats were bred for the purpose of serving as pets. A guy would manage to catch two wild ones, and every time a litter was born he'd give the babies out to whoever wanted one. They grow up with you and won't bite or scratch. The snakes would wander into the yard and suddenly find themselves stuffed into someone's pants and smuggled indoors.

The biggest rat I've ever seen in my life was raised by a guy here. It was as big as a Chihuahua, and he even fashioned a collar for it. It was as tame as any household pet and slept in the same bed as the guy who had trained it.

His pet rat was not the only thing that made the prisoner seem out of the ordinary. He was nicknamed "Butterfly," even though calling him that made him angry enough to strangle someone. This name spread like wildfire, along with the rumor that had started it. It was said that this gentleman had a giant tattoo of a butterfly on his rear end—one wing tattooed on each cheek—and that by doing a certain dance he could make it appear as if the butterfly were flapping its wings. As revolting as the thought was, it was still fodder for a great deal of humor. The only one not laughing was Butterfly.

The bird belonged to a prisoner I knew named Earl. Earl had gotten his pet bird from the yard. Every year when the weather begins to turn warm the birds build nests and lay eggs in the razor wire surrounding the yard. Inevitably, baby birds will tumble out. Earl smuggled one in and kept it in his cell. You would hear it every morning before sunrise, chirp-chirp-chirping like mad. This would be met with a volley of curses from the prisoners it had awakened.

Earl was an interesting character. He was about five feet eight inches tall and weighed about 160 pounds. His hair had turned prematurely gray. Earl never cracked a joke and spoke only if he had something important to say or a question to ask. He never raised his voice or argued with anyone. Earl was on Death Row but had never actually killed anyone. He had escaped from prison with another guy, and the other guy had shot and killed someone. Since Earl had been with him, they were both given the death penalty. I believe he was one of the few people here with enough intelligence to comprehend the full horror of his predicament. When they set an execution date for him he became violently ill and couldn't keep anything in his stomach until they killed him. For some reason Earl haunts me more than anyone else they've killed. Perhaps it's because I knew that, like me, he hadn't taken anyone's life.

They led Earl out to the Death House with the guy who had actually done the shooting. They were both executed at the same time. As they took them out I was standing at my cell door to say good-bye. It was four o'clock in the morning. The other guy passed me first, and he was chewing a piece of gum as if he didn't have a care in the world. He nodded in my direction and uttered a nonchalant "Catch you later." I nodded back to him. When Earl came down next there were tears in his eyes. He struggled to keep his voice under control. "Damien," he said, and nodded once. "Earl," I said, and returned the nod.

The guards later said he couldn't even finish his last meal, because he was continuously vomiting. Now, years later, I still feel something in my stomach turn over every time I think of him. He left me nearly everything he owned before he was executed—his books, a leather belt, all his drawing pens, and some origami paper. I couldn't keep them, because it bothered me too much. I gave everything away.

Where was I? Ah, yes. All alone on the third floor. It was just me and seventeen other dark, empty cells. One night, from the corner of my eye, I thought I saw movement in one of the vacant domiciles. My head snapped in that direction and the hair on my neck and arms stood on end. I stood staring, body taut, like a gunslinger at high noon. There was no repeat performance that night. Over time you grow accustomed to such things and no longer pay them any mind. Sometimes you'll wake up in the middle of the night and feel like you were awakened by someone speaking, but there's no one around and it's as quiet as a crypt.

The silence on Death Row is something that seems to unnerve guards when they first get assigned here. That's because every other barracks sounds like a madhouse. There are people screaming at the top of their lungs twenty-four hours a day. It never stops for a moment. Screams of anger and rage, begging, threatening, cursing—it sounds like the din of some forgotten hell. These are the "regular" prisoners. As soon as you step through the door of Death Row it stops. More than once I've heard a new guard say, "My God—you can hear a pin drop in here!"

The only time I even register the silence is late at night, when I would sit up to watch the midnight movie, keeping my fingers crossed that it would be a horror flick.

Horror movies were a family tradition in our house. I remember when I was a child, still in kindergarten, I would sit up and watch back-to-back horror movies—Godzilla, the mummy, vampires, werewolves, or a disembodied hand that somehow made its way around town in search of its victim. I would stare wide-eyed and unmoving at the flickering screen until I fell asleep, then my dad would carry me to bed.

I'd remember those times as I sat in the silent barracks watching a cheaply made horror movie. It filled me with nostalgia and made me want to go back in time to a place where I was safe and had no doubt that my mom and dad would take care of everything.

At one time I lived in a cell next to a guy who got a little nervous in the silence. One night as I was watching *The Texas Chainsaw Massacre 2*, the guy in the next cell whispered my name every few minutes, to be certain I hadn't fallen asleep and left him alone. Finally I said, "Man, if this movie scares you that much you should quit watching it." Others who overheard started laughing. He swore at me, stung because I'd leaked his secret. Moments later he crept back to the door to watch some more. I don't believe he slept at all that night.

Six

In 1986 came the joys of junior high school. Many significant events and rites of passage took place during the time I inhabited the halls of this repugnant example of our educational system. It was beyond rural; there were probably about a thousand students in the entire school. I had my first taste of beer and my first look at pornography, I took up skateboarding, and I met Jason Baldwin.

The beer and pornography were compliments of my stepbrother Keith Echols, who was actually a pretty decent guy despite having a drinking problem. He gave me the first of only two experiences I've ever had behind the wheel of a vehicle. He drove an old pickup truck with a jacked-up rear end and super-wide back tires. One day as I sat in the passenger seat listening to Alice Cooper on the radio, he tossed out the empty beer can he'd been holding between his legs, looked at me with bleary eyes, and asked, "Wanna drive?"

I responded with the phrase every southerner uses on a regular basis: "Hell yeah."

He pulled over and exchanged places with me, then instructed me on how to drive the last couple of miles to his house. Keith was extremely laid-back (out in the middle of nowhere there's not much to crash into) and told me repeatedly, "You can go faster."

By this time all of Jack's kids had long since moved off on their own, but Keith, along with his wife and infant daughter, were forced to move into the tin-roof shack with us after their house and all they owned burned to the ground. While there he taught me many practical skills, such as how to shoot and take care of your gun and how to replace the engine in your car, all while maintaining a beer buzz. I never did develop a taste for the stuff and have never been able to drink an entire bottle. He'd hand me his girlie magazines while belching, "Don't tell Dad I showed you these." All in all, he was a pretty fun guy to be around, even though his tact was sometimes questionable (once, years later, when witnessing a neighborhood girl flirting with me, he called out a cheerful, "You better get on that, boy!"). I looked up to him then, but haven't seen or heard from him since I was imprisoned.

My first year of junior high I befriended a mildly retarded and majorly weird kid named Kevin. I was most likely the only friend he'd ever had, and you couldn't make him shut up. It was as if he'd been saving up conversations his whole life. He could talk about literally anything for hours at a time—a cartoon he'd watched the previous afternoon, a magazine he'd looked at in the grocery store, or a new stuffed animal he'd acquired. This kid was a freak when it came to stuffed animals, and he had a huge collection—it's where every cent of his money went. I never had to say much of anything;

he'd carry the entire conversation. He couldn't even make himself stop talking during class. Everyone else did their best to avoid him, so we had our own table every day at lunch.

I believe the reason I didn't extend myself or try to make other friends is that I couldn't compete. We were dirt poor, so I didn't have the latest sneakers, I had no idea what videos were playing on MTV, I hadn't seen the latest movies, and I didn't own a single article of trendy clothing. I didn't have to compete with Kevin. I could be wearing sackcloth and no shoes for all he cared, as long as I listened to him talk about his stuffed animal collection and nodded every now and then. Other than that, there were no expectations. I think pretty much everyone else in the world abused and made fun of him, but as long as I let him hang around, he didn't care. In hindsight, I also believe some part of me had given up. By the age of twelve or thirteen, I had decided life was hopeless.

I had to repeat my first year of junior high because I failed. I don't remember completing a single assignment during the entire year, and it showed when report cards were handed out—I had an F in every single subject. I didn't pass anything, and I didn't care. As the school year came to a close, I was looking at another long, brutal, lonely summer in what my family still refers to as "the white house." This year I would carry an extra piece of darkness home with me. Right before we were released for vacation, another thirteen-year-old tried to commit suicide by hanging himself.

Joseph was in three or four of my classes. He even sat right in front of me during one of them. He was never without a large duffel bag full of books, paper, colored pencils, protractors, and anything else you could possibly need to navigate your way through the seventh-grade world. He was no friend of mine, but I knew who he was. A couple of weeks before the end of the year he stopped showing up at school. Soon the entire student body knew he'd tried to hang himself. He survived, but spent the next few months in a mental institution. The image would haunt me all summer long with a power that nothing before had. I couldn't get it out of my head.

Late at night I'd lie in bed with my ear pressed to my little radio so that no one else could hear it. If Jack heard the slightest hint of music he would throw a fit and claim that I had kept him awake all night. I would lie there wondering if perhaps Joseph had been listening to music when he decided life was no longer worth the effort. Did he wait until nightfall, or did he do it in the daylight? What did he tie the rope to? Did he jump off a chair? Why didn't he succeed? If I had said anything to him, would it have made a difference? It drove me to tears more than once. Lying in bed covered in sweat and staring at the darkness, I didn't even feel the mosquitoes biting me as I replayed the scenes I'd imagined over and over. I thought that if anyone knew how lonely and miserable I was, it was that kid. The anguish and the ghosts that haunted me evaporated like mist under the light of the morning sun, but would be waiting on me when darkness fell. I couldn't seem to shake it off. That's how I spent my summer vacation.

The beginning of my second year of seventh grade didn't start out a great deal differently from the first. I wore my secondhand clothes and collected my free lunch. Kevin wasn't around this year, as it was decided over the summer that he was better suited to attend a special school for kids with learning disabilities. I was on my own.

One day a week during study hall we were allowed to spend thirty minutes in the school library. It was on one of these excursions that my life was drastically changed when I came across a superior literary publication called *Thrasher*. For those who don't know, it was *the* skateboarding magazine. This was the first time I was exposed to the world of skateboarding. It wasn't just an activity—it was a culture. I don't remember seeing any skaters in our school, so I don't know how the magazine found its way into those humble archives. That magazine became my bible. All I could think about was skating, and after months of begging I received my first skateboard for Christmas. It was a cheap, heavy thing, with no nose and very little tail. It was piss yellow, with a Chinese dragon graphic on the bottom. Definitely not the best of equipment, but it gave me my start.

Day and night I did nothing but practice tricks and read *Thrasher*. I would stare at the ads for the new decks like a sex fiend in the porn section. I also became acquainted with a different world of music I'd never before heard of, and discovered The Cure, Dinosaur Jr., Primus, Black Flag, Circle Jerks, and many other classics.

Nanny moved into a trailer park located between Marion and West Memphis with the dubious title of "Lakeshore Estates," and when I went to see her, a couple of the neighbors would give me five dollars to mow their lawns. I saved the money to order clothes from skateboard companies, and replaced the cheap parts on my board with better-quality stuff, one piece at a time. Skateboarding became my life, and I did just enough work to get by in school that year. Soon enough, summer vacation was on me once again.

That summer was as hot, miserable, and lonely as the others, but it seemed to pass a little more quickly just because I now had a little life in me. I'd skate up the old deserted highway between the cotton fields, all the way to the courthouse and public library. Once there I made use of every curb in the parking lot until I was drenched in sweat and on the verge of heatstroke. If not for the old librarian allowing me to guzzle from her water fountain like a horse at a trough, I would have likely suffered terminal dehydration. I never walked anywhere—the skateboard became an extension of my body. I knew the name of every pro skater, I knew who they were sponsored by, and I knew what tricks each of them had invented. I could have quoted any of these statistics to you without even having to think about it.

Skating had an unexpected side effect, too. It started when I noticed that people who saw me skating would stop and watch. I'd never thought about it before, but this made me realize I was actually good at something. It occurred to me for the first time that this was something not everyone else could do, and they were impressed with my ability. It gave me self-confidence and raised my self-esteem. I walked with my head higher, and any feelings of inferiority withered away. It was as if I had become a completely new person. A new era had begun for me.

When I entered eighth grade the next year, school was vastly different. I was no longer invisible. It seemed that a few others had learned the pleasures of skating, and we drew together to form our own little group. We had our own style of dressing, our own obscure references, and our own rules of conduct. The way we looked made it easy for us to identify other skaters in the crowd of students, and made it easier for them to identify us. Things have changed in the years since, but back then skaters drew quite a bit of attention, and often enough it was not of the positive sort.

Perhaps I stood out a little more than the others. One side of my head was shaved to the scalp while the hair on the other side was long. I wore combat boots while everyone else had the latest Nikes. I had earrings in both ears and in one nipple. No one looks twice at that sort of thing these days, when even housewives have tattoos and every kid on the street has some part of their face pierced. A nose ring is now about as shocking as a glass of milk. Things are always different in the South, though.

My behavior wasn't exactly low-key, either. I was thrown out of class at least once a week for disturbing the peace in general. Part of the problem was that I was just so happy to be away from the hell of home. I mocked teachers, screamed out bizarre and nonsensical answers when they asked questions, and made a nuisance of myself in a variety of ways designed to drive authority figures mad with rage. One teacher even threatened to "slap that bird nest off of your head," in reference to my haircut. I was delighted.

When I met Jason Baldwin, he was quite the opposite. I don't recall hearing him ever speak during his first year of junior high. I was the immature pervert who liked to amuse himself by looking up vulgar words in the dictionary during study hall. I certainly wasn't going to waste my time on such pointless exercises as homework. One day after exhausting my sexual vocabulary for the millionth time I slammed the dictionary shut and looked up with the intention of finding someone to bother.

Looking back at me was a skinny kid with a black eye and a long, blond mullet. He was wearing a Mötley Crüe T-shirt, and judging by the paper on his desk he'd been drawing and doodling to kill time. There was a backpack propped next to his feet that turned out not to contain a single book. Instead it held a large collection of cassette tapes—Metallica, Anthrax, Iron Maiden, Slayer, and every other hair band a young hoodlum could desire. He often brought a small Walkman with him and would pass me one of the earpieces during study hall or, months later, on the bus so we both could listen. I'd see him eating lunch every day in the cafeteria and would nod in greeting as I was walking out. I never did ask how he got the black eye.

Jason usually had the latest *Metal Edge* and *Heavy Metal* magazines, and I would look at them while he examined my *Thrasher* collection. All of our interactions took place during school, because I still lived in the shack far outside city limits and my mom drove my sister and me to school in a blue pickup truck. The only class we had together was study hall, so there was little or no talking. Most of our communication was through gestures—finger pointing, eyebrow raising, head shaking, and so on. This didn't change until the day Nanny nearly died.

Nanny had already suffered one heart attack, so she knew the symptoms well. Luckily she had time to call 911 and then to call my mom when the second one hit her. It was late in the evening when my mother began to shout that we had to go. We moved as quickly as we could, but the ambulance still got there before we did. We arrived in Lakeshore to see the paramedics bringing my grandmother out on a stretcher.

It was surreal because it was late enough that the sun was down, but it wasn't completely dark yet. The sky was a beautiful mix of dark blue and purple. There was a special, magickal feel in the air that I've felt only a few times in my life. It touches something in you and it's so damned beautiful that you think you'll die because it's too much to take. A time like that isn't part of any season. It's not spring, summer, winter, or fall. It's a day that stands alone, like a world unto itself.

There was something about the way the red ambulance lights flashed through the entire world without making a sound that hurt my mind. No loud siren, just that red light flashing. I knew my grandmother would be okay. Everyone is okay on an evening like that.

My mother jumped from the truck and explained who she was. They let her into the ambulance to ride with my grandmother, who was barely conscious. We followed behind. At the hospital she was quickly rushed to surgery, where her heart doctor was already waiting.

We sat in the waiting room flipping through magazines without seeing what was on the pages, pacing the halls, and staring blankly at the television screen perched high in the corner. When the doctor finally came out, after what seemed an eternity, he pulled my mother to the side and explained that he had done what he could, but that my grandmother wasn't expected to live through the night. We slept in the waiting room, expecting to hear the worst every time a doctor passed through. The news didn't come that night, or the next day, either.

That afternoon the doctor came to talk to my mother again. He said my grandmother was still alive, though in critical condition. The new problem was that she had developed blood clots in her leg, and it was going to have to be amputated. He had doubts about her making it through the surgery, but she would surely die without it.

We all lived in that hospital waiting room for nearly two weeks. I didn't mind; it was more comfortable than home. The air was nice and cool, everything was spotlessly clean, and there was even cable television. Jack brought sandwiches from home to eat or, when he scraped up enough money, hamburgers from a fast-food place. We ate in the cafeteria only once, because the food was so expensive. Every so often I'd sneak down to grab a few handfuls of crackers or breadsticks from the salad bar when no one was watching. I loved the hospital food. I thought it was delicious.

When I was allowed to go in and see my grandmother, she was so high on morphine that she didn't know what was going on around her. She weakly raised one hand to point at a mirror on the wall and asked me to change the channel. She called me a "little shit" and told a story about how we would become vampire hunters, because you could get a huge reward for bringing in a vampire egg. She started coming back to reality once the doctor gradually decreased the morphine dosage. She was going to survive after all, though now she would have only one leg.

A sixty-five-year-old amputee with two heart attacks under her belt, she was in no condition to take care of herself. She couldn't be expected to move into our squalid palace, so we had to move into her trailer in Lakeshore.

I couldn't pack my few belongings quickly enough, knowing that this was my last time in the shack. It seemed too good to be true; I was escaping hell. I'd never have to see this place again. I didn't waste time taking a last look around, as there was nothing I wanted to say good-bye to. We didn't own a great deal that was worth taking other than our clothes and a few appliances. The furniture was all ready for the trash.

Ah, but I did find a treasure in that place before I left. A parting gift from the ghosts. There was only one closet in the house, and it hadn't been opened in years. It was packed full of clothes that no one wore and other assorted trash that should have been thrown out years ago. My mother and Jack decided to go through it to make certain they weren't leaving behind anything useful (yeah, right, like a pirate might have crept in and buried a treasure). Jack was pulling things out and tossing them on the floor while my mother looked on. At one point he climbed into the closet so he could reach an area that extended up to the ceiling. This was the area where the fire had started. He handed everything he found down to my mother, and she tossed it all onto the floor with her nose wrinkled in disgust.

Suddenly something dusty and black caught my eye. Until that point, I had no interest in anything they were doing. I was just eager to leave. Something about that dusty black bundle drew my attention, so I picked it up. It was a filthy, tattered, dry-rotted, moth-eaten trench coat. My heart skipped a beat because of its perfection. I had to have it.

"Whose is this?" I asked.

My mom said, "No one's, it's just trash." I was slipping it on before she even finished speaking. "That's filthy, you need to wash it," she told me.

Jack, who had just climbed down, took one look and said, "It'll probably come apart if you try to wash it."

And that was how I came to own my very first trench coat. From then on, I was never without one. That seemed to be the one thing that people remembered about me more than anything else. Everyone who described me always began with "He wears a long, black coat." It became the symbol that people associated with me. That particular coat would eventually disintegrate, but I would go on to find others. I would feel safe when wrapped in them, covered up and shielded. It was the greatest security blanket of all. I felt hidden when wearing it, as if bad things couldn't find me. Without it, I felt exposed and vulnerable to the world. I was never self-conscious or a victim of self-doubt when draped in all that black cloth. There's no reason to fear anything when you float through the world like a dusty black ghost.

Seven

Once ensconced in my grandmother's "Lakeshore Estate," we had to build two ramps—one to get her into and out of the trailer, and one to bridge the slight drop between the kitchen and living room. It was next to impossible for her to navigate her wheelchair through the narrow hallway, so we put her bed in a corner of the living room. My mother and Jack took her old room, and at long last I had a room of my own. I rarely ventured outside that room while at home. It was small and dark since the lamplight was covered by a smoky glass globe. I had a black vinyl couch to sleep on and a small metal shelf to store my things. One entire wall was covered by a three-panel mirror. The closet had an odd folding door on it, and the floor was covered with short, brown carpet. I immediately covered the walls with pictures and posters of pro skaters and set up the cheap, secondhand stereo that had been my Christmas present. I made it my place.

I've heard many jokes about poor people living in trailer parks, but I no longer considered myself poor. I was now in the lap of luxury—I could take a shower whenever I wanted, there was central heat for the winter, and a window air conditioner for the summer. The toilet flushed, there were no crop dusters, and we had neighbors. It was heaven.

This narrative would not be complete without a word about Lakeshore itself. It was a pretty big place, as far as trailer parks go. It consisted of two hundred trailers, give or take a few. They were nearly all run-down and beat-up, having put their best days long behind them. Nearly every one of them had a small yard surrounded by a chain-link fence. The majority of those fences held dogs, which were the only form of "home security" we knew. Without a dog and a fence, it was just a matter of time before everything in your yard would be stolen and the gas sucked right out of the tank of your car. The latter was accomplished with nothing more than a piece of hose and a bucket. The residents and locals rarely had regular jobs, although some worked at a box factory nearby. People were more often self-employed thieves or scroungers—for scrap metal, copper, anything you could sell. Addiction of all forms—drinking and meth were the most popular—were daily recreational activities.

People who have seen it in the many years since I left have told me it's changed quite a bit, that it's no longer the same place. Now it's clean, the residents plant flowers in their yards, and they wash their cars. People are neighborly and friendly, and even cops live there. Old people live there after they've retired. I suppose it would now be considered lower middle class. That's a big difference from the days when I knew it. To hear of these changes saddens me, because I feel that the last vestiges of what I knew as home are now gone. The world has moved on while I've been behind these walls. I no longer feel as if I have any roots. It seems that there's a whole new world out there, and I've become an old man in body and mind if not in years.

The heart of Lakeshore was indeed a lake. A lake so green and scummy that most fish no longer inhabited it, and you were strongly advised against swimming in it, because it would not be wise to swallow the water. The bottom of the lake was an old boneyard of newspaper machines, wheelbarrows, box springs and mattresses, rusted bicycles, tangled fishing line, busted tackle boxes, broken fishing poles, and anything else your mind could conceive of. Before we went on trial, the cops claimed they found a knife there that had been used in the murders. I don't doubt that at all, and I would not be surprised if they found a dozen more. My attorneys thought it was most likely planted there to make me look bad, which could very well be true. I also believe it's just as likely to have been thrown in there by one of the many people who used the lake as their own personal dumpster.

That lake was a monster. I miss it terribly. I now think of it as being beautiful in its own green, scummy way, although I can understand why those who lack my nostalgia would not. In my mind, that lake has become like the Ganges, capable of washing away the pain, fear, suffering, and misery caused by years of incarceration for something I didn't even do. That lake has become a magickal thing to me now and has come to represent "home" more than the Mississippi itself.

When writing about your life, it's impossible to include every detail, or even the most uneventful life would require several volumes to record. You have to look back over your life and ask yourself, "What really mattered? What were the big moments that shaped me and made me who I am?" For me, one of those big events was becoming a member of the Roman Catholic Church.

As far back as I can recall, I've always been extremely interested in religion, spirituality, and spiritualism. For me those words cover a wide range of topics, including clairvoyance, ESP, apparitions and hauntings, druids, reincarnation and rebirth, prophecy, and even attending Mass or praying, among others. Around the fourth grade I started to read books on Nostradamus, Edgar Cayce, astral projection, and the healing properties of crystals and stones. If it was connected to spirituality in any way at all, then I was interested. I believe this may have somehow been in response to all the sermons about hate, fear, and the wrath of God that I'd been hearing. I suppose I needed something that would balance that.

One day, while looking through the stacks in the library, I encountered a shiny new book on Catholicism written for teens. It was intended to teach young Catholics the meaning behind each thing they're supposed to do during Mass. I was about fourteen or fifteen when I found it, and I had never been to a Catholic church in my life.

I took the book home and sat up late into the night reading it. I took it to school with me and read it when I had a spare moment. I was absolutely entranced, and I fell in love with the Catholic Church.

All my life I'd been forced to go to Protestant churches against my will. Now I wanted desperately to be allowed to go to a Catholic church. I wanted to see the things I was reading about; I wanted to experience them firsthand. Genuflecting, holy water, praying with a rosary, the Stations of the Cross, and especially receiving the Eucharist—I loved the idea of it all. This was Christianity the way I had never before seen it. The entire process from the moment you enter the door, genuflect, and bless yourself is about respect, and about a dignity of the spirit. It was beautiful.

At first I was afraid to tell Jack or my mother that I wanted to go to a Catholic church. There's still a large amount of prejudice in the South when it comes to Catholicism. The word "Catholic" is often said in the same tone of voice one uses when issuing an insult. I once heard someone comment that a Saint Christopher medal was "satanic." These days the South is the land of the Baptist Church, and it can be a cruel place for anyone not of that persuasion.

I knew Jack was the one who would have to agree to it, and I knew I had to tell him in a language he'd understand. So one day I informed him that I felt I had a "calling" from God, and that I needed to find the place I was supposed to be. In the type of churches he attended, to say one had a calling meant that you were directly hearing God's voice or feeling His presence, and that He was compelling you to do something. A calling could be seen by the rest of the world as anything from intuition to a psychotic episode. Still, he understood. And if I felt God was telling me to do something, then Jack Echols would be the last to interfere. He may not respect me, but he would respect what he perceived to be God's will.

When he asked where I wanted to go, I knew I couldn't just blurt out, "The Catholic Church," because he would have looked at that suspiciously. Instead I told him I thought it best if I went to different places, and that I'd know the right one when I found it. He nodded, and that was the end of the conversation.

There was only one Catholic church in West Memphis; it was called St. Michael's. It was a small place when compared with the huge cathedral-like buildings that housed the local Baptist churches, but it was well taken care of and in pristine condition. There were stone benches outside, and a small statue of Saint Francis. The lawn was raked and there was no debris or even a stray leaf to be found on the grounds. The word I keep coming back to over and over is "dignity." The place had dignity, and it encouraged all who entered to have the same. The entire atmosphere announced that this was not a place where you would find people rolling on the floor and screaming.

I was dropped off and went inside to take a seat. I followed the lead of people around me and knelt on a padded bench to say a little "Hi, I'm here" to whatever power in the universe was listening. The place was completely silent—no screaming children or men in cheap suits bellowing obnoxious greetings to one another. Everyone quietly took their seats and waited. It was not an uncomfortable silence. On the contrary, it was very relaxing and peaceful; you could sit engaged in your own contemplations without fear of being disturbed. I felt very welcome there.

The organ began playing softly and everyone stood as the procession of the priest and altar boys made their way down the central aisle and to the front of the church. I couldn't take my eyes off the small parade. The robes, the candles, the book held aloft—I was witnessing pure magick. I enjoyed every moment and savored the experience. After the opening ceremony the priest spoke for about thirty minutes in a calm, quiet voice about what he'd just read. There was no shouting, he didn't beat his fist on the podium, and there was not one single word about the end of the world being at hand. I regretted having to leave once it was over, and would rather have spent the day there examining the scenes on the stained glass windows, admiring the statues that stood in the corners, or even watching the flickering of the votive candles.

That evening when Jack asked how it was, I told him that I'd found my place. When he asked how I knew, I said because it felt like home. He didn't say another word, and dropped me off again a week later.

This time I waited around afterward until everyone had trailed out into the parking lot. I approached the priest, Greg Hart, who was a small, balding man with wire-framed glasses. I introduced myself and with no preamble asked, "How do I become a Catholic?" We sat and talked for a while, and he explained how I would have to attend conversion classes, as there was a lot to learn. He himself would teach the classes every Monday night. After getting all the information I needed, I walked outside where Jack was waiting in the truck to take me home.

I attended every single class, never missing one. Father Hart arranged a ride back and forth for me with a woman who would also be attending the classes. There were fewer than ten of us in all. We learned everything, from the teachings of the church on different points of dogma to how to pray the rosary. I enjoyed the classes almost as much as Mass itself. For my confirmation, I chose to name myself after Saint Damien.

When the day finally arrived that I was to receive the sacraments of baptism and first communion, a deacon who'd sponsored my conversion, Ben, gave me two gifts. One was the rosary his wife had used up until the day she died. The other was a suit to wear for the occasion. I was very touched by both. Unfortunately, I lost contact with these kind and supportive people in my life relatively soon afterward.

The only time my mother or Jack ever stepped inside the church was on the night of my baptism and first communion. I was fifteen or sixteen at the time. They sat in the very back row, looking uneasy and out of place throughout the ceremony. When it was over they stood and clapped along with everyone else. I was happy that they came, because I felt a sense of accomplishment and wanted someone to witness it.

I didn't stop attending Mass until my life went straight to hell a couple of years later. I've long since outgrown any belief in mainstream Christian theology, and I even have some degree of animosity toward Christianity in general because of what has been done to me by people declaring themselves Christian. But I still love the ritual and ceremony of the Catholic Church. A little old priest comes here once a month, and I watch as he gives the sacraments to the Catholic convicts on Death Row. It comforts me just to watch it, and I often find myself remembering the pleasure I used to take in it.

Today, on Good Friday, I began performing the Holy Guardian Angel ritual as described in *The Book of the Sacred Magic of Abramelin the Mage*. It's a prayer that asks a higher self or outside intelligence for guidance, protection, and for forgiveness of all my weaknesses and sins. Expert practitioners wear white robes and burn candles and frankincense, and use other esoteric paraphernalia. I obviously don't have all the materials he suggests, but I don't believe they're needed. I was reading through the scriptures that would be read during Mass for today and was suddenly overcome with the feeling that I need to begin *now*. I felt a sense of power and peace that I wanted to be closer to. I showered and put on clean white clothes, and then knelt to pray. If Aleister Crowley could do the ritual on horseback, then I could do it in a prison cell.

I prayed that I be forgiven all my transgressions, that I be protected and watched over, that I be granted the strength I would need, and that I be granted the knowledge and conversation of the Holy Guardian Angel. I haven't prayed like that since I was a child. Afterward I just wanted to sit and bask in the sense of peace that I felt. I know I will have to be on guard so as not to be completely swept up into devotion, or I won't be able to remain objective. Aleister Crowley stressed the importance of neither believing nor disbelieving; I have the tendency to become a zealot.

The ritual was very informal and spur-of-the-moment, but I wanted to do it, if only for symbolic reasons, it being Good Friday. Tomorrow I'll begin in a more formal manner, by setting up an altar and scrubbing this cell from top to bottom.

Today at 8:15 a.m., I prayed for the knowledge and conversation of the Holy Guardian Angel. I repeated the prayer at 9:55 a.m. almost as a compulsion. I love how clean and focused I feel afterward. I asked for the knowledge and conversation of the Holy Guardian Angel, along with the strength and intelligence I need to complete and endure the ritual. I swear that I will never use it for evil, but only for the glory of God, and to aid myself and others. Last, I ask for help and guidance in following the one true Way. I always end with the phrase "In Christ's name I ask this, amen," and then I make the sign of the cross. Afterward I feel refreshed and rejuvenated. I wonder what the difference would be if I had *all* the tools—the oil of Abramelin, Cakes of Light, incense, and wine.

I realized that while going through the Holy Guardian Angel prayer everything inside me becomes incredibly still. It's like a very concentrated form of meditation. When you sit zazen, the first twenty minutes or so are maddening. Your legs ache, your nose itches, you can't seem to find your center of gravity and so on, but once you make it past that first stage it starts to feel *good*. Like you could do it forever. That's how the HGA prayer starts to feel. There's an incredible stillness. The only thing moving inside you is the prayer itself, moving up and up. You begin to feel it seeping into the times when you *aren't* praying, too. I'll be just reading a book, and there it will suddenly be, bringing me into the present moment. I can now find that still, small point without even doing the prayer. It's *always* there inside me; it takes only a split second to locate it. It's there even when there's no hope in it.

The prayer makes you focus. The focus makes you alert enough to notice the crack when it appears. The angel comes through the crack. The crack is somewhere inside me, as dark as a hole the sun has never touched. The angel is electric blue. I saw all of this in a matter of one-tenth of a second. It was nothing more than a flicker of endless black and electric blue.

That still, silent point of focus is back today. As soon as I knelt to begin, the feeling came over me. It's like being the only thing that exists. Like being in an endless, silent vacuum. It's both peaceful and powerful. My life is becoming more compact, like a tremendous amount of energy that has been compressed into a tiny sun. That's as it should be. It feels good, as if I've discovered exactly what I'm meant to be doing right now. For a long time I have been overextending my reach, desperately snatching at every strand that floated my way in hopes of discovering some shred of inspiration. I've now come to realize that the only names I need are the ones that have been in my book of destiny since the very beginning. If I want to keep moving forward, then I have to keep looking back. I am rejuvenated by drinking from the oldest and deepest wells. I have found my way back to the source from which my magick flows. I am home.

One of the reasons I am now pushing my body beyond all its known limits is that over the years I have erected a barrier between my mind and body. I have elevated the mind until the body became next to worthless. It shows in my physical posture—the way my shoulders unconsciously slump and my head hangs. I can correct this only for short periods of time, and only by applying all of my will to it. I have to find a way to heal myself, to bring both mind and body into harmony. If I don't, disease will set in.

Today my feet bled through two pairs of socks. It was bliss. Watching those coin-sized crimson stains bloom through the white fabric has become Holy Communion for me. Bringing my body to that point of pain and exhaustion has become my religion.

My life has taught me that true spiritual insight can come about only through direct experience, the way a severe burn can be attained only by putting your hand in the fire. Faith is nothing more than a watered-down attempt to accept someone else's insight as your own. Belief is the psychic equivalent of an article of secondhand clothing, worn-out and passed down. I equate true spiritual insight with wisdom, which is different from knowledge. Knowledge can be obtained through many sources: books, stories, songs, legends, myths, and, in modern times, computers and television programs. On the other hand, there's only one real source of wisdom—pain. Any experience that provides a person with wisdom will also usually provide them with a scar. The greater the pain, the greater the realization. Faith is spiritual *rigor mortis*.

I can vaguely remember life in what I call the real world. It seemed to be a chain of events that flowed one into another, not always seamlessly but at least naturally. There is *nothing* natural about my current situation. Nothing flows—or even *moves*—without someone applying a tremendous amount of willpower to one of reality's pressure points. Even then, it's like trying to keep a beach ball aloft just by blowing on it. Life without momentum is not truly life. A person needs movement, or they eventually begin to forget that they even exist.

I've read stories in which bliss, through some bizarre form of emotional alchemy, becomes lethargy or malaise. Perhaps it's the boredom that causes a prince to give up all he knows and become a beggar. I can't say. What I began to wonder is if the opposite may be true—if by following the thread of pain to a deep enough level, I could find something else. I knew I wasn't the first to wonder about such a thing, because in certain Native American tribes, the men would sometimes undergo tremendously painful ordeals in search of spiritual or psychic insight.

One of the most torturous and well-known paths to opening the senses wider than usual is fasting. On my first attempt, I went for two weeks without consuming anything but water. For the first four days or so the pain of hunger, combined with the physical deterioration, was maddening. My skin was hot with fever. It reminded me of the powerful periods of fever and sickness that would come upon me suddenly as a child. There would be no warning; I would just wake up in the middle of the night with a high fever. I would be so weak that I couldn't move, but it felt like I was floating. I could feel currents of energy passing through my consciousness, and realized they were always flowing through the world, but that I could feel them only when I was in that fevered state. The closest I can come to articulating it even now would be to say that I could hear a river of pink voices. Once I became a teenager, it stopped. During the very last fit, my fever went so high that my mother submerged me in a tub of ice-cold water in order to bring it down. The touch of that ice water on my skin was one of the most horrific experiences of my life. I wanted to scream and fight, but could only lie there gasping. I couldn't even cry. My mother kept muttering reassurances to me and smoothing my hair out of the way as she poured the frigid water over my face. I kept thinking, *How can she not know that I'm in hell?* The fever never bothered me. It was comforting in a way. It was the ice water that I thought was going to kill me.

While fasting I would fall asleep fevered, hungry, and exhausted, but I was closer to that current than I had been since childhood. Still, there was something separating me from it. I could hear it on the horizon like a distant train whistle, but I wasn't *experiencing* it. I needed something else to bring me closer.

I don't know why I started running. I don't even *remember* starting; I was suddenly just doing it. Being trapped in a cell meant I had to run in place, so that's what I did. I ran so hard that I lost all track of time. Eventually, I passed out. The world just went black, and sounds seemed to be coming from the far end of a very long hallway. I did it again the next day, only this time I put on two pairs of socks, because of the blisters on my feet. I ran until I found myself crawling toward the toilet on my hands and knees, retching and dry-heaving as I slipped in my own sweat. What should have been horrible was somehow beautiful. It was one of the most wonderful experiences of my life. I felt closer to all things divine than I ever did in any church. I had run for over two hours without stopping for so much as a drink of water, and I had discovered a new world.

By the third day, my feet had started bleeding, leaving little smudges and droplets all over the floor, but I wouldn't even notice them until later. I don't understand how there can be magick in the repetitive movement of the body, but I've found it.

There are times when my mind screams at my body to stop, that it's not possible to go for one more second. I ignore it and push beyond that point. Only by pushing beyond every boundary that my mind and body pose can I swim in the dark, deep waters that I need. That's the place where anything worth having comes from. It's the pain of destroying my boundaries that lets me scan the current for messages in bottles. They come from downstream with a ghost inside each one. I don't know who or what casts those bottles, at least not yet. Those with less curiosity or ambition just mumble that God works in mysterious ways. I intend to catch him in the act.

Eight

Eventually, Jason Baldwin came over nearly every single day after school, and we'd sit in my room listening to music, talking, and laughing at other people until we reached a fevered, manic pitch. I laughed harder in those early days than I have ever since. It was the kind of laughter that causes you to lose all control and fall over. Years later, Jason and I talk about those days, trying to remember exactly what was so funny. Neither of us knows; we only recall that it was the most hilarious period of our lives.

Soon every weekend would find either me sleeping at Jason's house or him sleeping at mine. When we were at my place we'd stay in my room, eating chips, drinking cans of generic soda, and listening to heavy metal cassettes. We were always trying to be quiet so that Jack wouldn't hear us—if he heard even the slightest sound he'd go into a rage. He automatically hated anyone I befriended and went out of his way to make it unpleasant for all of us.

The very first night I stayed at Jason's we decided to sneak out. I had never done this before, so I was doing it more for the thrill than to go anywhere in particular. The evening started out with Jason's mom, Gail, dropping us off at the bowling alley in West Memphis, with the instruction to go nowhere else. As soon as she left the parking lot, Jason's younger brother Matt departed the scene in search of other excitement. Jason and I went inside to play pool and associate with all the other hoodlums. This was the hangout for degenerates, and there were mullets everywhere you turned.

After playing a couple games and exchanging greetings with the locals, we decided to go find Matt. Perhaps there were more interesting things to be found wherever he was. We crossed the parking lots of grocery stores and strip malls to reach Walmart, which we knew to be his most likely location. While there we paid a visit to the music section, put our money together, and bought the newest Metallica tape, then sat down to read the lyrics. We finally found Matt playing video games, and all three of us made our way back to the bowling alley, where Gail soon picked us up.

The night was so cold that everything seemed crystal clear, magickal, and a little scary. The world suddenly felt very large. I remember every detail because that was the first time I had so wantonly and completely disobeyed all orders. We were free to do whatever we wanted, with no interference or adult supervision. A whole new world had opened up. The feeling of adventure and absolute freedom was amazing.

When Gail pulled up we quickly piled into the car and made our way back to Lakeshore. Back at Jason's place we all three went into his room to listen to the new Metallica tape and play video games on the Nintendo system and old television that sat on the dresser. I can't remember who first suggested sneaking out, but we immediately seized upon the idea. Time seemed to tick by at an agonizingly slow pace as we waited for Jason's mom and stepfather to go to bed. After the lights went out we gave them another hour just to be certain they were sleeping.

We made our exit through the window in Matt's room, because it was bigger than the one in Jason's room. We could also step out onto the fence by stretching our legs out as far as possible, and from the fence it was only a short hop to the ground. Jason and Matt had both done this before and had no difficulty. I, on the other hand, got hung up with one leg inside and one leg outside. They decided to "help" me by yanking on the leg that was outside, and nearly crushed my testicles in the process.

We had no particular destination in mind, so we walked the streets of Lakeshore for a while, leaving a trail of barking dogs in our wake. It was so cold that all the puddles next to the street had thin sheets of ice over them, and the streetlights sparkled on them like diamonds. I was giddy with excitement and considered Jason to be wise in the ways of the world for having done this before.

We decided to pay a visit to the nearby train tracks, where Jason said there was a tree house in which people sometimes left bottles of wine. To get there we had to cross an empty field, and we didn't take into account the recent rains. Our feet punched through the thin glaze of ice, and the three of us were standing in ankle-deep water. But the shivering and teeth chattering barely dimmed our sense of excitement and we plodded on.

When we finally made it to the tracks, not only was the tree house smashed but the whole rotten tree had fallen over. We continued on our way, following the tracks for about a mile, with the intention of making a full circle and ending up back at Jason's trailer. We were quite a distance from any lights or trailers, and the night was silent. We talked about ghost tales and horror movies, urban legends and things we'd seen in Time-Life's Mysteries of the Unknown books. Soon every hair on our necks was standing straight up and we were jumping at our own imaginations. We walked in a single file, Jason leading the way, Matt in the middle, and me bringing up the rear. Matt insisted on being in the middle so that nothing could sneak up on him. In quiet voices we discussed how some kid had claimed to see a dead man hopping back and forth across the train tracks on Halloween night. It was like we couldn't keep from feeding our own terror. Sometime later I saw the movie *Stand by Me* and was overcome with nostalgia because of how much it reminded me of us.

Back at the trailer, we peeled off our wet footwear and fell asleep in front of the TV watching *Headbangers Ball*. I'll never forget a single thing about that night as long as I live. It's part of what makes me who I am. I've often wondered if Jason and Matt have thought about it much over the years.

As we grew older, the thrill of sneaking out lost much of its appeal because in such a small town there's nowhere to go and nothing to do. Everything is closed by ten o'clock and there's not much thrill in walking empty streets after the first time or two. Instead, we'd rent low-budget, straight-to-video horror movies every weekend and sit up all night watching them and making wisecracks. That was the closest thing to a "satanic orgy" I ever witnessed. The police had very vivid imaginations. I'm inclined to believe they may have seen a few too many of those cheap horror movies themselves.

Often at the end of these festivities we'd collapse onto the bed and sleep until noon the next day. We couldn't fall asleep without music. I never slept better than with Iron Maiden or Testament playing in the background.

Over the years Jason and I became as close as brothers because we knew there was no one else to look out for us. We shared everything we had—food, clothes, money, whatever. If one of us had it, both of us had it. It was known without having to be said.

After we were unceremoniously released from school for summer vacation every year, we would spend the long days sitting on the ragged dock in Jason's backyard, fishing, feeding the ducks, or making foul comments and put-downs to whatever neighborhood teenagers showed up to hang out. Sometimes we'd play video games, stare blankly at the afternoon cartoons on television, pick at each other, or listen to one of the geniuses make prank calls. Other times we'd explore out-of-the-way places in search of snakes. In our neighborhood snakes were as valuable as cash and could be traded for anything. The days were slow and lazy, hot and long, each the same as the last. This was the extent of our lives, and we thought nothing would ever change.

The first time I met Jessie Misskelley was completely unintentional. One day after school I knocked on Jason's door, and Gail answered. Before I even asked, she said, "He's not here, he's at Jessie

Misskelley's." She called him by his full name—Jessie Misskelley—
and I would later learn that's what everyone did.

Leaving Jason's front porch, I began to head back toward home,
because I had no idea where "Jessie Misskelley's" was. I'd heard the
name before, and from the sounds of it he was supposed to be one of
the Lakeshore badasses. About halfway down the street I heard Jason
yell, and I looked to my left to see him standing in the open doorway of a trailer. It turned out that Jessie Misskelley lived only about
four or five trailers down from Jason. I entered the gate and Jason
led the way inside.

The trailer appeared clean and kept up, no roaches or mice to be
seen, and everything was in its place. Sitting in a living room chair
next to the door was Jessie Misskelley. He was wearing blue jeans, a
T-shirt, and tennis shoes. His feet were propped up on the coffee
table, and he had a bologna and cheese sandwich in one hand, and
he was twirling an orange flare gun in the other. His hands had
something black smeared on them all the way up to the forearms, as
if he'd been working on a car. There was a mesh baseball cap perched
atop his head; the emblem on the front was a Confederate flag and a
grinning skull—typical truck-stop fare. From beneath the hat, long,
straight, brown hair hung down to his shoulders.

Before my eyes even had time to adjust to the inside, a female
voice screeched with deafening fury, "Get out from in front of the
TV!" This seemed to be directed at me, and it came from a skinny,
dark-haired girl sitting in another chair. This bundle of feminine
charm turned out to be Jessie's girlfriend, who was notorious in cer-

tain trailer park circles. Some guys had their girlfriend's name tattooed on their chest. Jessie had the word "bitch" tattooed on his, in reference to Alicia.

Jason and I took a seat on the couch. Jessie's girlfriend fell back into a silent stupor. Jessie became more animated and began to bebop around the living room. He took a glass figurine from a shelf and started making kissing noises. "This is my girlfriend," he announced, holding up the glass figure. It appeared to be a small black woman with breasts bared, perhaps a novelty saltshaker.

An older man came out of a back room, and I took him to be Jessie's dad. I was correct. He didn't so much sit in the chair that Jessie had vacated as collapse into it with a groan and a sigh. He looked tired and weary, as if every day of his life had been a long day. He eyed Jessie's sandwich and asked, "That ain't the last of that cheese, is it?"

Jessie's response was "Oops." When his dad informed him he'd been saving it to take for lunch the next day, Jessie pulled the cheese from between the bread and flapped it in the air. "You can still have it," he said, holding the cheese aloft and casting a grin in our direction. It was several bites short of being a whole piece.

His father paid him no attention. Instead he said Jessie needed to get ready to climb under the trailer and make sure all the tires were on and aired up. They were preparing to move it to another trailer park, called Highland.

Jason was suddenly very ready to leave. As we were going through the gate Jessie called out, "Y'all come back later so you can help me." Jason said, "Okay," over his shoulder without slowing down. A little farther down the street he told me that's why he rarely went over there—they always tried to put you to work while they did nothing. Needless to say, we did not go back later to help, and Jessie took no offense. He knew he'd try to get out of unpaid manual labor, too.

I never did see Jessie a great deal, but we became familiar enough with each other to talk when we met. Jason and I would run into him at the bowling alley and spend an hour or two playing pool, or hang out for a little while at the Lakeshore store. Jessie was no great conversationalist, but his antics could be amusing, and the odd things he said were usually worth a chuckle. It was very apparent to anyone of even average intelligence that you weren't dealing with the world's brightest guy. He was a great deal like a child. He was harmless.

Nine

Going back to school the next year was like starting from scratch. I was going to high school, while Jason was staying behind in junior high. In the preceding three years, I had developed a sense of security or stability, and now it was gone. Even though the high school was only about ten feet away from the junior high, it was a whole different world.

Marion High School drew ninety-five percent of its student body from middle- and upper-middle-class neighborhoods. This was a place where kids drove brand-new cars to school, wore Gucci clothing, and had enough jewelry to spark the envy of rap stars. This was a place where I definitely didn't fit in. Everyone who used to skateboard seemed to have given it up and moved on to other things, which meant that my circle of acquaintances had grown much smaller. In truth, I wasn't even skating all that much anymore.

In response to my new environment, my behavior became even more outrageous, and I was viewed as a freak. Freaks were a definite group of people, but it's sometimes hard to explain what causes a certain person to fall into that category. Freaks weren't really popular, but everyone knew who they were on sight. One boy had huge muttonchop sideburns, wore short pants, and had stuffed animal heads on his shoes. Another guy rarely took a bath and had a tendency to show up every now and then wearing a skirt. He wasn't gay; he just liked skirts. A girl named Tammy (whom I had a crush on) was harder to define. She was gorgeous and a gymnast, but she wore nose rings, thermal underwear under her shorts, and white socks with black sandals. We had an odd relationship because she'd insult me and create a whole new genre of derogatory names to call me, but she'd jump down anyone else's throat if they even looked at me funny.

I began an intense and unlikely friendship with a guy named Brian that year. He sat next to me in a couple of classes and was always very quiet, but in an arrogant fashion. He dressed as if he had a business meeting to attend every day, had immaculately groomed blond hair, and wore tiny, round, gold-rimmed spectacles. When he finished whatever work had been assigned to us, he'd pull out a novel and quietly read until the end of class. When he acknowledged anyone's presence, it was with contempt. I couldn't resist bothering him. When I demanded to see the book he was reading, he refused, saying that it had been a birthday gift and I looked like the sort who would damage it. When I declared that I wished to try on his spectacles, he once again refused and said he had no desire to clean my greasy fingerprints off the lenses. He seemed to think me an ill-mannered barbarian. These exchanges continued on a daily basis while class went on around us. He once hissed at me furiously, "Why can you not whisper? Even when you're being quiet you're still screaming." This came after several warnings from the teacher. He had never been thrown out of a class in his life, and he had no intention of this being his first.

One day I noticed he had a cassette sitting on top of his books. I leaned over to get a look at the title, and it was no one I had ever heard of. "What's that?" I asked. Handing me the cover so I could read the lyrics, he said it was a Christian rock band and that it was the only kind of music he listened to.

I was appalled and outraged that such a thing existed—how dare they defile the sanctity of rock 'n' roll? He claimed he had quite the extensive collection, was active in many fundamentalist youth programs, and never missed church. He even had the nerve to invite me to come with him. My first instinct was to make a nasty gesture, but I suddenly stopped. Why not? It could be very interesting. My own religion felt so personal to me, a private thing, that his religion seemed viral, its only purpose to recruit more followers. It was all about "saving" others; once you "saved" somebody, you just moved on to "saving" others.

The function we attended was some sort of youth gathering. The Baptist church had a gym, and that's where we went. There were teenagers playing basketball, Ping-Pong, and even a few board games. I took part in none of the above. Instead, Brian and I took a seat in metal folding chairs at the back, so we could watch everyone else. While we were talking, a group of about five girls approached us, obviously friends of his, judging by the way they greeted him.

Despite what I had been expecting, I soon found that I was enjoying myself. I struck up a friendship with one of the girls that would last for a couple of years—we talked two or three times a week on the phone, for hours at a time. Contrary to what my past experiences had led me to expect, no one preached, tried to convert me, or seemed to be even thinking about religion. We sat and talked while everyone went about their business all around us.

It also seemed to be quite the hot spot for teenage romance. Just like any other place where young people tend to congregate, you would often see boys and girls looking at one another as if they were about ready to eat each other up. We went back to this place several times during the year and there was only one awkward moment.

The awkward moment came when I showed up one night dressed in a long black coat, black pants, black shirt, and shiny, knee-high black boots that looked like they'd been stolen from a dead Nazi. This was my everyday garb now. I no longer dressed like a skater. In fact, I now never wore anything but black. Anytime I replaced an article of clothing it was with something black. I never again wore any color until after I was arrested. My appearance had been changing gradually, too. I had allowed my hair to grow long and tangled until it looked like Johnny Depp's hair in the movie *Edward Scissorhands*.

I noticed Brian talking to an older man, who I later discovered was the "youth pastor." When Brian came back and sat next to me, he said the youth pastor didn't like the way I was dressed, that it appeared "satanic." Brian suggested that I at least take off the black duster, so I did as he requested. His eyes grew large as he urgently said, "Put it back on!" Evidently my shirt, which was emblazoned with the Iron Maiden slogan "No prayer for the dying," was a church "don't." I hadn't even thought about it before that moment, but it drew a great deal of attention from everyone else. That moment became one of the nails hammered into the coffin that sealed my fate and sent me here.

As I sat in the Monroe County jail some years later, waiting to go to trial for murder, I saw that youth minister on the television screen. He was practically rabid as he ranted about "pacts with the devil." He seemed psychotic. Simply the fact that I wore such a shirt to a church function was enough to convince a great many people that I had to be guilty.

My influence on Brian's life crept in gradually. His manner of dressing changed, his hair grew long and shaggy, and he no longer listened to Christian rock bands. He soon fell into the "freak" category. He wore silverware for jewelry and chain-smoked clove cigarettes. He was no longer above sneaking into his mom's cabinet for a drink or two every now and then. He took up skating and became better than I had ever been.

He was better because he was fearless. It was as if the possibility that he could fall and damage himself never even crossed his mind. Some part of me was always scared that I was going to fall when trying something new, so there would be a slight hesitation or a sense of holding back. Brian never had that; he hadn't yet learned that pain waits for you around every corner—and it was apparent just by watching him.

Soon I was staying at his place on weekends, or he at mine. On spring days, we'd go to the convenience store down the street from his house to get chocolate milk, Popsicles, and cigarettes, then sit on the curb and watch people going in and out. It doesn't sound like much fun, but it was relaxing to me.

For some reason I can no longer remember, I began keeping an odd sort of journal during this time period. It was a plain black notebook with no special characteristics, but in the years since it has become one of the most embarrassing and humiliating aspects of my existence. Everyone else is free to forget their period of teenage angst. I am not. That damnable notebook is always there to remind me. To be honest, I'm always amazed that I still get letters from people telling me how much they've enjoyed reading the parts that are known to the public and asking for more. There is no accounting for taste. I'm appalled that I ever wrote such trash. One day while watching my favorite sitcom a character on the show remarked, "Ever since they decided poems don't have to rhyme, everyone thinks they're poets." How true. He may as well have been pointing at me.

I wrote about typical teenage bullshit: depression, loneliness, heartache, angst, free-floating anxiety, thoughts of suicide. Even after I tired of it I was enticed into writing more by the only factor that has motivated boys since the beginning of time—a girl. Ultimately she kept the notebook, and I forgot all about it. I never even saw it again until I found myself on trial a couple of years later. Not only would I find myself on trial for something I was innocent of, but the prosecutors would rub salt into my wounds by reading my most private thoughts and feelings before a packed courtroom, television cameras, and newspaper reporters. Somehow this was considered "evidence." A bad hairdo, a black wardrobe, teenage angst-ridden "poetry," and a taste for hair bands is enough to send you to prison. Death Row, no less.

The notebook became filled with all sorts of things I hardly remember—quotes, bits of information, lines from my favorite stories, and "poems" I had written. I can bring myself to call them that only with tongue in cheek. When I hear or read someone quote from them now, I want to crawl under a chair and hide. Ultimately, it is only my bad taste that has been immortalized.

The evening following our last day of school, Brian stayed at my house and we ordered pizza to celebrate the beginning of summer vacation. We sat at the kitchen table eating and watching the occasional person walk past on the darkened street outside. When I informed him that during the course of the day I had met a girl and we'd found ourselves attracted to each other, his curiosity was piqued. I told him her name, Laura, thinking he'd have no idea who I was talking about, but he surprised me by saying, more than once, "Are you *serious*?"

It turned out that he saw this girl and her two sidekicks on an almost daily basis, because one of them, Ashley, lived on the street directly behind him. That set the tone and daily routine of our entire summer. Every single day after Ashley's parents left for work, Brian and I would head straight over to her house, and all five of us would spend the day watching music videos or passing the hours in her backyard pool. The third girl's name was Carrie, and before the summer was over Laura and I broke up and Carrie and I paired off. Brian and Ashley were an item all summer. There was something magickal about that season and the small group the five of us formed. When the summer ended, so did we.

We didn't meet them often on the weekends, because that would have involved the hassle of dealing with parental figures. We kept in constant contact by phone, but had no in-the-flesh meetings. Instead, Brian and I would spend the weekends ice-skating at a nearby shopping mall, riding around the streets of Memphis with his older brother, or watching videos and talking. That was the summer of much talking.

I also got my first job, and it was one of the most horrendous experiences of my life. I woke up one morning and decided I was tired of being broke and penniless; it was time for me to join the workforce.

I started by putting in applications at all the usual places that hire teenagers—grocery stores, fast-food joints, Walmart. No one was hiring. Then one day I remembered a small seafood restaurant next to the highway. I had never been inside the place, and I was growing desperate because potential employers didn't seem to value the exceptional intellectual giant who was presenting himself to them. The seafood restaurant was my last option.

I stepped inside the place one afternoon, and it was so dark that it took my eyes a minute to adjust. The floors were bare concrete, and the tables were small and covered with red-and-white-checkered plastic tablecloths. The cash register stood a few feet away from me, and sitting on a bar stool next to it was a small, gray-haired, humpbacked man. He seemed to be engrossed in paperwork of some sort.

I approached him and asked if this fine establishment might be hiring. He looked at me for a moment in a way that would lead one to believe he was calculating shrewdly, then asked, "Can you start tonight?" I responded in the affirmative, and he told me to show up at five o'clock.

I returned home elated. I had a job and would soon be able to afford whatever I wanted. The future was wide open and my mind was filled with possibilities. Reality would soon smash my youthful idealism.

When I arrived at five I was told that I was the new busboy. My uniform was an apron that looked as if it might have once been white in previous years. I distinctly remember using my fingernail to scrape off pieces of eggshell that were cemented to the front of it. After putting it on I was shown to the kitchen, where I witnessed a vision from the very bowels of hell.

This restaurant was the only place on earth I've seen that was filthier than prison. You could have literally vomited on the floor and no one would have noticed it. They would have stepped over the puddle and kept right on walking. The place was family-owned, and the family consisted of a father, mother, and three children. The hunchback who hired me was the father.

The mother was a 250-pound lump who never made eye contact with anyone and never spoke a word. She was filthy from laboring day and night in this kitchen. The three children—two boys and a girl—were hell spawn. The youngest, a boy about two years old, wore nothing but a pair of filth-caked underpants. The older son, who was about three or four, usually wore shorts but no shirt or shoes. The little girl couldn't have been older than five, and she wore a set of superhero-themed underwear and T-shirt every day. All three had crud-smeared faces, runny noses, and tangled hair.

The kids had to be kept in the kitchen and out of sight of any customers at all times. They weren't even allowed to use the restroom. Instead, they used a five-gallon bucket with a toilet seat balanced precariously atop it. This meant there was a five-gallon bucket of shit and piss sitting right in the middle of the kitchen at any given time.

The kitchen itself looked much like a room from the house in *The Texas Chainsaw Massacre*. The walls were greasy and stained black from smoke, the countertops looked like tiny garbage barges, and the entire place carried the aroma of rotting fish. As a matter of fact, my first task was to clean about ten pounds of spoiled fish out of the sink, which I did while swallowing my own vomit. More than once I walked in to find the mother giving one of the kids a bath in one side of the sink as fish fillets or crab legs soaked in the other half. On my first night, I moved a large bag of cornmeal only to discover a large rat nursing a litter of hairless pink babies.

I had been working there about three weeks when several of the other workers showed up at my door. They said they had to round everyone up and get to work quickly because someone had called the health department and they were coming to inspect the place. We cleaned, scrubbed, and hauled garbage from two-thirty in the afternoon until after eleven that night and still seemed no closer to making the place presentable. At that point I knew I couldn't take this for another second. I stood before the hunchback with my clothes looking as if they had been plucked from a dumpster and every inch of my body covered in sludge, filth, and crud that defied any attempt at description. I told him that I was going home and would not be returning. I couldn't escape that place in my nightmares, though. I dreamed about it much longer than I worked there.

B rian and I began to drift apart once we started school again. One reason was that I had once again failed and would be spending another year as a freshman. This meant I'd be celebrating my seventeenth birthday in the ninth grade. Coincidentally, one of my childhood heroes had managed to do the same. His name was Andy, and he was the only guy in eighth grade with a five-o'clock shadow. He paid no mind to trends or changing fashions; he always wore jeans with the knees ripped out and a battered green army jacket. He had shoulder-length black hair and wore a long, dangling earring that looked like a crucifix. Andy was the most laid-back guy in the school, and he'd either sleep through every class or draw. Nobody messed with him, and he didn't mess with anyone. During the summer Brian and I had gotten rides from his little sister, Dawn, who was our age. She loved both of us, and was great just because she was so normal. She didn't care about high school politics and didn't fit into any particular group. She also consumed more vodka than a teenage girl should be able to.

Brian advanced to tenth grade and grew closer to the freak crowd. I completely quit skating and became what people now call "goth," though I had never heard the word, and there were no goths in our school. I did what I did because it was aesthetically pleasing to me. In addition to Slayer, Testament, and Metallica, my musical taste expanded to include things like Danzig, The Misfits, Siouxsie and the Banshees, and Depeche Mode. All the old skateboarding posters disappeared from my room and were replaced with old prints I found in odd books. Most of them looked a great deal like images from Goya's etchings and sketches. I caught a couple of filthy, vindictive pigeons and allowed them to fly around the room as they pleased.

I spent much less time with Brian and found myself falling back into the old patterns Jason and I had established. Brian was becoming much more melancholy. One day in the fall we found ourselves standing on Ashley's street. He was looking at her house, lost in thought, when he asked, "Do you miss it?" I knew exactly what he was talking about, but still asked what he meant. "The way things were during the summer."

I said, "No," and realized it was true. Of all the people, times, places, and things in my life that make me nostalgic, that was not one of them. By that time I had other things on my mind. I was in my first real relationship.

Ten

My sister could not sing to save her life, but that never stopped her from trying. The problem was that every song sounded the same as the last one when it came from her mouth. My mother said it was because she was hard of hearing, but I have my doubts. I'm more inclined to believe it was simply a lack of talent, but no mother wants to tell her daughter she sounds like a bag of cats being beaten with a stick. Michelle was allowed to join the school choir only because the policy was to refuse no one who signed up.

The choir director had thought it a good idea to hold the first concert less than two weeks after the beginning of the school year. My sister put on her best dress and my mother prepared to drive her to the gymnasium and stay to watch the show. Normally I had no interest in extracurricular activities, especially if it was a bunch of thirteen-year-old girls caterwauling their way through "Amazing Grace," but that night something compelled me. At the very last minute I decided to go along.

When we pulled into the parking lot, my mother, sister, and Jack all hustled inside to take their places. I stayed outside for a while longer, dragging my feet and exchanging words with people I recognized. There's something very odd about being on a school campus at night. It doesn't feel the way it usually does. It's an entirely different place, and there's a crackle of excitement in the air. I was feeling this more than thinking it as I finally made my way to the gym.

I could hear the piano playing and people singing as I approached the building. There was a greasy yellow light shining through the front windows that suddenly made me feel as though winter had arrived, even with the temperature close to eighty degrees. When I pulled the front door open and stepped into the foyer, the click of my boot heels on the hard tile only increased the winter feeling.

Ten feet in front of me were two large wooden doors that covered the entryway into the main part of the gym. There was a girl standing with her eye pressed to the crack between the doors, looking in. Her back was to me. When she heard me enter she let the door slip closed and turned to ask, "Would you like a program, sir?" She grinned at me like she knew something amusing I didn't. Not a smile, a grin.

I've thought about it since, and there's a difference. A person smiles when they're happy. A smile indicates warmth and friendliness. A grin is a whole different animal. A grin implies pleasure. A person who grins is usually someone who is being pleased, even if it's your misfortune that pleases them. My grandmother used to say that when I grinned you could see the devil dancing in my eyes. That's what I saw that night—the devil dancing. It wasn't a waltz, either. More like a mosh pit.

The girl had skin as white as my own and shoulder-length hair that was just as black as mine, with no help from dye. (Over the years many sources have erroneously stated that I dyed my hair black. That is indeed its natural color.) She was wearing a pair of slacks that were so tight many would call them vulgar, and a low-cut blouse one could only say matched the slacks. She had a handful of programs for the choir concert, and I refused the one she offered.

I never went in to see the choir that night. Instead I stayed out in the lobby with this girl who reeked of sex. It emanated from her like static electricity and was present in every gesture—the way she stood too close and looked up at me, the way she hooked her arm through mine, and cocked her hip to the side as she talked. She didn't seem to be able to control it, like a cat in heat. It wasn't me that brought out this behavior—it was any man. I spent the evening entertaining her, and the sound of her laughter twice brought someone to the door to cast us a warning glance.

Her name was Deanna, and she informed me that if I'd bothered to look back I would have seen her in at least three of my classes. I didn't understand how I could have sat in the same room with her for almost two weeks and never even registered her presence. We had lunch together every day after that night. We sat alone at our own table at first, and gradually a small but loyal group of people formed around us—other couples, two younger guys who had started trying to dress like me, and a large gentleman by the name of Joey, who claimed to be my "bodyguard."

In the evenings I often went to Deanna's house. Her family was very pleasant, a proper and quiet southern family. They invited me into their home and allowed me to take part in their routine. Sometimes we'd watch movies, play games, or listen to music. Nothing harder than country music was allowed in the house, and watching MTV was an offense that would get Deanna and her two sisters grounded. Deanna's parents could be very strict and even intolerant at times. After all the bad stuff went down, I thought they were evil tyrants who wanted to force religion down the throats of their children while ruling them with an iron fist. I still believe that's an accurate picture in many ways, and I often heard Deanna make declarations of hatred against her mother, but all the years that have passed have given me a new perspective. They were looking out for their children in the best way they knew. I can see both sides of the coin now.

In the beginning they accepted me as family. I didn't realize the honor I was receiving, because I'd never known anything like it before. I'd never met a girlfriend's family. Every time there was a family gathering I was invited. It was so long ago that most of the memories have faded away and only the feeling remains. I can recall only a few of the more powerful ones. I remember being at their Christmas party, where Deanna gave me a stuffed gorilla and a tin of Hershey's Kisses. We sat next to the fireplace eating chocolate while the rest of the family laughed and celebrated all around us.

Deanna was secretly a pagan, she told me quite soon after we met. What was called a witch in the old days. A Wiccan. I had never before heard the term. All that I knew of "witches" was what I had read in the old books that said they flew to meetings where they danced with the devil and cursed crops or caused babies to be born with birthmarks. I knew only the nonsense—that all religions outside Christianity are at best misguided, and at worst, satanic—

passed down by the Catholic Church and the Inquisition. She kept a small green diary filled with all sorts of things: names of ancient, pre-Christian goddesses; plants and their medicinal purposes; and prayers written in flowery verse.

This was just before Wicca exploded in popularity (and notoriety) in the United States. Now there are many books written on the subject every year, and it is recognized by the United States Department of Defense as a valid religion. Times have changed. Back then I had no idea that such a religion existed. I was amazed and flabbergasted.

I began doing my own research into Wicca, reading about it and even meeting a group of local teens who were followers of the religion. They were a good source of information, but I couldn't stand being around them. They were all extremely flaky and melodramatic. I felt embarrassed for them, as they didn't have the sense to realize how socially inept they were. Wicca is a beautiful religion in theory, but I distanced myself from anything to do with it because I couldn't take the people. Many of them are people in their thirties who still try to live and behave like teenagers. Wicca seems to draw a great many people who cannot or will not grow up.

It did serve as a springboard into other areas of knowledge later, though. I've since learned much more about Kabbalah, Hinduism, Buddhism, meditation, yoga, the tarot, Theosophy, Tantra, Taoism, the Rosicrucians, the Knights Templar, and the Hermetic practices of the Golden Dawn. At the time, I couldn't get enough, and devoured what I could on Wicca. I found it infinitely fascinating for a great while, not knowing my curiosity and interest would one day be used against me in court.

The beginning of the end came when Deanna's parents found out we'd been having sex. We would get away with it for a while, but a simple mistake gave us away.

The very first time, we planned it out. When she was dropped off at school I was there to meet her. We immediately left and walked to my place. We took a back path, following railroad tracks that kept us out of view of passing cars but also tripled the distance we had to cover. It took an hour to get there, and when we arrived we went straight into my room, where we stayed for the rest of the day. My mother and Jack both knew, but neither cared. Fittingly enough, the sound track that played in the background was Suicidal Tendencies singing "How Will I Laugh Tomorrow When I Can't Even Smile Today?" This became our routine.

We'd been together for most of a year when the slip occurred. The problem was that one day we arrived back at school a few minutes later than normal, and her bus had already left. I had no idea, so I left her there and returned home. She had to walk home. Her mother asked her why she hadn't told someone in the front office, so she could have gotten a ride. Instead of giving the typical teenage response of "I don't know," she said she had told someone, and they refused to help. Her mother promptly went to the school to complain, only to discover that her daughter had not been in school that day. That's when the proverbial shit hit the fan.

After Deanna told her mother the entire story, she was forbidden to ever have anything to do with me. She wasn't even allowed to speak to me. They couldn't stop us during school hours, but they made it impossible for us to meet once she was at home. I tried, though. I tried everything I could think of, but they weren't stupid. They even informed school officials to call them if she was ever absent from school.

We tried to work it out for months, but her parents were relentless, and it was like beating our heads against a wall. Early one foggy, gray morning Deanna met me and said she couldn't do it anymore. She couldn't take the pressure her family was putting on her, so she was breaking up with me. This was the last thing I was expecting to hear, because all we had talked about were ways to make it work. We had never even discussed the alternative. I was in shock, and my mind was having trouble comprehending her words. When the pain came it was like being stabbed in the chest with a blade of ice. I said nothing, so there wasn't a great deal of talking. She severed everything as quickly as a razor. "I can't do this anymore."

I turned and wandered away like someone who'd been in an accident. "Wander" is the perfect word for what I did, because I didn't really go anywhere. I just walked. Walked and walked and walked. It would become a hobby for me. I was the Forrest Gump of Arkansas.

The nights were the worst. Every night I'd wake up racked with sobs because of the dreams. It was the same general dream, with slight variations: Deanna comes to me and says it was all a mistake, that she's back now and the hurt will all be gone. Each one seemed so real that waking up would drive me almost to the point of madness.

In addition to having to deal with this, I had to deal with Jack, who had quit his job and was always home. Not only did he never leave the house, he never left the couch. He festered with hatred and made everyone's life miserable. The only time he spoke was to spew venom at someone, and he and my mother fought constantly. She complained of a new ailment every week because the stress was wearing her down. Jack always managed to make us the most miserable when it was time for supper. He'd sit at the table with a hateful expression on his face, daring anyone to speak. I just tried to stay out of his way, but it was impossible. He made sure everyone was as miserable as he was. It was hard to swallow a single bite, much less make it through an entire meal, when he was present. My sister later claimed that he molested her during this period, but I wasn't aware of it at the time.

I stayed out as much as possible. I didn't really care where I was; I just drifted from place to place, hoping to dull the pain. I took up smoking because the nicotine helped me fall asleep at first. Later it would keep me up.

Grief sometimes causes people to do strange things. It once caused me to plant a pumpkin patch. I didn't tend it like a farmer or anything; I just left it to grow wild, like a baby raised by wolves. I had saved every love letter Deanna ever gave me, as if they were a priceless treasure. Perhaps they were, in a way. Over the years I've searched my brain trying to remember what words were inscribed on those pages, but I can only draw a blank. Whether the letters were playful, passionate, or filled with longing, I'll never know. Not that it matters much now, but it just seems like I'd be able to remember something about them because I once thought they were so important.

I needed to create a doorway through which I could enter the future and leave the past behind. I needed closure. I drifted through the days brooding and sullen, heartbroken and at a loss. My favorite holiday, Halloween, came and went. That year I didn't feel the sense of excitement and possibility that the season usually exuded. It didn't make me happy. Normally Halloween was like Christmas for me. I would anticipate it for weeks, decorating myself and the house, as well as strolling around the neighborhood, admiring everyone else's decorations. Nothing lifts my spirit like a scarecrow in the front yard.

There was a magickal crispness in the air that matched the fallen leaves underfoot. One of the things I always loved most was sitting on the porch and breathing the scent in the air as I handed out candy. I always thought it was more fun to hand it out than to collect it. That year, however, not even that appeased me.

A few days after Halloween, I was at Jason's house. He sat on the couch, staring dully at the television as I milled around in the kitchen. An old school box sitting on the table caught my eye. It was the sort that elementary school kids kept their crayons, glue, and pencils in. It appeared to be well used and was missing its top. Inside was a large quantity of pumpkin seeds that the family matriarch had deposited when carving the jack-o'-lantern. "What are these for?" I called out, picking up a handful and letting them run through my fingers and back into the box like gold coins. He looked over, shrugged, and went back to watching television. I put a handful into the pocket of my jacket.

I stayed up late into the night, lying on the couch and eyeing the canister that contained all of Deanna's letters. It was a form of self-torture. I felt the need to do *something*, to take some form of decisive action. I knew it was the only way to begin reclaiming my life and enter a new stage of development and growth. I was tired of the stagnation.

Making up my mind, I got off the couch, grabbed the letters, and went into the bathroom. Using a cigarette lighter I lit each letter one by one and let it burn all the way down to my fingertips before dropping it in the sink. I went through the entire collection, consigning the past to a funeral pyre. The entire bathroom was filled with smoke by the time I was finished, and my eyes were bloodshot. It didn't bring the sense of relief I thought it would. Still, I had committed myself to a course of action and would follow it to completion.

I collected all the ashes from the sink and put them back into the canister. I sat with that can of ashes and waited for the sun to rise. When the first rays of light touched the world I started my trip. I walked back to that spot between the hills where we had spent the spring day that now seemed to have been an eternity ago. Autumn was now in full sway; the grass was no longer green. Everything was brown, more like stalks than foliage. The sky was dark gray, warning that rain was on the way. The wind whipped my hair around my face, and the trench coat I was wearing made a sound like the sail on a pirate ship as it flapped behind me.

Using the lid of the canister I began to churn up the earth on the spot that would have been beneath us that day. I was on my hands and knees, digging in the rich soil and sprinkling pumpkin seeds like some demented creature in an ancient children's tale. When I finished, I sprinkled the ashes of the love letters over the seeds, then covered it all up with dirt. I knew it was awfully late in the year to be planting anything, but I was hoping for a miracle. Pumpkins are pretty hearty and can withstand frost.

I don't know if they grew or not because I never returned to the spot. I left the empty canister there and walked away. I was tempted to go back a couple of years later, just to see what the scene looked like. I fantasized that pumpkins would still be growing there, the descendants of the ones I had planted and fed with ash. Perhaps they still are, decades later. The thought pleases me. It would be a mark I left on the world that the winds of time had not worn away. Perhaps when you sit down to carve a jack-o'-lantern this year, or are enjoying a piece of pumpkin pie at Thanksgiving dinner, it'll be with one of my magick pumpkins that has made its way to your table. I'll be part of the festivities by proxy.

My life seemed to have no point. I went on living because that's what my body was used to doing. I drifted from one day to the next, not really caring about anything. I began sleeping with someone else just because she was there.

Domini was a transfer student from Illinois, where she had been living with her dad. She came to Arkansas in the middle of the school year and moved in with her mother. Since her parents' divorce she'd alternated living with one and then the other.

I was sitting through some sort of civics class when she first walked in. Deanna was sitting behind me (we were still together at the time), and two friends, Joey and Jamie, were sitting on my right. The teacher was a bad-tempered Italian man who had just finished lecturing us on how we'd have time to finish our homework if we weren't out riding around and "partying" every night. I pointed an accusing finger at Joey and voiced a loud "That's right," only to have him do the same back at me.

Deanna laughed, and the bad-tempered Italian said, "Look at Damien, pointing them out." He gave me a narrow-eyed look to let me know his comment had been directed at my crew. There was a knock on the door and he stepped out into the hallway. The class erupted, as it always did when there was no disciplinarian in sight. When he came back in, Domini was with him. He introduced her as Alia and told everyone she'd be part of the class from now on. Joey shivered as though he found her repulsive. I paid very little attention. She was a red-haired girl with green eyes who looked strangely like Axl Rose in the "Welcome to the Jungle" video. She was dressed in jeans and a denim jacket. I turned back to Jamie and Joey and continued to discuss where we would go that night once Jamie picked us up, just as we had been doing before the teacher caught us. I didn't give Domini another thought for several months.

I encountered her out of school for the first time about a month after Deanna and I had broken up, while I was on one of my Forrest Gump walkathons. Jason was with me and we were walking through a store a couple of miles from Lakeshore. Domini was there with another girl. I never did understand why she used her middle name, Alia, at school and Domini at home. At school she seemed painfully shy—she never talked, and kept to herself. At home she was a little more outgoing. The four of us began talking and ended up at the nearby apartment complex where Domini and the other girl lived. A guy who lived there seemed to have an open apartment policy, because his front door stood open to let the breeze in and people seemed to come and go as they pleased. I figured he was a friend of Domini's because she wandered in and started talking to him as if she had just left. Jason and I followed.

I sat in a chair minding my own business and staring blankly at the television screen while other people talked, drank beer, teased each other, or stood at the door, shouting to people in the pool outside. I didn't care about any of it; this was not my place and I did not fit in. I could tell Jason was just as uncomfortable. The only people I spoke to were Domini and her friend, who introduced herself as Jennifer. We weren't there long before Jason and I got up to leave. Domini tried to get us to stay, but we said Jason had to check in at home. She wanted us to come back later, and I said I would, even though I had no intention of doing so. As we were walking home Jason asked, "You're not really going back, are you?" My answer was "Of course not." In the end I didn't have to, as she came to me.

That night I was alone in my room with the lights off. The radio was on and I was staring at the ceiling. I couldn't sleep much at night anymore because that was when the hollow, empty feeling was the worst. At night there's nothing to hold your mind to the earth, and you spend the entire time falling into an abyss. The only cure is the rising of the sun. I was following my usual routine of waiting for daylight when my mother opened the door and told me someone was there to see me.

When I entered the living room, Domini stood looking back at me. She knew people who knew where I lived, and had taken it upon herself to come calling. It was late and she stayed only for about fifteen minutes, but before she left I kissed her. I don't really know why; I guess I felt like it was expected of me. I was still in mourning and felt no desire for her. In hindsight I know I did it for the same reason I walked nonstop—because I didn't know what else to do, and doing something was better than doing nothing.

There wasn't much of a courtship, no scenes of seduction. We started sleeping together two days later. It took my mind off things and gave me something to do on autopilot. It was something to lose myself in, and we established a routine. Every day Jason and I would go hang around the apartments where she lived, or she would come to Lakeshore. Jason and I did a great deal of "hanging around" and must have appeared to be pretty shady characters.

Perhaps Domini saved my life, just because I needed someone to be near me then. I didn't want to be alone where I had to think. We had some fun moments together, but when I ask myself if there was ever a burning love for her in my heart I must be honest and say no. Domini is a good person, straightforward and loyal, and she doesn't play games. She keeps things simple and never makes life complicated the way so many people love to do. Maybe I praise her so it doesn't seem so harsh when I say I was never in love with her. She was and still is a friend of mine.

One other thing of interest happened at this time. I heard a piece of information that wasn't meant for my ears and committed the only act of violence I've ever been guilty of. Early one morning I stood talking to a couple that Deanna and I had been close to, Josh and Lisa. Lisa let slip that Deanna had performed sexual favors for another young man while still with me.

If my wounds had started to develop scabs, they had suddenly been ripped off. This was a "whole 'nother story," to quote Matt. Lisa immediately knew she had made a mistake, and if I weren't so white she would have seen the blood drain from my face. I knew just where this young man would be, so I turned to go find him. I could feel fire in my blood and a gleam in my eye that let me know I was alive. I hadn't realized how much I'd been dying inside until I felt that flame of life. I had no plan and no idea what I was going to do; I just let the current carry me.

I approached him from behind and saw something I hadn't planned on—Deanna was standing with him. This was new. She must have realized I knew by the look on my face. I was hurt and mad as hell, and it must have been obvious, because as I walked down the hall many people stopped and turned to watch. I still don't think my course was unalterable, even at that point. What pushed me over the edge was seeing her glance nervously at him and say, "He's behind you." I felt a world of betrayal come crashing down on me. She didn't say, "Damien's behind you." She said, "He's behind you," like it was something they had been expecting. I knew the whole story when I heard those words.

"Hey!" I screamed at his back. The moment he turned around, I was on him. He was bigger than me, and I'd never been in a real fight in my life, but he wasn't expecting the pure, raw fury that came from being hurt the way I had been. It happened so fast that all he could do was try to ward me off. He backed up, trying to escape what must have seemed like a cyclone, and tripped over his own feet and fell. I went down on top of him and about twenty people jumped in to pull us apart. As they pulled me away I desperately tried to hang on to him, grabbing at him, and left scratch marks across his face.

Later there was a rumor that I had tried to pull his eye out, but it wasn't true. I was just trying to hang on to him. This rumor spread and grew with time, darkening my reputation. Or as they say in prison, "casting a shade on my character." I was suspended from school for three days over this incident.

I regretted it almost as soon as it was over. It wasn't the guy's fault. I've wanted to apologize to him ever since, but haven't seen him in many years. I truly am sorry, though, and I wish I could take it back.

Ah, but talking about such things tends to depress me, and a man in my shoes can't afford to become depressed. And we are talking, you and I. Just like old friends. Who else would I be telling my life story to? Let us now skip ahead to when things became more cheerful, however briefly.

I had one of the greatest teachers to ever lend his skill to the realm of academic learning. His name was Steve Baca, and he taught physical science. What made him so interesting and effective was that he didn't stick to a script or enforce rote memorization. He made you think. Sometimes he would hand us a video camera, assign a certain scientific principle to us, and then we had to invent and conduct our own experiment, while videotaping the whole thing. Instead of grading us himself, the entire class would watch the tapes and grade one another. He showed us movies like *The Manchurian Candidate* and introduced us to the music of Pink Floyd. Sometimes we'd take the day off and play a quick game of baseball. This is a guy who made you want to go to school. He could also tell a joke that appealed to the teenage mind, a task most adults aren't up to. He was open to any topic you cared to discuss, and he would give advice. You don't find many teachers like that.

It was in one of his classes that Deanna came back to me. Mr. Baca had sent us out to work on one project or another, and he assigned Deanna and me to the same team, along with three others. It's one of the times that are fixed crystal clear in my mind. We all went into the gym, and one guy operated the video camera while another guy and girl interviewed the janitor. I was sitting on the stairs and looking out a back door that had been propped open. Summer was just arriving and the sunlight was so bright it dazzled the eyes. There was just the slightest breeze blowing in. Deanna came and sat next to me, and I was scared to move or say anything, lest she move away like a frightened deer. My throat closed up so I could barely breathe, and I wanted to cry. This was the closest she'd been to me since she left me.

"Want to talk?" she asked.

"About what?" I managed to croak. I knew damned well what. My heart beat like it was trying to escape my chest.

"Why did you do that?" she asked, referring to the fight that had taken place almost a month ago by this time. We hadn't spoken since. I shrugged, not knowing what to say. We talked about other things for a while—the guy, who was now her boyfriend, and Domini, who was now my girlfriend. She asked me whether or not I still wanted to be with her.

If I'd known then what I know now, I'd have run for my life. I didn't know, though. "Yes," I said, almost hissing the word, hoping she could sense the force and determination behind it. She nodded her head as if she'd just made a decision, then without another word left me sitting there. What did this mean? Was she coming back to me?

I never even came close to sleep that night. I felt like I was on the cusp of something big. The next morning Jason stopped by and we walked to school together. My nerves were too jangled for me to be much of a conversationalist.

Deanna was standing there waiting for me when I arrived, and she indicated that she wanted to talk to me alone. I told Jason I'd see him later and followed her over to what used to be "our corner." She was crackling with happiness as she told me she had dumped the other young gentleman. She said that since she had been the one to mess things up, she wanted to fix them properly. In a very official tone she asked if I would take her back.

I should have run like I was on fire. I should have shaved my head and taken a vow of celibacy. I should have instructed this raven-haired package of pain to go bugger herself. I did none of the above. Instead I crushed her to me, buried my face in the top of her head, and inhaled deeply. Her face was against my chest and she said she was breathing my scent. When I asked her what she smelled, her response was "home."

She asked if I'd broken up with Domini, and I explained that I'd yet to see her, so I hadn't been able to. She folded her arms across her chest and looked at me through narrowed eyes, but there was no real anger or jealousy, because she knew there was no competition.

Did I seek out Domini that night and tell her that it was over? Indeed I did. All was right with the world and I cared about nothing else. Domini has earned the right to call me an asshole many times over. I could tell her heart was broken and I offered no comfort. I couldn't get away from her fast enough, because I was living in denial. I wanted to believe the split with Deanna had never happened, the tryst with Domini had never taken place. Because I knew that a vase that has been broken, even if it's been glued back together, is never the same.

Eleven

Sleep deprivation is a direct result of the lights. They turn the lights off every night at ten-thirty. Then they're turned right back on at two-thirty, when they start to serve breakfast. If you could manage to fall asleep the moment the lights went out, then sleep through all the guards' activity, you would still get only four hours of uninterrupted sleep. It's not possible, though. Doors slamming, keys hitting the floor, guards yelling at one another as if they're at a family reunion—it all wakes you up. During the four hours when the lights are off you can expect to be awakened *at least* once an hour. The activity continues throughout the day, with the addition of bright, fluorescent lights. Any attempt at a nap leads to further frustration. You can never sleep very deeply here anyway, because you have to stay aware of your surroundings. Bad things can come to those caught off guard. The strain of keeping one eye open wears you down.

When Death Row was housed in Tucker Max, we at least had control of our own light. It was an older building, and each cell had a wall-mounted fixture with a bulb you screwed in to turn on and unscrewed to turn off. You had to be quick about it, or it would burn your fingertips.

One of the first things I learned when I arrived was how to cook on a 100-watt lightbulb. This is accomplished in one of two ways. The first is by using the bulb directly, as a heat source. To use the bulb like an oven, you first cut the top off a soda can with a disposable razor blade. You then fill the can with whatever you want to cook—coffee, or leftover beef stew, for instance. You make certain the can is completely dry, not a single drop of water on it, and then balance it on the lightbulb. After twenty or thirty minutes, whatever is in the can will be hot enough to burn your mouth. You have to be absolutely certain the can is dry, because the bulb will explode in your face if water drips on it. You can always tell when someone has made this mistake—the explosion sounds like a shotgun blast.

This technique can be modified to create a sort of hobo microwave. You simply flatten out a few soda cans and line the inside of a saltine cracker box with them, then fit the box over the bulb. This contraption can be used to prepare some of your more delectable treats, such as bologna or Spam.

The second way to cook with the bulb is by using it to start a fire. If you prefer to cook over an open flame, you must first create a "burner." You do this by wrapping toilet paper around your hand a few dozen times and then folding the ends in on themselves. If you do this correctly, you have something that vaguely resembles a doughnut. There's an art to this technique. If you roll the paper too tight, it will only smolder and you'll choke on the smoke. If it's not rolled tight enough, the whole thing will go up in flames in a matter of seconds. You need a nice, controlled burn that lasts for at least five minutes.

Next you wrap your bulb in toilet paper—twice around should be sufficient. All you have to do is wait for it to begin smoking, which shouldn't take longer than three minutes. When the paper is smoldering, pull it off the bulb and blow on it, which should cause it to erupt into flames. Light the burner from this fire, and you're well on your way to being the Wolfgang Puck of the prison world.

Set the burner on the edge of the toilet seat so that when you're finished you can just nudge it into the toilet and flush it away. You can flush *anything* down a prison toilet—socks, plastic spoons, busted-up whiskey bottles, smashed cassette tapes, orange peels— I've seen it all go down with no effort. Once you get used to these big, industrial-sized prison toilets you will thumb your nose at the home variety. The *only* good thing about this place is the toilets.

I used this method to brew myself some tea on many occasions: fill a soda can with water, tie a piece of dental floss or a string from a bedsheet to the top of the can, then dangle it over the flame until the water begins to boil. Put your tea bag in a cup and pour the water over it. I love tea. Others make hot chocolate, or even chili.

One other trick that people always seem to find interesting for some reason is "fishing." Fishing is what you do when you can't get anyone outside a cell to pass something to someone else for you. You yell to the guy you're trying to pass something to—"Hey! Send me your fishing line!" Soon a string will land in front of your door. You tie whatever it is to the line, and the guy reels it in. You need fifty to a hundred yards of string and something to use for a weight to pull this trick off.

Most people obtain their string by slicing sheets into thin strips and tying the ends together so that you have one long strand. The most commonly used weights are batteries, a bar of soap, or a travel-size bottle of lotion. If you use batteries, you can even fish in the toilet. It requires two people to do this. Each of you flushes about a hundred yards of string down the toilet while holding on to one end of it. If both of you keep flushing, the strings will become entangled somewhere in the pipes. One man wraps whatever he is passing to you in plastic—a cigarette, for example. He then ties it to the end of the string, and the other guy pulls the whole thing back up through his own toilet. Some men frown on this practice and refer to those who do it as "shitty fingers."

I have no idea what it is about fishing that people in the free world find so amusing, but some of them ask me to describe it to them every time they come to see me. They know the story as well as I do by now, but still want to hear it over and over. To me it's just another aspect of daily life in the Arkansas Department of Correction.

Most people in the outside world look at you in a different way if they find out you've spent time in prison. They can hold it against you for the rest of your life. You're never trusted and always made to feel like an outcast. For most of the people in here with me it's a different story. It's nothing out of the ordinary for people in here to have friends and family within the prison system. It's accepted as an everyday part of life, as if everyone goes to prison at least once. Several men on Death Row have sons, brothers, uncles, and cousins who are doing time within the ADC. None of their friends or family members would ask for a description of a prison cell because most of them have already seen one.

One of the first things people always ask is what a cell looks like—my cell in particular—and they want to know whether it looks like what they've seen on television or in the movies. To begin with, you have two types of walls. Some of them are made of cinder block; others are simply smooth, poured concrete. The one I live in at Varner Unit is smooth concrete, which is what I prefer. Perhaps that's because I had to look at the cinder blocks for a decade and simply appreciate the change.

The color is a very pale blue. Everything here is blue of one shade or another. The walls are so light they're almost white, while the door is more of a powder blue. The floor is plain, unfinished concrete, and it's very harsh on the feet. In seventeen years I have not taken a step that wasn't on concrete. I miss grass and dirt. Sometimes I believe one of the most beautiful things on Earth must be grass. The green of summer or the brown of winter—both are equally bewitching. I'd love to be able to touch it.

My bed is a concrete slab that stands about eighteen inches off the floor. I have a thin mat to place on top of it that greatly resembles the ones given to kindergartners to nap on. We're given the cheapest, most horrid blankets ever designed by mankind. When you wake up in the morning you have to pick bits of fuzz out of your nose, eyebrows, and hair. Not to mention the fact that they just aren't very warm. My pillow is composed of extra clothes—socks, T-shirts, sweatpants. We have to buy these clothes ourselves. Being that there are no chairs, or anything else to sit on, you spend a great deal of time on or in the bed.

Next to the bed is a three-foot-tall concrete block that serves as a table. You can never see the top of mine because it's beneath a jumbled mound of books, magazines, journals, letters, pens and pencils. No matter how often I try to organize or straighten it up it will be mayhem an hour later. I can never find anything I'm looking for. Sometimes when I pass other cells I see spotless, well-organized tables, but I can never figure out their secret.

There is one wall not made of concrete, and it serves as your "bathroom area." This wall and everything on it is made of steel. It's nine feet tall and houses the toilet, sink, mirror, light, and shower. The toilet and sink are made of one big chunk of steel. The sink is where the tank would be on most toilets, so you have to straddle the toilet to shave or brush your teeth. The mirror is nothing more than a square of the steel wall that is slightly more reflective than the rest. It's not very clear, and it's impossible to make out small details in it.

Over the sink and toilet resides the hated fluorescent light. It's the same sort of light found in the ceilings of office buildings, hospitals, and public schools. The only difference is that mine is in the wall instead of overhead. About two feet over from the toilet is the shower, which consists of a spout on the wall with a button underneath. When you push the button, the water comes on for about thirty seconds. There's no way to adjust the temperature of the water; you must accept whatever comes out. There is a drain in the floor, which barely works. I have a small brown plastic rosary hanging on my shower button. I've loved holding a rosary all my life. Just running the beads through my fingers calms me.

Nanny gave me my first rosary on my fifteenth birthday. She took me to a small bookstore and allowed me to pick out the one I wanted. I chose a long turquoise strand of beads with a thin, sleek, silver crucifix. I always carried it in a small pocket of my leather motorcycle jacket. It was the first of many, though I no longer have any idea what happened to it.

The cell door is made of solid steel. It has a plexiglass window so the guards can play Peeping Tom, and a small letterbox-type opening heavily bolted from the outside that the guards open to slide your food inside. This door ensures that there will be no fresh air circulating or communication between prisoners. It took a while to get used to because I had been behind old-fashioned bars for nine years at Tucker Max.

The window is a four-inch-wide slit through which I have a panoramic view of a concrete wall and chain-link fence. The most exciting things I ever glimpse are the flocks of pigeons and sparrows that come here to roost.

My television is inside a steel box suspended high up in a corner of the cell. It picks up three channels, but there's not much that comes on that I'm interested in watching. I have two addictions when it comes to television: David Letterman and professional wrestling. David Letterman is someone I've only recently discovered, but I've indulged in pro wrestling all my life. It's a tradition in my house. My grandfather and father both watch, and when my son comes to visit once a year, we compare notes, too. I grew up watching it and as a child often had tag team matches with other neighborhood kids. We all argued over who got to be Jerry Lawler. Jerry "The King" Lawler was a huge deal in the Memphis area. He was *the* wrestler. For a while he was so well-known you'd see him on various commercials for local places, and he had his own talk show, which aired every Sunday morning.

My loyalty to *The Jerry Lawler Show* once outraged and embarrassed my grandmother. A woman from a local church used to make rounds through the neighborhood with a purse full of bubble gum. She would stop at houses and try to lure the kids into coming to church on Sunday. If you promised to come she would give you gum. When she arrived at our house she chatted amiably with my grandmother for a few moments before turning to me and asking, "Do you want to come to church with me on Sunday?" The gleam in her eye spoke volumes. It said, "You know you can't resist bubble gum. You may as well sell me your soul." Thus, she was quite shocked when I responded, "Absolutely not." The smile on her face turned into a puzzled frown as she asked, "Why not?" I looked at her as if she'd lost her mind and said, "Because I'd miss *The Jerry Lawler Show*."

My grandmother was mortified. I had just proved myself to be a heathen of the highest order. She gaped at me in disbelief. In her view I had just chosen Jerry Lawler over Jesus, which made her look bad. After the shock wore off she promised the woman, as she ushered her from the house, that I would indeed be in church on Sunday. Not only did I miss *The Jerry Lawler Show*, but I didn't get a piece of gum.

At any rate, that's the nickel tour of my cell. The only other things in here are two big plastic boxes in which I keep everything I own. They're filled with small packs of Tylenol, packs of mustard, bars of soap, books, extra paper, and various other odds and ends I've collected over the years.

The best fortune I can wish for you is that you never have to see the inside of such a place for yourself. This is a hell, void of anything that makes life worthwhile.

Once I was looking through a magazine and I came across a piece about an art show opening in New York. The artist was a female photographer who had been badly burned as a child. She had taken photographs of herself as she slowly went through the healing process. She had to have an ungodly number of surgeries to help her along, and they continued well into adulthood. Throughout the years she kept her trusty camera in hand, documenting every step. Above the tiny article there was a photograph of her laughing, and at first glance I didn't even notice the light ripples of scar tissue on her chest and collarbones. Only after reading it did I backtrack and realize there was indeed still evidence of her childhood trauma.

The thing that really struck me about this article was a comment the woman made. What she said was that she was much stronger as a child than she is as an adult. She had to have an understanding and appreciation for the subtle mechanisms of the mind to have come to this realization. Perhaps sometimes the memory is worse than the pain at the time of its happening. And sometimes it's not.

The older I grow, the more I understand what the burned woman meant. Things I was able to walk through unscathed in my youth would mark me for life or damage me beyond repair now. Things I once shrugged off without thought would now bring about my collapse. I was much more flexible in both mind and body as a youth. I could absorb the impact and roll with the punches.

Twelve

It was amazing how quickly the hurt stopped. Humpty Dumpty had indeed been put back together again and he was a grinning fool. I sat slouched far down in my desk, lolling lazily as if there wasn't a bone in my body. Deanna sat directly behind me, tracing the pattern of hair at the back of my neck and laughing low in her throat when I shivered. She leaned forward to whisper, "There's only three days of school left. I don't want to lose you again now that I've just got you back." This was something I'd been contemplating but could find no solution to. We still had no way to see each other outside school hours. After a few moments she continued, "We can still do what we talked about."

She meant leaving, of course. We had discussed running away together as a last resort. I hadn't believed it would come to that; I was certain a solution would present itself. But time was quickly running out. "I'll be your huckleberry"—never have I spoken truer words.

"Bring your things with you on the last day and away we'll go." That answer sealed my fate.

We talked about it nonstop, yet had no specific plan. We had no destination or goal in mind. We would be going on an adventure, and our excitement was palpable. We settled on the vague notion of "going west." Neither of us had any idea what the magnitude of our actions would be.

When the final day of classes arrived, we came to school as usual. We would leave when it was over, simply drift off into the crowd, which would be delirious with the realization that school was over for another year. No one would even notice us. It was a daisy of a plan and came off without a hitch.

We took an extra-long route that I had never before explored. Jason walked with us. If you're roaming aimlessly, then why not begin with the magickal land of Lakeshore? It normally took only about fifteen minutes to walk from school to our places, but this day it took two and a half hours of constant walking. We trod through empty fields far from any road, where there was zero chance of anyone eyeballing us.

At first Jason and I carried on with our usual bantering while Deanna laughed uproariously at our antics. She was amazed, because Jason never spoke in school, yet here he was chatting like a magpie. He and I could play off each other's words all day, until eventually we were incapacitated with laughter. Not many people know it, but Jason is pretty hilarious. He has a caustic, smart sense of humor. After the first hour we got pretty quiet, though.

It was the heat, which was right at one hundred degrees. The sun beat down on us without mercy, baking our brains in our skulls. On a day when the television was warning others to stay indoors and out of the heat, we were outside maintaining a strenuous pace. Every step we took sent bone-dry clouds of dust into the air, and my mouth was so dry I could barely speak. There was nothing but flat, feature-less fields in every direction. No trees, no buildings, and no shade. Not even a living blade of grass. The three of us were dressed in black, which didn't help matters any. At one point I thought I would collapse from heatstroke. I was positive that I couldn't force myself to keep going, yet I still did, one step after another. One foot, two foot, red foot, blue foot.

We finally arrived in Lakeshore and proceeded to an abandoned trailer that we knew would be empty. The door was unlocked so we went inside and collapsed on the floor to rest. Even that hot trailer was a relief after facing the blistering sun. I handed Jason a wad of sweat-soaked dollar bills and moaned, "Drinks." He left and made his way to the Lakeshore store. While he was gone Deanna changed into a set of my clothes that weren't wet with sweat, as I'd had the presence of mind to bring along some extras. I didn't bother chang-ing, but I became obsessed with one idea. All I could think about was how wonderful it would be to wait until nightfall, then slip into that cool, crusty green lake. I no longer cared that it was filthier than a septic tank; I could practically feel its coolness against my skin. My tongue was stuck to the roof of my mouth. We were alone, but so hot, tired, and nauseous that we could do nothing.

Jason finally returned with a paper sack of Mountain Dews and Dr Peppers. I drained a Mountain Dew in one long swallow, then popped open a Dr Pepper to drink at a more sedate pace. I felt life returning to me. He'd even had the wisdom to pick up some candy bars, so I quickly scarfed one of those. Full of sugar and caffeine, I was ready to juke and jive.

I investigated my surroundings while Jason told me breathlessly, "Man, every freak in the world is out there." When I suggested it might help if he were slightly more articulate, he explained that all the neighborhood kids were looking for me like a pack of hounds, because the police had been looking for me, and they were now convinced they might receive some sort of reward for finding me. It seemed Deanna's parents had wasted no time in calling the authorities to report her missing once they realized skulduggery was afoot.

"No shit?" I asked as I sat down in front of a piano, the only piece of furniture in the entire place. I found it slightly odd that someone lived in a trailer park but could still afford a piano. A few of the keys were busted, but I could still manage to play it a little (Nanny had taught me as a kid how to play church hymns on the organ), which I did while Jason told me they had tried to follow him, thinking he'd lead them to me. Deanna came and sat next to me on the piano bench while Jason peeked out a window. He turned to me and said something that hadn't crossed my mind—"You better stop that, because if one of those freaks hears a piano playing in here they're going to be pretty sure it's not a ghost." I snatched my fingers from the keys.

I sat quietly in thought for a few minutes before telling Jason that Deanna and I would sleep there that night, then say good-bye to him in the morning. There was no chance of him going with us because he was the only pillar of stability in his home. His mother,

Gail, was unstable and suffered from schizophrenia; she might take medication for a period of time and improve, but once that happened, she frequently stopped taking it. She might tell Jason she was going out for a few hours and return several days later. If he was not there to take care of his two younger brothers, they would go feral like the Lakeshore dogs. He truly did have to be like a father figure to them, and I was always impressed by how competently he handled the task. Most people twice his age couldn't do the job half as well. He left to go make supper for them.

The moment he was gone Deanna and I fell upon each other. Next came a mystery that I have never found the key to. Somehow, we were found.

For the last half-hour the sky had grown steadily darker, until the sun that had scorched us earlier was no longer visible. It signaled not the approach of night but the coming of one big, God-almighty storm. The wind picked up until I was absolutely certain a tornado would arrive at any moment. The sky was black as night and the wind continued to howl and blow so fiercely that it seemed the trailer would roll over, but not a single drop of rain fell.

The wind suddenly stopped. It didn't die down, it just stopped all at once. A really bad feeling rippled up my spine. I stopped what I was doing and cocked my head to the side like a dog listening for a strange sound. "What is it?" Deanna asked.

I waited seconds before reluctantly admitting, "I don't know." All I knew was that my every cell had just been flooded with the fight-or-flight feeling, and I had a terrible sense of urgency.

"Then pay attention to me," she said.

As I leaned forward to kiss her I heard glass shatter. "Shit!" I hissed as we grabbed our clothes. Even though I knew it was pointless and the jig was up, we still attempted to hide. It was a cop. Instead of opening the door and walking in, he felt the need to smash in a window and fulfill some sort of SWAT team fantasy. He later lied and said that we had busted out the window. He was a real piece of work—about four and a half feet tall, with the sort of mustache you see only on cops or seventies gay porn stars. He was the kind of guy who needed a badge and gun just to stop people from laughing at him. He found us almost immediately and started jerking us around.

As he was escorting us out the door, Deanna's father approached. He put his hand on my shoulder and began breathing hard, as if he were having trouble restraining himself. I looked straight into his eyes and grinned like a jackal. I wanted him to know he could do nothing to me that was worse than what I'd already been through. The cop pushed him away and said, "Relax, just let me handle it." He backed off and the cop put Deanna and me in the back of his car before returning to talk to her mother and father. I noticed that even her older sister had come out for the occasion, and I gave her my most charming smile.

While we sat in the car Deanna held my hands and said, "Whatever happens, you have to come find me." I promised that I would, no matter what. She kissed me then, like she had seen the future. It was the last time we would ever touch. Another cop had pulled up, and they split us up, putting her in his car. She blew a kiss at me and waved good-bye as it drove off.

I arrived at the Crittenden County jail on the outskirts of West Memphis, and was escorted to my suite. It was a dark, dank cell that smelled like feet and corn chips, a tiny space with a brown solid-steel door. There was no entertainment except for the graffiti, which covered every square inch of the walls. I was amazed at the things people had thought important enough to write there. For instance, someone thought it vital that the world know someone named "Pimp Hen" was adept at certain sexual maneuvers. I felt a bit like an archaeologist in a tomb.

I was left alone for what I estimated to be two or three hours, but it's impossible to really tell time in a place like that. It's a form of mental torture, and I only knew that it seemed like an eternity. I kept wondering, *Where is she? Is she in this building? Do they have her in a filthy hole like this one?* The graffiti offered no answers to these questions. I was pacing like an animal when a guard came and opened the door, motioning for me to follow. I was led to an office in which sat a bloated, corpulent man with beady little rat's eyes. Jerry Driver, juvenile officer for the county, and I came face-to-face for the first time.

He had a pleasant-enough attitude as he introduced himself. He started asking questions and I answered honestly, thinking there was no reason not to. He asked why we were in the trailer, and I told him we had run away because her parents wouldn't leave us alone. No, we didn't know where we were going, and no, we didn't know what we were going to do once we got there. We figured it would come to us in time.

This is where things started getting weird. The smile never left his face, which looked like folds of uncooked dough. "Have you heard anything about Satanists around town?"

I thought that a bit odd, but answered, "No."

He continued to press on. "You haven't heard anything about Satanists, plans to commit sacrifices or break into churches?" Those beady little rat's eyes gleamed at me, like he was really starting to get off on thinking about this stuff. You could tell something just wasn't right about him.

I was pretty certain I would have remembered a roving pack of bloodthirsty devil worshippers if they had passed me on the street while chatting loud enough about such topics, so I told him, "I'm pretty certain I haven't." He seemed to be considering something as he chewed his bottom lip with tiny, yellow-stained rat teeth. Finally he shifted his obese bulk to pull something out of his desk.

I could practically see his whiskers twitch as he said, "What can you tell me about this?" The object he held was Deanna's little green diary. I wanted to reach out for it but knew it was pointless. I didn't answer his question, knowing that it would be futile.

"Where is she?" It was my turn to ask questions. He told me she was being held at a women's detention center in a town called Helena. He watched me closely as he said she had had "psychiatric trouble" in the past, and her parents thought it might be best if she was sent for treatment. She was being held until tomorrow, when she would be transported to a psychiatric hospital in Memphis. This was news to me. I knew nothing of any past "psychiatric trouble." It may not even have been true, because I would soon learn that nothing he said was trustworthy. I didn't know that then, though, and I sat there seeing images of Deanna in an insane asylum. All I could picture was the Anthrax video called "Madhouse," in which everyone wore straitjackets.

I was told I'd spend the week in Craighead County jail, in Jonesboro, about an hour north of West Memphis, where someone would come talk to me. Jerry Driver himself drove me there. Everyone wore an orange jumpsuit that said "Craighead County" on the back, and you slept in a cell. There was a dayroom where inmates played Uno with an ancient deck of greasy, creased cards. Time seemed to come to an absolute standstill. Later I discovered that it made no sense for me to be there, because anyone else who had been picked up the way we were would have received nothing more serious than a warning, or a year of probation at the most, before being sent home. Deanna and I were being put in jail because Jerry Driver was not finished with us.

One day during that week I was escorted to a small room in the back of the courthouse to see a mountain of a woman who looked like she applied her makeup with a spatula. She talked to me for about an hour, then gave me a test, which consisted of showing me flash cards, before telling Jerry Driver, "We have a bed for him." I was puzzled about the meaning of this until it was explained that I, too, would be going to a psychiatric hospital within the next few days. I suddenly saw myself in that "Madhouse" video.

I was left in the jail while they made arrangements for me to take a vacation in the nuthouse. I had about three days to wait for my transportation, and during that time I continuously paced from one end of the cell block to the other. There were about ten to fifteen other guys there at any given time, and I would later learn they were all typical jailbirds. I say "typical" because over the years I've had the opportunity to observe many people behind bars, and most of them have a tremendous amount in common. Greed, anger, frustration, lust, hatred, and jealousy, all housed in one body. I've always come to the same conclusion—it's no wonder these guys are where they are.

There's not much to do in jail, so one day I thought I'd call home and check in. My mother had known about my plan, and she had even given me a little money, saying that if I needed anything I should call. She was at the courthouse when Jerry Driver argued before a judge that he should be allowed to keep me in jail until my court date instead of allowing me to go home, as any first-time offender would have been permitted to do. I called my mother to see if perhaps she knew more than I did. I was in for quite a shock—it had been a dramatic week for everyone. My father was back.

It seems that my mother finally came to her senses and gave Jack the boot. It wasn't like she had much choice, either, because my sister had made accusations against him concerning molestation. Social Services sent a representative, and they informed my mother that Jack was not to be in the house under any circumstances. Records show an investigation was conducted but I'm not aware anything conclusive was ever found or decided on where that was concerned.

After Jack was gone—and by gone, I mean that he moved to another trailer on the next street over—my sister started calling people, searching for my father. I never asked her why and she never explained. Joe was in Arkansas visiting his family, and he and my mother were talking about getting back together. I was stunned. It felt like the whole world had been turned upside down overnight while I was sitting in a cage. Under other circumstances I would have been ecstatic, but right then there were other things on my mind. I'd given Deanna my word that I would find her, but time was slipping through my hands. I was beginning to feel that I would never again know what life was like beyond those walls. After being locked in a cage for weeks, the thought of ever getting out became one of those things that are too good to be true.

My mother and father came to see me the next day. There was no way to touch, and we had to talk to each other through two-inch-thick bulletproof glass. My father hardly recognized me. When he and my mother walked through the door I heard him ask her, "Is that him?" We were allowed to talk for fifteen minutes, they on one side of the glass and me on the other. That's not much time to get reacquainted, but my father promised that he would be part of my life from then on. The guard then came and told them it was time to leave.

I look back now and find myself filled with a tremendous amount of anger at how unjust it all was. The punishment for a first-time breaking and entering charge and an accusation of sexual misconduct didn't fit the crime by any stretch of the imagination. All I did was walk into an abandoned trailer. This made no sense.

At my court date a couple of days later Jerry Driver recommended to the court that I be put in a mental institution, which he told my parents and me was the alternative to holding me in jail for nine months until going to trial. At the time, it didn't seem logical but it did seem like the lesser of two evils. I was given my clothes and told to get dressed. If you've never had to wear jail clothes, then you can't comprehend what it's like to finally be able to put your own clothes back on. It takes a while to get used to. The jail clothes are designed to strip you of any identity and reduce you to a number. You don't even feel like a human being when you're wearing them. You have no dignity.

The four of us traveled in Driver's car, and it was a long ride. It took several hours to get from Jonesboro to Little Rock, where Charter Hospital of Maumelle was located. He restrained himself from asking more insane Satanist-related questions in front of my parents, but I could tell it almost caused him physical pain to do so. Every time I looked up I saw his beady rat's eyes staring intently at me in the rearview mirror. For some unknown reason he had visited my mother while I waited in jail, and asked her if he could see my room. She let him in and left him back there alone. He told her that he was "confiscating" a few things, even though that was blatantly illegal. He took the Goya-like sketches from the walls and a new journal I had started. (It was in a funeral registry book, morbidly enough.) He also took my skull collection.

It sounds kind of odd to have a skull collection, but I'll explain. There's a hard-packed dirt path behind Lakeshore that the local youth would wander on. It doesn't go anywhere specific, just sort of meanders around a small lake and a few fields. I often found odd pieces of the skeletons of possums, raccoons, squirrels, birds, and even the occasional dog or cat that had died out there. I began collecting them because my teenage mind thought they looked cool. I'm not the only one, and I've never denied having questionable taste when it comes to interior decorating. The oddest thing Jason and I ever found was a beer bottle with two tiny skulls inside. The problem was that they were slightly too large to get out of the bottle. We spent hours trying to figure out how they got in the bottle in the first place.

At any rate, Jerry Driver took my personal possessions as "evidence." Evidence of what, he didn't say. I wouldn't know this for quite a while, as it would be some time before I ever saw Lakeshore again. For now, I was on my way to the funny farm.

By the time we arrived, all the other patients had been put to bed. It was about ten o'clock at night and the place was silent. My mother and father had been completely convinced by Driver's authoritative tone, that this was Driver's right and they had no choice in the matter. They sat in a small office giving my personal information to the woman in charge of filing paperwork on new patients. The process took about thirty minutes, and Jerry Driver sat silently listening to everything. I was exceedingly nervous, never having been in such an environment before. The only thing I had to base my expectations on was the jail I had just left, so I was expecting the worst. To me, as to my parents, Driver's authority was not to be questioned; I believed he was a legitimate cop. None of us understood that we could protest or contest his decisions. We were simply operating out of fear of the consequences—and in the meantime, without knowing it, our rights were never explained to us and were taken from us without our knowledge.

A nurse came to escort me through two large doors, back into the heart of the building. My mother was still answering questions as I left—was I allergic to anything, my birthday, family history of illness. Nothing about my mental state or behavior. Beyond those doors, it wasn't nearly as nice as the lobby we had just left behind, but it was also no chamber of horrors. The furniture appeared to be made of plastic, so if anyone vomited or pissed themselves, there would be no stain. It possessed the added bonus of only needing to be hosed off after the occasional fecal smearing.

I was told to sit at a small table, where I was introduced to a tall, thin black guy named Ron. He looked through my suitcase, wrote down everything I had, then showed me to a room. There were two beds, a desk, a chair, and a small wardrobe. I was alone; there was no one in the other bed. I'd been through so much stress and trauma during the past few weeks that I immediately fell into a deep sleep, which lasted until morning.

The days there began with a nurse making wake-up calls at six a.m. She'd turn on the lights and go from room to room telling everyone to prepare for breakfast. Everyone would get up, take a shower, get dressed, and perform whatever morning rituals the insane carry out in privacy. We'd then march down to the dayroom, sit on the puke-proof couches, and stare at each other until seven o'clock.

On my first morning there were only three other patients. The first patient I saw was a blond-haired girl who was sitting with her back to me and singing a Guns N' Roses song. I looked at the back of her head for a while, until I became curious about what she looked like. When I could no longer take the curiosity I walked around in front of her. She looked up at me with ice-blue eyes that seemed either half asleep or fully hypnotized, and she smiled. By her gaze alone you could tell that something just wasn't right with this picture. She seemed happy, and rightfully so, as she was being discharged later in the day. Her name was Michelle, and she told me she was there for attempting suicide by swallowing thumbtacks and hair barrettes.

Soon a second patient entered. He was wearing Bermuda shorts and flip-flops and could have easily passed for Michelle's twin brother. I never knew what he was there for, and he was discharged in less than three days. The third patient was a young black guy who seemed to be the most normal of the trio. He went home the next day.

If I had any fear of being left alone, it would soon be laid to rest. Patients began to come in on a daily basis, and soon the entire place was full. I had to share my room with an interesting young sociopath who was sent there after being discovered at his new hobby— masturbating into a syringe and injecting it into dogs. The entire ward was a parade of bizarre characters.

We lined up every morning and strolled down to the kitchen for a tasty breakfast of biscuits and gravy, orange juice, blueberry muffins, hash browns, scrambled eggs, toast, sausage, and Frosted Flakes. The insane do not count carbs. The food was delicious, and I enjoyed every meal. Conversation around the table was never dull and covered such topics as who had stolen whose underwear, and whether or not Quasimodo had ever been a sumo wrestler.

Once breakfast was over we walked single file (in theory) back down to our wing and had the first of four group therapy sessions for the day. At this session you had to set a daily goal for yourself, such as "My goal for the day is to learn the rules," or "My goal for the day is to deal with my anger in a more constructive manner than I did yesterday." This task made everyone irritable, because it's hard to come up with a new goal every single day, and you couldn't use the same one twice. Your last group session would be right before bed, during which you had to say whether you had achieved your goal, and if not, then why not.

Next came our weekly visit to the psychiatrist. We'd all sit on the couches and fidget while she called us in one at a time to talk. She had a small, dark, pleasant office filled with bookshelves. This was the doctor in charge of making your diagnosis and deciding what medication you needed. My diagnosis was depression. No shit. My life was hell and showed no signs of improvement, I had a step-father who was a ten on the asshole scale, I'd spent two or three weeks in jail for reasons I still didn't understand, I didn't know where my lover was being held, and I was now locked in a building full of sociopaths, schizophrenics, and other assorted freaks. You bet your ass I was depressed. I'd be more inclined to believe I had a problem if I *wasn't* depressed. At any rate, I was prescribed antide-pressants, which I was given shortly after I got there.

Antidepressants were a horrid invention. The only thing I could tell they did was make me so tired I couldn't think straight. I told one of the nurses that something was wrong because it hurt to open my eyes and I kept falling asleep every time I quit moving. I was told not to worry, this was natural and I'd get used to it. That's not something you want to hear. Over time I did grow used to it, and in another month I wasn't even able to tell I'd taken anything.

After talking to the doctor, we went to the gym for a bit of morning exercise. There was a stationary bike, a punching bag, a rowing machine, and a StairMaster. Everyone spent time on each one. There was also a foosball table and a basketball hoop we could use after lunch.

Every so often we would go to an arts-and-crafts room to work on individual projects. I made two ceramic unicorns that I took home with me when I left. I've no idea what eventually happened to them, but I was proud of them at the time.

For lunch it was back to the kitchen, then another group session, which was usually greeted with outraged cries of "This is bullshit!" I agreed wholeheartedly but kept my opinion silent. After suffering through this indignity, we were allowed to take a thirty-minute nap.

In the evening we went outside to a large fenced-in area to walk around and enjoy the air. We talked, looked out into the woods, or bounced tennis balls back and forth. Before bed we were allowed to choose a snack. There were granola bars, chocolate milk, peanut butter and crackers, or a cup of pudding. It wasn't a bad place to be, as far as psych wards go.

We were rewarded for good behavior by being taken on field trips. Once, we were all loaded into a long white van with a giant handicap symbol on the side and taken to the circus. It was hard to tell if there were more clowns in the show or in the stands. Another time we were taken swimming, and I never even got in the pool. I stood under an umbrella, dressed head to toe in black, and waited to go back to the hospital. The last and most wretched trip was to a movie theater, where we watched Whoopi Goldberg in *Sister Act*.

Life went on, with my anxiety continuing to build. After I had been there for about three weeks, I was given a twenty-four-hour pass and my mother, father, and sister came to visit. A therapist met with them privately to describe how and what I'd been doing over the past few weeks, and to tell them that the hospital had deemed me well enough to be discharged. Before leaving us alone, she informed them that they could come to her with any questions they might have. This was the first real chance I'd had to talk to my father in many years. He hadn't kept in touch with us during his absence, and we discussed both the future and the past.

He lived in Oregon and had been preparing to come back when my sister contacted him. He had been married several times since he left, and I had an eight-year-old half brother who lived with him. I was amazed to learn that he and my mother were planning to get married again, and as soon as I was out of the hospital we were all moving to Oregon. Ordinarily I would have been thrilled, as this was everything I could possibly have wanted—Jack was gone, my father was back, I was receiving a twenty-four-hour pass to spend the next day with my family, and we were moving up in the world. Now it was a nightmare. I would be leaving Deanna behind. I started to rock gently in my chair as I silently cried. I didn't make a sound, but the tears came so fast and heavy that I couldn't see the room. I was looking at the world from behind a waterfall. I was sad and desperate, but something in my guts turned to steel. I knew I would keep my word to her no matter what.

I barely slept that night: one moment I was excited about the potential adventure ahead, and the next I felt devastated about what I was leaving behind. This was a whole new life. I could leave my past behind like an old skin, something at one time I would have given anything for.

When morning arrived, I got dressed and packed my things, because I would be staying in a motel that night. I love hotels and motels. There's something exciting about them, even though you're only sleeping. I hadn't had a chance to go to one in many years—not since the last time my mother and father had been married.

They arrived to pick me up in my father's Dodge Charger, and I was impressed. Chrome mags, a nice paint job, and a top-of-the-line stereo system. I loved the car immediately. They asked me what I wanted to do, so we went to McDonald's, where I saw some people I knew. They were in the high school band and were in Little Rock for some sort of competition, and by some amazing coincidence they had wandered into this very McDonald's. When a girl named Becky asked what I was doing there, I informed her that I was out on a twenty-four-hour pass from the nearby mental institution. After she realized I was serious, she erupted into peals of laughter.

We got a motel room, and my father and I went down to rent a VCR and some tapes. We got every Steven Seagal film they had, and went back to watch them. He already had all of these movies at home, and they were some of his favorites. I enjoyed myself more that night than I had in a very long time, even though there were things nagging at me. We ordered pizza, watched movies, and talked about what it was like in Oregon. They tried to please me and kept the curtains drawn and the air turned low so that the room was like ice. It was almost as if it were my birthday. They knew I'd been through hell lately and were being extra nice. I fell asleep early, emotionally exhausted.

The next morning I had a breakfast of doughnuts before heading back to the hospital. Before they left, the doctor told my parents I would be discharged in twenty-four hours and they could pick me up. I never understood the point of having to come back for one more day, but it passed quickly enough. After saying good-bye to the other patients, I was on my way to Oregon.

Thirteen

The trip to Oregon took almost a full week, and I enjoyed every moment of it, even with a sadness in my heart that felt like a weight. I was leaving my home behind and I was more than a little scared that I'd never see anyone or anything I knew ever again. I cried so hard I couldn't see the road before me until we were halfway through Oklahoma. I could tell it made my father nervous by the way he kept glancing at me out of the corner of his eye. After the first day I had exhausted my grief supply and could cry no more for a while. That's when it became more fun.

The trip took so long because we made it in my father's car while pulling an orange U-Haul trailer. We listened to music all the way, alternating between my father's collection and mine. The Eagles, Conway Twitty, and Garth Brooks were followed by Ozzy Osbourne, Anthrax, and Metallica, all played at ear-shattering volume. We ate every meal at roadside places and slept every night in cheap motels. This was the life I had loved as a young child, when my mother and father were together and we moved to a new state every month or so.

My father was in rare form throughout the entire trip, and I laughed at his insanity until I lost my breath. He spent all of one morning pointing out the prairie dogs along the side of the road and around rest stops. With the grave air and facial expression of one imparting divine wisdom, he explained that I should keep my eyes open because if I saw someone run over a prairie dog I would then see all its friends run out and start eating it. The manner in which he relayed this tidbit of knowledge caused me to erupt into uncontrollable laughter. He looked at me for a moment before snickering, then abruptly stopped, and his eyes darted around as if he feared someone might be listening in. This made me laugh even harder because I could tell he had no idea what I found so funny.

Watching my father interact with restaurant employees was an interesting and humorous experience in itself. It's hard to put my finger on specific things, but when looking at the overall picture it's hilarious. He'd order a cup of coffee and then look intently at the waitress as he emphasized the words *two* and *sugars*. When she turned to walk away, he'd call out to her with a "Hey!" When she looked back, he'd make direct eye contact while solemnly and slowly holding up two fingers to remind her, "Two."

My little brother, Timothy, was a quandary, too. It sounds odd when I say he was just like my father yet completely different, but it's true. His mannerisms were completely his own, yet everything he did seemed like something my father would do. I lost all contact with him though; when I was arrested, he went to live with his mother, yet I often think of him and wonder what kind of person he turned out to be.

We arrived in Oregon and moved into a three-bedroom apartment in a town called Aloha. It was a very nice place and I was given the biggest room, though I had nothing to fill it with. Unloading furniture from the trailer, I realized my mother had brought almost none of our personal belongings. I asked her where everything was and she said she'd left it all in Lakeshore. This was almost impossible for me to believe. She didn't try to sell anything to get more money for the trip, she didn't even give it to others who might need it—she just abandoned it. The only thing of mine brought along was a single suitcase containing my clothes and music. This blew my mind.

When I later returned to Arkansas, Jason told me he was walking past one day and noticed everything I owned in one big pile by the curb—television, stereo, baseball bat, antique Japanese rifle, skateboard, electric guitar, and more that had been in the house. I asked him if anyone looked through it and took anything, to which he shook his head and said, "We figured it must not have been any good, or they wouldn't have thrown it away." Things we had spent a lifetime collecting were now gone as if they never existed. I would have been more upset if not for the fact that in two days I'd be starting a new job. I figured I'd soon be able to replace everything since I'd be working full-time.

My father was the manager of a local chain of garages and gas stations, so he gave me a job working for him. I would be bringing home well over four hundred dollars every two weeks, and the job was easy enough. I was assigned to work shifts with an old Vietnam War vet named Dave, in a garage that attracted very few customers.

We mostly sat and watched the traffic pass while sipping cold drinks and listening to country music on the radio. Dave was a cynical, cantankerous old bastard, and he became the closest thing to a friend I had in Oregon. Despite our age difference, we got along quite well together. Most of Dave's vocabulary consisted of swear words, and he fired them like bullets at everyone and everything on earth.

Now that I had a full-time job, I was no longer in school. I never made the decision to quit; it was more like my parents made it for me. They didn't actually say, "You're quitting school," but they didn't have to. It was pretty obvious when they enrolled my sister and brother in a new school and didn't do the same for me. I was resentful but said nothing. At least I was making money now.

My little brother began developing some odd habits. He would watch *The Texas Chainsaw Massacre 2* over and over, even though it scared him so bad he couldn't sleep at night. He mimicked characters from the movie, walking around the house scratching his head with a coat hanger while pretending to eat flakes of dandruff. He had a small plastic sunflower that wore sunglasses and a bow tie, and when placed next to a radio it danced to the beat of the music. He carried it everywhere with him, and as far as I know, it was his only playmate. My sister began to hang out with some pretty shady characters and was always drinking or partying with them. This was the first time in her life she'd experienced any freedom, and she was taking advantage of it. When we were with Jack he'd rarely let her leave the house.

After we'd been there about a month, I decided the time had

come to call Deanna's house. When her mother answered I had my sister ask for Deanna. The second she was on the line I took the phone and said, "It's me." Her voice sounded odd, almost like a little girl, when she asked, "Where are you?" I told her I was in Oregon and asked if there was someone hovering around her, to which she said indeed there was. My heart sang just at hearing her voice, being in contact again. It was more than just her—I was talking to home, to my familiar world. I was on the phone with someone who didn't sound like they had a Yankee accent. I felt alive again. I felt like myself, and that was a rare thing of late.

It's hard to describe what had changed. Ever since I walked through the doors of that mental institution I'd felt like an old man shuffling his feet along the halls of a nursing home. Talking to her sent a wave of energy through me that shook the rust off and I felt ready to get moving again. That all ended in less than sixty seconds. "Do you still want me to come for you?" If she said yes, I would leave right then, even if I had to walk.

She didn't say yes, though. What she said was, "I don't know." She was hesitant, uncertain. The magick was broken. The last thing she ever said to me was "I have to go now." She hung up the phone and we have not spoken again to this day.

Up until that point my life had at least had a purpose, a direction; some part of me still had faith that it would all work out. That was now gone and I was infinitely tired. I sat on the edge of the bed and stared at the wall for a very long time, not knowing what else to do.

My parents were going to visit relatives in California and would be gone for a few days. Nanny was flying out to meet them there because she didn't think she was strong enough to make the road trip when the rest of us came, and would return to Oregon with them. I chose to stay at home. Once they were gone, I walked to the corner store and bought two of the cheapest bottles of wine they had—Wild Irish Rose. I spent the entire night sitting out on the balcony looking down at the street and drowning my sorrows with the foulest-tasting alcohol ever dreamed of by man. I guess I was at the point most people call "rock bottom." I was so lonely that I no longer felt like expending the energy necessary to keep living. When the sun began to rise I went to bed and didn't get up for several days.

Little did I know, Jerry Driver had been a busy bee in my absence. Deanna's reluctance came from the fact that Driver had told her parents that I was a satanic monster and the head of a very large cult that was up to all sorts of skulduggery in the area. Driver had no doubt Deanna's life was in danger as there was no telling what foul plot I had devised to trap her in. He told them he was positive I had been committing sacrifices all over town, that I'd burned down churches (even though no church in the area had burned), and that I had a hand in infinite other untold crimes. He wove a tale in which I was the very incarnation of evil, come to create hell in Arkansas.

Why did he do this? I don't know. I didn't learn all these facts until later, when local teenagers told me he questioned them about me every time they went out into the streets of Lakeshore, burning gas and taxpayers' dollars as he terrorized teenage boys. He was beyond doubt a very sick individual, and I never have understood why it was me who became his obsession. He once went so far as to make

Jason take off his shirt so he could "inspect him for satanic markings." I was also later told that during the investigation after my arrest in the summer of 1993, he persuaded Deanna's parents to send her to a "deprogramming center" to be certain she was no longer under the influence of my nefarious spell, and that they should contact him at once if they ever saw or heard from me again. That's precisely what happened.

After I got off the phone with Deanna, her parents questioned her about the call and she eventually told them it was me. They called Driver and sent up a red alert. Driver's reaction was to call the police in Oregon and tell them that I was on probation in Arkansas for all sorts of satanic crimes and that I should be arrested at once. The police seemed to think it some sort of joke, but when he kept demanding that I be arrested for calling Deanna, they sent someone out to talk to me. I found out about this from Driver himself, who told me in an effort to prove that at any given moment he always knew what I was doing.

An officer in plain clothes came to our apartment to find out what was going on. He sat at the kitchen table drinking, a cup of coffee as he asked me and my family questions. I told him that I had indeed called Deanna, but that I was no satanic kingpin and had no idea what Driver was raving about. The officer reported that I was breaking no law, didn't seem to be abnormal, and that the apartment was not the hotbed of satanic activity that Driver seemed to want them to believe. I can only imagine the tantrum Jerry Driver threw when they refused to arrest me.

Meanwhile I became more lethargic and lackluster by the day.

I no longer cared about anything. My mother expressed concern that I would harm myself, though I never seriously considered it. Everything exploded one night over a simple misunderstanding.

I had some Kahlúa and planned to drink it in milk. I've never been a regular drinker of alcohol of any sort, but this stuff had a nice chocolaty taste and helped me sleep. I poured it into the milk and stirred it briskly. My sister went and told my mother that I was in the kitchen "doing something sneaky." Of course I was being sneaky—I was trying to spend what little money we had on the pint without being caught!

My mother didn't bother to come and ask me anything; she went behind my back and as I was walking back to my room I heard her talking very quietly on the phone, so I stopped to listen. She was telling whoever was on the other end that I had been depressed and quiet lately, and she feared that I might commit suicide. I couldn't believe what I was hearing. This was the lowest thing anyone had ever done to me in my life. This was a betrayal of epic proportions.

You must understand my mother to be able to really understand why she did this. If you don't know her you could easily mistake her action for the concern of a caring parent. In reality it was the action of a drama queen. My mother loves to create drama, as I've already said. She still does. These days, anytime a reporter comes around she can't keep her mouth shut and goes into her "poor mother" routine, complete with copious tears. I've seen it too many times.

I continued on to my room and listened to the radio for a few minutes, knowing she had set an unalterable chain of events in motion. I don't know if she called Driver for advice, but within a very short time, someone knocked on the door and I opened it to discover a police officer. He asked if I would talk to him, so we took a seat in the living room. I couldn't believe the difference between the police in Oregon and the police in Arkansas. The guy was well groomed and fit, very polite, and spoke proper English. He treated me like a human being, and I may have even liked the guy under other circumstances. The upshot of communications between my mother and the police—and possibly others—was that it was decided I should be taken to the psychiatric unit of St. Anthony's Hospital in Portland, nearby. The cop left, and I got in the car with my parents.

I sat at the hospital, waiting to see a doctor and wondering why the hell this was happening to me. My parents had been utterly convinced by strangers that their son was suicidal and mentally unstable, and their solution was to lock me up. My mother has made more than her fair share of stupid mistakes, but I believe this one was the most ridiculous. My relationship with my father also changed that night.

It's been so many years that I can now no longer even remember exactly what he said, but it was something along the lines of "You need to straighten up and fly right. I'm tired of you moping around all the time, blah, blah, blah." He followed it up with some kind of threat. He was trying to be a hard-ass because I refused to speak to either him or my mother. I had nothing to say to them, not after doing this to me. I listened to his whole angry spiel without saying anything, but every word he spoke changed the way I saw him.

In that moment, I saw my father not as a man but as a boy. He was a child who had never lived up to a single responsibility in his life, and he had failed me in every way conceivable. He had abandoned me, left me to live in poverty and squalor with a hateful, religious zealot of a stepfather and a mother who wouldn't raise a hand to protect us from his tyranny. I saw him as weak, knowing he wouldn't have survived the despair of a life like the one he had left me to. I didn't want to hear anything else from him. With absolute contempt I spat the words, "I'd eat you alive." During my trial the prosecutor tried to say that I meant those words literally—that I was a cannibal, lacking nothing but a bone to put through my nose. Of course I meant nothing of the sort. What I meant was that I realized I was stronger than my father, that I had survived a life he had crumbled beneath the weight of and abandoned years earlier. I had survived without him, and he was doing me no great favor by being back in my life now. I was disgusted by his childishness.

When I finally saw a doctor, he admitted me and I was given a room. The psychiatric ward was nothing like the hospital in Little Rock; it was more like an asylum. There were no group therapy sessions, no interaction with staff, no scheduled routines, no anything. The patients spent all their time wandering the hallways, looking out the windows at the city below or whispering among themselves.

My parents came to see me the next day, and my mother behaved in her typical fashion—as if all would now be forgiven and we'd go back to being friends. Not this time. I was fed up with her. I told her that if she didn't check me out of this place immediately, I never wanted to see her again. Her only response was, "If that's what you want," and they left. It was too much to ask that they stay away, and they returned the next day.

I was taken into a doctor's office and found my parents sitting on a couch inside. I was in no mood to make friends and behaved rudely. The doctor finally asked me, "What is it you want?" Perhaps this is a question only a medical doctor has the intelligence to ask, because my mother and father certainly never did. I no longer trusted my parents and could see just one option—"I want to go home." I didn't mean the apartment in Oregon. When I said "home," I meant Arkansas. I didn't believe there was a chance in hell of it happening, so I was stunned when my parents agreed to it. As I sat there, the doctor—who had been in communication with Jerry Driver and was aware that I had been "institutionalized" prior to this—actually called Driver to tell him I would be returning to Arkansas. Arrangements were made for me to be discharged the next morning, and I would take a bus back down South.

There wasn't much sleep for me that night. I went to bed but mostly just tossed and turned. I kept trying to form a plan of what I would do once I got to Arkansas, but I couldn't keep my mind on it. I didn't even have a place to go once I got there, but I didn't care. I knew it would all come together in time. All that mattered now was that I would soon be back home. The month I'd been gone seemed like years.

At daybreak I showered, dressed, and ate breakfast. A security guard led me downstairs and out the front door, where I saw my mother and father standing on the sidewalk next to a cab. My suitcase was sitting at their feet. My father handed me a bus ticket and the money left over from my last paycheck. I hugged him good-bye, but his body was stiff and rigid, as if he was reluctant to touch me. He didn't say much. Same with my mother. I put my suitcase in the cab and climbed aboard for the trip to the bus station. I was nervous, I was excited, and I was on my own at the age of seventeen.

I'd never been on a bus before, so the experience was a little surreal. I had been waiting in the station about fifteen minutes when the intercom announced that everyone should board now. My suitcase was placed in a storage compartment and I took an anonymous seat in the middle of a row.

As I watched the bus fill rapidly, I noticed the passengers all seemed to have quite a bit in common. They were all unshaven and appeared to be in need of a bath; most were ill-tempered and barked at anyone who got too close to them. Somehow all the dregs of society had found their way onto a single bus. It was the smelly, grouchy Greyhound from hell.

I put on my fiercest facial expression in hopes of scaring away anyone who might be tempted to sit next to me. It seemed to work. No one had the inclination to sit next to a scowling creature with unbrushed hair and dressed in black leather.

The entire magickal voyage lasted for five enchanting days. We stopped mostly at gas stations and convenience stores for people to buy supplies, then we'd be off again. I survived on a steady diet of chips and soda, with an occasional sandwich. Sometimes we'd stop at a McDonald's for breakfast, but I never went in. I stuck close to the bus in a constant state of anxiety that it would leave without me.

On the second or third day I was reluctantly pulled into a con-versation with two other gentlemen who had come aboard at the last stop. One guy was young, about nineteen or twenty years old; the other guy looked to be about fifty, but it was difficult to tell because of the layers of fat and road dirt. The young guy had long black hair and was wearing a leather jacket with a picture of Madonna air-brushed on the back. He spoke in a soft, quiet voice and chain-smoked clove cigarettes every time the bus made a stop. The old guy had a loud, obnoxious voice, greasy, gray hair, and was dressed in cutoff sweatpants and a filthy teal-colored shirt. They were travel-ing together, and both set out to convince me that I should join them in working at a carnival that traveled from state to state. They spoke nonstop about the glories and riches I could acquire if I chose to undertake this noble profession. I thanked them but declined the offer on the grounds that I was holding out for a more lucrative deal in the porn industry. Somewhere between Oregon and Missouri they departed the scene, and I continued my journey alone.

The longest layover was in St. Louis, where I spent six hours. I left the bus station to go exploring and stumbled upon an extraordi-nary number of dubious individuals. An old black man who looked like a fugitive from the intensive care unit tried to sell me drugs be-fore I was more than ten feet away from the station. This was a neighborhood in which one definitely didn't want to be caught after dark, and since night was rapidly approaching I soon beat a hasty retreat to the station. I spent the remainder of the time talking to a guy from Germany who had come to the United States in search of his father.

We crossed the Arkansas state line somewhere between two and three a.m., but I still had trouble believing I was there. A part of me was certain the place no longer existed, that it had disappeared once I left. I looked out the window into the darkness beyond and kept thinking, *I'm back, I'm back, I'm back,* projecting it out into the night. It was a Saturday morning, and everyone else on the bus was asleep. I couldn't sit still. Every landmark I recognized pushed me to a new level of excitement. When we passed the cemetery where my grandfather was buried, it took all my self-control not to tell the bus driver, "I need off *now*! Let me out *here*!"

We pulled into the bus station just as the sun was rising. No one else stirred; I was the only one getting off. I got off the bus, retrieved my suitcase, and looked around. Everything I could see looked exactly the same as when I'd left.

Fourteen

I was stopped by a cop less than ten minutes after getting off the bus in West Memphis. There was no one to pick me up, so I was going to have to walk while carrying my luggage. The closest person I knew was Domini, and she lived about three miles away. I thought that perhaps I could leave my suitcase there while searching for a place to stay, so that's where I'd started off to.

As I crossed the street from the bus station, a cop car pulled around the corner. I was greeted with flashing blue lights and a blaring siren. I have no idea what I did to arouse his suspicion, but he pulled up next to me and rolled down the window. Behind the wheel was an insolent slob with a stomach so huge he could barely squeeze into the front seat. With a voice somewhere between a hare-lipped drone and an obnoxious whine, he began to ask, "What's your name? Where are you going? Why are you dressed like that?"

I had broken no laws and was doing nothing wrong. He was harassing me simply because he could. The only reason he eventually left me alone is that he got a call on his radio. If not for that, there's no telling where the situation would have gone.

Walking three miles with a large, heavy suitcase took forever. I had to stop every so often to rub my hands, which were quickly developing blisters. The day was rapidly growing hot, the morning turning into a fine example of the brutal Arkansas summer. When I reached the apartment complex where Domini lived, I was exhausted and covered in sweat.

I had an odd sensation as I made my way between the buildings. It was a complex mixture of thoughts and feelings, one of which was amazement (and perhaps pleasure) at how nothing had changed. When I had gone there to see Domini in the past, I was always struck by how different the place was from Lakeshore, and as an outsider returning home, it was surreally familiar. I was sleep-deprived and hungry, and I couldn't decide which was more dreamlike—the time I'd spent in Oregon or being back there now.

My feelings about West Memphis and Arkansas in general have always been something of a paradox. The people there have often been cruel and hateful toward me, and I've been so lonely there that I thought the ennui would kill me. I didn't fit into the social scenes, and there aren't many opportunities to be had there, but it's been my home. The place itself is alive with a kind of magick that can cause my heart to feel like it's bursting. There is a scent in the air I can't describe. I wish everyone who reads this could feel it just once. You would remember it forever.

When I stepped in front of Domini's apartment, she was on the second floor looking out an open window. She glanced down and saw me, looked shocked for a second, then disappeared back into her room. A few seconds later the front door opened and Domini ran out. All she said was "Hi" when she hugged me. She felt familiar to me in her own way, but there was no power or passion to it like there was with Deanna.

The word I associate with Domini is just "pleasant." Hugging Domini was pleasant. I told her I was back for good and asked if I could leave my luggage there until I figured out what I was going to do with it. She helped me get it inside and out of the way, then said she'd come with me to Lakeshore. My next step would be to let Jason know that I was back.

As Domini and I walked the mile or so to Lakeshore, I told her all about being sent to the hospital, the return of my father, and the great Oregon adventure. She was explaining that she would let me stay with her if it wasn't for her aunt and uncle's objections when a cop stopped me for the second time that day. It wasn't even lunchtime yet. He pulled up next to us, got out of his car, and struck a pose like some sort of obese superhero. This one asked all the same questions the first one did, and I had to go through the same routine.

As a child, I was taught in school that living in America automatically entitles you to certain freedoms, yet the older I've gotten the more I've come to know the harsh reality. These cops could stop me anytime and anywhere, and make demands of me that left me no choice but to comply. Even though I was doing nothing wrong I was forced to tell them where I was going, where I was from, and any other personal information they demanded of me, all because they didn't like the way I looked. The only freedom I had was to obey or go to jail. They never taught me that in school.

When this cop finally released us, we continued on to Lakeshore. I hadn't realized how much I'd missed that dilapidated hell-hole until I saw it again. That trailer park was a magickal place. I still miss it now, even though the Lakeshore I knew is gone. The scummy green water and the dead fish smell in the air said "home" to me like nothing else.

As Jason's trailer came into view, I wanted to break into a run. I knew he'd still be sleeping, so I slapped the window next to where his head would be. He peeked out the window, looking irritated and half asleep, then realized who it was and quickly ran to open the front door. He was highly excited and ushered us inside, where he was the only one home. Once we were all seated I had to explain again where I'd been and what had happened. I hadn't seen or spoken to Jason since he'd left Deanna and me in the abandoned trailer that afternoon, so the whole thing had been a mystery to him.

He told us how he'd knocked on my door one day to discover a whole different family inside, and none of them had ever even heard of me. It was as if I had disappeared from the face of the earth without a trace, and he was certain he'd never see me again. When I told him about Oregon he just shook his head and said, "I would have never come back." I'd have said the same thing myself before I had the actual experience.

We discussed the fact that I didn't know for certain where I was going to stay yet and how great it would be if I could stay with him. We both knew his mother would never agree to it, but later that day he tried to convince her anyway. As we expected, the idea was met with much hostility.

My only real option was Brian. I made the trip to his house accompanied by both Jason and Domini. He started laughing the moment he opened the door and saw who it was. We all sat on the patio and I explained for the third and final time where I'd been. Brian was more amazed than I expected him to be, because he had thought I was still around and had simply dropped out of sight for a while. He found the entire story to be very amusing and laughed as if my misfortunes were the epitome of stupidity and hilarity. He asked questions when he wanted me to clarify certain points, all the while staring at me like he couldn't believe what he was hearing.

Brian had a plan that was both simple and ingenious—I would stay with him, but we would tell no one. As long as his mother didn't know I was living in the house, she could not object to it. I was impressed with his logic. After much pleading and cajoling, we persuaded his brother to drive to Domini's and pick up my suitcase.

The weekend was a flurry of excitement because I was so happy to be back and around the people I knew. We talked about what I'd missed, drove around Memphis like old times, got reacquainted with people I'd forgotten about, and generally enjoyed ourselves. I slept on Brian's floor Saturday and Sunday night, and on Monday morning I went with him to school.

Attempting to reenroll in school turned out to be one more thing on a long list of disappointments. The principal informed me that I needed a parent present to sign me up because I was not yet eighteen years old. I explained that this would be impossible as both of my parents were now living on the other side of the country. He suggested that I consider getting a GED instead. I found the idea to be distasteful, but I could see that I was making no progress in pleading my case. Dejected, I returned to Brian's house, where I ordered a pizza and watched television for the rest of the day.

When Brian returned home from school, I told him what had happened and we put our heads together to form a solution. In the end, the conclusion we came to was to see if the school would allow his mother to enroll me. She didn't know I was actually staying with them, but we did get along well. We never had a chance to test this plan, and school would soon be the least of my worries. The very next day would find me back in jail.

Tuesday morning, Brian got up and followed his usual routine of preparing for school. I was jealous that he got to go and I did not. I loved going to school; I just didn't like doing the work. I always thought school was more fun than a carnival. Everyone I knew was going to be there, so the day would be impossibly boring for me during school hours.

Brian left and I settled in for another long day of watching television. When lunchtime came I ordered another pizza. I knew I couldn't eat the food in the house, or Brian's mom would become suspicious. I was pretty sure I could live on pizza until my money ran out, but then I'd have to think of something else.

Twenty minutes after I placed my daily pizza order, there was a knock at the front door. Thinking that my provisions had arrived, I opened the door to discover Jerry Driver and one of his two cronies. Driver was trying his best to look official; he wore a pair of mirrored sunglasses stretched across his rotund face. His partner was a skinny black man who would one day meet the wrong end of a shotgun after sleeping with another man's wife.

"I'm here to arrest you," Driver wheezed.

This was quite a shock to me, as the only crime I had committed was not being in school, and that was not for lack of trying. "For what?" I asked him.

He began stuttering as if my question had caught him off guard. His jowls quivered as he managed to insult my intelligence with the crime of being under the age of eighteen and not living in the household with my parents. I seriously doubted his assertion that this was a criminal offense, but once again, I simply didn't understand that Driver was operating outside his jurisdiction, and I didn't know my rights. I was put in chains and shackles like a convict while Driver ushered me back to the Crittenden jail.

This time Driver's questions became even more bizarre and outrageous. I was taken into a small office and chained to a chair, while he and the black guy tried to entice me to read texts to them that were written in Latin. He showed me odd objects that I'd never seen before, such as glass pyramids and silver rings with strange designs. He wanted me to explain the significance of these items to him. I had not the slightest clue what any of it meant, but he refused to accept that answer. When he was finished with this, I was left in a jail cell for a few more weeks.

I knew what to expect this time, but that didn't make the ordeal any less horrendous. The endless days in a cage, the fights that erupt all around you, the inedible gruel, the humiliating orange clothes, and the way the jailers treat you like scum—it all comes together to create an incredible mental pressure that's maddening. You feel defeated and hopeless. What made it even worse was that this time I knew I had done nothing wrong. I was being punished at the whim of an obsessive, delusional, power-hungry liar. I just couldn't figure out why this clown had become obsessed with me.

After my time in jail, I was once again sent back to Charter of Maumelle. Jerry Driver took me himself, as he had obtained a court order for my institutionalization. He'd given me the same two options as before: either go to the hospital or wait in jail for months until a trial. It was the equivalent of a plea deal—and again I was caught between a rock and a hard place. In the absence of my parents, Driver arranged for my father's sister Pat to give her consent, sign the paperwork, and offer answers to the questions posed at the hospital all over again. I was chained and shackled for the entire trip. When we arrived, the other patients were quite disturbed by the sight of me. Some later confided that they had believed I must be a madman of the highest order to require all the restraints. You know you've hit rock bottom when mental patients question your sanity.

Luckily, I had to spend only two weeks at the hospital this time. During my first conversation with the doctor she said, "I have no idea why they brought you back here, because I see no reason for it." It would have taken too long to explain Driver's fixation, so I just shrugged as if to say, "I don't know why you're asking me, I only live here." I was kept there for two weeks just for the sake of following procedure, and then I was discharged. On my last day, I said goodbye to all the other patients, some of whom I really liked. There's always a huge emotional scene anytime someone is released.

I walked to the front desk and standing there was none other than Jack Echols. Driver had contacted him while I was hospitalized, told him where to pick me up, and said that I was his responsibility since he had legally adopted me. If I had had a choice I would have checked myself back into the hospital. Unfortunately, I didn't have a choice. I would now be living with Jack Echols again. I was caught in an endless cycle of hell.

Fifteen

The guards brought another tour in today. That happens every month or so. Sometimes they bring in a group of teenagers they want to scare into submission. The kids stand around shuffling their feet as the guards tell them that if they continue living the way they are now, then sooner or later they'll wind up here. They always say that Death Row is the worst. They tell the tourists that in this barracks are the people who would murder their children and rape their grandmothers. In truth, the people who commit the most heinous crimes aren't on Death Row. They're out in the general prison population with much lighter sentences. Most of the people on Death Row are here for no other reason than that their case got more publicity than others. The difference between a man receiving a prison sentence and a man receiving a death sentence could be decided by nothing more than a slow news day.

The tours aren't always just kids. Sometimes they bring in church groups, or people taking certain college courses. One thing they have in common is that they all know my name. I'll often hear them ask the guards, "Where's Damien Echols?" The guards point me out, then the people in the group gather in a circle and whisper as they stare at me. They do it without any trace of self-consciousness, as if I am an animal that has no idea what's going on. As if I don't have the slightest trace of humanity. Most haven't a clue as to how socially inept their own actions are. My family has been here visiting me when a tour comes through, and they'll stand around staring at my family and me as if we were put there for their entertainment. It would probably be humiliating if my feelings weren't buried under a mountain of disgust.

I have always lived in my head, but once I was locked in a cell I *completely* retreated into the world of the mind to escape the horrendous environment. I leave my body here to cope with the nightmare while my mind walks other hallways. I have to sometimes listen to my body, but it's hard. If my attention wanders for even a split second I automatically retreat down into those psychic rabbit holes. People tend to think of the soul as a man-shaped thing composed of a vague ghostlike substance. In reality it's more like some God-almighty haunted house, in which the rooms are constantly shifting, moving, and reconfiguring themselves. A small broom closet becomes a cavernous ballroom behind your back. You always see movement in your peripheral vision, but never can find the source of the faint noises that seem to be coming from around some forever distant corner.

Ghosts can haunt damned near anything. I have heard them in the breathy voice of a song and seen them between the covers of a book. They have hidden in trees so that their faces peer out of the bark, and hovered beneath the silver surface of water. They disguise themselves as cracks in concrete or come calling in a delirium of fever. On summer days they keep pace like the shadow of our shadow. They lurk in the breath of young girls who give us our first kiss. I've seen men who were haunted to the point of madness by things that never were and things that should have been. I've seen ghosts in the lines on a woman's face and heard them in the jangling of keys. The ghosts in fire freeze and the ghosts in ice burn. Some died long ago; some were never born. Some ride the blood in my veins until it reaches my brain. Sometimes I even mistake myself for one. Sometimes I am one.

Sixteen

Living with Jack was worse now than ever before. I could tell he really didn't want me there but felt like he had no choice in the matter. While I was in Oregon he had been renting a small room in West Memphis that was barely bigger than a closet, so he had to find a new place. That place turned out to be a tiny trailer back in Lakeshore. It was barely big enough for us to stay out of each other's way. I can't recall speaking to my parents at all during this time, although my mother may have been in touch with Jack.

Unsurprisingly, Jack didn't have a single friend in the world. Every moment that he wasn't at work was spent in a chair in front of the television. Other than yelling at me, the only topics of conversation he employed were how my sister had ruined his life by telling Social Services that he had molested her, or how wrong my mother had treated him by filing for a divorce. He was sickening to me, and I hated the very sight of him in his sweat-stained shirts.

He went to bed at eight o'clock every night, which meant that I was forced to do the same. After eight I was not allowed to turn on a light because he said it would keep him awake, so there was no reading. We didn't have a phone. I couldn't watch TV or listen to

the radio—not even a Walkman. He claimed he could hear it playing in his room even with the headphones clasped firmly to my ears.
I couldn't go out after six o'clock because he would have to sit up
and let me in. When I asked why he didn't just give me a key, he said
because he wouldn't be able to fasten the chain lock, and I'd wake
him up coming in. He had three locks on the door and still felt the
need to prop a chair against it every night so no one could break in.
The only thing a thief could have taken was the jar of pennies next
to Jack's bed or the huge picture of Jesus hanging in the living room.
Only a true crackhead would break into that place.

Jack Echols was always angry. Sometimes it was at a simmer and
other times he erupted into a screaming fit, but there was always
anger. I couldn't tiptoe around him or stay invisible in such a tiny
place, so his rage was always directed at me. He did nothing but sit
in his chair stewing and brewing, filling the rooms with misery and
hatred. It was unbearable. Brian had moved to Missouri the day
after I got out of the hospital, so my only refuge was Jason's house. I
slept there as often as possible.

For reasons unknown, Jerry Driver had also told Jack that I was
to check into his office once a week. Every Monday I made the five-
mile trek to Driver's office, where he and his two sidekicks (Steve
Jones and another, whose last name was Murray) would question
me. Their approach no longer seemed friendly. They had switched
tactics and become downright antagonistic. Most often Driver and
I were alone, but if one of the other two were there, they'd appear to
be deep in thought while Driver asked one "satanic activity" question after another.

Jack worked at a roofing company, and during the winter months and rainy days jobs were often postponed, so he would take me to Driver's office. As long as Jack was present, Driver would refrain from his usual insanity. His beady eyes gleamed and his whiskers twitched as he stared at me across the desk, but he managed to restrain himself. After Jack came with me every week for over a month, Driver must have grown exasperated, thinking he'd never again be able to see me alone. Admitting defeat, he said I no longer had to check in.

While Jason and Domini were in school, I had nothing to do but read. I educated myself since I couldn't go to school. I spent most of every day in the West Memphis Public Library devouring book after book. I loved that library. I reread the Stephen King novels so often that the two librarians who worked there would hold a new release in the back for me to read first. There was something a little creepy about all that knowledge housed in one place. It gave the books a slightly sinister aspect.

I eventually took my old principal's advice and got my GED. I was hoping I'd have to attend classes or something, but no such luck. I passed the test with flying colors.

Being that I was still on the antidepressants given to me during my first visit to the hospital, I had to make periodic visits to a local mental health center, where a doctor would refill my prescription. They never bothered to reevaluate me or question whether I still actually needed them; I'd just be handed a prescription like it was a hall pass.

I thought my life was pretty dull, but Jerry Driver must have believed otherwise. One day Jason and I were sitting in Jack's trailer watching television while he was at work. I answered a knock at the door to discover Bo, one of the local Lakeshore youths. He was sweating and breathless as he came in and helped himself to a soda before telling me that Driver was around the corner at the Lakeshore store, asking questions about me. "He asked me which street you live on and I said I didn't know," Bo informed me, without a trace of irony in his voice. Driver had also told everyone at the store to stay away from me because sooner or later I was "going down," and anyone who was with me would meet the same fate.

Upon hearing this news, Jason looked at me with an irritated expression on his face and said, "What the fuck are we doing? We never do anything, but this freak is telling everyone we're 'running wild.' Doesn't he have any real crimes to solve?" Apparently not.

The last time I saw Driver before my trial was the night of the high school homecoming football game. Jason and I went to it because there was absolutely nothing else to do. We had to walk home after it was over, which is when we were intercepted by my old friend. He was driving up and down the streets of Lakeshore, probably looking for me. He asked where we were going, what we were doing, and so on. When he finished the interrogation we continued on our way to Jason's trailer, where we passed the night watching horror movies. I forgot all about this incident until I was on trial for murder and Driver testified. He told a great many lies, some of which were that Jessie Misskelley was walking with us that night, that we were all three carrying staves and dressed in satanic regalia, and that he believed we were returning from some sort of devil-worshipping orgy. The jury ate it up like candy and loved every sordid detail. A story straight from the tabloids, right next to "Bigfoot Sighted!" or "Bat Boy Born in Cave!" This was *evidence.*

The misery of living with Jack reached a fever pitch when he decided that I should have a job and that I was incapable of finding one for myself. The truth is that it's almost impossible to persuade someone to hire you when you don't have a car or anyone willing to drive you to work. I had tried everywhere. Jack persuaded his boss to hire me to work alongside him doing roof construction.

The job was hard, boring, and dangerous, but the worst part was that I never had a second in which I was out of Jack's presence. We got up at sunrise and didn't get home until nightfall. The only thing I could do was come home, eat supper, go to bed, and rest for the next day. I was chained to him day and night. This went on for months. I began to hate my life and could easily see myself trapped forever. Jack became more of a bastard by the day, and it wasn't just me who noticed it. The people we worked with tried to be friendly to him but were met with hatefulness.

I grew more and more desperate to escape his presence. I racked my brain attempting to come up with an idea that would allow me to break free. Finally I discovered the answer, which Jerry Driver himself had handed to me. He had insisted that I be confined to a mental institution on two separate occasions, and now I would take advantage of it.

At my mother's suggestion, I went to the Social Security office and applied for disability benefits. They looked over my application, which detailed my stays in the hospital, and declared me mentally disabled. I would be entitled to a check every month. I wasn't allowed to work and draw the check at the same time, so this was my escape from working with Jack. The chain was broken. When I told Jason about it, he laughingly called them "crazy checks." The name stuck, and that's what we came to refer to my income as. "Have you gotten your crazy check yet?" Yes, indeed.

Doris and Ed, my paternal grandparents, moved to West Memphis, and I began to spend time at their house a few miles away. I would keep my grandmother company while my grandfather was at work. I dearly love my paternal grandparents. No matter how old I get I always feel like a kid around them. To have that feeling around anyone else would be irritating, but I didn't mind it at all around them. It made life seem clean and simple. You can't stay in a black mood when visiting my grandmother; it's impossible. Jason usually went with me because he knew there would always be food there. As soon as we walked in she would begin preparing huge bowls of chili for us, or bacon and eggs with toast, sometimes pork chops or fried chicken. Dessert was always Dolly Madison cakes and ice-cold cans of Coke. My grandmother is a saint.

One day while I was visiting her, my mother called. My grandmother told her that I was there and then handed me the phone. I talked to my mother and father, who were both still in Oregon. It wasn't unpleasant; they mostly asked what I was doing, where I was staying, how Domini and Jason were. I had my reservations, but didn't mind talking to them. It became a routine that when I was at my grandmother's house I'd speak to them on the phone. We were getting along, but I remained wary of them to a certain degree, like I would a dog that had bitten me in the past.

Domini now skipped school more often than not, and she stayed with me while Jack was at work. We never had a burning romance, but we kept each other company. I had no desire to get into another situation where I risked the sort of trauma I had experienced with Deanna, and Domini was safe. We were friends who had sex, and that's the only type of relationship I was willing to have then. Perhaps that makes me sound selfish, but I will be nothing if not truthful. My worst fear in the world was having my heart broken. When she called me one day and said to come over, I already knew what was happening.

I knew exactly what she was going to say once I got there, but curiously I felt nothing. I knew my life was about to change forever, yet I was strangely detached. I wasn't especially happy, nor was there sadness to speak of. There was neither excitement nor dread. I was a Zen master for a day.

When I arrived, Domini was smiling, glowing. She had an assortment of papers scattered across the kitchen table and her mother was with her. The papers were medical pamphlets. I sat in a chair; she sat on my lap and put her arms around my neck. She said the exact thing I knew she was going to. She told me she was pregnant.

Seventeen

For a split second today I could smell home. It smelled like sunset on a dirt road. I thought my heart was going to break. The world I left behind was so close I could almost touch it. Everything in me cried out for it. It's amazing how certain shades of agony have their own beauty. I can't ever seem to make myself believe that the home I once knew doesn't even exist anymore. It's still too real inside my head. I wish I had a handful of dust from back then, so that I could keep it in a bottle and always have it near.

Time has changed for me. I don't recall exactly when it happened, and I don't even remember if it was sudden or gradual. Somehow the change just crept up on me like a wolf on tiptoe. Hell, I don't even remember when I first started to *notice* it. What I *do* remember is how when I was a kid every single day seemed to last for an eternity. Time was as long and drawn-out as a politician's speech. I swear to God that I can remember a single summer day that lasted for several months. I was a sweaty boy with no shirt, sitting on my grandmother's front porch while the gnats dreamily circled me. The days were so long that my young mind couldn't conceive of a block of time that would make up an entire week. There had been summer, shorts, crew cuts, and Popsicles ever since the Big Bang, and only a fool thought it would ever end.

Then one day I turned around and realized that entire years were slipping through my hands like water. Youth had been stolen from me while my back was turned. It's still happening now. It seems like no sooner does the sun rise than it's already setting again. Now I watch while years flip by like an exhalation, and sometimes I feel panic trying to claw its way up into my throat. Time itself has become a cruel race toward an ash-colored sunset. It opens doorways to disease and leaves me empty-handed. I truly don't understand how it happened. How it *continues* to happen. Even looking directly at it doesn't change anything, no matter what the old people say about watched pots never boiling. Forever can be measured with a ruler, and eternity is no longer than a stiff breeze.

God, I miss the sound of cicadas singing. I used to sit on my front porch and listen to those invisible hordes all screaming in the trees like green lunacy. The only place I hear them now is on television. I've seen live newscasts where I could hear them screeching in the background. When I realized what it was I was hearing I nearly fell to my knees, sobbing and screaming a denial to everything I've lost, everything that's been stolen from me. It's a powerful sound—the sound home would make if it weren't a silent eternity away from me.

Hearing the cicadas is like being stabbed through the heart with blades of ice. They remind me that life has continued for the world while I've been sealed away in a concrete vault. I've been awakened on many nights by the feel of rats crawling over my body, but I've never heard summer's green singing. The last time I heard it, I had yet to see my twentieth birthday.

People in places like West Memphis don't like *anything* that stands out, including intelligence and beauty. If a woman is smart enough to take care of her body so that she doesn't become a sexless lump, she will get looks of hatred from the local women. They will cast the evil eye at her as they help themselves to another plate of biscuits and fried pork chops. If a man is a little too intelligent for the taste of the locals, he will soon find himself ostracized. Most don't have either the self-discipline or the self-respect to better themselves, and they despise anyone who does, because it makes them feel small and inadequate. Unless you want to be the target of resentment you have to keep your head down and shuffle your feet along with the rest of the herd. The one thing above all else that is not tolerated is magick. Any trace of wonder or magick must be snuffed out at all costs. Then instead of mourning its loss, they'll pat themselves on the back. Nothing can be mundane enough to suit the herd. Bland country faces in bland country places.

When I was a kid, somehow a story started circulating in West Memphis. I can only guess at its origin, but something about it horrified me. In fact, the whole town was pretty on edge. People were claiming to have seen a dog with a man's head. It was rumored to have escaped from a traveling carnival freak show that had come through the area. A preacher swore that he spotted it looking through a window of his house. Neighbors stood on their lawns in the evening with the same facial expressions they wore when scanning the skies for tornadoes. "Get back in the house," they would snap at the children who were drawn out by the hovering sense of excitement. I'm certain I wasn't the only one who began having bad dreams about the dogman.

Eventually people seemed to forget about it, and it faded from the conversations. The *feeling* never left, though. A vague atmosphere of dread and dangerous fear seemed to hover like a fog for the next decade. It was the sort of fear that robs people of their ability to think clearly. It was the kind of fear that usually ends up with a frightened mob hurting someone.

In this part of the world all shrines are built to honor the great spirit of mediocrity. The celebrations are for mediocre events, and everyone praises a mediocre god. Heads upon pillows dream mediocre dreams and loins all give birth to mediocre offspring. At the end of a pointless life awaits a mediocre death. Love comes wrapped in a bland little package and fulfillment of the biological urge leads to swift decline. There are no monuments to greatness in this land of stupor.

Down here in the deep, dark South we know and live with the real world. Candy-Land idealism is quietly suffocated in the relentless humidity. This is the world where fist meets face. This is where the calluses on a man's hand are bigger than his conscience, and dreams get drowned in sweat and tears. Mutually assured destruction rides the roads on gun racks in the back windows of pickup trucks. The goodness of human nature gets packed away with childhood toys, and the only third eye I have is the one I use to watch my back. Everyone puts on their Sunday best and pays tribute to religion's slaughterhouse and then dines on a cannibal communion.

People put their backs to the stone in the field and push until their entrails rupture, and they drag their meals from the earth with bleeding hands. Education is foreign to the sunburned beasts of burden, and the painkiller comes in black-labeled Tennessee bottles. No one here moves quickly, but *everyone* moves with absolute certainty.

Eighteen

My eighteenth birthday, in December 1992, came and went on silent feet. There was no cake, no celebration, no well-wishers. Jack didn't even remember it, or if he did, he made no mention. I'm certain his hatred of me equaled my disgust with him by this point. Having me in his house was a reminder of his failed relationship and disgrace. At least I was now officially an adult, and outside Jerry Driver's jurisdiction. As a juvenile officer, he was only allowed to harass children.

Domini's aunt and uncle had decided to move and were leaving her and her mother behind. Domini's mother was in extremely poor health. She was diabetic and needed insulin injections, not to mention the fact that the left side of her body was almost completely paralyzed from a stroke. It took her ten minutes to walk the length of a room, and she often needed help getting dressed. Needless to say, the doors of opportunity weren't exactly banging open for her.

After searching for a place to stay, they located a rapidly disintegrating trailer in Lakeshore. They had procured a van to move their things, but a one-hundred-pound pregnant girl and a half-paralyzed woman proved to be less than adept at the moving process. In the end most of the loading and unloading fell to me, but I didn't really mind. It gave me a chance to look at all the interesting things they had accumulated—old birdcages, roach clips shaped like snakes, mildewed books, and other assorted treasures they hoarded. They were more than a little worried about how they were going to make ends meet.

Meanwhile, pressures continued to mount with Jack. He constantly accused me of things I hadn't done, such as having parties and letting people go into his room while he was at work. I didn't know enough people to put together a party, and there was nothing in his room worth going in there for. He would rant and rave, screaming at me, pressing his face right into mine, but he drew the line at hitting me. I could tell he sometimes wanted to, but he never did.

Late one night I could take it no more. He was bellowing at me as usual and I simply got up and left. I walked out while he was in mid-tirade.

It was dark, cold, and drizzling as I walked up and down the streets of Lakeshore. It must have been winter still because I remember I was wearing a leather jacket at the time. It seems it's always cold, dark, and drizzling when I go through momentous emotional changes. I used to wear an old black slouch hat, and I liked to watch the rain drip off the brim. It made me feel like a character in a spaghetti western. That's what I did for a couple of hours before finally going to Domini's, where I slept that night.

I went and got my things the next day while Jack was at work and brought them back to Domini's. Between my "crazy check" and the money Domini got from her father, we managed to pay rent and survive. We even started buying a few items for the baby we would soon have. We couldn't afford a car, so a decent job remained beyond my grasp. I was certain that if I just had a way to get across the bridge to Memphis every day, I could find something good.

Domini quit high school because of the pregnancy, and we spent the days together. We went on walks, watched television, fed the ducks that came to the lake, or kept her mom company while listening to music. We passed the days in this fashion for several months. We talked about what we should do once the baby was born and agreed that we should get married, although we never laid solid plans.

I continued talking to my parents on the phone, and not long after I told them Domini was pregnant, they told me they were moving back to Arkansas. It seemed that things weren't going so well for them in Oregon. I wasn't certain how I felt about this, because I knew it meant they'd be back in my life. Could be good, could be bad. Time would tell. They would be back in about a week or so. I told them our address so they could come see us once they were in town.

During those calm, quiet, uneventful months with Domini, I fell prey to the belief that things would never change. It wasn't that I wanted things to remain that way forever; it just seemed that I didn't have much choice in the matter. I was wasting away. Ever since I was a child, I'd felt like I was doing nothing but waiting for my special place in life to be revealed to me. Often I was frightened that I'd miss it when it happened. I felt that the stagnant life I was living was not what I was destined for, but I had no idea what to do about it. All I could do was wait, wait, wait. I knew I wasn't meant to live and die in a trailer park the rest of the world had never even heard of.

My parents arrived in Arkansas early on a weekday morning in the early spring. Domini and I were still in bed sleeping when my mother and sister knocked at the door and Domini's mom let them in. I could hear them talking in the living room and figured I'd better get up. If anything, my mother's southern accent seemed to have deepened while she was away. It was very odd hearing her voice in person again; it made the day seem special somehow, like a holiday.

I deliberately took my time getting dressed and brushing my hair before going into the living room, mostly because I didn't know what to do. I had no idea how to behave in this situation. When I finally entered the room I saw my mother and sister in chairs; my sister was wide-eyed but silent. My father wasn't there. I wondered if that meant anything. My mother turned to see me looking at her, then quickly bustled over to hug me. The first thing that struck me was how much I'd grown. I now stood a full head taller than her. While my mother theatrically shed the few requisite tears, I hugged my sister and asked where my father was. He was at their new place, unloading their things. My little brother was with him. He would meet us at my grandmother Doris's house for breakfast.

Domini and I went with them and listened to tales of their adventures in Oregon on the way. They seemed to be well rested and

cheerful despite their weeklong drive. When I first laid eyes on my
father I could see something like doubt in his face, as if, like me, he
didn't know what to do. He was nervous and uncertain.

Not having a clue what to say, I hugged him. Domini did the
same. That seemed to put him at ease. The awkwardness faded away,
and he began behaving like his normal self. The single most familiar
thing about my father to me is his cough. He coughed a great deal
because of his lifelong smoking habit, and hearing him cough put
me at ease for some reason. It softened my heart toward both of my
parents. Perhaps because it reminded me that they were only human,
subject to the same failings as everyone else. My mother had gotten
pregnant with me at the age of fifteen; they were both high school
dropouts and had never known any other life.

At least I was capable of knowing there was some other kind of
life possible, even if I was having trouble achieving it. They believed
that the way they were living was the only kind of life that existed.
They had no imagination to envision anything else, and no desire to
reach it. I felt sorry for them. I still do sometimes, although that
doesn't mean their constant idiocy isn't capable of driving me to the
brink of madness. They never have learned from their mistakes. It
would probably be easier on everyone if I stopped expecting them to.

After they settled into their new place, I began spending time
with them. I alternated living with Domini and at my parents' place.
So did Domini sometimes, and Jason was known to stay over, too.
One day he laughingly called me a nomad after we made stops at
both places, then traveled to my grandmother's to see what tasty
dishes she would serve. Once he mentioned it, I did feel like a bit of

a gypsy. I didn't quarrel with my parents at that point, maybe because I could always escape them.

I was now legally an adult, an expectant father, and in a relationship I was certain would end in marriage. I never would have abandoned Domini. Sometimes I think that comes from sheer determination not to make the same mistakes my father did. But I was not in love.

I thought of Deanna frequently, wondering what had happened. Through sheer coincidence (I use that word but don't believe there's any such thing) I found out where Deanna's family had started attending church. The possibility of seeing her again plagued me. I couldn't drive it out of my head. I constantly wondered what would happen, how she would react, what I would see in her eyes, and I had a plethora of questions I needed answers to. I couldn't understand how she had so thoroughly and completely severed our connection. I needed an explanation.

Sunday morning found me preparing to descend into the hellish realm of fundamentalism. From the outside, the church looked like a Kentucky Fried Chicken shack with a steeple. I knew I didn't belong there, but I had to do it or I would get no rest. Slinking inside, I took a seat on the last bench of the congregation and watched the activity. People obnoxiously called out greetings, shook hands, and slapped one another on the back as if they hadn't seen each other in years. I saw people glance at me from the corner of their eyes, but no one approached me. No one smiled at me, shook my hand, or slapped me on the back. No one even said hello.

Scanning the rows, I saw Deanna sitting in the dead center of the room with her family. I hadn't seen her in a year, but she hadn't changed at all. I'm not sure what it was that I felt, but my heart was in my throat. I couldn't breathe. She looked at me . . . and looked away. I didn't see even a flicker of recognition. What did that mean? I had been expecting something—anything—but her eyes passed over me as if I were not even there.

I sat through the entire hour and a half of the red-faced preacher bellowing and beating his fist against the podium, but never heard a word of it. I stared at Deanna's back, willing her to turn around and give me some sort of reaction, but she never did.

When it was over, I walked outside and stood on the sidewalk. I was trying to figure out what this meant as I watched her family get in their car and drive away. I turned to leave and heard someone call out, "Hey! I want to talk to you for a minute!" The preacher was staring at me without blinking as he approached.

He stood before me with crossed arms, not offering to shake my hand. "What's that?" he asked, pointing to a pin on my jacket. It was the iron cross from the cover of the Guns N' Roses album *Appetite for Destruction*. "That some sort of satanic thing?"

I told him it most certainly was not, but he still looked dubious.

"I don't want you coming here making people uncomfortable." He looked like he was working himself up into a state of anger.

"Don't worry, I won't be back." I walked away, still trying to figure out what it all meant.

Nineteen

By May, Domini and I had been arguing a little, though nothing serious. It was mostly in the vein of people who have spent too much time together and just need a break. I had slept at my parents' house for a couple of nights to create some breathing space. One morning I got up and went out to have a nice big bowl of Froot Loops for breakfast. Toucan Sam makes a mean box of cereal. While I was happily munching and contemplating the fact that I would soon have a bowl of pink milk, I flipped on the television. Nothing goes better with Fruit Loops than cartoons. There were no cartoons that day. Every channel was showing the same special news coverage of three murdered kids who had been discovered the day before. The reports all said the same thing: the bodies of three eight-year-old boys had been found mutilated in a wooded area nearby. It looked like every reporter in the world had descended upon West Memphis.

It wasn't just the people on TV talking about it—the whole town was abuzz. It was the conversation on everyone's lips, and the rumors were already starting to fly. I heard the same two words countless times over the next month: "Satanists" and "sacrifice." Each day that passed without a suspect being arrested only increased the talk, as the words cemented themselves more firmly in the minds of every gossipmonger in town.

The very same day, Friday, May 7, I saw the first news coverage is when the police began to sniff around my door, although they later denied it and said they never considered me a suspect until several weeks down the road. Not long after the coverage began, a cop named James Sudbury and Jerry Driver's sidekick, Jones, came knocking. I found it interesting that Driver himself didn't show up. They came into the house and said they wanted to talk to me privately. Evidently they did not want my family to hear what they had to say. My mother, sister, and paternal grandmother watched as I led Sudbury and Jones into Michelle's bedroom and closed the door. They sat on the edge of the bed, one on either side of me.

This was the first time I'd ever seen Sudbury. He was potbellied, with a horrible comb-over and weak, watery eyes. He also sported the same seventies porn mustache so popular among his colleagues. He didn't say much, and just sat quietly while Driver's cohort asked the questions. Jones was all saccharine and lying eyes as he said things like "Something bad has happened, and we really need your help." Instead of questioning me about the murders, he stayed on topics such as "What's your favorite book of the Bible, and why? Have you ever read anything by Anton LaVey? Who is your favorite author?" It seemed they couldn't decide between conducting a murder investigation and filing a book report. Of course eventually came the inevitable "Have you heard anything about devil-worshippers in the area, or any plans to sacrifice children?" I found it sickening. Instead of attempting to find out who had murdered three children, they indulged in these childish fairy tales and grab-ass games. A fine example of your tax dollars at work.

Before leaving, they took a Polaroid picture of me. Later, I found out they showed it to nearly everyone in town, using it to plant ideas in the minds of an already frightened public. In court they denied taking the picture or ever even coming to see me that day. They had to, because Jones and Driver were from a different office and weren't supposed to be involved in the investigation in any way. By that point in the courtroom, the blatant lies would no longer shock me because I'd seen them do it too many times.

This visit was the first of many. They were soon coming at me every single day. They came to my parents' house, to Domini's trailer, and to Jason's house. It wasn't always the same two; there was a rotating crew of about six of them. It was the same questions, day after day. It became pretty apparent that these clowns weren't looking for a murderer. Jerry Driver and his two cohorts, Jones and Murray, put a bug in the ear of the West Memphis police department, and they couldn't shake it. Instead of conducting a real murder investigation and checking the forensic evidence, the police started immediately chasing stories of black-robed figures that danced around bonfires and chanted demonic incantations.

Beginning that day, that's all anyone talked about. The entire town was petrified because they were convinced hell had broken loose in Arkansas. Every redneck preacher in the area was preaching sermons about how we were in the "end times," so you better get right with God or else the devil would come for you, too. You must keep in mind that this is a state in which one out of every four people can't read above a fifth-grade level. Ignorance breeds superstition. People believed these stories and helped them grow. After being shown my picture, one man swore to the police that I had caused him to levitate. Another swore that the police told him they had found body parts under my bed. These sorts of stories passed for investigation.

The constant harassment continued to escalate. Within days, instead of coming to my house they were taking me to the police station. It was easier for them to play good cop, bad cop there. One of them (usually Sudbury, whose breath smelled as if he ate onions morning, noon, and night) would get in my face and scream, "You're going to fry! You may as well tell us you did it now!" The other cop would then pretend to be my friend and act as if he were rescuing me from Sudbury's "wrath." I was only a teenager, and the whole thing looked pretty pathetic even to me.

This continued day after day for a month. My grandmother grew worried and sold her rings to hire an attorney to come to the police station with me, but the police refused to let him in. They lied and said I never asked for him, even though I did so several times. My grandmother lost her engagement and wedding rings for nothing.

I didn't think there was anything wrong with answering their questions, because I had nothing to hide. I had done nothing wrong, and figured they would sooner or later get this insanity out of their system. It didn't work that way. The more I cooperated, the more abusive and belligerent they became.

In spite of their abusive behavior, the threat didn't feel any more escalated than the tone of the harassment we'd been through for nearly two years where Driver was concerned. That changed permanently the last time I was picked up and brought into the police station before the arrest. I was kept there for eight hours. I was not allowed a drink of water, a bite of food, or even to use the restroom. They screamed and threatened me the entire time, trying to force me to make a confession. The psychological pressure was enormous. They would have kept me all night if I hadn't finally demanded they either charge me with a crime or let me go home. I suffered from extreme exhaustion, my head was pounding, and my body kept trying to vomit, although there was nothing in my stomach. I felt like I'd been run over. If you've never been through anything like that, there's no way you can understand. There's no word that describes what they did to me other than "torture."

On the evening of June 3, my mother, father, and Nanny left to go to a casino for a night of gambling. My grandmother loved playing blackjack more than just about anything else in the world, and my parents were more than happy to keep her company at the table. They would be gone all night. Michelle, Jason, Domini, and I had all settled down for an evening of watching horror videos. We were making fun of a movie that seemed to have been put together with more imagination than money when someone started beating on the door. Not knocking, beating. You could feel the vibration through your feet on the floor. Outside someone screamed, "This is Sudbury. Open the door!"

My first thought was, *To hell with that.* I was sick of those ass clowns tormenting me day after day. I figured it was more of the same and that they'd eventually get tired of waiting and leave. When the beating continued and grew even more persistent, I knew something wasn't right. They were being even more aggressive than usual. I went to answer the door to see what they wanted.

When I opened the door, there were three cops standing on the steps, all pointing guns directly at my face. The barrels of their weapons were less than three inches from touching my skin. Another cop stood on the ground pointing a gun at my chest. Sudbury nearly tackled me in his eagerness to handcuff me and get me into a cop car. Looking over my shoulder, I told Domini, "Don't worry about it." *After all, it's impossible for them to prove you've done something you haven't done, right?* At least that's what I thought.

It was a scene of utter chaos. I don't recall whether my rights were read to me amid the noise and police stampede. I didn't see them arrest Jason; I was rushed out too quickly. I later found out they took him out right after me. After I was put into a car, I was driven straight to the police station and escorted to a small office by a cop who looked disturbingly like a pig that had been taught to walk upright. I never saw a single cop in the station who was even close to being physically fit, but this guy was the worst of the lot. He was so fat he was suffocating under his own weight. He weighed at least 350 pounds. He had no neck, and his nose was turned up like a snout. I've learned over the years that sooner or later a person's physical appearance comes to resemble whatever is in their heart. I shudder to think what this guy's true nature was. For some reason I couldn't stop thinking of him as "Piggy Little."

Piggy Little was an old-school asshole. You could tell he'd never succeeded at anything in his life, and he was out for revenge. He seemed to think his personal God-given mission in life was to harass and torment me in every way possible. He kept his hands on me at all times—he pushed, pulled, and jerked me around continuously.

After ten or fifteen minutes, the chief inspector came into the office and sat behind a desk. His name was Gary Gitchell, and I'd seen him at the station a couple of times before, but I'd never had to deal with him. Gitchell was slightly more intelligent than his co-workers, which is most likely why he was the boss. He was no intellectual giant, but he didn't have to be when compared with the rest.

"Is there something you want to tell me?" he asked.

I stared at him blankly, saying nothing.

"You may as well tell me something now because your friend has already confessed. This is your only chance to make sure you don't take all the blame." I felt like I had somehow gotten lost in this conversation, or that I must be missing something, because it wasn't making sense to me. Friend? Confessed?

"Who are you talking about?" I asked. It was his turn to look at me blankly. I had no idea who he could be talking about, because I knew it couldn't be Jason.

He continued along the same lines with statements like "You should just tell us something, because your friend is already pointing the finger at you. If you want to make sure he doesn't put everything on you, this is your only chance." This went on for at least half an hour, Gitchell talking while Piggy glared. When he finally realized this wasn't going anywhere, I was put inside a cell that wasn't much larger than a phone booth. I was left there throughout the night, confined to a space so small I couldn't even stretch my legs out. There was no water, no restroom, nothing. Every so often Gitchell came in and asked more of the same. At one point he came in and said, "One of the officers told me you wanted to talk to me." I hadn't even seen an officer in hours. "He lied," I informed him. This continued until well after sunrise.

When I wasn't being questioned, I was trying to solve this mystery. Who could Gitchell be talking about? What had this friend said I had done? None of it made any sense.

A cop came in and demanded my clothes. I'd never experienced anything like this in my life and thought him some sort of pervert, judging by the looks of him. I was given more clothes—an old, ragged police uniform that was at least twelve sizes too large. I had to gather the waist and tie it in a knot to keep the pants from falling down. This is how I made my first court appearance.

At ten in the morning on June 4, I was arraigned. Jason, Jessie, and I were called separately. I was walked down a narrow hallway that suddenly opened up into a courtroom. I was stunned by the contrast. The jail itself was filthy and roach-infested to the point of making you not want to touch anything for fear of contamination. It was a place the general public was never meant to see. I'd grown used to that, so the dazzlingly clean and well-lit courtroom was jarring.

I blinked like an animal pulled from its hole and looked around me. The place was packed from wall to wall, and the only faces I recognized were my mother's and father's. Everyone else in the place watched me with hatred in their eyes. Every few seconds someone popped up as though in a Whac-A-Mole game and snapped pictures of me. I hadn't slept in about thirty-six hours, so everything had an even more surreal quality to it.

The judge—his name was Rainey—began rambling while I leaned against a wall to keep my knees from buckling. Four cops kept their hands on me at all times, as if they expected me to break and run at any second. In the course of maybe ten minutes, I was charged with three counts of capital murder. I didn't hear the charges outside the panic, fear, and exhaustion in my head. When the judge got to the "How do you plead?" part of the show, I said, "Not guilty." I was following the instructions of a lawyer temporarily assigned to me, who'd told me minutes before the hearing what to say. My voice sounded flat, dull, and small. I felt a wave of outrage directed toward me from the peanut gallery. The judge's droning voice sounded strangely like an auctioneer as he began talking about a confession. I was so exhausted and in such shock that I could follow very little of what he was saying. It finally dawned on me that he was asking if I wanted the confession read out loud or just entered into the record. I was starting to feel a little pissed, and my voice was a little more forceful this time as I said, "Read it." I could tell he didn't like that idea at all. As a matter of fact he seemed downright uncomfortable as he looked down and started shuffling papers.

Finally he stuttered that he wasn't going to do that, but that he would call for a recess until after I had read it. During the recess I was taken into a broom closet filled with cleaning supplies, and was handed a stack of papers while two cops stood staring at me. My brain was so numb I could comprehend only about one-fifth of what

I was reading, but at least now I knew who had made the confession. The name written at the top was "Jessie Misskelley." My first thought was, *Did he really do it?* Followed quickly by, *Why did he say I did it?* Even in my shell-shocked state I could tell something about his "confession" wasn't right. For one thing, every line seemed to contradict the one before it. Any idiot could plainly see he was just agreeing with everything the cops said. That's when I knew why the judge didn't want it read out loud. Anyone with even an average IQ could see it was a setup. The whole thing seemed shady.

It's no great wonder to me how the cops could make Jessie say the things they wanted him to say. If they treated him anything like they did me, then it's quite amazing that he didn't have a nervous breakdown. They used both physical and psychological torture to break me down. One minute they'd threaten to kill you, and the next they'd behave as if they were your best friends in the world, and that everything they were doing was for your own good. They shoved me into walls, spit at me, and never let up for a moment. When one of them got tired, another came in to take his place. By the time I'd been allowed to go home after previous interrogations I'd had a migraine headache, and I'd been through periods of dry heaving and vomiting. I survived because when pushed hard enough I acted like an asshole, just like the cops themselves. My point is that we were just kids. Teenagers. And they tortured us. How could someone like Jessie, with the intellect of a child, be expected to go through that and come out whole?

It makes me sick and fills me with disgust to think about how the public trusts these people, who are in charge of upholding the law yet torture kids and the mentally handicapped. People in this country believe the corrupted are the exception. They're not. Anyone who has had in-depth dealings with them knows it's the rule. I've been asked many times if I'm angry with Jessie for accusing me. The answer is no, because it's not Jessie's fault. It's the fault of the weak and lazy "civil servants" who abuse the authority placed in their hands by people who trust them. I'm angry with police who would rather torture a retarded kid than look for a murderer. I'm angry with corrupt judges and prosecutors who would ruin the lives of three innocent people in order to protect their jobs and further their own political ambitions. We were nothing but poor trailer trash to them, and they thought no one would even miss us. They thought they could take our lives and the matter would end there, all swept under the rug. And it would have ended there, if the world hadn't taken notice. No, I'm not angry at Jessie Misskelley.

From everything I'd seen on TV and read in books, I came to believe the cops were the good guys, and that dirty cops were few and far between. So why was no one stepping up to expose this for the bullshit it was? Why were they all going along with something so fraudulent? The answer: to save their asses. The police assigned to my case were members of the West Memphis drug task force—cops who normally would not be investigating these murders; they were also offered additional help from the Arkansas State Police and they turned it down. It seems quite a few of the cops on

the drug task force were being investigated by the FBI for drug dealing, money laundering, and tampering with confiscated evidence,
and the last thing they needed was the entire world watching them
as they bumbled around ineptly, pretending to conduct an investigation. They needed to solve this case quickly, and we were the easy
solution. As one of the cops told Jason, "You're just white trash. We
could kill you and dump your body in the Mississippi, and no one
would care." We were disposable, subhuman. Feed us into the meat
grinder, and the problem goes away. It's not like we were ever going
to amount to anything anyway.

After I read the script/confession, I was taken back into the
courtroom. The judge was rambling again, and I was on the verge of
collapse. Suddenly everyone sprang to life as an overweight man
with bad skin jumped from his seat and tried to run down the aisle.
He was screaming something incoherently as the cops tackled him
and I was hustled from the room. I later found out that he was the
father of one of the murdered children. I couldn't really blame him.
I have a son of my own now, and I might have done the same thing
if I thought I was looking at the man who had harmed him. He just
needed someone to blame, to take his grief out on. He wasn't interested in facts or evidence.

Once I was back in the dark and dingy part of the building, they
began putting chains on me—around my waist, my hands, my feet,
and anywhere else they could think to attach them. I saw Jason a
few feet ahead of me, and they were doing the same to him. He was
also wearing one of the old, ragged police uniforms. In front of him

was Jessie Misskelley. He, too, was shackled, but he wore his own clothes. Perhaps this was another small way of punishing Jason and me for not giving them the confession they wanted.

They rushed Jessie through a door, and outside I saw sunlight and heard the roar of a crowd. It sounded like a referee had made a really bad call at the Super Bowl. Next they walked Jason and me out the doors at the same time. There was a circle of cops around me, all trying to drag me. I would have had to run to keep up with them, but there were chains on my legs and I had no shoes on. They dragged me across the concrete, ripping off two of my toenails and a fair amount of skin. The crowd went into a frenzy at the sight of us. It looked as though the entire city had turned out to see us, and they were all screaming, yelling, and throwing things. They wanted to crucify us right then and there. I imagine that was the closest a modern man could come to knowing what it was like in the Roman Colosseum.

I was tossed into the back of a car and told to stay down. There were two cops in the front seat, both fat and wearing the standard mustaches. They could have passed for brothers. The one behind the wheel quickly started driving at a high rate of speed. I was curled into the fetal position on the backseat, vomiting and dry-heaving. One cop looked back at me, cursing and swearing. In disgust, he spit, "That's just fucking great." No one said another word to me for the rest of the trip. I had no idea where I was being taken.

When we finally came to a stop sometime later in the afternoon, it was at a small white building with several cop cars parked outside. A few old, crusty-looking men with a hose were halfheartedly spraying the cop cars. As I was being escorted inside, I heard the cops tell them to wash out the backseat where I had gotten sick.

Once inside the Monroe County jail, the chains were removed and I was told to strip. I stood naked while one cop sprayed my entire body with some sort of lice repellent. Four or five other cops looked on while conversing nonchalantly. This was nothing new to them. Soon enough I myself would begin to view such events as nothing out of the ordinary. After my flea dip, I was given a pair of white pants and a white shirt to put on. One of the old car-washers from out front handed me a towel, a blanket, and a mat like preschoolers sleep on. The induction ceremony being complete, I was pushed into a cell that would be my home for most of the next year.

Twenty

The cell I was confined to on June 4 had four concrete slabs that served as beds. There was a small metal table bolted to the floor, a shower stall, and a television suspended high in one corner that picked up two channels. For the first week or so there was only one other person in the cell with me. His name was Chad, a white guy with a terrible case of acne and unwashed curly hair. He was there on a capital murder charge. He'd killed someone with a sawed-off shotgun while burglarizing their house. His back had already started to curve into a hump, like an old man, even though he was only sixteen.

Chad seemed a bit slow in the thinking department, if you catch my drift. He claimed he had been there for years and was quite excited that he now had company. He couldn't answer a single one of my questions: he didn't know where we were, or how far we were from West Memphis, or how to make a phone call, or anything else I could think to ask him. He'd just smile really big, throw his hands up in the air as if to say, "Who knows? Only the gods can say," then rock back and forth for a while. Not so encouraging.

I didn't find out where I was for a week. My thinking was that perhaps my whereabouts were being kept secret from everyone, including Domini and my family. I was worried about how Domini was taking it. My family and I weren't on the greatest of terms, but when you're drowning like I was, you'll reach for anything. I was lost and alone and empty. Floating deep in outer space would have been no more frightening. I had done nothing to deserve this, and I was goddamned if these assholes were going to make me the sacrificial lamb.

I was still taking antidepressants, which the guards gave me every night. That very first week, I had the ingenious idea of saving them up and taking them all at once. That was the only way out I could see at that point. The situation was getting worse. There was no Sherlock Holmes coming to solve the case and let me out. Besides, what did I really have to live for, anyway? I would regret not being there for the baby. It would have been nice to stick around for that.

When I was in one of the hospitals, I had heard that 800 milligrams of the particular antidepressant I was on was enough to put you into a coma you'd never come out of. I wanted to be certain I did it right, so I took 1,200 milligrams. I swallowed the pills and sat down to write a quick note to Domini and my family. It was only a few lines scratched out quickly with a pencil. I don't recall what they were and I don't want to. That being taken care of, I stretched out on my concrete slab and flipped through one of Chad's magazines. He wasn't much of a reader, but he loved those pictures. He wasn't too fond of losing the only company he had, either. I hadn't bothered to hide what I was doing from him, thinking there was no need.

The main sensation I had was of being so tired it was physically painful. I wanted to sleep more than I'd ever wanted anything in my life. I closed my eyes and just let go. That's when all hell broke loose. About ten guards came for me. Chad had told them what I'd done, because he didn't want to be left all alone again, especially with a dead body. I could hear them talking but couldn't make my eyes open. Someone opened them for me and shone a flashlight in them. Someone else poured a vile-tasting liquid in my mouth and told me to swallow it. It was some sort of vomit-inducing syrup. They put me in the backseat of a car and drove about 150 miles an hour to get me to a hospital. By that point I was so confused I kept asking myself if the drugs were taking effect yet, or if I was already dead. I tried to tell the cop behind the wheel that we would have been there by now if we'd all ridden on the back of a giant spider. Unfortunately, my mouth wouldn't work the way I wanted it to.

I don't remember much about the hospital that night. I know it was somewhere in Monroe County. I woke up for a moment when someone put a tube up my nose and down my throat. Two cops were sitting before me, watching, while all the doctors and nurses were moving double-time. Can't let the star of the show die, can we?

Strangely enough, all the doctors and nurses looked like therapists from the mental institution. I was so discombobulated that I hardly knew what was happening to me, much less could think about where I was at that point. I was awakened a couple of times during the night by someone shining a light in my eyes and asking if I remembered my name, but I slept through the entire stomach pumping procedure. When I finally woke up sometime the next day, I found myself in the intensive care unit.

My court-appointed lawyer, Scott Davidson, first came to see me while I was in the hospital. He stayed for maybe ten minutes, just long enough to introduce himself and tell me my family knew where I was being held. He looked incredulous when I told him I was innocent. I would see him about three more times over the course of the next year, and never for longer than thirty minutes at a time. You would think that if a guy were going on trial, and could very well be sentenced to death, that his lawyers would spend a lot of time preparing him for court. Mine did not. He didn't tell me what he would be doing to prepare for the trial or give me any idea of what to expect or to do in the meantime. Perhaps this is how capital cases are handled, I thought. After all, this guy is a lawyer, so he must know what he's doing, right? Surely they wouldn't appoint me a lawyer who was ineffectual or uncaring. I had a lot to learn.

The same court that was putting me on trial was also paying my lawyer. Look at it this way—are you going to employ someone who makes you look stupid and rubs your face in your own mistakes? No. You're going to pay the guy who knows his place and sticks with the program. These guys get paid the same amount whether they win or lose, so why try too hard? Later, during the trial, when I asked why they didn't push a point or challenge a ruling, they answered, "We have to work with the judge on a daily basis and don't want to piss him off."

"Beyond a reasonable doubt" disappeared, and "Innocent until proven guilty" had left the building. Once they go through all that trouble to accuse and arrest you, you're going down unless you've got a couple million dollars on hand to hire some real gunslingers to come to your aid. I was a fool back then, though. Still wet behind the ears. I thought the purpose of the justice system was to see that justice is done. That's the way it works on TV. While I was counting on divine intervention, they were plotting my demise.

The court system does not have the sane man's mentality, even though it's built on his back. It's an insane snake of mammoth proportions, all tangled up in itself. It's vicious and demented, biting any flesh it can reach. It's so entangled and drunken that it will eventually strangle itself to death. There's no way to convey its madness to anyone who hasn't come into contact with its sluggish embrace. The people who operate within it have become as deranged as the lunatic snake itself, and justice is a foreign concept. They accept pointless and drawn-out procedures as religion. Nothing outrages them more than an idea that makes sense, and there's nothing they'll fight harder against. It's no wonder there are so many jokes about lawyers. It's only growing worse since the time of Kafka. There's no way to understand it. It is a world without logic.

Once I was released from the hospital and taken back to the jail, I was put in a padded cell with no clothes. I lived in only my underwear for days. I'd heard of padded rooms all my life and imagined them to be like a giant pillow. It's nothing of the sort. Everything is coated in a thick, greasy substance similar to rubber. More like a bicycle tire filled with cement than a pillow. Since I had no clothes, it was pretty chilly. One of the guys passing by slid some copies of *National Enquirer* under the door. I read them during the day and covered up with them at night. There was nothing else to do in there. It was just an empty room.

There was a small opening in the door, and sometimes one of the other prisoners on the block would sit by the door and talk for a while. Everyone on the block, with one exception, was a young black guy who had already been to prison at least once in the past. The only exception was an old man in his fifties. His hair was as white as his skin was black, and all the other guys would abuse and take advantage of him. He was given absolutely no respect. He would sit by my door and cry for a half-hour straight at times, like I could help him somehow. He was there for having two children with his own daughter. He was their father and grandfather at the same time. He tried to stay quiet and out of everyone's way, but it didn't always work.

I spent a week in the padded cell, talking to people through the opening in the door and freezing. Contrary to what I had been led to believe by movies and TV, none of the other prisoners seemed like hardened criminals who would kill their mothers for a nickel. Some of them were pretty funny. Every night after lockdown, someone would call to the guy in the next cell, "Hey, man, come here a minute, I need to show you something." There would be laughter, then, "Shut up, fool, I'm trying to sleep." Several times a day someone would beat on my door and ask, "You all right in there?" Their constant antics kept me from feeling quite so sad, at least until the lights went out. Once the lights went out and everyone was in bed, the despair came back full force. I cried myself to sleep many nights.

After I was back in jail for a couple of days, I was taken into an interrogation room by a guard. There I was introduced to two visitors: Ron Lax and his associate, Glori Shettles. Ron was a private investigator, he said to me, and had taken a particular interest in the case as soon as he saw the media coverage of our arrests. They started to ask me questions—did I know the children or the families, where had I been the night of the murders—direct and specifically about what had happened. They told me they had a strong interest in the case because they were very much against capital punishment, and could see that my being singled out made me the defendant most likely to receive the death penalty. They had contacted my attorneys immediately and requested to be the court-appointed investigators—a common part of a defense team—on my case. I was too shattered to take in what they were saying or to understand that they might prove helpful to my case.

When I got out of the padded cell a week later, I was taken back to the cell block with Chad. He was as pleased as could be because, counting me, he now had three roommates. While I was gone, two more guys had come in. Both were black teenagers, one named James and one named Nikia (everyone called him Kilo). Kilo turned out to be the second-best friend I've ever had in my life. This guy was really smart and extremely funny. We'd often say the same thing at the same time, or when I would try to explain something he would get excited and say, "Yeah! That's it exactly!" He would slide across the cell-block floor on his knees, doing a flawless Michael Jackson impersonation, and I would laugh until my sides hurt.

We got a chessboard from somewhere, and I taught him the game. I had learned at some point to play by reading the instructions on the box. After playing several games a day for about a month, I could never beat him again. He kicked my ass every time, unless we played speed chess by my rules. This was a variation that I invented, and its purpose was to prevent you from thinking about your next move. Your opponent had until the count of five to move a piece, or you could legally start thumping him in the forehead. It was a very fast five-count, which gave you slightly under two seconds to grab a piece and move it.

Chad's family brought him some games, too, so the four of us passed the time playing Monopoly, checkers, and dominoes. We all pooled our money, so that even the person with the smallest amount wouldn't have to play without stakes. If my family left me twenty dollars, I'd buy twenty dollars' worth of candy and chips, which was considered to belong to all of us. Kilo, Chad, and James did the same. We never had a single fight, which is a very rare thing when you've got guys who are forced to be in each other's faces twenty-four hours a day.

The guards at the Monroe County jail were different from any I've ever seen since. They were nice, polite, well groomed—not abusive in any way. I was fooled into thinking all guards were this way. I didn't realize I was experiencing a miracle. They treated us like human beings, and even let us do things the other prisoners didn't get to do, like stay up all night. The four of us never were locked up alone; we made small pallets in the common area between our cells, and lived like we were having an eternal slumber party.

Kilo and I both looked with great anticipation to Saturday at midnight, when a television show called *Night Flight* came on. We were so starved for music that we'd listen to anything, and this was our only fix. It wasn't the music either of us loved, but it was all we had. You never know how much you need music until you don't have it. I missed it so much my heart hurt.

M y mother, father, and Domini came to visit me once a week. We were allowed twenty minutes, and had to talk through bulletproof glass. Domini had been almost five months pregnant when I was arrested, but you still couldn't tell it by looking at her. In the last three or four months of the pregnancy, she grew at an alarming rate. By July, her body was still the same size it had always been, but her stomach had become huge and tight.

On August 4, I was taken to a pretrial hearing with Jason and Jessie, where all three of us pleaded not guilty. Judge David Burnett, who had been assigned to the case after the first hearing with Rainey, presided. He was a Craighead County judge, his demeanor administrative and assuming—in his eyes, we were already convicted. He was just going through the formalities and paperwork of a trial. He did at this point "sever" Jessie's trial from mine and Jason's—Jessie's lawyers were effective in arguing that the publicity surrounding all of us would damage his own case. In the back room, seated just a few feet from Jessie and Jason, it was impossible to speak. The three of us were shell-shocked. Jessie never lifted his head; he sat staring at his feet. Jason appeared angry, and if we managed to make eye contact, he shook his head at me in sheer bewilderment and disbelief.

I wouldn't get to be there for the birth of my son. That was one more thing taken from me. A guard stuck her head in the door on the morning of September 9 and told me that I was now a father. So much for a celebration.

We had a boy. Domini gave him my first name, only spelled differently—Damian. I gave him the middle name of Seth, which is what everyone calls him. We gave him a third name, Azariah, just to be certain he'd never have an inferiority complex. I wasn't there to sign the papers, so he has Domini's last name. She brought him to see me for twenty minutes every week, but I couldn't touch him. The only time I was permitted to touch or hold him was during the trial, a few months later; while the cameras were running, the court allowed me to hold my son for the sake of the film.

My father or grandmother would bring me five paperback books from a local secondhand bookstore every week, and I'd usually have read them all by their next visit. I had always loved reading, but at that point those books became my only way to forget about the nightmare of my life. I would hide in them and go someplace else for hours at a time. The other guys were amazed by how much and how quickly I could read. It was a trend that has continued to this day. I've read a few thousand books over the time I've been locked up. Without books, I would have gone insane long ago.

Five months passed in this way. I was still being given anti-depressants, and there were the momentary distractions but they lasted only a short period of time—the unknown threat of an up-coming trial hung over me daily. In an October hearing, it was de-cided that Jason, only sixteen when he was arrested, would be tried as an adult. Despite the evidence that Ron and Glori told me they had uncovered, their findings often only underscored the thought that I would likely be given the death sentence. They told me that I would surely be convicted of murder, and that they were working toward the possibility of winning a case later on down the line by appeal. But first I would be convicted of murder.

Christmas Day came and went—it may as well have been the Fourth of July, such was the vacuum I lived in. Everything I'd known was gone, absent completely. Between this time and February 1994, I rarely saw or heard from Ron in person, though I was told he was investigating the case, and coming up with useful information on an almost daily basis. He reviewed the West Memphis police records and discovered inaccuracies, inconsistencies, and un-reliable information and leads in the reports and offered them to my defense lawyers. Unfortunately, my lawyers (I was assigned a lawyer named Val Price in addition to Davidson) didn't use or follow up on any of the information he found or leads he offered. They didn't even call the witnesses who could have testified to my whereabouts on the night of the murders, witnesses Ron had tracked down and interviewed. In order for the information to be used, my lawyers needed to get a sworn affidavit from those witnesses, the extra "mile" that they never bothered to go for me. They never attempted to prove my alibi.

Glori did come to see me nearly every single weekend, and she always brought pizza. It seemed to me at the time that she really cared about the case, because she and Ron both went to tremendous lengths, visiting me on off-hours and telling me about their progress.

I found out later that they were being paid by the court and hadn't in fact done anything beyond what any investigator is obliged to do in this situation. But on my birthday Glori even brought me a box of cupcakes. We sat alone in a small office eating cake and going over the case. She gave me hope. What I've discovered in the years since then is that this is their job, to give hope. It's a ploy, really, because they are just as much a part of the predetermined courtroom defense formula.

O n January 26, 1994, Jessie went to trial. I watched news coverage from my cell—it was utterly painful to see. Jessie's false confession was the centerpiece of the proceedings—it was the only so-called evidence the prosecutor, John Fogleman, had. It cemented our guilt in everyone's mind and ensured our conviction before we could go on trial ourselves. On the eighth day, Jessie was convicted and sentenced to life plus two twenty-year sentences.

We were also being made the subjects of an HBO documentary. On June 5, the day after the West Memphis police held a press conference to announce they had caught the alleged perpetrators of the crime, an HBO executive named Sheila Nevins saw an article half-buried in *The New York Times* and shared it with two filmmakers, Joe Berlinger and Bruce Sinofsky. The headline, "3 Arkansas Youths Are Held in Slayings of 3 8-Year-Olds," offered the potential for a provocative and salacious film about Satanism, human sacrifice, and debauchery of gothic proportion. Joe and Bruce immediately took a production crew to West Memphis and began interviewing locals, the parents of the victims, my friends and acquaintances, my family, Jason's family, and Jessie's. What began to emerge for them was a far different picture of the circumstances. Joe and Bruce both acknowledged that after speaking with locals, it was clear to them that the three of us were being put on trial for crimes we didn't commit.

A few weeks before my trial, I was transferred to Craighead County jail in the town of Jonesboro—ostensibly, I was moved there to be closer to my lawyers, so we could strategize in the weeks before my trial. It was nothing like the Monroe County jail. The guards were all cruel and abusive. They talked to you as if addressing a lower life form, no matter how polite and civil you were to them. I witnessed them beating prisoners on an almost daily basis. Years later, as I was lying in my cell on Death Row watching the news, I saw that five guards had been fired in Jonesboro because they had handcuffed a prisoner and beat him unconscious. They were fired. No charges were filed against them. Most of the time they're not even fired, only demoted. If you walk up to a man on the street and punch him in the face, you go to prison for assault. Do the same thing to a man in prison and you get demoted.

There was a small Mexican guy in jail there who suffered from catatonic schizophrenia. He would sit or stand in odd positions for hours at a time because of his mental illness. The guards would beat him just to see if they could make him move. It was a game to them. They often spit in your food to see if they could get you to fight. If you said anything at all, they'd call in five or six of their friends to beat you. Once you're behind the walls, there is no help. The world doesn't care.

Me, around second grade. This is the only picture of me I know of that survives from this time.

At Tucker Max, 1996. After nearly two years in prison, I had only recently begun to have visits from strangers who were sympathetic to my cause. (Grove Pashley)

Both of these photos were taken outside hearings, probably around 1997 and 1998. (Grove Pashley)

In 1996, I met my future wife, Lorri Davis, when she wrote me a letter telling me she'd seen the first documentary made about the West Memphis Three. She gave me these photos, which I kept hidden in my cell for years.

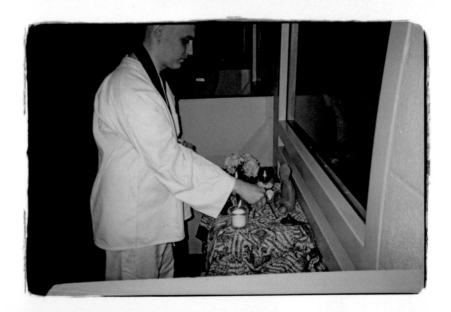

(FROM TOP)

The wedding altar. The ceremony, December 3, 1999. Lorri and I are married. It was the first time we were permitted to touch each other. Afterward, author Mara Leveritt and her partner, Linda Bessette, hosted a reception at their home in Little Rock. (Grove Pashley)

Lorri and me; with Lorri's parents, Harry and Lynn Davis; and my adoptive mother, Cally Salzman, visiting me. The prison charged five dollars for each Polaroid, and to judge from the stacks and stacks of them that Lorri has—one from nearly every visit—the prison photo business was lucrative during my tenure.

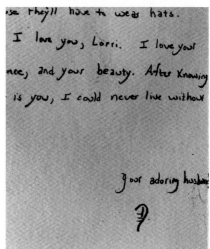

se they'll have to wear hats.

I love you, Lorri. I love your
nce, and your beauty. After Knowing
is you, I could never live without

your adoring husband

*A birthday card that I made for Lorri
one year. Occasions like this were especially
painful; I wanted so much to be with her,
to give her gifts, to spend the day with her.*

I felt truly blessed, though, just to know she had found me.

Domini brought my son, Seth, to Arkansas, and Lorri would meet them and take over, acting as stepmother for a day or two. These pictures were taken at Mount Holly Cemetery in Little Rock, a historic landmark. Lorri and Seth got along well, and it was a relief to share my anxieties about fatherhood with her. (Grove Pashley)

Lorri brought Seth to visit several times in the first ten years or so that I was incarcerated. The prison photographer, you may have noted, was not exactly a professional artiste. . . .

I made the piece above and those below to decorate my cell. I think the photo of the figure comes from a National Geographic; unfortunately I can't recall what the characters mean.

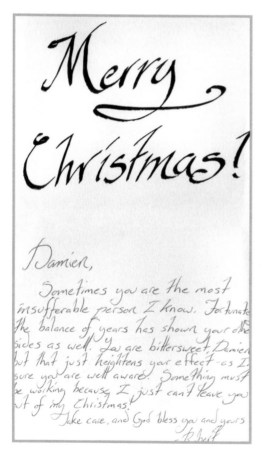

I wasn't the only artist on Death Row. A Christmas card I still have from another inmate, Robert Robbins. His sentence was commuted to life without parole, and he is still in an Arkansas prison today.

Most of my art was made from the inner casings of book covers. These are my paintings of the Egyptian god Anubis.

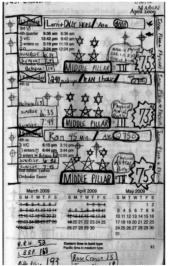
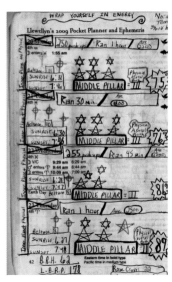

I kept an astrological pocket planner some years. These pages are from 2009.

Lorri showing some of my artwork to WM3.org cofounder Burk Sauls at her home in Little Rock. All the pieces I have left were for the most part smuggled out by Lorri while I was inside.
(Grove Pashley)

This piece was given to me by Harada Roshi, and I have it to this day.

State justices refuse to

BY LINDA SATTER
ARKANSAS DEMOCRAT-GAZETTE

Without addressing the merits of a petition seeking to throw out the conviction and death sentence of Damien Wayne Echols, the Arkansas Supreme Court refused Thursday to reopen the case in state court.

But the ruling clears the way for a federal court in Little Rock to clos_____ rors i_____ win's l_____

ered prejudici__ l information that they learned o_ _side the courtroom and whet_ _r some jurors were biased against Echols.

Echols, now 30, and Baldwin, now 27, were tried together in Craighead County in the deaths of three 8-year-old West Memphis boys whose nude bodies were found in May 1993 in a Crittenden County creek. A third de_____ isskelley, was _____ Clay County _____e Echols' and

Baldwi__
Bot__
of Critt__
publici__
of devi__
the fac__
was ca__
All
convic
capital
and Mi
withou
On (
torney

Me in 2004. It was a terribl
difficult and dark year. Even
though we had tremendous
support and sympathy in the
outside world, our case had
made no progress.
(Grove Pashley)

pen conviction of Echol.

e moved out
ty because of
luded rumors
emming from
f the victims

idants were
e counts of
ith Baldwin
tenced to life

Francisco at-
dan filed pe-

titions in state and federal court
in Little Rock raising the new
allegations of juror misconduct.
He said the allegations stemmed
from recent confessions of jurors
in Echols' and Baldwin's trial.

According to Riordan, the
jurors have said that during deliberations they made lists of
reasons to convict or acquit the
two men, and among the reasons
they listed in favor of conviction
was a statement that Misskelley
gave to investigators implicating

himself, Echols and Baldwin

The statement, however,
not admitted into evidence
Echols' and Baldwin's trial,
therefore was not to be con
ered during deliberations.

Riordan also alleges that c
ing jury selection, none of
people who were ultimat
seated on the panel admit
to being aware that Misskel
had given a statement or that
had implicated the other def

See **ECHOLS**, Page

*Once in a while I saved clippings about the case. This one, from 2005,
reports on the state's refusal to reconsider my conviction. But that denial
did provide the opportunity to take my case ultimately to the Arkansas
Supreme Court.*

*Jason and Jessie, around 2004. They were often incarcerated together in
prison, even sleeping in beds side by side for a time. (Grove Pashley)*

With several people who helped save my life, some of whom worked at it for years. Left to right: Miu and Burk Sauls, Chad Robertson, Kathy Bakken, me, Lisa Fancher, and Grove Pashley. (Grove Pashley)

With Lorri, August 19, 2011, at the party for Jason, Jessie, and me at the Madison Hotel, Memphis—my first day of freedom in eighteen years. I hadn't slept in nearly a week. (Grove Pashley)

With Eddie Vedder and Lorri.

With some of my family. Left to right: Lorri, my nephew August, my niece Shae, Lorri's sister Sherry, my niece Sydney, and Sherry's husband, Sam Chico.

My first visit to the Museum of Modern Art, New York, 2012, with friend Danny Bland. A far cry from the art scene on Death Row.

Lorri, Amy Berg, and me, spring 2012. Amy, who directed West of Memphis *beautifully, has become a dear friend.*

With Helen Carr, Peter Jackson, Fran Walsh, and Lorri, at an all-ice bar in New Zealand—the start of many surreal travels and adventures.

With Lorri at Sundance, January 2012. I'm starting to look a little less dazed here, right? It was a beautiful place, and the sight of that snow falling was better than just about anything else I'd seen since getting out.

With Marilyn Manson, on our way to the 2012 Revolver Golden Gods Awards in Los Angeles. I introduced Manson that night—my first "public speaking" appearance—and I was nervous as hell. Manson was a supporter of ours behind the scenes for years; he will always be a hero of mine.

With Johnny Depp, a true friend and brother, and tattoo artist Mark Mahoney, Los Angeles, 2012.

Lorri and me with Jacob Pitts, another good and deeply loyal friend.

Lorri and me, New York, June 2012.

*A recent photo shoot for a
magazine, 2012. I hardly
recognize the man posing for
the camera, but I know he's
a lot more comfortable in his
skin than I was for
many years.*

In Jonesboro, I was put in a cell block by myself. There was no one to talk to, no books to read, no television to watch, and no going outside. I was locked in an empty concrete vault all day and night. I knew Jason was in the next cell block, because it was so noisy I could hear the guys on that side through the wall. He was on a block with about ten other people. It would have been a huge comfort to be able to sit in the same room with him and talk, perhaps try to figure out what went wrong, but the guards made certain we never even saw each other.

I slipped deeper and deeper into despair. Without a miracle we would die in prison. Jason and I were scheduled to go to trial together, though the attorneys were all fighting tooth and nail. Jason's attorneys wanted a separate trial for him, to remove him somehow from my already established guilt. It seemed like the entire world was howling for my blood.

Twenty-one

february 19, 1994, the first morning of our trial, Jason and I were given bulletproof vests to wear to and from the courthouse. Emotions were running high and the cops were taking no chances. We would ride to court every day in a convoy of police cars—six of them, to be exact. When we pulled up out front we had to walk a gauntlet. There would be a huge crowd of reporters, and people who wanted us dead, and we had to walk right through the middle of them like Moses parting the Red Sea. The screams of hatred were so loud you couldn't discern individual voices. Reporters shoved cameras and microphones into your face at every step, all shouting questions at once.

An interesting thing began to happen as the days passed. People who supported us and believed in us began to appear in the crowd, one or two at a time. They would smile or give me a slight nod as I made my way in or out. They were mostly young boys or girls standing apart from the rest, many dressed in black. I started to receive little bits of poetry scratched on scraps of paper. Someone sent me a single red rose. The supporters never matched the haters in number or volume, but they mattered a great deal to me.

There were a few odd cases, too. Ron started a ritual of pointing out the girls he said were "eye-fucking" me. As I got out of the car one morning a girl screamed, "Oh my God, he looked at me!" like she had just seen John, Paul, George, and Ringo rolled into one.

The reporters were the worst. If people knew how much of what they read in the papers or see on the news is distorted or outright lies, media corporations would soon go out of business. I've seen more fiction on local news broadcasts than I've read in novels. Quite often, the newspaper accounts didn't match anything I saw go down in the courtroom. Valuable information went unreported and preposterous new developments were invented. One day, sitting in my cell watching coverage, the broadcast was interrupted with breaking news: a stick covered in a red substance and hair had been found in my mother's now abandoned trailer. The announcement was made and regular programming resumed—but in everyone's mind here was a possible murder weapon. In fact, it was a paint stick, the kind you use to stir a freshly opened gallon of paint. My mother had been disciplining her two Pomeranians with the end of a used stick—and before anyone did the logical thing, the media had their hands on it somehow. In a later example of the hysteria, during a post-trial hearing, new evidence was presented—they had found teeth marks on one of the bodies, and they did not match my teeth. There was no mention of it in the next day's paper.

Burnett and Fogleman welcomed the media's presence, and they (in addition to my attorneys and Jason's) agreed to allow Joe and Bruce to film the trial for their HBO production—one would suppose because they assumed that they were going to be the centerpieces of a major legal victory when the trial concluded. Since both Joe and Bruce had visited me often in jail, pretrial, at this point, I had gotten to know them fairly well and I was used to the cameras by then. They didn't discuss the specifics of the case with me, but asked me about my background and childhood, and often asked why the police might have focused on me as a suspect. They interviewed Jason and Jessie extensively, too. Their presence was comforting in the courtroom—amid the sea of outraged and angry people, their conversations and attention to me was the only familiar part of my life at that point.

It's maddening to sit there hour after hour, day after day, on trial for something both you and the cops know you didn't do. You feel hundreds of eyes drilling into you, taking in your every shift and move. Many seemed to think this was the greatest form of entertainment they'd ever witnessed. Vultures were stripping the flesh from my bones while I was still alive.

I never stood a chance. During breaks, the judge and prosecutors told jokes about me and smiled like they were awaiting a pat on the back. Burnett would comment on what a nice ass one of the female potential jury members had, and Fogleman's teeth would stick out while he yuk-yuk-yukked it up. Convincing twelve people they should vote to have me murdered was just another day at the office for them.

Whenever evidence was introduced that could have helped me, the jury was escorted out of the room so they wouldn't hear it. It was discovered that John Mark Byers, the stepfather of one of the children, had a knife with blood on it that matched the blood of at least one of the victims. My lawyers were not permitted to ask him directly, "Did you murder those children?" in the presence of the jury. Why? Because, they were told, he wasn't the one on trial here, I was. It wasn't really a trial. More like a formality to get out of the way before the guilty verdict. The parents and family members of the victims didn't speak or act out in any way in the courtroom, though they spoke often and volubly outside for the cameras. I'd watch them on the news later in my cell. My parents, Jack, and Michelle, as well as friends of our family, sat watching every day. When I looked back at them from my seat at the defense table, they would stare back at me helplessly. I believe they wanted to do something for me, to help with my defense, though they simply did not know what to do and hardly understood the proceedings unfolding in front of their eyes. After listening and paying attention for a short period of time, I stopped trying—it was too painful to register the blatant "railroading," a term everyone started using early on. Jason's attorneys were very strict about our communicating; they did not permit him to come near me or speak to me, though we made eye contact once in a while.

It would be redundant to go over every detail, because the murder case and the trials have been documented at length in four documentaries and several books—in fact, you can read more about the proceedings at damienechols.com, wm3.org, freewestmemphis3.org, or at my publisher's website. Many of the details that came to light during the trial I wasn't informed about until much later, and much of the evidence (or lack thereof) that finally established my innocence was not found or introduced until many years after this time.

Jason and I were both found guilty on March 18, 1994. Ironically, it was the longest trial in the history of the Arkansas criminal justice system. I didn't need to call a psychic hotline to see that coming, but it was still a complete shock. Perhaps it's human nature to clutch at any little bit of hope you can conjure up. I did, all the way to the very last second. It's devastating, even when you see it coming a mile away. As the verdict was read, I heard Domini start sobbing and run from the courtroom. I couldn't turn around to look because my legs would have buckled. I was determined not to let them know how badly they were hurting me. I refused to give them that satisfaction. I would not cry, I would not faint, and I would not show weakness. I had to hold myself up by placing my hands on the table, but I tried to make it look casual. Inside, I started to die. There was no safe place in all the world for me. My stomach was filled with ice water. Hearing Domini was the final straw. Something in me broke. All the King's horses and all the King's men would never be able to put me back together again.

I did not sleep. A trustee—a prisoner who works for the jail— was stationed immediately outside my cell to watch over me that night to make sure I didn't harm myself.

The following day I was sentenced to death, Jason to life without parole plus forty years. After the reading of the sentence, I was immediately rushed out of the courtroom and into a waiting car. As I walked through the crowd outside, someone screamed, "You're going to die!" Someone else screamed, "No you're not!" The car door slammed, and we pulled out of the parking lot. I was on my way to Death Row.

Twenty-two

To get from the Craighead County Courthouse to Tucker Max took about three hours. That's an eternity to a man who doesn't know what kind of situation he's walking into. Everyone in jail has horror stories to tell about prison. A lot of people think jail and prison are the same place, and that they know what the penitentiary is like because they were once picked up for being drunk. Jail is preschool. Prison is for those earning a Ph.D. in brutality.

My mind was numb and I couldn't think. I know now this was a combination of shock and post-traumatic stress disorder—the same thing experienced by soldiers who have been in a firefight. I shivered uncontrollably, though I didn't feel the cold outside. My life was over. That's the closest thing to a thought I could formulate. My execution date was set for May 5. That was a couple of months away. The attorneys had told me, "Don't worry about that, your first execution date means nothing. Everyone gets one of those, but getting a stay of execution is automatic." I'd like to see how well they'd laugh it off if it was their names on a piece of paper with a date next to it. Har har har, you jokers. That's a good one.

My attorneys were so incompetent that they didn't realize a motion needed to be filed in order to obtain a stay of execution. They found out before it was too late, but just by a hair. I managed to have a phone conversation with Glori, who told me that somehow one of them had discovered the oversight at the last minute.

Most people who go to prison first stay at what is called the Diagnostic Center. That's where they give you a complete physical and mental evaluation. Jason was there for about three weeks, I believe, and Jessie was there for the better part of a year, at least. If you're going to Death Row, there's no layover at the Diagnostic Center. What would be the point? Physical health and mental health don't really matter if you're going to be standing before a firing squad. I went straight to the big house itself.

It was dark outside when we pulled up, but the place was still lit up like a Christmas tree. The lights are never turned completely off in prison, and there are searchlights constantly moving to and fro. I was taken out of the car and into the base of the guard tower behind the prison building, where I was strip-searched and given a pair of "prison whites." That's what they call the uniform you're issued.

There was some fat clown in polyester pants, a short-sleeved shirt, and clip-on tie issuing orders. His air of self-importance would lead you to believe he was a warden or something. He had a horrendous little boy's haircut and the requisite seventies porn mustache. He was not the warden. During the first week, another prisoner told me he was assigned to the mental health division and had no authority whatsoever. And since there is no budget, no resources or structured mental health services for Death Row inmates, he had no professional reason for being there anyway.

That's a common thing in the prison industry: take some losers who have spent their life bagging groceries or asking, "Would you like fries with that?" and put them in polyester guard uniforms, and they blow up like puffer fish and march around like baby Hitlers. This is the only place they can feel important, so they fall in love with the job. It becomes their life, and they'd rather die than lose it.

The clown screamed in my face, "Your number is SK931! Remember it!" At that moment, I happened to glance at a digital clock, which read 9:31 p.m. I wondered if everyone's number was the same as the time they came in. (It was just a very bizarre coincidence.) A nurse checked my temperature, blood pressure, and heart rate. They seemed to find it hilarious that my pulse registered like that of a rabbit's in a snare.

After they finished, I was taken to a filthy, rat-infested barracks that contained fifty-four cells. Death Row. You'd be amazed at how many letters I've gotten from people who say they're sorry I'm on "Death Roll." I always picture that thing an alligator does when it grabs you and starts spinning around and around. It rips you to shreds and drowns you at the same time. The death roll. I was put in cell number four, and immediately fell asleep. I was exhausted from the trauma. Shutting down was the only way my mind could preserve itself.

I think my first phone call was to my parents, to let them know that I was alive. I don't remember when I made that call, because the phone system at the time was so convoluted. You had to fill out paperwork just to make a five-minute call. It took about a week for the paperwork to be reviewed and then approved or not. It's vastly different now, because the prison system has an agreement with a phone company to split the charges on any call; now, anyone can make a call just about anytime they want, as long as you can afford it. The prison profits enormously; a fifteen-minute call can cost you about twenty-five dollars.

When I arose from my concrete slab to begin my first full day of prison life, I noticed someone had dropped a package in my cell. Opening it, I saw that it contained a couple of stamped envelopes, a pen and some paper, a can of shaving cream, a razor, a chocolate cupcake, a grape soda, and a letter of introduction. The letter was from a guy upstairs named Frankie Parker. No one called him by that name, though. Everyone called him either Ju San or Si-Fu. He was a Zen Buddhist, and was ordained as a Rinzai priest before his execution. That's where the name Ju San came from. Si-Fu is a generic term that means *teacher* in Chinese. He was a huge white guy with a shaved head and tattoos of Asian-style dragons on his back. The package he sent was something he gave to every new person who came in, to help them get on their feet.

His constant companion was a guy who greatly resembled a caveman. His name was Gene, and he had dark hair that reached the small of his back and a full beard that reached his chest. Gene was a Theosophist, a follower of H. P. Blavatsky. They both loaned me books on Buddhism and Theosophy, and answered countless questions. Listening to them debate each other on the yard was like watching a tennis match. Both of them lit a fire in me that grew into a decade-long educational process. I made my way through texts such as *The Tibetan Book of the Dead* and *Isis Unveiled*.

These two guys were no dry scholars. They loved to laugh, and nothing was more hilarious to them than the perverse. They were completely irreverent. It was not unusual to hear one or the other make comments such as "I like the way your butt sticks up in the air when you bow to that little Buddha statue." Gene was a remarkable artist, and I once saw a canvas he had painted to look like a giant dollar bill. If you looked closely, you'd notice it wasn't George Washington in the middle, it was Jesus. Look even closer and you'd realize Jesus had a penis for an ear. Gene lectured for an hour on what such symbolism meant. Believe it or not, I actually learned quite a bit from him.

I also learned quite a bit from the guy in the cell next to me, though I've never put the knowledge to use. He was an old biker from a gang called the Outlaws—rivals of the Hell's Angels. He was a horrendous sight—three hundred pounds, blind in one eye, and barely able to walk. He was the epitome of hateful, old-age cunning. He was too old to fight, so he devised other ways to get revenge on those who did him wrong. He was known to befriend his enemies and then feed them rat poison and battery acid. A guy once stole five dollars from him, then found himself on the floor puking up blood after drinking a cup of coffee. He told me everything I needed to know in order to move and operate within the system. He also sold me my first radio. After not hearing music for a year, Lynyrd Skynyrd sounded like a choir of angels.

My first two weeks on Death Row were spent vomiting and sleeping. I suffered a pretty fierce withdrawal from the antidepressants I had been on for three years. The prison system spends a bare minimum on medical care for inmates, so there was no way in hell they were going to pay for a luxury item like antidepressants. Instead of gradually weaning me off the medication the way they should have, I was forced to go cold turkey. My sleep was troubled and I could keep nothing in my stomach. Even though it was agony, in hindsight it was for the best. After the drugs had made their way out of my system, I felt better physically and clearer mentally. I also lost all the weight I had gained while sitting in the county jail. You don't get much exercise when locked up in a cage, so I had gained over sixty pounds by the time I went to trial. I lost that and more. At one point I was down to 116 pounds. My attorneys visited me maybe once, telling me they would file an appeal—none of it made sense to me, and nothing they said offered me any idea as to how I might take the next steps legally to appeal my conviction. Their primary goal was to keep me from participating in my own defense, and so nothing was explained to me clearly, and nothing was asked of me.

Almost immediately, though, I started to get requests from media sources asking me to do interviews. I thought this could be my chance to tell my story to the rest of the world, since no one else had articulated my side of the story. It was obvious that no one else was going to do it for me. So I granted a couple interviews, with disastrous results. A local news station got ahold of the footage of one of my interviews and claimed I had talked "exclusively" to them. In truth, I never talked to anyone from their station; they cut and spliced the footage to make it appear that I had done so. A newscaster would say something like "Here's Damien Echols, talking about his leadership of a satanic cult!" They would then show clips of me speaking about something completely unrelated to anything they had said. That wasn't the worst part, though. The worst was when the prison administration decided to teach me the folly of my ways.

People in prison have their own language, and it takes a while to grow accustomed to it. For example, "Shoot me a kite" means "Don't discuss business out loud—write it down and pass it to me." "Catch out" means "Shut up and leave, or violence will soon follow." "Reckless eyeballing" means you're looking at someone a little too closely. "Ear hustling" or "ear popping" means someone is trying to listen in to your conversation. "Shakedown" means the guards are coming to destroy your cell in search of contraband. A shakedown is how my lesson started.

I was listening to the radio one day not long after my arrival when two guards came to my cell and barked out, "Shakedown!" They began knocking my things to the floor and walking on them, deliberately trying to destroy what little property I was allowed. My family had sent photos to me, along with a few books and the radio. One of the guards pulled a knife out of his boot and tossed it onto my bunk, then called for a camera. He took a picture of the knife and wrote a report saying he found it in my cell. I couldn't believe what I was seeing. I thought being set up for things I didn't do would stop once I got to prison. I was wrong.

One night at almost twelve o'clock I heard keys jingling in the hallway and knew they were coming for me. Two guards came into my cell, handcuffed me, and took me up to the warden's office. One guard held me up by the hair as the warden choked me. I could smell the alcohol on his breath as he ranted and raved about how "sick" I was. One of the guards kept punching me in the stomach while repeatedly asking, "Are you going to tell anyone about this? Are you?" I had never been subjected to anything like that in my life. I thought adults were that barbaric only in movies.

They threw me in "the hole." The hole is a group of cells located at the back of the prison, out of sight and hearing of everyone else. Temperatures can reach nearly 120 degrees in the summer, and it's even darker and filthier than the rest of the prison. You aren't allowed to have anything when you're in the hole—no toothbrush, no comb, no deodorant, and no contact with the outside world. Its purpose is complete and absolute sensory deprivation. If sent to the hole, you spend a minimum of thirty days there alone, no matter what your offense. Beating someone half to death or making a homemade lampshade to go over your light both carry the same penalty: thirty days in the hole. The only thing that differs is how you're treated while you're back there.

While I was in the hole, I was beaten, starved, spit on, threatened with death, and subjected to various other forms of abuse, both large and small, all at the hands of guards. The reason? Because the warden said I had made the ADC look bad in the interviews I was doing.

It happened more than once during this particular episode. On three more occasions, guards came into my cell and beat me. Once I was chained to the bars of the cell while three of them took turns. Another time it was five of them. I was told that they planned on keeping me in the hole for a very long time. Every time the thirty days were up, they could just give me another thirty for something else. What saved me was that word leaked out to the rest of the prison, and a deacon from the Catholic Church heard about it. He told the warden that if it didn't stop he would start telling people what was going on. They didn't want to risk it, so I was taken out of the hole and put back into the barracks.

The thing about the prison administration is that they will abuse you as long as you're quiet. The only way they can't hurt you is if someone is paying attention. I started talking to more people, doing more interviews, because I knew only that would make them leave me alone. They can't afford to harm you if the world is watching. They could not drag me into a dark alley if I had a spotlight shining on me. I even filed a lawsuit against the warden and some of the guards responsible.

In the end the suit was a waste of my time, as they once again chose the attorney who would represent me. I saw him once, about ten minutes before the "trial" began. He wouldn't do one single thing to help me. I was refused the right to a trial in front of a jury, and he just shrugged as if to say, "Oh, well. That's life." Instead, a judge alone decided my case. I wasn't even allowed to talk during the proceeding. We didn't go to a courtroom; the judge came to the prison so the session could be held in a small room out of public view. The lies the administration told were pretty incredible. They "proved" that the warden couldn't have done anything to me because he was in the hospital recovering from a heart attack. Did the lawyer appointed to me investigate that claim? No. He sat quietly, drinking a soda.

Ultimately, that warden was fired, although it wasn't because of anything he'd done to me. Some of his other foul deeds caught up to him. The worst of those particular guards were also either fired or promoted and shipped to other prisons in the state. The one who put the knife in my cell continued to work at Tucker Max for many more years, despite constant reports of abuse. Eventually, the ADC had no choice but to "take action" against him when he was caught on camera beating a handcuffed inmate in the face. No charges were ever filed against any of them. After all, it's not like they were actually abusing people, you know. Just prisoners.

The cells of my body store fear the way others' do fat. Every terrifying and traumatic thing I've ever experienced is still held within my muscle fiber as well as in my brain tissue. It pervades nearly every aspect of my life and influences nearly all of my actions. Everyone thinks of me as being so brave, but I recognize my own cowardice in all I do. Sometimes I feel fear building up in my throat like a scream.

One day a couple guys from another barracks had some sort of disagreement. They weren't on Death Row, but were often on the yard at the same time we were. The disagreement escalated into a shoving match, and soon enough one of them produced the most infamous of all prison artifacts: the homemade knife. The man who had no knife tried to climb the fence to escape the one who did. If he had succeeded, the guard in the tower would have shot him dead and called it an escape attempt. However, he did not make it over. Instead, he became entangled in the razor wire that lines the top of the fence. Razor wire is far more unforgiving than barbed wire and will produce horrendous damage when it meets with human flesh. As the gentleman cut himself to shreds in the razor wire, the other guy stepped up and began stabbing him repeatedly in the ass. It was horrific. I have no idea how many wounds were delivered to the gentleman's rear end; suffice it to say it was more than he wished for. This guy was none too liked by his comrades, who chose to taunt him by asking which hole he would now shit out of. This is a harsh world in which you often search in vain for a bit of sympathy.

As unpleasant as that scene was, there was one worse. There was an image that kept me staring at the ceiling on more than one sleepless night. The ignorance and cruelty of prison guards can't be overstressed. They make their living by abusing men who are down on their luck. Never was a more cowardly profession devised. They love nothing more than to have a man chained and shackled so they can torture him at leisure. If that same man were unchained and unshackled, the guards would run for their lives, or at least gather up ten or twelve of their friends to provide "moral support."

Two of these despicable men (I use the word "men" in its loosest sense) had been ceaselessly tormenting an inmate on Death Row. It went on for several weeks before he finally snapped. They soon realized you can push a man only so far, especially when he has nothing left to lose. Some of the guys on Death Row were playing a game of basketball on the yard when someone tossed the ball over the fence. When the guards opened the gate to toss the ball back in, all hell broke loose. Kurt, the man they had been tormenting, began to viciously stab both guards over and over. The one with the least amount of damage had been stabbed about seven times. Blood was everywhere. His weapon of choice was a piece of the chain-link fence he had pulled free.

I couldn't even begin to tell you how this affected me. To see two men curled up in the fetal position and lying in puddles of their own blood is not something that ever fades from your memory. For quite some time afterward I would walk around in a daze, thinking to myself, *What kind of world is this where such things happen?* The only thing that's ever affected me the same way was footage on the TV news of Iraqi terrorists beheading an American hostage. It's hard to comprehend that such things still take place in this day and age.

As for Kurt, he didn't look much better than the two guards once it was all over. When I was really young—about nine or ten years old—my stepfather took me on a form of hunting expedition called "frog-gigging." My stepfather, stepbrother, brother-in-law, and I would go out at night into the swamp and float silently in a twelve-foot boat. I was the light man. This means while the other three were armed with implements that looked like extremely long pitch-forks, I was in charge of sweeping a spotlight up and down the banks to find the frogs. I never was much good at it, because I found the whole affair to be entirely repulsive with not a single redeeming quality. At any rate, by the time twenty guards were finished beating Kurt to a pulp, he looked like a team of frog-giggers had been at him. That's what I thought of every time I saw him after that. In my mind I saw him as a giant bullfrog. They had beaten him so badly it looked like he had two heads. It was even worse than it sounds. They tortured him right up until his death. You could see fear in their eyes because of what he had done to the two guards. They were so scared of him that they would go out of their way to appear unafraid. I'll never forget it for as long as I live. What makes it all worse for me is that I know I should never have been sent here to witness it in the first place.

Twenty-three

The crew from HBO were still working on the documentary they'd started before we went on trial. I had mostly forgotten about it after I had been in prison for a year or so, thinking nothing had come of it. They had interviewed me, Domini, my family, the cops, the victims' families, and anyone else who would talk. They had also filmed the entire trial, from beginning to end. I didn't see the documentary when it finally aired in 1996, but many other people around the world did.

On a daily basis I started receiving letters and cards from people all over the country who had seen the film *Paradise Lost*, and were horrified by it. The overwhelming sentiment was, "That could have been me they did that to!" If you are to understand the impact this had on me, you have to understand that up until that point I had received no sympathy or empathy from anyone. Everywhere I turned, I found nothing but disgust, contempt, and hatred. The whole world wanted me to die. It's impossible to have any hope in the face of such opposition. Now I was suddenly receiving letters from people saying, "I'm so sorry for what was done to you. I wish there was something I could do to help."

A single letter like that would have been enough to kindle a tiny spark of hope in my heart, but I received hundreds. Every day at least one or two would arrive, sometimes as many as ten or twenty. I would lie on my bunk and flip through the letters, savoring them like a fat kid with a fistful of candy, whispering, "Thank you. . . . Thank you," over and over again. I clutched those letters to my chest and slept with them under my head. I had never been so thankful for anything in my entire life.

I don't want a "holy" life of prayer and contemplation. I want a life of strife, lust, striving, seeking, struggling, and debauchery. I'm not content to settle for one experience when there is a whole life-time of experiences to be had. I am so hungry for knowledge that I live several lives at once to acquire it. A Catholic and a Buddhist, a reader and a writer, a sinner and a philosopher, a husband and a fa-ther, a Native American and a white man—I no longer have any desire to fit into any one category. I see no reason why I can't love pornography and the art of Michelangelo equally. I want to see life from every angle. I feel as if I've learned a tremendous amount from my excursion into the realm of Eastern thought, philosophy, and practice—things I'll carry with me to the end of my days. Still, it doesn't come close to the lessons I've learned from, and with, the woman who is now my wife.

I had been on Death Row for about two years when I received an odd letter in the mail, in February 1996. It was from a woman who loved movies and had recently seen the documentary about my case at a film festival in New York. Her name was Lorri Davis, and she did something no one else had ever done—she apologized for invading my privacy by seeking me out. That really struck me, because I felt like I no longer had any privacy. My entire life had been exposed for anyone and everyone to examine and poke at with a stick. I was a fly that had its wings ripped off by a malicious kid. I was the proverbial ant under the magnifying glass. Every day I received letters from people who did nothing but ask questions about the most intimate aspects of my life, almost as if everyone in the world felt entitled to demand anything of me they wanted to know. Imagine being hounded by the paparazzi, but instead of taking your picture they throw rocks and try to dissect you.

Here was a lady who understood the value of common courtesy. She said she felt horrible about what I'd been through and was compelled to contact me, but she didn't want to intrude. I immediately wrote back to her, and ever since we have tried to write to each other every single day. Our letters to each other now fill up an entire closet.

She's the most magickal thing on earth, but it took me at least a year to be able to understand her, because she was so foreign to anything I'd ever known. She was from New York, college-educated, a world traveler who'd been to South America and as far away as the Middle East, and an architect who had worked on projects for people I'd heard of only from Hollywood movies. I was introduced to a whole new way of life through her.

We wrote to each other obsessively, and we spoke on the phone for the first time a month or so after that first letter. I just decided to call her one day—I was terribly nervous, knowing I'd need to improvise the conversation rather than script it ahead of time. She always laughs now when she tells anyone about the first time I called her. She picked up the phone to hear a deep, Delta accent ask, "Are you okay?" It was such a shock to her system that it took a second for her to reply. She said it nearly killed her. She still sometimes teases me about my accent, but her friends in New York often tell her that she's started to sound like me.

Lorri came to visit me about six months later. I remember it was summer because she wasn't wearing a coat. We had no idea what to expect, and both of us were on autopilot, for lack of a better way to describe it. We both knew we needed to talk to each other, and then to see each other. Lorri flew in the night before to be at the prison at eight a.m., when the three-hour visitation period began. She flew back to New York the same day.

It was a slow and gradual process, forging ahead together. In the beginning, I couldn't have even articulated what we were doing because I had no concept of subtlety. Now it's a personal obsession of mine, to know more of subtlety. I believe this obsession started with literature. The Latin American writer Julio Cortázar had had a huge impact on her life, and his books were among her most valued possessions. When she sent them to me, I was dumbfounded. I truly couldn't understand why anyone thought these stories important enough to commit to paper. They made no sense to me. I had been raised to believe a real story had a beginning, a middle, and a conclusion in which the loose ends were tied up. These stories seemed to defy logic.

I knew I was in love with Lorri when I started to wake up in the middle of the night furious and cursing her for making me feel the way she did. It was pain beyond belief. Nothing has ever hurt me that way. I tried to sleep as much as possible just to escape. I was grinding my teeth down to nubs. Now, years later, it's exactly the opposite. Now there is no pain, yet she still makes my heart explode. Now there is only fun and love and silliness. She drives me to frenzy, because I can never get enough.

For the first two years we knew each other, Lorri flew from New York to Arkansas about every other month, so in addition to the phone bill, this was an extremely expensive relationship for her.

When she came to see me, there was a sheet of glass separating us. It was maddening, and we would often blow through the screen at the bottom of the glass just to feel each other's breath. I loved to sit and look at Lorri, as she has an absolutely perfect body. It's every man's fantasy, like a 1950s pinup model. To have such intelligence in a body like that is a miracle. She takes exquisite care of herself, and it shows. It inspires me and makes me always try harder to be better for her.

The thing is, I do things just to dazzle her. She says I know everything, and she is always amazed by the information I can supply on any topic she thinks of. I devour books by the boxful, just to impress her with what I know. I exercise twice a day—push-ups, sit-ups, jumping jacks, running in place, and yoga—just so she'll be as enamored of my body as I am of hers.

Lorri and I weren't able to touch each other at all until December 1999, when we were married. We had the only Buddhist wedding ceremony in the history of the Arkansas prison system. The guards had no idea what to make of it. It was a small ceremony that lasted about forty-five minutes, and we were allowed to have six friends there to witness it. They were friends and supporters of us both. Afterward, people said it was so beautiful they forgot it was taking place in a prison. At one point, I broke out in a cold sweat and nearly fainted, just because that's every man's genetic predisposition to weddings. After we were married, Lorri and I were permitted to be in the same room with each other, but every visit we had while I was imprisoned was chaperoned.

Lorri had moved to Little Rock in August 1997 to start a whole new life and to be near me. She kept and still keeps every aspect of my life—and my ongoing legal case—neatly filed and managed, even when I rebel against it. She now represents me to the world at large. When she attends a meeting on my behalf, everyone has learned that it's the same as if I were sitting there. She's the only person I've ever trusted to take care of me as if she's taking care of herself. When things need to be done "out there," I can rest easy knowing she will tend to it.

I spend every day of the week looking forward to Friday, when we have our weekly "picnic" in a visitation cell. Everything else is just a countdown to those three hours. We don't spend all our time waiting on some distant day when I'm out of prison, because we have a life together right here and now. This is our life, and there is not a moment when we're not in each other's minds and hearts.

Her parents are extremely supportive of our relationship and make trips to the prison for occasional visits. They've been a hell of a lot more accepting than I would have been if I had a daughter and she announced that she'd married a guy on Death Row. My son loves her as well, and she gets to take on the role of stepmother whenever he comes for a visit. She's better suited to the role of parent than I, because I've still not gotten used to someone addressing me as "Dad." In the early years, Domini brought Seth to visit me twice—after that, she would send him by plane to meet Lorri, who brought him to visit, though after he was about twelve, he and his mother just stopped visiting. This happens all the time: in the first year or two family will visit weekly or monthly; after that, their lives continue on, and the visits taper off.

I would go through everything I've been through again if I knew that's what it would take for Lorri to find me. She found me when I was drowning and breathed life into me. I had given up and she gave me hope. For the first time in my life I am whole.

Any friendship that is worth its weight is like a dark and secret place where you hide bits of yourself. The door can be opened only by the two people who have the key, and you carry it with you wherever you go. Magnify that by a billion, and you begin to get an idea of what marriage is like.

Lorri and I have struggled, fought, wept, and laughed as we were forced to discover new connections. She's the only person I've ever known who has the tenacity and willpower to keep going when all others would have given up and walked away in defeat. We've had to take turns guiding each other through dark places. In the end it has helped us create a stronger bond than those who get to live together under the same roof. We've grown together as a single organism.

Times have been both hard and magickal. I'll never forget the Christmas we spent brokenheartedly whispering to each other on the phone, listing all the presents we would so dearly have loved to be able to give the other. Sometimes we decide on television programs to watch at the same time, and it's as if we're going to the movies on a date. We adjusted our sleep schedules so that we go to bed and get up at the same time. We talk to each other all day long. For example, I'll think of something she said or did when she was last here and suddenly find myself laughing at her antics and saying, "You monkey!" out loud, forgetting for a moment that I'm alone in a prison cell. Instead, for that time period we are playing and cavorting together. We both do this.

I have a propensity to glance around the visitation area to see what others are doing or talking about. You see a wide variety of experiences and activities taking place. Some people are incredibly happy to be there with a loved one, and others show up late and act like they'd rather not be there at all.

One father showed up every week hoping to persuade his son to drop his appeals and allow the state to execute him. He had two reasons why this was such a good idea. The first was that he believed it was the Christian thing for the son to do. The second reason was that the trip to and from the prison was difficult to make when he came to visit. I turned away in disgust, unable to comprehend a parent who would encourage his child to commit suicide.

A great many visitors appear awkward, because they don't know what to say to the loved one they came to visit. They glance around, clear their throats, and ask, "How 'bout them Cowboys?" thinking football the only safe topic. When visitation time comes to an end some people jump up, relieved the painful experience is over and eager to be on their way. Others clutch hands and hug, trying to get in one last kiss. A few cry as they leave; a few more laugh and call out raucous good-byes. Some convicts shuffle their feet and look at the floor; others stare at the retreating forms of loved ones until they're out of sight.

Some convicts and visitors don't even get to touch each other and have to speak through a pane of glass, like Lorri and I did for the first three years of our relationship before we were finally approved to sit in the same room together. Some people never get approved at all. Children stare at fathers without being able to hug them, sometimes for years at a time.

My parents separated again during the first year I was in prison. They both continued to live in the West Memphis and Marion area. My father came to visit regularly during the first year, and brought his new wife. He stopped visiting after 1997. My mother also remarried. She usually came to visit me two, maybe three times a year in the early years. She couldn't come more often, because she couldn't afford it. She has never owned a car that cost more than a few hundred dollars and so had no means of making the long trip to the prison—nor could she afford a trip to the vet when her beloved cat got into a fight with a possum.

During one visit she sat across from me in a hard plastic chair, slowly eating her way through a bag of pork skins bought from the prison vending machine and describing every detail of performing an amputation on the family pet. She spoke with a tremendous

amount of pride in her accomplishment as I squirmed in my chair
and tried to keep from becoming violently ill. She was clearly pleased
with her handiwork and couldn't understand why anyone would not
be in awe and pat her on the back. She seemed to view herself as the
Mother Teresa of the cat world.

The unfortunate feline came home with one of its back legs bitten most of the way off. She held the little guy's leg together and
bandaged it up, hoping it would miraculously grow back together. It
did not. Soon the cat began to stink of rotting meat as gangrene set
in. After she realized the smell was not going to get any better, she
called the vet and asked for advice. The vet told her she had two
choices—the cat could either be "put to sleep," or they could ampu-
tate the leg, which would cost what amounted to a small fortune
when you're poverty-stricken.

My mother couldn't stand the thought of having the animal put
down, and she couldn't afford the amputation, so she decided to do
it herself. From old movies she had learned that ether renders people
unconscious, so she figured it would work on the cat. Her first step
was to buy something from an auto parts store that was in a can labeled "Ether." Since ether isn't something a person can just march
into a corner store and buy, God only knows what the can contained.
She poured the liquid into a Mason jar and held the cat's head over
it, forcing her patient to inhale the fumes. Other than causing the
creature to struggle, it didn't seem to have any effect.

She decided pills were the next-best option, and she scoured the
medicine cabinet. The cat was promptly forced to swallow both a
Valium and a muscle-relaxer that had been prescribed for my mother.

The cat had ingested enough painkiller to fell a large adult human. After a few minutes it was no longer even moving. The only sign of life was the loud, nonstop purring that emanated from its small, inert form.

Her next step was to lay out her surgical instruments, which were limited to a garbage bag, a large pair of shears, and a small sewing kit. The garbage bag was used to cover the kitchen counter and contain the mess. The unlucky bastard was placed on the makeshift surgical table, where my mother stood with shears in hand. She realized she couldn't bring herself to do the actual cutting "because the cat trusted me too much," so she recruited her new husband to take part in the operation. The husband took up the shears and severed the tiny leg with one good chop while my mother held the cat's head and gave it what comfort she could.

The stump was then washed with cold water under the kitchen faucet ("I figured the cold water would help stop the bleeding") and the wound was drenched in hydrogen peroxide and rubbing alcohol. After finding it impossible to sew the wound shut, she decided to experiment with a new product on the market called Liquid Skin. This stuff would normally be used in place of a Band-Aid to cement together the edges of a minor cut. My mother used it to seal off the cat's stump.

I was doubled over and clutching my head in my hands. When I managed to sit up straight I saw my mom dusting the last of the pork skin crumbs from her hands, and Lorri looking like she was going into shock.

"So the cat's okay?" I asked.

"Oh, yeah, he's just fine. He falls over sometimes when he loses his balance, and sometimes he forgets he doesn't have a leg and his stump twitches when he tries to scratch his head with it, but other than that he's hopping around just fine." She was clearly proud of herself and beamed with pleasure.

Mothers are odd things. We're quick to think of their nurturing aspects, but there is also some sort of strange darkness there. It tends to be much stronger in connection with sons than with daughters. It's easy for a mother to cross an invisible line and enslave a son with kindness. There's nothing more revolting than a man incapable of slipping his mother's apron strings. He will always revert back to a boy in her presence. I see boys with unnatural attachments to their mothers all the time. It's a sign of the times in which no one ever grows up. We live in soft times.

My mother's just not capable of feeling things very deeply. Or at least not as deeply as I do. Not anger, love, hatred, or anything else. You could insult her, tell her you hated her, and she'd play off the drama of the moment, but the very next day she'd act as if nothing ever happened. My grudge is always there, and my moods are not flippant.

Twenty-four

I am a Sagittarius, a fire sign. Sagittarians are known for their need to keep moving, exploring, learning. Much like fire, Sagittarians must be fed or they will die. What they must be fed is a constant stream of new experiences. There aren't many journeys to be undertaken when locked in a cage. Outward motion comes to a complete standstill. You have two choices: turn inward and start your journey there, or go insane.

There is no time in prison, unless you create it for yourself. People on the outside seem to believe time passes slowly in prison, but it doesn't. The truth is that time doesn't pass at all. It's an eternal vacuum, and each moment is meaningless because it has no context. Tomorrow may as well be yesterday. That's why there's so much stagnation inherent in prison life—because there is no momentum of any sort.

There is only one way to avoid being swallowed whole by malaise, despair, and loneliness, and that is to create a routine you stick to no matter what. A physical routine, a mental routine, and even a spiritual routine. You don't pass time—you create it.

I began measuring time by doing thirty push-ups a day, and

pushing myself until several years later I could do one thousand. I began doing ten minutes of meditation a day, and then pushed myself until I eventually reached five hours a day. It was only by becoming more disciplined, more focused, and more driven that I could prevent myself from falling into entropy and internal death.

One of the first things that both Ju San/Frankie and Gene told me was that you must turn your cell into a school and monastery. You will spend a minimum of twenty-three hours a day in that cell, all alone. After I was moved to Varner, I spent only three hours a week out of my cell, when Lorri visited. Most people can't take being forced to come face-to-face with themselves, so they become loud and mean, like baboons looking for a shiny object to distract themselves. The number one distraction is television. Most people in prison grow fat and out of shape as they spend endless hours in front of the TV. They'll watch football, basketball, baseball, soap operas, *The Jerry Springer Show*, *Judge Judy*, and anything else that crosses the screen. They watch TV from the moment they get up in the morning until the moment they go to bed. If I didn't want to become a brain-dead, shuffling, obese Neanderthal, I had to nip it in the bud and not allow myself to fall into the pattern.

I moved from one area of study to another. In addition to the Theosophy texts from Gene and the Buddhist texts from Ju San, I began practicing a kind of Christian mysticism described in *A Course in Miracles*. I was introduced to this school of thought by a gentleman named Mike. I never could figure out if the guy was a genius or a psychopath. He wasn't actually a Death Row inmate, he was what is known as a "porter." He was doing a life without parole sentence, and his job was to keep Death Row clean. Sweeping, mopping, washing windows, scrubbing the showers, dusting, et cetera—those were his jobs.

I awoke one morning at two because of a scritch-scritch-scritching noise. Getting up to see what it was, I saw Mike on his hands and knees scrubbing the floor with a toothbrush. When I asked him exactly what in the hell he was doing, he explained that he no longer needed sleep so he figured he might as well use his time constructively. That was a typical Mike answer. He said only the ego needs sleep. He was also prone to having visions. He once told me he was shown in a vision that if he fasted for a week, he could reward himself with ice cream. (If someone indeed sends you money for your account, the prison has a short list of things you can buy. Ice cream is one of them.) Just when you were positive he was insane, he would do something to stop you dead in your tracks with wonder.

A Course in Miracles is a book of practices that takes you a year to complete if you follow each lesson. Its aim is to completely change the way your mind has been programmed to think since birth. You come to experience reality in an entirely different manner, in which anything is possible. It's based on quantum physics but uses biblical terminology. It's become rather popular in recent years, and there are study groups devoted to *A Course in Miracles* all over the country.

Mike hung out in front of my cell every day, sitting on a five-gallon bucket. Our only topic of conversation was *A Course in Miracles* and how it related to the Kabbalah, a book of Jewish mysticism. The Kabbalah is what we dedicated our time to learning about after finishing *Miracles*. Mike was learning from a guy in general population who was a Kabbalist, then he would come and explain things to me. You'd be amazed by how many students of various forms of mysticism you can find in prison. These prisoners are usually determined to make the most of their time and not repeat the same mistakes. These are men starving for a kind of knowledge not given in the mundane world, ready to learn and pass on what they already know. I would continue my study alone for a while after Mike was sent to another part of the prison.

Next I went on to learn about the philosophy and practice of an organization known as "The Golden Dawn." This was a group of people who practiced metaphysical rites of passage to mark the different stages in the evolution of consciousness. It was all about the constant learning and growth process that everyone goes through, and how to speed it up. The great poet W. B. Yeats was one of the more well-known students of this school of thought. I had my nose in these books morning, noon, and night.

Many people donated money to a college fund that was set up for Jason and me, so I began taking courses from a local college here in Arkansas. At first I was interested mostly in psychology, but I mixed in a few other subjects, such as sociology and reading German, for good measure. Psychology seemed infinitely interesting to me, with all of its experiments and nature-versus-nurture debates—but I don't think anyone's surprised at this point to hear I became interested in psychology. . . .

I later realized psychology was not my love at all—it was history. I've grown to love history more than any other subject, and I have come to believe you can understand far more about the world through history than you can through psychology, especially military history. At first I delved into every aspect and every era of history, but gradually my scope narrowed as I began to realize what I was drawn to.

My love is Italian history, specifically the history of the cities of Florence and Venice, in the period between 1400 and 1800. My role model is Cosimo de' Medici, though I also like his grandson Lorenzo the Magnificent. What I love about the span of time during which the Medici were in power is the social structure and all the intrigue that accompanied it. Among aristocratic circles, life was like a chess game. You had to weigh your every word, as conversations were filled with subtlety. Social success or failure could hinge on whom you were seen making eye contact with. Not to mention the decadent styles and fashions that were all the rage. No one wore baggy jeans and backward baseball caps. These days no one makes an effort.

And yet no routine or spiritual practice in the world will dim the reality of daily life on Death Row. A normal person does not commit murder. For almost seventeen years I've waited for someone to walk through the door whom I could have a conversation with, but it just doesn't happen. The people here are all mentally defective in ways that range from mild retardation to extreme schizophrenia. Others are stuck in some no-man's-land between sanity and delusion. There are no criminal geniuses walking these halls. Most not only are culturally illiterate, but also can barely manage to express themselves in English. I have never met a prisoner with a college education, and I can count the high school graduates on one hand.

Nearly all lived in absolute poverty, and most were abused in one way or another. Not a single one of them is capable of functioning normally in society, and it's not a skill they're likely to learn when locked in a cell among others who are as bad or worse. I've yet to see any sign of "rehabilitation," or any program designed to bring about that aim. Most of the people you meet in prison have been here repeatedly. Some have been to prison three or four times before making it to Death Row. They claim to hate and despise everything about prison, but they always come back. It's like they're collecting frequent flyer miles in hell. They themselves can't explain it, falling back on excuses such as "It's hard to stay out once you've been in." Why? How? It's hard to refrain from snatching an old woman's purse? It's somehow difficult to prevent yourself from committing rape? Somehow you accidentally found yourself burglarizing a house and stealing a car? I don't understand why they don't learn their lesson the first time around. That in itself is evidence that they've got a couple screws loose.

On Death Row we used to have television sets that were in stands about five feet in front of the cells. The guards were supposed to make security checks every half-hour, at which time they could change the channel if you wanted them to, but that never happened. I've seen up to eight hours pass without a single guard coming by. A convict once lay dead on the floor all night long after having a heart attack, and the guards didn't find him until after breakfast.

With no guards around we had to devise a way of changing the channel on the television for ourselves, so someone invented what quickly became known as the "channel checker." A channel checker is made with construction paper, pencils, and bits of pilfered tape. You'd be surprised at what a sturdy spear you can make out of these materials, and in essence that's what a channel checker is—a spear. With it you can reach through the bars of your cell and change the channel on the TV set.

In the spirit of escalating warfare, a convict known as Chuckles and another known as "the hobo" modified their channel checkers in order to cause maximum damage. They used empty soda cans to fashion sharp metal tips, and then proceeded to stab each other in the face through the bars. They kept at it for at least an hour and both had shed blood before they finally tired. When someone asked what had started the whole thing, Chuckles pointed at the hobo and said, "He was trying to derogatize me." No one knew quite what that meant, but that was nothing out of the ordinary. Usually no one cared enough about Chuckles's conversation to try to follow along anyway.

I applied that moniker to him myself and it stuck. Soon the entire population of Death Row recognized him as such, and he even began to refer to himself by that name. It just seemed to suit him perfectly. Chuckles is about five and a half feet tall, of average build, and looks exactly like a possum. In fact, his alias is "Kid Possum." He has only one tooth left in his mouth, and it's situated right in front. He claims that drugs rotted his teeth, though I'm more inclined to believe it was the simple lack of good oral hygiene. I say this because Chuckles has the breath of a baby dragon and has never been seen in the presence of a toothbrush. I once tried to use the phone after him and the smell he left on the mouthpiece made me gag. I washed it for several minutes with soap and water, but the smell remained. In the end I had to pour cheap cologne over it. He was overheard making the statement "I don't drink coffee because it will stain my tooth."

It's not only his mouth that stinks, as Chuckles chronically avoids all forms of cleanliness. He's the only person on earth who smells worse when he gets out of the shower than he did before he got in. He doesn't actually wash himself, he just sort of splashes around while trying to talk to other people. The guards argue about who has to escort him, because no one wants to get close.

Chuckles arrived on Death Row after he was convicted of chopping two old ladies to death with a hatchet. Other inmates used to drive him into a frenzy by tormenting him with hatchets made out of construction paper. While making chopping motions they would imitate an old lady's voice and cry, "No, Chuckles! Please don't kill me! You'll catch a capital murder charge!" Chuckles would go insane with rage and threaten to kill everyone in sight.

Chuckles and the hobo had more than one altercation over the years, and most involved throwing either feces or urine at each other. I once witnessed the hobo dash a coffee cup of urine in Chuckles's face, after which Chuckles didn't even bother to wash up. He simply dried his face with a towel and went back to business.

Men who cultivate filth are a regular occurrence in prison. They justify it by saying, "I'm not going anywhere soon, so why bother?" They're referred to as either barbarians or Vikings. Although those called Vikings are crude, those considered to be barbarians have given up any pretense of civilized humanity.

Each day men are selected to work in the fields. They swing a hoe from daybreak to suppertime, and when they come back inside they are sweaty, filthy, and mud-caked. A Viking will strip off his clothes and go to bed without even showering. A barbarian, though—well, a barbarian will crawl straight into bed without even taking off his mud-encrusted boots. You can smell a barbarian from the next cell. I know from firsthand experience. I once lived in the cell next to a barbarian for about three months. I couldn't even sit at the door to watch television without holding a washcloth over my nose and mouth. This particular barbarian even had his teeth pulled so he could avoid the formality of brushing them. Dentures would save him the effort. The thing that struck me as being the most odd was the barbarian's insistence that he did not stink despite everyone in the barracks telling him otherwise.

I also had the misfortune of living next to another barbarian whom everyone called "Big Blue." This name was in reference to the fact that he wore the same pair of underwear every single day until they turned a dingy bluish-gray color. In truth it wasn't even underwear, but long johns that he had cut the legs off of. After about a year they were nothing but a tattered rag filled with holes and dangling fringe. Unlike Chuckles or the barbarian, Big Blue had a valid excuse—he was stark raving mad.

I noticed that Big Blue watched the news every morning with the intensity of a cat sitting outside a mouse hole. He confided in me that it wasn't the news he was watching, it was the time and temperature readings in the corner of the screen. He wouldn't take his eyes off those tiny numbers because he believed it was a secret message being sent to him. Who was sending him these messages? It was "they." He either couldn't or wouldn't be more articulate than that, nor did he elaborate on what those messages were. I must admit that after he told me this I found that my eyes kept drifting to the corner of the screen, as if to be certain there was nothing there but numbers.

I live with men who haven't been in contact with reality for years. The truth is that insanity is rampant on Death Row, as is retardation. The law says that the insane and the mentally retarded (the law's terminology, not mine) cannot be executed, yet it happens on a regular basis. It's both sad and frightening. It's sad because many of them don't even comprehend that they're on Death Row or what awaits them.

The mentally handicapped are executed on a regular basis while the politicians all give speeches about being tough on crime. I've never come across a single murderer who possessed the mental faculties required to fully comprehend the horror of what they have done. They are not emotionally developed enough to feel empathy. They live lives of nightmare, yet are not even capable of realizing that. They are the dregs of humanity, by both birth and choice. Prison and the prison mentality are not what society has been led to believe they are. These people cannot even take care of themselves, and they suffer from every health problem imaginable. There are no attractive murderers here. It's like the ugliness inside them manages to transform their facial features so that the outside resembles the inside. There are no conversations here. There are threats, taunts, and screams, but a conversation is an impossibility. Concepts such as love, honor, and self-respect are as foreign to this place as French cuisine. I waver between the extremes of pity and disgust.

The prison system makes no effort to help the mentally ill. There are no therapy sessions, no treatments, no cutting-edge drugs. The only thing they do is shoot them full of Thorazine if they start to get riled up. You can spot a man doing the Thorazine shuffle from a mile away. His every action takes ten times longer than it should, because it takes him a Herculean effort to move.

For many people in prison their worst fear is going insane, because once you do all hope is lost. You will be locked up not only within these walls, but also within your own rapidly degenerating mind. There is no help, and you wouldn't even be able to work on your own case in order to get your death sentence converted. You would sit in a cell playing with feces and screaming at phantoms that no one else could see. This is not the place you want to lose your marbles. If it begins to feel like the walls are closing in on you, then you have to come up with a way to work through it or shake it off.

Sometimes it's even more disturbing to see the cases of mental retardation on Death Row than it is to see the insane. I say this because there is often something very childlike in the actions of the retarded. To see a retarded person being led to execution is an abomination. It's something that should never happen, yet it does. Sometimes even innocent retarded people are executed, which is a double travesty.

There was a guy here who had the IQ of a child, and it was common knowledge that he did not commit the crime he was convicted of. He was here because he was taking the blame for something his brother had done. He was eventually executed in his brother's place. The guy was blatantly and obviously retarded, and he lived on a diet of potato chips, candy bars, and cake. He acquired the money for these things from a nun who came to see him every so often. Sometimes his mother would come see him, and since they had nothing to talk about they would both put their heads down on the table and sleep. It was heartbreaking to witness. I don't recall ever seeing him take a shower. He just sat silently in his cell until the day he was killed.

Everyone seems to agree that it's wrong to execute the retarded, yet it continues to happen. There are retarded people awaiting execution right now. There's one who often has to repeat himself several times because no one can understand what he's saying. Another strings words together that make no sense. He calls people names such as "Fish More" and "Fuck Bart." He paces his cell at four o'clock in the morning yelling, "Twiddle your fingers! Twiddle your fingers! Let's roll!" and then follows it with a string of obscenities.

A sane man can be reasoned with and talked to; you can guess his motives and predict his actions. A madman, on the other hand, may try to kill you, because he's convinced it's God's will. Like Nu-Nu.

The threat of violence hangs over Nu-Nu like a black cloud. He's not someone you would want sleeping under your roof or hanging around behind your back. If ever there was a clear-cut case of schizophrenia, this man is it. Nu-Nu shot and killed a man in a coin-operated laundry. When the cops came to investigate they found a security tape with footage of Nu-Nu break-dancing around the body. I've often been awakened at two o'clock in the morning by Nu-Nu screaming at the top of his lungs. He claims that the nurses in the inmate hospital are drinking his blood and defecating in his food. The entire barracks has listened to him argue with a mirror for hours at a time, threatening to kill his own reflection. He'll then stop and begin preaching a sermon in a very calm voice, instructing his congregation to "open up to the Book of Psalms and hold it down by your left nut."

Others are equally insane but more harmless. I've no doubt that they murdered someone at one time, but it's almost as if their drive to kill died along with their victims. Now they're just burned-out lunatics.

We have a character here who is stuck with the unfortunate name of "Patches." Patches despises this name and would gleefully murder anyone who uses it. Anytime you call him by that name he stares at you with the glint of pure, unadulterated hatred in his eye. He was given this name because he sports a hairdo exactly like George Jefferson in the old sitcom *The Jeffersons*—an Afro around the sides and nothing on top. Someone once pointed out that he had patches of hair missing, and it stuck. Patches was born.

Patches isn't the sort of guy you'd want to strike up a friendship with. He goes out of his way to cause more frustration for anyone he can. Patches is the guy who will change the channel just because he knows you're watching television. He'll pretend to be on the phone just so you can't use it. To put it bluntly, Patches is an asshole. No one stays in a cell next to him for very long, because they quickly grow to despise him, then do whatever it takes to get moved away from him. Patches loves nothing more than to see misfortune visited upon others, and that is the only time you will ever hear him laughing.

Patches has a rather interesting collection, even by prison standards, and he's rather touchy about it. If you approach him when no one else can hear the conversation he'll show it to you. If you say something about it where others can hear, he'll deny that it exists and then swear at you for the rest of the day. The odd thing is that nearly everyone has seen his collection at one time or another and knows that he is lying when he pretends ignorance. Those who wish to torment him will yell out across the barracks and ask him about it. This action is met with either explosive rage or deathly quiet. The only other thing that infuriates him even half as much is when someone starts singing that song from the seventies, "Patches, I'm depending on you, son."

So what exactly is it that Patches collects? She-male porn. Patches collects pornography that falls under such colorful titles as "chicks with dicks." Not only does he hoard it like treasure, he turns it into pop-up books that are cleverly disguised as birthday cards. He guards them like a Fort Knox of perversity, as if he believes everyone is out to steal his hard work. You see, this hoard of pop-up she-male porn is interactive. He takes a razor blade and combs through porn magazines in search of penis pictures. He carefully cuts out the picture of the penis and then cuts slits in the pictures of his half-men, half-women so he can slide the penis in and out of the slit. It is indeed disturbing, but no one can deny that Patches is a man who knows just what he likes.

As odd and unpleasant as Patches can be, there are those here who more than match him. A fine example of this sad species would be J.C.

I first noticed J.C. after I'd been here a few months and was moved up to a cell on the third floor. I could not look at him without being reminded of a scarecrow, and he greatly resembled Iggy Pop. He had long, graying hair and was rail thin, every muscle in his torso greatly defined. He constantly worked out, which is what he was doing the first time I really paid any attention to him. I looked over to see him doing squats and wearing nothing but a pair of boxer shorts. I did a double-take to see what the little black spots scattered over his body were. Closer scrutiny revealed them to be crickets. Big, black crickets. They were stuck to his shoulders, chest, and stomach with tiny pieces of Scotch tape. There was even one on his neck. He was fond of calling them his "babies" and knew how to make them chirp simply by touching them in a particular way. He had them, or their descendants, for quite a while before the guards went into his cell and flushed them all down the toilet. J.C. seemed to be genuinely torn up over their loss, as if he were truly attached to them.

J.C. was an artist of tremendous skill, though his subject matter came from the darkest reaches of a disturbed psyche. One day he was casually standing in the doorway wearing his uniform of nothing but boxer shorts. There was a hand-rolled cigarette hanging from the corner of his mouth and his eyes were squinted against the rising smoke. He seemed to be looking at something over my head as he tossed me a piece of thick art paper. It was rolled up and inserted into a cardboard tube such as you find in a roll of toilet paper.

"Check it out and tell me what you'll give me for it," he mumbled before retreating into his cell. I unrolled the paper to see a flawlessly drawn naked woman's body in a reclining position. The horrible part was that J.C. had drawn his own head on the woman's body. I stared at it in shock, unable to move. It came as such a shock to my mind that I had no idea what to do. Scream? Laugh? What? In the end I did the only thing I could do—rolled it back up, tossed it to him, and said, "Sorry, J.C., but I've already got one just like it." He accepted this explanation as completely plausible and passed the drawing on to his next potential customer.

Drawing was not his only medium of creativity. He once made matching handheld crossbows out of tongue depressors, Elmer's Glue-All, and heavy-duty rubber bands. These were no mere toys, but were strong enough to pierce flesh. Some people got a little jumpy when they'd see him holding one, even though he never actually shot anyone. He wasn't above whizzing one by your ear, but the only thing he'd actually shoot with them were rats. He thinned out the prison rodent population for a while. One day the hobo got nervous when J.C. started waving the crossbows in his direction, so he snitched to the guards. That put an end to J.C.'s gunslinging days.

J.C.'s most irritating habit was walking stark naked to and from the shower. He'd stroll up and down the tier at a leisurely pace, like nothing was out of the ordinary. This wouldn't have been so bad if you could have ignored him, but he'd walk right up to you and try to carry on a conversation. This would tend to make people pretty uneasy. Everyone dealt with it in different ways. As soon as he opened his mouth some men would bellow in outrage, "I done told you! Don't try to talk to me when you ain't got no drawers on!" Others would glance around nervously, eyes shifting left and right to see if anyone was looking, and then try to answer him as quickly as possible so he'd move on. All in all, he could be a very amusing character, and no one was happy when the state finally executed him.

Another potentially dangerous schizophrenic was recently executed after spending twenty-two years on Death Row. He was here so long because he had been judged too insane to execute. The state finally medicated him so that he would be sane enough to appreciate the fact that he was about to die. There was no question about his insanity for those who met him. I'd known it since the day he spit in my face and accused me of giving him ingrown toenails. He was still screaming at me as the guards took him to the hole.

That's something you never get used to. One day a man is there, the next he's gone. It's hard to make yourself believe that someone you were just talking to a couple of days before is now gone forever. These are men you've lived with for years, yet you don't even get to attend the funeral, so there's no sense of closure. The preachers all get a disgusting gleam in their eyes when an execution is at hand. They hover around the condemned man's cell like flies, threatening him with damnation unless he buys the mentality they're selling. They don't have time for you unless you're about to die. They never even stop to say hello until that point. Many men vow that they'll verbally abuse them if they hang around their cells when execution is imminent. The sentiment is "You had no time for me when I was living. Now that I'm dying I have no time for you."

The worst part of the weeks preceding an execution is the guards.

You can tell they get off on it, because it adds a little excitement to their jobs. A spokesperson for the Arkansas Department of Correction will go on television to give a speech about how hard it is on them, but it's nothing more than words to convince a gullible public how humane they are here. The truth is that the guards stand around and tell jokes about it before and afterward. They'll actually be friendly to the condemned man for a few days before the execution, even if they've abused and neglected him up until then. This is done out of sheer morbidity. They want to be able to tell others that they had a conversation with the dead man.

Some of the prisoners can't remember what you said to them or what they said to you just hours before. If you remind them, they will argue with you that such a conversation never took place. Others are grown men in their thirties who still behave like mean-spirited teenagers. Their mental development (what little there was) stopped once they began abusing drugs and alcohol.

To say that someone can't hold their mud is prison slang for anal leakage. With that in mind I leave it to you to figure out how an inmate earned the name "Mudpie." Mudpie could be no more oblivious to reality than if he walked around with a bag on his head. His greatest talent is lying to himself, and he makes it his life's work to distort every piece of information that passes through his senses. If self-deception were an art, Mudpie would be a master. He's the only person who can't see through his own smoke screen. He says things that leave everyone staring at him in disbelief.

An example of his self-deception would be his addictions. Mudpie would sell his soul for cigarettes or marijuana. Anytime he knows someone in the barracks has some, he goes into a frenzy. He'll beg from everyone and sell everything he owns to get it. He smokes so much that everything in his cell stinks of it. I once overheard him tell his father that he was soon going to be executed just so his father would send him money. It worked the first time, but the second time he tried it, his father called Mudpie's lawyer and found out the truth—that Mudpie was nowhere near an execution date. Who in their right mind would fake their death for cigarettes? Ah, but Mudpie becomes very angry when you call him an addict and a dope fiend, and constantly informs people that he has "quit." What that means is that he can't find any right then. When called upon to explain why his father no longer speaks to him, he insists it's because he broke off contact with his family so they wouldn't have to worry about him anymore. And he *forces* himself to believe it. He doesn't see the contradiction in his actions—that if he truly didn't want to worry his family he would not have called them with news of a nonexistent execution date.

Mudpie has been known to launch into a sermon about how he doesn't believe in gratuitous violence, after which he threatens to kill another inmate for trying to change the channel on the television. At least once a day he'll condemn someone for something he himself did the day before. He can be quite interesting to watch. I'll see him screw something up, then tell myself, "There's no way in hell he can put a spin on that. He'll *have* to live up to it." I'm wrong every time. He always pulls some trick out of his bag. It seems he would learn from his mistakes, but he never does. He brings a world of trouble upon himself time after time, and ignores the pattern. I've become convinced that this is now a necessity, because he'd probably commit suicide if forced to take a long, hard look at himself.

A great many of Mudpie's habits and antics are repugnant, though some of them are hilarious. There have been many times when I've laughed at him until I couldn't breathe. One such time was at the end of 1999, when he was making Y2K preparations.

Mudpie listened nonstop to a radio station that was home to a string of shows all focusing on conspiracy theories. At least once a year they do a show insisting that a giant asteroid is heading straight toward Earth, and all of creation will be wiped from existence on a given date. That date comes and goes with no dire consequences, but that never stops them from doing another such story in a year or so. It also doesn't stop Mudpie from accepting every word as the gospel truth. Bigfoot sightings, UFO crashes, alien abductions, Chinese plots to take over the world, et cetera. Mudpie couldn't get enough of it. Once they began doing shows predicting the Y2K computer crash, it was all he could talk about. He nearly drove us all insane with his constant prophecies of doom. The second that the calendar flipped over to the year 2000 we were all going to die, he told us.

One day as I was on my way to the yard I noticed a large stack in Mudpie's cell. He had several cases of ramen noodles, a pyramid of sodas, boxes of saltine crackers, and about fifteen rolls of toilet paper. He explained that he was stockpiling supplies because once Y2K arrived we would no longer have food or water. I gave this a moment's thought before asking, "If there's no water, how are you going to cook all those noodles?" He described to me his secret recipe—he would boil the noodles in Dr Pepper while holding them over burning toilet paper. He had already been sampling the concoction in order to accustom himself to eating it. Alas, the delectable enterprise turned out to be in vain, as our imminent destruction was postponed.

The Y2K debacle wasn't Mudpie's only questionable culinary habit. Mudpie is a cheapskate of the highest order. Once, after he had eaten the last of the peanut butter from a jar, I saw him fill it with hot water and set it aside. I thought perhaps he was washing it out to use as a storage container. Instead he went back and drank the cloudy water in which the peanut butter scum was floating. Just getting his money's worth. Others witnessed him do the same with a "squeeze cheese" bottle. From that day on, anytime he would argue with people, they would fire back with "At least I don't drink cheese water."

Mudpie was often seen wearing what he called "fart masks." He fashioned these contraptions out of cologne samples he would tear out of magazines and position over his nose and mouth with rubber bands that stretched over his ears. They resembled surgeons' masks. He wore them, breathing in pure cologne, at least twice a week, during the times he said the hobo had gas so bad it was gagging him.

In prison, pornography is more valuable than money. You can trade it for anything you may want. Mudpie collects pornography so that he can swap it to dealers who are capable of feeding his habits. I once had the chance to view his collection and found it more disturbing than erotic. One large sheet of paper featured nothing but row upon row of breasts. Another sheet was covered with vaginas.

Yet a third featured anuses. There were no heads, arms, or legs. They had all been cut off. When I inquired about this, his response was that he did not need to see an elbow in order to "get off." Although I found his taste to be crude and not very aesthetically pleasing, it made a certain amount of sense. Or at least it seemed to make sense until I saw that he also had a matchbox full of eyes. He had gone through a stack of magazines and meticulously cut the eyes out of every picture with a razor blade. He seemed deeply offended when I suggested that this might be abnormal, and insisted it related to a work of art he was creating. The tiny box of eyes then disappeared and was never seen again.

You can tell the long-term users by sight because of the toll it takes on their bodies. The most obvious are the ones whose teeth are crumbling in their mouths. Sometimes their breath smells like they're rotting from the inside out. They smile with ruined teeth as they tell you how good dope is. No, thank you. I'm far too vain to indulge in anything that's going to damage the way I look.

Just because they're in prison doesn't necessarily mean they no longer use. For the right price, guards are more than willing to help them get a shot of whatever they need. Some are alcoholics who brew their own. That's *very* common. It's made from the most God-awful ingredients you can imagine, and just the smell of it can turn your stomach The prison slang for such unpalatable crud is "boot-leg." It's no Merlot, and you won't see this stuff being bottled by Turning Leaf anytime soon.

I watch as men hand-roll cigarettes in pages they ripped from the Bible. They call it "smoking the Holy Ghost." The ones with no tobacco will smoke anything they find—old tea bags, toilet cleanser, whatever. I saw one man fall to the floor jerking and foaming at the mouth after smoking something that looked like a handful of baby-blue rock salt. His eyes rolled back in his head while his feet tried to propel him across the floor in a concrete backstroke. These are hard days for fiends, and the addicts have long since sold their souls.

You don't make many memories in prison—at least none you'd want to keep, or look back on fondly. It's more like you have horrific scenes and situations burned into your psyche like a branding iron. The ability to create good memories, though . . . is gone. The ones you came in with are the only ones you'll ever have. I would revisit mine constantly, trying desperately to wring every ounce of nourishment out of them that I possibly could. I was like a vampire, sucking them dry and then sifting through the dust in hopes of finding a drop I'd overlooked the previous hundred times. Sometimes I'd revisit a profound life experience; other times I'd chew over a minuscule detail like a hyena trying to find the marrow in the center of an old bone. For two weeks I remembered the handle on my grandmother's front door. I remembered what it was like to look at it on a winter morning, knowing it was going to be as cold as ice in my hand. I remembered the way it felt to raise my arm and reach for it, to curl my white fingers around the gray metal. And then the best part—the gush of warm air that poured out as I pushed the door open. It wasn't just warmth pouring over me, it was home. Bathing me, enveloping me, welcoming me. And then the door was closed again, the process beginning anew for the tenth time that day, or perhaps the hundredth. I lost count. The number was insignificant—

only the experience mattered. You'd be amazed at all the little things you begin to remember when there are no new experiences to distract you.

Gradually, as the years passed, I could slip more and more deeply into this state of remembrance. Eventually the prison disappears altogether, and only the world in the mind's eye holds any importance. I called this state by many names, one of which was the Land of Nod. Nod was the city Cain was banished to in the book of Genesis, and that's how I felt—exiled, cast out. The world didn't want me, so I would retreat deep into the Land of Nod.

Other times I thought of it as December. In my memories it was always December. December became another word for home to me. Then there were other times when I would swear the past almost had a personality. At those times I thought of it as Nostalgia. Nostalgia is the only friend that stays with you forever.

The most potent and powerful means I had of entering the Land of Nod was through writing. Every day I disappeared into the pages of my journal, scribbling from margin to margin, wallowing in the memories of a thousand December afternoons as my hand moved the pen. I filled a dozen leather-bound journals, many with the same memory examined from every angle. I never wanted to go back and read what I'd written because it didn't really matter to me. I hoped, too, that perhaps someday the pages would be of importance to someone, somewhere—but not to me. The memories were for me, but the journals were for someone else. The journals were a castle I was building for some future magician to find and explore. There were rooms full of beauty, pain, magick, love, horror, despair, and wonder. Every page was a hidden corner. When I was inside those journals, deep in the Land of Nod, the prison ceased to matter. I was no longer slowly dying in a godforsaken cage. In the land of Nod I was more alive than ever before.

On August 22, 2003, I was transferred from Tucker Max to the Varner Super Maximum Security Unit in Grady, the same prison where Jason and Jessie were (though ironically, Jason was soon after transferred to Tucker). I was awakened at two a.m. by a group of madcap guards, funsters with M-16 assault rifles and attack dogs. They roused all thirty-seven of us in the barracks and two others who were in the hole, wrapped us in chains, and packed us into vans like sardines. There were eight prisoners and two guards in each van. It was a tight fit and a long, uncomfortable ride.

Once we arrived, we were placed in what amounts to solitary confinement. It's a concrete cell with a solid steel door. We never came in contact with other inmates, and you could talk to the person next to you only by pressing your face into a crack and screaming. It was filthy. They cleaned the hallways and visiting areas if an inspection was coming through, but never inside the cells. I hadn't felt sunlight on my skin in months. It took a while to adjust to the absolute confinement and isolation, but I had a hell of a lot more privacy, which is a rare commodity in prison.

I was forbidden to communicate with Jason and Jessie, per prison administration orders, though nothing had been declared legally and in spite of the fact that they were housed together and had been sleeping in beds side by side for a couple of years.

My first appeal was turned down by the Arkansas court system in 1994. Big surprise there, eh?

My second appeal, known as a Rule 37, encompassed the myriad complaints of ineffective counsel in my defense, and ultimately opened the door to the incomprehensible and unending legal labyrinth that became my ongoing defense and effort to be freed.

As I already mentioned, Joe and Bruce's efforts culminated in the documentary *Paradise Lost*, which was released at Sundance and other festivals in 1996 and played in several small theaters, including the Quad Cinema in Manhattan and a theater in Little Rock. It had a huge impact on our case and raised awareness about the murders. Among the many people who saw it over the next several years was Eddie Vedder, of Pearl Jam, who was intrigued enough to reach out to my attorney at the time. Unfortunately and ironically, my attorney had never heard of Pearl Jam, so it took some time for Eddie to find someone receptive to his offer of support. In 1999, he finally made contact with my team and became involved in the fight to prove my innocence. His financial donations to my legal fund and his sheer devotion and energy in advocating for my release marked a pivotal moment in the years spent on my case. Eddie has shown himself to be a true friend time and time again. How many rock stars do you know who visit guys in prison when they come through town? It's always a tremendous amount of fun whenever he stops by and tells of his latest adventures.

After ten years, Jason and I caught sight of each other on a Friday afternoon in 2004, while Lorri and I were in the midst of our weekly picnic. I looked up to see him about thirty feet away in the hallway, looking at me through the glass. He raised his hand and smiled, then he was gone, like a ghost. I wish I could have talked to him, if only to say, "Just hang on."

That's the same thing I keep telling myself.

Just hang on.

Twenty-five

I went through the HGA prayer ritual three times today. At about
8:30 a.m., around noon, and at about 6:30 p.m. I've been reciting
the prayer exactly as written in Abramelin and then praying the prayers
again in my own words, making them as heartfelt as possible. Some of
the newness is beginning to wear off and cause it to seem like actual
work. However, for some reason I can't define I feel my faith in the procedure growing.

I had a dream that I was fighting with a lion and a dog on the street
where I used to live in Lakeshore. I was holding the lion's jaws open
with my hands, even though it was tremendously painful. I kept the lion
between myself and the dog, so that every time the dog lunged at me it
would bite the lion instead. I eventually managed to dart through the
gate and close it behind me.

When I was going through the last prayer today I had a pleasant experience. I was on my knees, head bowed, when I suddenly felt as if I were looking down into a room. The only description I can offer is that everything was white and, I'm tempted to say, made of marble. I was looking down on it from a height of between fifty and one hundred feet, but I wasn't seeing it with my eyes.

From ecstasy to drudgery. I move from feeling as if I'm on the verge of something huge to dread at the thought of one more round of prayer.

Same as yesterday. All work and no joy in the ritual. I'm hoping for a second wind. I did about twenty minutes of hatha yoga asanas today to loosen up. I find that once I begin the HGA ritual it's very pleasant. There's something about it that has a timeless quality. It's just the thought of beginning that I dread. I look at it as a child does homework.

There is no angel. There is nothing.

Everything is fractured, the pieces of everything come together, collide, then move away to collide again.

There is no such thing as magick.

I have lost all faith, lost all belief. I teeter on the edge of hopelessness. Everything is a fight, and I'm so tired. I'm so tired of struggling; I want to scream until I'm gargling my own blood.

The dreams are coming fast and fierce. Dreams of freedom. It hurts so much to wake up.

Time is coming apart for me. At some moments I can no longer feel a past, any past, trailing behind me like a snakeskin. At other moments it feels like the past is all that's real. Today I was two people, one laughing at the other.

The summer is on me like a ghost. I'd cry with longing if it weren't so pointless.

Nothing makes any sense. There doesn't seem to be any point in trying. Everything falls apart. I'll be thirty-two years old exactly six months from today.

My exhaustion is beyond bone-deep. It has seeped into my soul, and every day it robs me of a little more of what I once was. Of what I was meant to be. There is no rest here, and there is no life. When I try to look ahead the light seems a little farther away each day. There is despair on my breath and no savior in sight. They say it's only death if you accept it, but more and more these days I'm feeling like I don't have a choice. I keep saying to myself, "I will not stop. I will not stop." If for no other reason than that I will it to be so. If everything else fails, I will keep moving ahead on willpower alone. There has to be some magick in something, somewhere.

It used to be that a certain wrongness danced across the ocean's surface, crackling like chain lightning. Now the despair is more subtle, sinking silently beneath the waves and coming to rest in dark and poisonous places. The surface becomes pallid and exudes a sick, gray, greasy feeling that eventually drives you mad. It's an endless cycle that breeds a never-ending supply of frustration. Its heartache is the color of lead, and nothing in the world can heal it.

Summer makes me suicidal. It sucks all the magick out of life, and even sleeping becomes an exercise in fruitless brutality. I cannot comprehend what is in the souls who await this misery. Nothing worthwhile can survive the heat. The birds and the bees are harbingers of hell, ushering in a season of disease. There is nothing in these months that speaks to me. It conspires to keep me from ever reaching home.

If you were to go down the line and ask each man what it is that he hates most about prison, you'd probably come up with a different answer for nearly every person asked. Some things are universal, like not being able to go out at night and see the stars, or not being able to be with your family—but each person also has his own pet peeves. For me they are the mosquitoes and the sleep deprivation.

It's better here at Varner, but Tucker was hell where the mosquitoes were concerned. Tucker was surrounded by fields on all sides, and there's one crop or another growing as long as it's warm enough. The entire ground is like one giant mosquito hatchery. If you think you know what a swarm of mosquitoes is like just because you've been camping or sat in the backyard on a summer night, then you're badly mistaken. I've seen entire walls covered by blankets of mosquitoes. Every time you take a step, a cloud of them rises from the ground.

I've literally cried in frustration more than once because the mosquitoes were such a torment. My hands have been bitten so many times they've become swollen and miserable. The skin on my knuckles was so red and tight that my fingers looked like sausages. You have to keep moving because if you are still they land all over you. Every year the walls look like abstract paintings because of the blood spots from the smashed mosquitoes. You can't rest because they buzz in your ears, bite your lips and eyelids, and drive you to the edge of a nervous breakdown. This continues all summer long. It gets even worse when the mosquitoes discover they can breed in the toilets in the empty cells.

As you lie on your bunk trying to get what little sleep you can, there's nothing more annoying than having mosquitoes buzz in your ears and bite your face. When you combine the torment of the mosquitoes with the suffocating heat it becomes more than you can bear—except that you have no choice. You can either try to sleep while fully clothed, with socks on your hands and your face covered (but then the heat is worse) or you can strip down in hopes of cooling off, at which time the mosquitoes will feast.

I've seen times when the entire barracks was filled with smoke because people were burning paper in an attempt to smoke the mosquitoes out. It doesn't work. I've also seen a gentleman who couldn't take it anymore, so he started to plot his revenge. He would trap mosquitoes in a small plastic cup, pull their wings off, and then urinate on them. Judging by the cursing and insane laughter that accompanied the act, I'd say he obtained a great deal of satisfaction through his efforts.

Today a bird landed on my dingy windowsill. The window itself is only as wide as the bird was tall. It sat there as still as a stone and stared directly at me for over an hour. I stood on my bunk with my face right up to the glass, but it didn't fly away. Our eyes were only about two inches apart as we gazed at each other. The bird's entire body was a dusty gray, but it wasn't a sparrow. I know what a sparrow looks like. The odd part is how it sat perfectly still, with its mouth wide open. A thin string of saliva hung from the top section of its beak to the bottom, reminding me of a strand of a spider's web. After a few moments I raised my hand and tapped on the glass right by its head. The bird didn't even blink. It continued to stare at me with a beady black eye and an open beak. I've never seen a bird behave that way before. It feels like it meant something, as if it were some sort of bird omen. I'm positive that bird smelled like a coming rainstorm.

and veins. The holiday spirit is less than rampant.

11-25-05

Lorri is going mountain climbing today with Jennifer F. A place called pinnacle point. I'd love to be able to do that today. That's where I belong right now — by myself on the side of a mountain, the physical activity making thinking un necessary. It reminds me of something I heard on the news this morning. I was half asleep, so I didn't hear where it was at, but somewhere a sixteen year old boy has been sitting beneath a tree and meditating for six months. They say he's had no food or water. People are saying it is the Buddha reincarnated. They've even nick-named him "Buddha boy."

Today feels empty. All the energy that lets you know it's a holiday seems to have dispersed. That void has always made me feel more lonely than spending the holiday alone. When I was a kid, this was the day we'd put up all of our Christmas decorations.

I finished reading "True Lies" and am now starting on "Magical Thinking" by Augusten Burroughs.

They took Eric Nance to the death house first thing this morning. The death house is what the call the building that has the executing chamber in it. They usually move the intended victim over there a couple of days in advance. That way if he were to fight them, have a nervous breakdown, or a panic attack, we wouldn't see it. They want it to seem as clinical as possible to the rest of the world. It's necessary if they want to continue passing the practice off as "humane"

I always have trouble remembering all the executions that have taken place in my time here. Hoyt Clines, Bill Holmes, Daryl Richley, Charles Pickens, Jonas Whitmore, Barry Lee Fairchild, Earl Van Denton, Paul Ruiz, Kurt Wainwright, Marion Pruett, Clay Smith, Mark Gardner, Alvin Willett, Eugene Perry, Frankie Parker, Richard Snell, Charles Singleton, Gypsy Henderson, Debie Noel — and it seems like there's someone I'm forgetting.

Once again there's trouble with the D.N.A. testing. This time the analyst who was conducting the testing is quitting. No one knows what's going to happen. I am frustrated nearly to the point of insanity. The entire legal process is like dealing with a truckload of clowns. I finished reading the book about Ruben "Hurricane" Carter, and I could see my own situation mirrored all the way through it. The only reason he got out is because he had supporters who forced his attorneys to take the offensive. Otherwise he'd still be sitting in a prison cell, just as I am. Overtime, a person in this situation grows to be as angry with their own attorneys as they are at the cops and prosecutors. You start to see it all as one big machine that grinds the life from you.

One of the guards just said that Darel Hill has died. For some reason this reminds me how over and over again in my life I've felt like things would never change. Just let enough time pass and eventually even the unchangeable changes.

John Lennon has been dead for 25 years now. People have gathered at his grave all day today. He was a sad, dark and magickal man. I can smell him.

2-19-06

Lorri is scheduled to leave San Francisco and come back to Arkansas today — if the airport isn't too iced over. The roads are littered with the wreckage of slacked-jawed knuckledraggers who have slammed into one another.

The Dickens biography is very inspirational. He was a man who was driven. His ambition was a fire burning him up inside, causing him to always look towards the future. Even while working on one project, he had another in mind. I can relate to that more than nearly anything else I read about. I feel the same way when I hear stories of Benjamin Franklin. It makes me want to build worlds. The only thing I've been building so far today is another collage. It's all about monsters and freaks.

There are now four very visible bald patches on the back of my head, thanks to the ingenuity of the prison barber. He must be insane to believe this is somehow a normal haircut. It's like something a child would do if given a pair of scissors. I've actually considered shaving it all off and starting over again.

Twenty-six

The twelfth year I spent in that cage, was the worst one for me by far. My nerves were at the breaking point and my life was misery. That was the year I nearly gave up and lost all will to live. My physical health was rapidly deteriorating, the strain of trying to hold a marriage together in these circumstances was breaking my back, and I had used up every last ounce of willpower that I had. Then a miracle happened. The Boston Red Sox won the World Series. My sanity was saved by Johnny Damon.

There's something mystical about baseball. Some wholesome and gleaming quality that makes it as much myth as game. I watch it because it soothes and comforts, it bedazzles and bewitches. When a player steps up to the plate with a bat in his hand he ceases to be a man. He becomes the embodiment of hope. He becomes a magickal force capable of battling sickness and black despair. When someone knocks a ball over that back wall you can make a wish on it like a shooting star. A man who swings that bat becomes a force of nature, an act of divine intervention. He punches a hole through the darkness and reminds us that miracles have not vanished entirely. He is a sibyl in a sport jersey, a conduit through which all that is good shines its light.

There are only two things within these walls that can soothe or relax me. One is to go to Mass, the other is baseball. There is a priest who comes to visit and takes up to three of us into a broom closet that functions as a chapel. He performs the whole Mass right in the closet, and he brings a bishop in for Christmas Mass, too. Having a baseball game on the television has the same effect on me as sitting on the front porch in a rocking chair. It's a security blanket. When I have reached the very bottom of hopelessness, I will turn on a game, lie on my bunk, and pull the covers up over my head. I leave a tiny opening so that I can see the television with one eye. The sound of the announcer's voice lulls me toward relaxation in a way that's almost hypnotic. It helps me to heal.

Perhaps the comforting quality that baseball has for me stems from the fact that some of my best childhood memories have to do with watching games with Nanny. She was a lifelong fan of the St. Louis Cardinals and never missed a game. When she would glance at me from the television screen, I would see that she had the eyes of a young girl. Something about that scared me back then, because I was too young to understand it. I didn't understand that in those moments she was no longer a grandmother. She was no longer old, no longer the victim of creeping arthritis. She was light and young. She was a stranger to me. She was in another world.

I would sit next to her on the couch as she watched, or quietly lie on the floor. For Christmas she would buy me baseball cards, protective sleeves for them, and albums to store them in. Even though I grew up to be a Boston fan, there's still a soft spot in my heart for St. Louis. When I watch them play I can still feel my grandmother near me.

Baseball is my escape hatch. When I'm watching it I become enveloped in the feeling that everything will turn out okay. It reminds me that if I just hang on long enough, anything can happen.

One morning in 2006, I called Lorri at our usual time, eight a.m., and she told me that several of the forensic experts had reviewed much of the evidence and come back with the same conclusion: that the vast majority of the wounds on the bodies were made postmortem, and they believed animals were responsible. It was a major development in my favor; however, there had been many of those.

The forensic testing had been facilitated by Peter Jackson and Fran Walsh, who saw *Paradise Lost* in 2005 and sent money to my defense fund. They also reached out to Lorri, who welcomed their support and their resources with open arms. It was a turning point for me and for Lorri; although it would take several more years and certainly wasn't guaranteed, Peter and Fran had much to do with my actual release.

Rumors have continued to mount that animals of a more mundane variety are responsible for most of the damage to the murdered children. It's beginning to persuade even me, and I am a skeptical sort *by nature. If I hadn't grown so jaded I'd probably be growing excited. These days I don't hold my breath when waiting on anything, because the nature of the game is false hope. They'll string you out like a junkie time and time again unless you grow wise to the tricks. I'm not ungrateful, but I'm also not as young as I once was. The hair-trigger reflex of enthusiasm and hope I had when I was young has died a hard death in this lonely land. My eyes won't light up until the rumors begin to take on the weight of material form.*

There was some part of me that always knew I would walk out of prison one day. It wasn't something I knew on an intellectual level, and it went beyond the level people call instinct. It was something I knew not in my head, or even in my heart, but with my soul. I knew it in the same way that I knew the sun would rise and set. It didn't occur to me to question it, or even think about it. It simply was. Perhaps it was like watching a movie when you know the hero has to win in the end. You expect him to face peril, hardship, and heartache, but you know that in his darkest hour he must still prevail. I knew that the people subjecting me to a living hell were evil, and I couldn't conceive of a universe that would allow evil to succeed. Don't get me wrong—I know all too well that horrors and atrocities take place every single day, in every corner of the world. However, those stories were not mine. I grew up on stories, fed on them, lived in them. I grew up knowing that my own life was a story, and the stories I read always had magick in them. Therefore it was ingrained in me, into the deepest levels of my being, to expect there to be magick in my life. I had all the faith in the world that magick would guide me and save me.

I never really had much to do with the technical, legal work in my case. Anytime I even attempted to delve into it, read about it, or understand it, I would feel empty inside. The system was a soulless husk. Coming into contact with it sucked the hope and magick out of me, so I avoided it at all costs. I left the technicalities and legal nit-picking to the attorneys. It wasn't that I had any faith in them— at least not the early ones—because I did not. Who I had faith in was Lorri.

During the first two years of my incarceration, not one single thing was done by anyone on my behalf. It was Lorri, and Lorri alone, who changed that.

It didn't happen all at once. As Lorri became a part of my life, she began to educate herself, learning more and more about the legal process. When it became apparent that the public defender was going to get me killed, Lorri started doing research into defense attorneys. When she found someone she believed could do the job, she'd hound them until they agreed to take the case. When it was time to pay them, she begged and borrowed until it was done. She took loans from family members and friends, too.

The daily struggle was endless. The attorneys early on in my appeals would get lazy or go off to work on other cases they thought would bring them more prestige. Every day Lorri would have to plead and threaten in order to keep them moving forward, even at a snail's pace. It was maddening, draining, and exhausting. There were times when the stress and frustration of dealing with callous and greedy people pushed her to the point of collapse, yet she still would not stop. To do so would have meant my death.

She had to learn every single detail of the case, inside and out—names, dates, places, everything. She had to be my spokesperson, my representative. There is no one else in the world who could have done what she did, accomplished what she accomplished.

In many ways Lorri was like a general, fighting battles on many fronts. Sometimes she fought against defense attorneys as hard as she fought the state. Some of those battles were won, others were lost. One loss came from Jason's attorney right away. The cornerstone of his defense strategy from the outset was to make me look guilty. His plan was to dump the weight of the entire case on me and say that Jason had been sucked into the situation only because of his proximity to me.

To accomplish this goal, the attorney lied to Lorri and me. He asked us to talk to a mitigator, who he believed could be helpful; in capital murder cases, a mitigator comes in after conviction and works to lessen the sentence—ideally to eliminate a death sentence. We agreed. I spent a day talking to a woman who wove together a mental health report that came to be known as Exhibit 500. In it she claimed I was schizophrenic, bipolar, and suicidal, and suffered from extreme hallucinations, and anything else you could think of. To this day that report is still cited as the most damning piece of evidence against me. The woman who wrote it couldn't even testify in court because she'd already said in the past that she had lied on the witness stand in another case. To circumvent that little problem, she simply had another person file her report on me. That person's name is on that report to this day. Events like this honed Lorri's skills, sharpened her claws, and turned her into the warrior she became. Without her strength and drive, I would have been dead long ago.

The attorney I had at the time didn't really care one way or the other. And Lorri and I were not yet educated enough in the legal process to know what was happening. By the time we understood what Jason's attorney was doing, it was too late. The damage had been done. It had become a stain on my life that would shadow me forever. Jason himself still doesn't know any of this as I write it. He was blameless. Throughout all of this, a new execution date hovered in the background, though one was never actually assigned to me because the legal wranglings never resulted in my case being brought to federal court. After a stay of execution, a new date isn't assigned until the state appeals are exhausted, and from 1996, the date I was supposed to enter federal court, until my release in 2011, federal court remained out of reach.

As soon as I was sentenced and incarcerated, people far and wide sent letters of support and often monetary donations, too—anywhere from a dollar to thousands of dollars—which were used by my defense team. Inquiries were made on countless levels, from investigating the murders to the missteps in our trial to finding new evidence and witnesses we could use in future appeals and ultimately to effect a second trial for ourselves. All of these efforts cost money that we didn't have, and nothing happened without it, apart from the hiring of new lawyers (I had seven working on my case at various times through the years) for my defense, who in turn were tasked with opening new investigations, finding forensic experts, and filing paperwork. One of the costliest aspects of a major defense is paperwork—you wouldn't believe how the cost of photocopies and more photocopies can add up.

In 2001, a new law regarding DNA testing went into effect, which ostensibly would open the door to proving our innocence. The law dictates that the state will pay for all necessary testing, although then one has to wait for the state to get around to one's case. In order to get anything moving, we had to pay for all of the DNA testing up front—the evidence tested included articles (clothing and so on) that had been found near the crime scene and beyond, as well as a number of items that had not been kept in the courthouse or crime lab. Quite a few of these items had been kept for years at the West Memphis police department, where any number of people had had access to them without supervision or even gloves.

The person who helped us tremendously at this point was Henry Rollins, who not only appealed to his celebrity and musician friends but also produced an album, took it on tour, and raised enough for the first round of DNA testing. In 2002, the motion for DNA testing was filed, although we wouldn't hear anything resembling results until 2006.

I 've also got my fingers crossed right now, hoping the results of a DNA test come back soon. It seems to take forever sometimes. DNA testing has come quite a ways in the eleven years I've been locked up. They can do things now that they couldn't do a decade ago. There was no way to *do it until now because no one could afford it. The difference now is a one-man army named Henry Rollins, who has worked his ass off to make sure it happens. I'm still stunned every time I see a letter in the mail with a return address for "H. Rollins," because it hits me that I'm trading correspondence with a living legend. He's determined to see the truth come out, and nothing stops him once he's made his mind up about getting something done. It's things like that that really let me know how far this case has come. Still, I'd be lying if I said I wasn't scared sometimes. Every once in a while I'm damn near petrified, but I have no choice but to struggle on.*

In 2004, I was, oddly, adopted (again). I had been exchanging letters and phone calls with a woman who had seen *Paradise Lost*, and had contacted me around the same time Lorri did. She was a psychologist who wanted to help me. We spoke on the phone often, and she became a therapist for me in many ways. It was an escape to talk to her. We never talked about the case—instead she was humorous and entertaining, and we would bicker and laugh with each other nonstop. And so she adopted me in order to visit and spend time with me. Cally, also known as "Mama Mouse," decided she was no longer content with a houseful of cats and decided to adopt me despite my constant sarcasm. The nastier I was, the more she bragged to all her friends about me. Her job is to help shape the minds of today's youth by giving advice at a school in California. And people wonder how Californians gained the reputation of being fruitcakes. I point the finger of blame at Cally.

This is a woman who has pictures of barnyard animals on her socks and listens in on every conversation around her in the coffee-house. She insisted on sending me progress reports on the health of her ninety-nine cats, including which ones had diarrhea. You know she can't be normal—she voluntarily chose to adopt me, after all. Cally lives in San Francisco, where she says the weather is pretty much the same all the time. There are no tornadoes, no blizzards, no scorching heat waves that leave the earth dead and brown. It's just one eternal, mind-numbing seventy-degree day. At first I was in-trigued by this. In fact, it seemed somehow magickal. However, the more I contemplated it, the more uneasy I became. Then I realized why. It's because something about it is vaguely prisonlike. It seems almost dispassionate in some way. How is a person supposed to ex-perience different emotional and psychic states while living in an eternally static environment? Because that's what life comes down to in prison—a continuous, soul-stealing environment. Something like that can lull you into a stupor long before you realize it's happening, and before you know it, your spirit has atrophied and calcified.

Cally also donated extraordinary sums of money to our defense efforts, and she never wavered in her support and affection for me through all the years I was incarcerated.

In the early years, Jason and I actually exchanged letters through our various visitors. We told each other not to give in, not to give up hope, to keep fighting no matter what. He described living con-ditions in the general prison population—everything you've read about prison is true, only more so. The violence is incomprehensible, and Jason was brutalized in unspeakable ways. Among other things, he suffered a fractured skull and had to be hospitalized after he was thrown headfirst onto the concrete floor by another inmate. He told me he never saw his attacker. He'd been my closest friend and I missed him during those years, though he lived just nearby. The guards and wardens were obsessed with making sure we never spoke; when a letter was discovered, Jason was threatened and so we didn't try communicating often.

I was still a child when I was sent to Death Row. I grew into adulthood, both mentally and physically, in this hellhole. I came into this situation wide-eyed and naïve. Now I view most everything and everyone with narrow-eyed suspicion. I've learned the hard way that the world is not my friend. I thought that pretty much the entire human race wanted me to die a slow, painful death, until a miracle occurred. It seems my hopes of receiving divine intervention weren't completely ignored.

One thing I've noticed time and time again in prison is how quickly people in the outside world forget you. Their lives do not stop simply because yours does. Sooner or later they get over the grieving process and move on. Even your family. Two years is a very long time for someone to stick by your side once you're in prison. Most don't even last that long. Domini moved on with her life; she's now married, has a beautiful daughter, and lives all the way on the other side of the country. I haven't seen my father in many, many years. He has another family to worry about and care for now. There's not much he could have done for me anyway.

Between October 2009 and September 2010, we filed a motion

to make an oral argument in front of the Arkansas Supreme Court requesting a new trial based on all of the new evidence and DNA findings we'd accumulated over the past ten years. A hearing isn't guaranteed, and by this point Lorri and I were both worn down by the process. We had exhausted every possibility in terms of uncovering new proof of my innocence, and none of it had worked. We had all of the elements we needed in this battle—we simply could not get the court system to pay attention and we were running out of time. In fact, it looked to us like we would spend the rest of our lives in pursuit of something just out of reach.

All around me were people who had been abandoned to their fates. No one came to see them or offer encouragement. No one wrote them long letters with news from home. They had no one to call when they were so sad or scared they felt they couldn't go on. No one sent them a few dollars so they wouldn't have to eat the rancid prison food.

They are the true living dead. The world has moved on, and they are forgotten. The thought that I could have so easily been one of them fills my heart with terror. I'm fortunate beyond my ability to describe because I've had a few friends who have stuck by my side since almost the beginning.

*M*orphic field. That's what it's called when a certain kind of energy pattern is repeated over and over until it creates some-

thing like an aura. This prison, for example. All of the hatred, igno-rance, pain, humiliation, and greed constantly being put out by everyone in here has created one hell of a negative morphic field. The thing about morphic fields is that they behave like magnets. Like attracts like. It draws more of the same energy to itself, and it touches everyone who comes here. The people who come to see me immediately feel disgust, anger, and repugnance for the kind of people they have to deal with here. It also explains why every new batch of guards who come to work here are a little more brutal and ignorant than the last. As the morphic field grows increasingly worse, it draws in the kind of people who reso-nate with it.

Even the best-laid plans seem to go bad in a split second. All you can do is stand there in a state of shock, wondering what went wrong. It's one of the worst feelings possible, to helplessly watch as the world slips through your fingers like sand. Your heart seems to run out with it.

What happened to me was a great disruption. It was the violent shud-dering jerk of something that has slipped horribly off track. I sit in this cell now, filling someone else's place. It is a murderer who should be here, not me. I often wonder if this mistake was made deliberately, by those who have something to hide. Other times I wonder if it's for some great and secret purpose known only to a power much higher than my-self. But I believe the most important question of all is what will it take to set things right? What will it take to restore my life to its right track and clockwork precision? Is it already happening?

I come from a line of men with no fathers. I have no paternal traditions to pass on to my own offspring, and can count the number of times I've seen my son on one hand. They say that blood calls to blood, but I have thirty-two years of doubt and no contradiction. No one was there to teach me how to knot a necktie or explain the mechanics of sex. I had to learn on the run, wherever I could. My own son doesn't even know me. All he has is a handful of someone else's dusty memories, most of which aren't even accurate.

There are long stretches of time that fly by so quietly that another year has crept up on you before you realize it. The year can feel as oily as the steel of a gun barrel. Other times the stress comes in and floods out everything. It steals your sleep and your clarity of mind. Consciousness becomes a mental misery that takes a toll on the body. All the worldly concerns drop in to introduce themselves at a time you least suspect. Hairline fractures trace their way across the skull and settle into a deep throb. There is never enough time, patience, money, or enthusiasm. The pressure is relentless, and I twist in the wind like a sheet on a clothesline. The constantly shifting strategy wears me down and tires me out. The cycle is endlessly repetitive and I have no distractions. Matters of life and death are no more than afterthoughts to the cogs that turn the wheels. I *keep feeling that if I could only get one break, then I could find a way to get ahead. It never comes. I am at the end of my rope.*

Last night I dreamed that a bunch of rednecks burned me at the stake in a Walmart parking lot. Surprisingly enough, it wasn't entirely unpleasant. I was still conscious after I became smoke, and it felt good to spiral in the air. I didn't just float around the way smoke tends to. I flew quickly, and with a purpose. I was following someone, but can't remember who or why. I only remember watching them cross a gray winter field from a great distance as I formed a giant white spiral in the sky. I felt free and strong, vibrating with purpose. Sometimes we forget the raw power of that feeling when we leave the purity of youth behind. I recognized and remembered it in the dream. When I awakened, it lingered like an aftertaste.

In my best dreams I always run on all fours, like an animal. I still have the same body, but I travel like a quadruped. I'll be running and suddenly realize that I can move much faster if I use my hands. I lean forward just enough to get my hands on the ground and then use all four limbs to thrust myself forward like a rabbit, a cheetah, or a deer. It's a feeling of absolute freedom and power. These dreams feel ten times better than the few dreams I've had in which I can fly. I've had these running dreams for as long as I can remember, and it's always seemed like the most natural thing in the world. Someone once told me that in these dreams I am becoming my totem animal, that I am taking the form of my spirit guide, and that it probably has something to do with my Native American bloodline. The only flaw in that theory is that when I see myself in these dreams I don't look like any animal. I look like myself, only running faster than any human ever could.

The trauma of living circles me like a pack of wolves. It waits for the exhaustion to drive me to my knees so that it can devour me at leisure. It lingers over my bones, taking pride in its ghoulish feast. When life eats you, it always starts with your heart.

I've always sneered at weakness, and at those who need a painkiller to make it through the day. My sneers were caused by false pride. The only thing strong about me is the grip I have on my masks and delusions. Now all I feel is surgery without the anesthetic. All that I know is fear, and I can't find my way out.

I have a new next-door neighbor. He hasn't slept in several days. He paces his cell throughout the night, arguing with himself in several voices. One is a deep bass mumble, one is a screeching shrew, and a third does nothing but curse and swear at the other two. Sometimes they all merge into a bug-eyed, strangling gargle. It doesn't stop until daylight comes.

For the first time I see how I've spent my entire life on a pendulum, swinging back and forth between the two faces of God—the face that

hides in shadow and the face that shines forth from the light. The ciga-
rettes, the yoga, the sleeping pills, the meditation, the trashy horror mov-
ies, the music of Bach, the losing of myself in sex, the Catholicism, the
self-destructive urge, and the abandonment of myself to the ecstasy of
love. I saw the face of light as I struggled to understand life through the
heart of the Rose.

What I crave more than anything today is to sit at an outdoor café on a
cool autumn day. I just want to feel that end-of-the-year breeze as I sip
a cup of green tea and take my time with a piece of pumpkin pie. I
would slump in my chair and allow my mind to roam wherever it chose.
Nothing else in the world epitomizes absolute freedom to me more than
that thought. I could be alone or with a friend I know so well that we
wouldn't have to speak. Sometimes I wake up in the morning thinking
about pumpkin pie.

I'm convinced that people see the ghosts of themselves all the time,
but most just choose to block them out. The words don't even make sense
to me, and I know it's true. When I was seven years old I saw the ghost
of myself at the age of eighteen. Ever since that day I've kicked myself for
not asking questions. I've no idea what my eighteen-year-old self could
have told me at that point—perhaps nothing at all. Still, I can't help
but think of it as a lost opportunity. Somehow there was a slight fluctua-
tion in the current, and two of me bled through the fabric at once.
*   Trying to figure out the meaning behind such events can drive you*

mad, because there is no answer. Perhaps it was some sort of hiccup. Then again, perhaps I was making some Herculean effort to reach out to myself, and that was all I could manage.

I used to wonder if some other me had died on Death Row, causing all of my selves to snap back like a broken rubber band and haunt each other. Now I doubt it, even though no other answer is any more likely. It just doesn't feel right.

These things are always strongest in December, when the year is as thin and transparent as plastic wrap. Something in the center of my chest rejoices that this is my birth month—it swoons like a religious zealot with a mouthful of Hallelujahs.

DECEMBER 11

I have never seen the sun on my birthday. It simply does not shine. This one single day is immortal, eternally waiting for me to return to it once every year. It is a sentient gray room that sits outside the world's rotational authority. This is the day of the winter eclipse, and the graveyard of my alienation. Time is marked with an hourglass filled with snow instead of sand.

This day is one of the closest things to ritual or tradition that my family ever embraced. It's the quietest day of the year—no birds sing, no cars backfire, and there is no laughter. It enwraps me in a soft and soothing cocoon, and it holds me like a secret. Even the pictures on the walls silently sing its grace. If there was ever only one day on Marlou Island, then this would be that day.

DECEMBER 25

Christmas Day itself is always bittersweet, because it's the last day of that beautiful magick that's been building up like a tidal wave for the past month. In just a week it will be hard to even remember what it's like. I'll be brokenhearted at the thought of it being gone again for an entire year.

At home I always preferred Christmas Eve to Christmas. All the family would come over for the party. There would be sandwiches, homemade cookies and candy, chips and dip, and everyone would be in a great mood. After they left, my sister and I would be allowed to open up all of our presents at the stroke of midnight, unless I was at St. Michael's for the Christmas Eve Midnight Mass. If I was, then we opened them the second I got home. The house was always so warm. No one was ever in a bad mood, because we were experiencing the magick that had been accumulating for months. It sparkled in my mother's eyes.

It's been about fourteen years since I've really celebrated Christmas, or even had a decent meal on this day. The feeling the day carries manages to seep in through these concrete walls, but there's no one here to share it with and nothing I can do with it. I'd be happy to pass a stranger on the street and hear them say, "Merry Christmas," or to be able to say it to them. I want to be bundled up as I walk beneath the slate-colored afternoon sky. I want to sit and look at twinkling trees while sipping eggnog. In the outside world the air would feel like a music box, just like in the old days.

This is the time of year when it hurts the most to be here. The summer may be a misery to my body, but missing this magick hurts me to my soul.

December tastes like Hershey's Kisses. The month of December and those little Hershey's Kisses candies are connected in a way that I can't quite articulate. For me, at least. I do know that eating a Hershey's Kiss is like an act of communion—like taking a tiny taste of December into myself. I don't like to eat them at other times of the year, because I don't want that special association to fade.

Sometimes I think the vast majority of the year is about anticipation for me. The year is the journey, December is the destination. On November 30, I always sit up all night long so that I can greet December as it arrives. I like to meet it at the door, so to speak. And then I stay up all night on December 31, not to see the New Year in, but to savor the last few moments of my favorite month. October and November are really, really good, but December is great.

My favorite time of year is from December 20 until sunrise on December 25. During that stretch of time I can feel the entire world come to an absolute standstill. On those few days the hair on my neck stands on end, and the world feels like a pendulum that has swung all the way to one side and hangs suspended for a split second before beginning the reverse swing. At sunrise on December 25 the spell is broken and we begin the swing back in the other direction. Those magickal days are gone for another year, and my vigil starts all over again.

Strangely enough, the song that sounds the most like December is a ballad called "High Enough" by the Damn Yankees. I have a whole list of December songs: "Love Is on the Way" by Saigon Kick, "Don't Cry" by Guns N' Roses, "Wait" by White Lion, "House of Pain" by Faster Pussycat, and "Don't Close Your Eyes" by Kix. That's the sound track for the month of December. Oh yeah, I forgot one—"Don't Know What You've

Got (Till It's Gone)" by Cinderella. Yes, I still love Cinderella. And yes, I can hear your snorts of disgust. Doesn't bother me one bit, though. I'm used to it by now, as I even hear it from Lorri.

When I try to picture heaven, I see a place where it's always December, every radio station plays hair bands, and every time I check my pockets they're full of Hershey's Kisses. There's a Christmas parade on every street, every day is my birthday, and the sun always sets at 4:58 p.m.

The inertia is killing me, wearing me out one day at a time. The legal system is content to let me die of old age. If someone doesn't do something soon there will be nothing left of me to save.

I woke up this morning to discover a spider on my breakfast tray. It was smashed to a piece of bread. Something about it seemed too malicious to have been an accident. I haven't felt right all day. Every time that spider pops into my head I feel my stomach lurch again.

Tonight I separated and saw myself again, just as I did when I was seven years old. Tonight I was the ghost of sixteen. It went so fast that I couldn't say or do anything. It was just a flicker. I was gasping for breath like a fish pulled from the water and my heart beat like thunder. It's the fasting that triggered it. I haven't felt like eating because of the spider. A dead spider has given me the ghost flickers. There is a field between me and the ghost of sixteen. *Things wait in that field, unable to cross the line that divides me now from the ghost of me then. Step lively and move with purpose, or the ghosts will swarm all over you. They almost never get the chance to touch us, but they're always waiting should the chance arrive. They can't usually even see you unless you ride the ghost flickers. I am moving forward and backward at once. Some part of me is always in the ghost flickers.*

Or the flicker is in me. It's getting hard to tell. Everything is happening at once, and I can't pinpoint anything. It's all too much. The flickers are like inhaled gasoline fumes. They are a vulgar shimmer with no false grace, and a world unto themselves. The flickers are a place where everything exists as a series of jerky movements.

I can't stop my hands from shaking, but I cannot feel the cold.

Last night the Rose had a dream of prophecy and bureaucratic bullshit. She was swimming in a competition, able to literally pull herself through the water by finding handholds in it. After she easily won, the judges disqualified her over some small technicality. She was furious because she recognized it for what it was—pointless bureaucracy.

She knew it symbolized the case. We've seen it time and again. The good thing was that the dream filled her with certainty. She knew that if she could win once, she could win again. Next time she would beat them at their own game. Fuck the lawyers, the prosecutors, the judge, the liars, the police, and everyone else that stands against us. They will never win, because we won't give up. Knock me down ninety-nine times, and I will get back up one hundred.

I was sealed inside a concrete box deep in the heart of a super-maximum-security prison several years ago, and since that time have not had fresh air, sunlight, the feel of grass, or anything else people associate with real life. My living space is as confining and unnatural as that of astronauts in outer space. It's all brought me to the conclusion that I am being treated like veal, and for the same reason.

The prison administration doesn't want you to be too healthy, because then you would be strong. The weaker they can keep you, the easier their job is—especially when an execution comes up. If they keep you soft by putting you in a tiny space so that you can barely move, then feed you nothing but grease and carbs, while maintaining a constantly elevated stress level, then when an execution comes up the man tends to die pretty quickly. Hell, most men are usually at least a quarter of the way dead by the time they make it to the death chamber. Actually, I don't even think I'm supposed to call it that anymore—the death chamber. In these politically correct times they've given it some other less self-explanatory name that I can't quite remember. Still, everyone here knows it's where they do all of the official killing.

A friend recently told me there was an article in a national magazine about how super-max prisons drive the inmates insane. I already knew that, because I see it every day. Not so long ago a guard made a mistake and pushed the button that opens all the doors in a cell block at once. One schizophrenic man immediately smashed another's skull with a steel bar, killing him. Neither man could have been considered sane by any stretch of the imagination.

Perception becomes distorted in here, which leads to bizarre behavior. It's because there is nothing for a person to compare themselves to. There is no barometer for judging what is "normal," so the thought processes begin to gradually drift in odd directions. The next thing you know, someone snaps and begins screaming that there is blood in his food. At first when something like that happened I was horrified and in a state that I can only describe as terrified awe. Now I find a raving lunatic to be only mildly annoying.

After a while it makes you wonder if you yourself may have lost your mind. How would you know if you had? And the crazy people all seem to think themselves completely sane, so they must not be able to tell the difference. I can't think about it for very long or I get stomach cramps. The last thing I need to add to my current list of woe-inducing problems is insanity.

The courts have ruled that executing an insane person is inhumane, so what they do now is begin pumping the lunatics full of drugs a few weeks before the execution date. By doing so they can make them lucid enough to comprehend that they're being murdered on a given date, which qualifies them as sane. Somehow that strikes me as being far more inhumane than allowing a person to remain in a state where they don't realize they're being murdered.

Don't get me wrong, I'm no bleeding-heart liberal who believes everyone is a victim and no one is responsible for their own actions. However, I do possess the intelligence and acumen to realize that something is horribly wrong with this system. I don't know what the answer is, but I know it's not veal.

FEBRUARY

The temperature dropped to around twenty degrees last night. I woke up at 2:30 a.m. when a guard began beating on my door with a metal bar and yelling for me to get up if I wanted a breakfast tray. When I got up it took me a minute or two to get my hands to work right because they were so cold. I slept in two sets of clothes, but my bones still felt like glass. Not that I'm complaining—I'll take the cold over the heat any day, and summer in here is hell. I actually like the cold. It fills me with nostalgia, reminds me of my youth. When I was a kid the fire would always go out in the middle of the night and the cold would roll in and coat the entire house. I was always amazed to see that the water in the toilet had frozen over. Something about the cold always makes me feel young again.

They set another execution date this week. There's now one scheduled for March and one for April. It's looking like there's probably going to be at least one a month for the next four or five months, not counting February. The non–Death Row prisoners like when there's an execution because it's the only time the prison serves fried chicken. I'm still not one hundred percent positive what the point of the fried chicken is—either placating the rest of us or celebrating the execution. Whatever it is, it's looking like the fried chicken may be coming fast and furious this year.

I can feel the daylight hours growing. I can't see it, but something in my core feels it happening. It's strange how I can still feel when the sun is up, even after not being out in its light in seven years. I've heard of experiments where people were closed away from sunlight for long periods of time, and eventually they lost the ability to feel if it was day or night. Perhaps I would have, too, were it not for the solar and lunar energy-

circulating practices I do. Last night was the full moon. The Storm moon, which usually falls in February. That means the Chaste moon will be in February this year, instead of its usual time in March. I would have loved to have been able to go out and look up at it. That's one of the things I miss most—the night sky. The stars, the moon, the crisp air. Maybe soon.

Time to get busy. My routine is not going to do itself.

The Boston Red Sox are big, big magick. I've heard that some analysts are saying they won't even make it to the play-offs this year. I don't like sports for the most part. It seems like a tremendous waste of valuable, precious time to me—time that could be used for something constructive, productive, or to further your growth: studying, meditating, working out, talking to loved ones, et cetera, but there's something about the Red Sox that soothes my nerves, like a security blanket or a rocking chair. I like to have them on the TV or radio playing in the background as I go about my business. It's better than one of those ocean sound tracks.

I'd better get to work. Talk to you soon.

I've been keeping an eye out for the Charlie Brown Valentine's Day special. I know it will be on soon, and I never miss a Charlie Brown special. The best one is the Halloween show about the Great Pumpkin—which I've only missed one year in my life, due to the local ABC station having technical difficulties—but all the Peanuts shows make me feel like I'm one step closer to Halloween.

When I was in second grade we were told to write a letter to some-one we admired. Most kids wrote to the president or an athlete. I wrote to Charles Schulz. He wrote back and even sent some autographed Pea-nuts drawings. The teacher took them and put them on display for the whole class to see—and I never got them back. She kept the drawings. I wonder where they are now.

The thing I like about the shows isn't the characters—it's the back-ground. The colors are so amazing it almost takes my breath away. Every time I watch The Great Pumpkin I feel like I'm going to have a seizure during the scenes where Snoopy is in a dogfight. Just look at the background in those scenes. It really is too much to take. I can barely keep from holding my head in my hands and involuntarily groaning like I have a mouthful of the best chocolate cake ever made. I look at them and can literally smell the crisp autumn air—even in this cell. No horror movie in the world makes me feel the magick of Halloween as strongly as The Great Pumpkin.

The Valentine's show is good, too.

I'm excited today, and happy. Not for any particular reason, other than the fact that good things are coming. Good things are always com-ing; sometimes we just forget it.

P.S. Wednesday, February 10. That's the night that love is in the air for Charlie Brown, on ABC.

In a way I'm thankful for all the physical pain and suffering I've had to endure in here because it has forced me to keep learning and moving forward. If I didn't have pain, I'd probably take the day off. And that day could become a week. And that week could turn into months. But as it is I know I have two choices—practice every single day without fail, or hurt so bad that life is a misery. So I keep reminding myself that the pain is a gift from the Divine, and that I should be thankful for it.

Today the guards made me bleed again. They chained my feet so tight I could barely move. I bleed through my socks—last month it was my left ankle, today it was the right. When I wash the soap burns like fire, but I have to keep my ankles clean because I don't have any alcohol or peroxide—nothing to kill bacteria or infections. And this place is filthy.

I can't remember what it's like to walk as a human being anymore. My cell is so small that I can only take two steps. Anytime I'm brought out—however briefly or infrequently—I have chains on my hands and feet as well as guards hanging on me. It's been well over sixteen years since I've actually walked anywhere. Sometimes I still can't wrap my mind around that. I'm working on my seventeenth year now. There are times when I've thought, "Surely someone is going to put a stop to this. Surely someone is going to do something." But no one ever does. Time just rolls on. It's insanity. I am truly amazed at what they've been allowed to get away with, and for how long—especially Burnett and the Arkansas Supreme Court. If Burnett gets that senate seat, I really do fear how many people he'll be able to hurt. If he's engaged in this much corruption as a judge, the thought of what he could do as a senator is horrifying.

Ah, well . . . does no good to dwell on it. Either I waste my energy by focusing on things I cannot change, or I conserve my energy and apply it to the small things I can change. That's what the I Ching calls "the *taming power of the small." Every great victory is made up of many smaller victories.*

Someone sent me a letter that had one of the best quotes I've ever read. It said "What is to give light must endure burning." It's by a writer named Viktor Frankl. I've been turning that quote over and over in my head. The truth of it is absolutely awe-inspiring. In the end, I believe it's why we all suffer. It's the meaning we all look for behind the tragedies in our lives. The pain deepens us, burns away our impurities and petty selfishness. It makes us capable of empathy and sympathy. It makes us capable of love. The pain is the fire that allows us to rise from the ashes of what we were, and more fully realize what we can become. When you can step back and see the beauty of the process, it's amazing beyond words.

All my life I've heard people say, "Why would God allow this to happen?" I think it's because while we can see only the tragedy, God sees only the beauty. While we see misery, Divinity sees us lurching and shambling one step closer to the light. I truly do believe that one day we'll shine as brightly as the archangels themselves.

To the person who sent me that quote—thank you. I stuck it up so that my eyes will travel over it several times a day. It's something I'll never forget.

Just about every time I do an interview they ask me what I miss most. When they do, a hundred things flash through my mind—the memories giving me that free-fall feeling in the pit of my stomach. I miss the rain. I miss standing beneath the sky and looking up at the moon and stars. I miss the wind. I miss cats and dogs. I miss wearing real clothes, having a real toothbrush, using a real pen, drinking iced tea, eating ice cream, and going for walks.

I'm tempted to say the thing I miss most is fruit. I haven't had a piece of fresh fruit in about eight years, and before that I only got it once a year. The prison used to give everyone two apples and two oranges on Christmas, but then they stopped, said it was a "threat to security," along with tea bags and dental floss. So I haven't had any in nearly a decade now. They prevent scurvy by giving everyone a cup of watered-down orange juice for breakfast. It doesn't have much taste, but enough vitamin C to keep your teeth from falling out.

In the end, it's not the fruit I miss most, though if you rolled all the deprivations into one thing, it would be this: I miss being treated like a human being.

FEBRUARY 12

This place is hell on the body. One of the reasons I cannot write letters the way I used to is that living in this cell twenty-four hours a day has destroyed my vision. I used to read three or four books a week. Now I average about one a month, if the print isn't too small. The eye works like any other part of the body—use it or lose it. A person confined to a small space never has a chance to see anything that's more than a couple feet away, so the first thing to go is your ability to see at a distance. Even *with my glasses on, I can see maybe ten feet. Without glasses, maybe four inches—anything beyond that is color and movement.*

The teeth go because dental care is practically nonexistent. Several years ago I was brutally beaten by a pack of sadistic guards, which caused nerve damage to several of my teeth. The prison gave me the choice of living with the pain or having my teeth pulled out. I've been in pain ever since (prison policy says no root canals, even if the guards themselves cause the damage).

Diabetes and heart disease come about from being unable to move. These cells are just big enough to take two steps forward and two steps back. Even if you work out for an hour a day, that leaves 23 hours when you are practically not moving at all. Add to that the cheapest diet you can find—plain noodles, white rice, white bread, grits, et cetera—and you've created a recipe for disaster. If you don't work very hard, and aren't very, very careful, you'll die in here.

Last year there was a brief mention on the news about a sick pris-oner who had to be put on life support after he was left lying in his own feces for several days. They eventually fired two guards for it, but only because it was mentioned on the news. Just about every guard in the prison had to pass that man's cell on a daily basis. They all saw him. The two guards who got fired were simply scapegoats.

I don't want to complain. No one likes a whiner, I know. Sometimes I just get so tired, though—tired of the abuse, tired of the cruelty, tired of the apathy. It wears you down to nothing. But I know that allowing myself to be sucked down into it, allowing myself to waste time dwelling on it, does nothing but create and feed more frustration. Tomorrow is a new day. I will put this one behind me and move forward into a more productive place. Today, however, what you get to read is me whining and complaining. As Billy Bob says in the movie Bad Santa, *"Well, they can't all be winners now, can they?"*

FEBRUARY 26

I've been asked by quite a few people why the prison serves breakfast at 2:30 a.m. The answer to that would be slave labor. The prison is run by what amounts to slave labor—planting crops, digging ditches, construction and maintenance—any job you can think of other than guard is done by the prisoners. They have the choice of doing whatever job the administration gives them to do, or go to the hole. They throw you in there, then drag you out every thirty days to ask if you're ready to go to work yet. If you say no, they toss you back in. This goes on until the person's mind or soul has been broken. So breakfast is at 2:30 a.m. because they want to have everyone out in the fields as early as possible so they can get as many hours of work out of them as they can.

It's a brutal system. In other states prisoners get paid, even if it's only five cents an hour. Not here, though. Here you get nothing. They still charge you if you need to see a doctor, even though many people have no money and no way of getting any. The reason other states pay prisoners to work is that in prison you have to buy everything—they don't give you even the basic necessities, from soap and toothpaste to coffee and candy bars. So they charge you for all of it and take back the money they've paid you anyway.

They can also put you in the hole for giving something to another

345

prisoner who can't afford it. For example, say the guards decided not to feed a guy one day to teach him a lesson. If you give him a candy bar, they can give you thirty days in the hole. Give someone soap who can't afford it—thirty days. A cup of coffee? Thirty days. It's cruelty and madness. I once saw a man get thirty days for giving another man construction paper. The only thing you can do is keep your head down, be quiet, and try to avoid notice.

FEBRUARY 27

I just received a letter from Amy in New Jersey, asking if I believe in God. What I think is that belief is irrelevant. Belief doesn't play much of a role in my life. What matters to me is experience. I experience the Divine in my life on a daily basis. For me, effort is far more important than belief, and the effort I put forth is to spend every single moment of my life in the presence of the Divine.

I like to compare spirituality to riding a bicycle. You can believe with every fiber of your being that it's possible to ride a bicycle, but until you start practicing you won't be able to do it. Spirituality has to be about action, not belief.

One of my favorite quotes of all time comes from Oscar Wilde. When someone asked him if he believed in God, his response was "No, I believe in something much bigger." I feel the same way. There is no old man waiting in the clouds to inflict pain on us for our failures. What there is is beyond words. Our concepts of God are tiny and insignificant compared to the reality of what Divinity is. Does that answer your question, Amy?

Speaking of such things, I gave up all cursing for Lent in an attempt to practice a more mindful way of speaking. It's harder than I thought it would be. I've slipped several times, but I'm still trying. What trips me up most is dealing with the abusive guards. When they're deliberately trying to hurt me, or when they're harassing Lorri, I find myself cursing them under my breath and have to remind myself "No cursing!" Lorri and I are supposed to be able to see each other for three hours once a week, but this week a hateful guard deliberately took an hour of our time. The more attention the case gets, the more hateful and vindictive the guards become.

FEBRUARY 28

I've never felt anything like what I've been feeling for the past few days. It's like there's a tremendous tidal wave hovering over my head. It's just been growing and growing ever since word of Johnny Depp being a supporter and friend began to make the rounds. Johnny contacted Lorri for the first time in 1999, calling her up on the phone while she was at work one day. From that moment on, he corresponded with us both, with emotional and financial support in equal measure. He learned everything he could about the case, down to the finest details, and when he appeared on 48 Hours his participation was startling where his knowledge of events was concerned. To be honest, it's a little scary. It just feels so huge. I can only imagine what the energy would feel like out there. One thing I've discovered is that I wouldn't want to be a celebrity for anything in the world. They have to live with far more energy than this directed at them twenty-four hours a day, seven days a week. I can't even imagine how it would be to have to try to lead a normal life when there are people constantly trying to ask you questions, catch you on film, et cetera.

I know there must be a lot of support being generated out there because the level of hatred directed toward me by the guards has increased tenfold. I don't even care. It just lets me know that good things are happening. The feeling in the air is almost the same thing I feel when a thunderstorm is coming. That's what I pray for—rain. Enough rain to wash away the corruption, the cover-ups, the darkness, and the apathy that has stolen the past seventeen years of my life.

March 16

The prison refused to let me see Harada Roshi. Communication between us has suddenly become a "security risk," even though nothing has changed since the last time. I gave up trying to understand prison logic long ago—Rolling Stone magazine is a security risk, sodas are a security risk, salt and pepper are security risks. The list goes on and on. It's incredibly disappointing that we didn't get to talk. It would have been like getting a breath of fresh air to have been able to see Roshi and Chisan. Chisan is Roshi's translator, and a female priest who does tarot readings in Japan. They carry an incredible energy with them wherever they go. It's like love, happiness, compassion, discipline, and fun all rolled up into one current of golden light. At least Lorri got to meet them for dinner and talk about where our practice has taken us. I can't wait for the day when we can go to Japan and visit the temple. It's a way of life that hasn't changed much in hundreds of years, and life in the temple is practically a world unto itself.

Roshi had no idea who Johnny Depp was when he heard about the 48 Hours episode. That's how I wish I could live—cut off from modern society and focused entirely on self-development. In a way I do live that way, except that my days are a dark and distorted version of monastic life.

In other news, the execution that was scheduled for tonight was not carried out. The attorney general is furious, and the guards are less than pleased. No one knows what to expect next.

APRIL 9

This is to the raven-haired lady I spoke to today from the Innocence Project: Thank you. Thank you for speaking to me like a human being. A lot of times they'll bring tours through here and they come to my cell and just stare at me as if I'm some sort of exhibit in a museum. I've had teenage girls from a community college criminal justice class stand and watch me in the shower, and they didn't even speak. They just stood around as if they had every right in the world to do so. You, raven-haired lady, were only the second person to ever speak to me. I was very happy to hear that you have been reading these letters. I have been slacking on the updates lately, but now I want to do a better job. In some ways I feel like I've been throwing messages in a bottle into the ocean, wondering if anyone is finding them. Now I know that someone is.

Not much is changing here. I've been moving deeper into my studies, my meditating, and my energy work. The days continue to fly past at an incredibly high rate of speed. The only thing of interest to anyone is that I think Marilyn Manson is quickly becoming my new best friend. Lorri loves him to pieces, too. He's going to be speaking out for us on VH1 at an awards show that will air in July. He's also painting my portrait, which I am incredibly excited about. Manson got involved to help with my case, although he has stayed behind the scenes—he thought his presence might be as hurtful as helpful in the public perception.

The air is filled with that odd, powerful energy that you only feel when the seasons are changing. It stirs up old memories of when I was young and free, and it nearly drives me mad. It was during this time of year that I experienced my very last days of freedom nearly seventeen years ago. The energy in the air makes those memories feel as if they only happened a few days ago. It hurts me somewhere deep in the core of my bones, but it's an exquisitely beautiful kind of pain.

APRIL

They stopped the execution that was scheduled to take place last night. They had already taken the man to the death house, where the executions are carried out, when the Arkansas Supreme Court issued the order to stop. Now there will have to be a hearing before anyone else is put to death. That probably bought an extra year for those scheduled to be executed soon. Maybe. You can never be certain.

More than anything, I'd like to go to a park today. I want to sit in a swing, drink chocolate milk, and not think about anything in the world except the pleasure of that moment. I want to know what a normal life feels like because I can't remember anymore. I want to drag my feet on the ground as I swing back and forth. I want to feel the fresh, spring chi on my skin. I'm very tempted to get out my Halloween decorations today because looking at them always gives me a little burst of excitement. I can't, though, because I have a rule: No Halloween decorations before June 21. That's the summer solstice, so after that we're officially in the second half of the year.

Another rule I abide by is no peppermint until November 1. I only eat peppermint between November 1 and January 6, because that keeps it special. If you don't do things like that in here, then there's nothing to look forward to.

April 18

Many people have asked me why I cut my hair. The answer is because I didn't have a choice. One day the prison decided it was a "security risk" if my hair were to touch my ears or my collar. If I refused to let them cut my hair, I would be thrown in the hole for thirty days, my visits would be taken for one year, and I would not be allowed to use the phone for one month. Same deal with facial hair. Sideburns that extend beyond mid-ear are "detrimental to the order and discipline of the unit."

The whole purpose was to rob everyone of their identity. Dress everyone exactly alike, give them the same haircut, take away their name, and give them a number. To the prison system, I am not Damien Echols.

I am inmate SK931. I still don't let them cut my hair, though. I cut it myself, with a disposable razor. It's a time-consuming process, but better than the alternative. The prison "barber" is just a prisoner they choose at random and assign to the job. It's usually someone who has never cut hair in his life, and I don't fancy being the training dummy.

April 27

With every day that passes I feel more and more as if I'm playing Russian roulette. It's nothing to do with the case, because I know that sooner or later someone will step in and correct this situation. The danger I feel comes from trying to survive in here. Every day the odds continue to stack up. Sooner or later the hammer will fall on a chamber with a round in it. Could be anything—diabetes, starvation, food poisoning, skull cracked by a bored guard, heat stroke, or about a million other things. I feel like the frog trying to cross the street in that old video game Frogger. Sooner or later he always gets squashed. The only question is how long you can prevent it from happening.

May 1

The next execution is scheduled to take place in three days. Chances are high it will be called off, since the last one wasn't carried out. There's another one scheduled for May 24, but it probably won't take place, either. Everyone seems to think they'll be put on hold until after a hearing about procedure. Arkansas is the only state in the country that has a law that says the prison director can carry out executions in any way he sees fit. This means it's legal for the prison to starve you to death. Or burn you alive. Or stone you. The law in Arkansas gives these people the power to do anything they want. What is legal and what is right are often two different things.

Even if the execution gets called off at the last minute, the man who is scheduled to die will never be the same. When someone comes back from the death house, they're far, far older than when they entered. There's no life in their eyes, they don't talk much, and when the guards take them anywhere they shuffle like someone in a nursing home. It's almost as if everything dies except the body. Guards are the opposite. When an execution date nears, they get a little pep in their step.

May 5

Today I saw a campaign commercial for Fogleman. He hasn't aged well at all. There is a tremendous sense of darkness about him. It was there when he was a prosecutor, but now it seems to have grown to horrendous proportions. Am I the only one who finds it repugnant that they began airing on May 5?

In the commercial he was bragging about how many years of experience he has. Anyone who wants to see that experience in action should just watch Paradise Lost.

I must admit that I was a little hurt that he didn't mention us in his commercial. I mean, he could at least thank all the little people he stepped on in his climb up the political ladder. Seriously, folks—please don't forget to vote on May 18. Don't let this guy keep hurting people, or get away with such corruption.

Today was our first ninety-degree day of the year. The humidity is already suffocating. Summer is here. Over the past few days I've been cleaning my cell from top to bottom and throwing out tons of junk. I've decided I want to live my life as if I am leaving this place at any moment. From now on I will live in a state of joyous expectation.

MAY 2010

I don't want to be a nag, or drive this into the ground, but I do want to ask everyone one more time to vote on May 18. The Good Ol' Boy Network, which includes everyone from the West Memphis police department to the Arkansas Times, *is out there promoting Fogleman. They want to promote a man who not only helped condemn three innocent men, but has also allowed a child-murderer to walk free for seventeen years. If this is to be amended, it will have to be you who does it. If you live in Arkansas and are reading this, please turn out on May 18 to make certain this man is not rewarded for his corruption. You have the power and ability to see that justice is done. All it takes for evil to triumph is for good people to do nothing. This is a chance to demonstrate that not everyone in Arkansas embraces ignorance and corruption. This will be my last plea on the subject. Please, people—vote. Shut Fogleman down May 18.*

And by the way, has anyone else noticed that on his commercial Fogleman looks exactly like Mr. Burns?

MAY 8

Today is the feast of the Apparition of Saint Michael. Old herbal almanacs say you should collect angelica root on May 8 because it's sacred to the archangel Michael.

They say that if you keep angelica in the house it will change your fortune for the better, because it brings blessings and healing energy into the home. The fact that angelica is so beneficial is the reason it was named after the angels.

You can eat it, brew it like tea, put it in your bath water, or just keep a piece in your pocket.

It's one of the most used charms in the herbal realm, along with St. John's wort (named after John the Baptist) and High John the Conquerer (Conqueror) root. Don't eat High John, though. He's poisonous.

The day after tomorrow is another interesting day. May 10 is the memorial day of Father Damien. Actually, now he's Saint Damien. I never thought I'd see that in my lifetime. I think it's a good sign.

It's only ten more days until the election.

MAY 10

Today is the memorial day of Saint Damien. Time is passing so quickly. September is going to be here before you know it. I often feel like I'm living on faerie time. In the old stories about the Fay, time is an unstable concept. People who find themselves in the realm of the Fay may pass a hundred years in a single day, or a single day in a hundred years.

They may return to the physical world after one night in faerie, only to discover everything and everyone they knew are long gone. Or they may return after having an entire lifetime of adventures and discover they've only been gone from the "real" world for a single night. Either way, time is not the same. When I learned that my case would be heard in September, I thought, "That's not long at all." Others asked, "Why did they set it so far away?" Then again, I can feel the closeness of Halloween on the Fourth of July, and I can feel Christmas looming at the end of August.

I wanted to ask if everyone will make plans to come to the hearing on September 30 while there's still plenty of time. The only thing the corrupt politicians in this state care about is people watching them. If the Arkansas Supreme Court sees how many people care about this case they may think twice about trying to sweep it under the rug. Your presence can make a huge difference. It sends a message. If you can come, please do. We need a packed house. This is the final stretch, and things will begin to move very quickly once September arrives. We need you there, folks. Please come.

June 5

The governor has now put together some sort of committee to figure out how the state can save money on prison costs. Perhaps it would help if they stopped spending millions of dollars to keep this case covered up. They're literally spending millions of dollars in taxpayers' money just to keep from having to admit they made a mistake.

Instead of doing what's right, they'll just cut the food budget again. That's what they usually do. They reduce the number of calories each person gets per day. They've also decided we're no longer allowed to have headphones. They used to sell us headphones for about thirty dollars, and that's how you listened to music. Unfortunately, one of the guards' favorite things to do was stomp on the headphones when they came into a cell. Prisoners began filing claims in small claims court, and the guards were being forced to pay for the headphones. Instead of telling the guards to stop maliciously destroying what little property people have, the prison just said no more headphones.

That's their answer to everything. Everything is always the prisoners' fault, no matter what. I've even seen them try to imply it was a prisoner's fault for being raped by a sadistic, homosexual guard.

June 22

I've been told there's a picture of Axl Rose on the Internet wearing a WM3 T-shirt. That made my month. Everyone who knows me is well aware that I believe there never has been and never will be another band that even comes close to Guns N' Roses. There have been months at a time when I've listened to nothing but GNR. I don't even care who else is in the band, as long as Axl is singing. When I was a kid I used to wear GNR T-shirts until they disintegrated, which makes it all the more amazing to me that Axl Rose has a WM3 shirt. Thinking about it makes me smile. It feels like getting exactly what you wanted on your birthday.

June 29

Two of the men on Death Row recently had to be shipped to an insane asylum. In these politically correct times, they're no longer called insane asylums, though. They're now called "long-term treatment facilities," even though a padded room is a padded room, no matter what name you stick on it. Both men snapped and went stark raving nuts. They actually went nuts years ago, but it took a while before a judge could be convinced to even look at them. That happens all the time in here. I once saw a man go nuts and start punching the wall until both his fists were broken and bloody. They simply bandaged his hands and sealed him back up in a cell.

The law says the state cannot execute the insane or the mentally retarded, but it's still done quite often. The prosecutors just get an "expert" to testify that the guy is okay. They've killed guys who had no idea they were even being killed. The most morally repugnant execution Arkansas has carried out so far involved a man who had shot himself in the head. He only managed to give himself a lobotomy with a bullet. When asked what he wanted for a last meal, he said, "Pie." He ate half the pie, then wrapped the other half up to save for after his execution. He couldn't even be made to understand that he wouldn't be able to finish the pie after his death.

These are the kinds of things I'll remember for the rest of my life. Sometimes I think the biggest challenge in life is overcoming the urge to recoil in horror when you see the blackness that lies slightly beneath the skin of the world.

AUGUST 16

Today I received a letter in the mail from Vice President Joe Biden. It was asking for money. The essence of the letter is that the Republicans are going to take over the Senate and violate my civil rights if I don't donate money. He says that even if I can only send $5 it would help. I had to look at the envelope three times just to ensure that it was actually sent to me and I hadn't accidentally received someone else's mail. This is insanity. I considered writing back and informing him that my entire existence has been violated, but he could help by donating a few dollars to my fund. I decided against it. The last thing I need is to be on some Secret Service watch list.

SEPTEMBER 11

Every so often the wind carries the radio signal of a classic country station to the prison, and I feel like I'll lose my mind. It's like hearing the sound track to my early childhood. My parents listened to this music all the time, so it constantly filled our home. Sometimes I'll hear Waylon Jennings's voice and for a split second the sensation of being twelve years old is so overwhelming it feels like I'm short-circuiting. When I hear that Eddie Rabbitt song "Rocky Mountain Music," it takes all my will to keep from sobbing or screaming. All of that old music—Willie Nelson, Conway Twitty, Dolly Parton—when I hear it I feel like my heart is being squeezed in a fist. It hurts me beyond words, but I won't be able to stop listening. I'll sit frozen, listening and remembering, for as long as it lasts. George Jones. Johnny Cash. Mickey Gilley. It's like drowning in some kind of beautiful, velvet pool of despair. Then the wind shifts direction and it's gone again, the spell broken. I'll completely forget about it until the next time it happens, which could be several months.

September 20

There are only three days left of Virgo, and then we move into Libra. Libra is ruled by the archangel Zuriel, which I think is an excellent sign for the upcoming hearing. Zuriel is the archangel you call on when you are in need of balance, fairness, or help with any kind of legal matter. I never even thought about the fact that the hearing would take place under the time ruled by her until now. And now I'm even more excited about the prospect of a fair hearing. I really do have a good feeling about this hearing. If you would have asked me a year ago I would have said there's no chance in hell of the Arkansas Supreme Court doing anything to help us in any way. I don't feel that way now. It's nothing concrete that I can put my finger on; it's just something in the air. Maybe it's Zuriel.

In addition to the archangels of the zodiac, there are also archangels that oversee the seasons. Raphael presides over spring, Michael over summer, Gabriel over autumn, and Uriel over winter. That means this week we move out of Michael's season and into Gabriel's. Not only does Gabriel rule autumn, she's also over the cups suit in the tarot deck and is the archangel of emotions. Anytime a lot of cups cards come up in a person's tarot reading you know that Gabriel's energy is very active in that person's life.

It's nine days until the Feast of the Archangels and ten days until the hearing.

SEPTEMBER 30

Today was the hearing before the Arkansas Supreme Court. I haven't heard all the details yet, but I've been told it went well.

I'm exhausted. The guards spent the day doing their best to destroy everything in my cell. They took my books, my journal, my shoes, and left a pile of destruction behind. I was told it's because the prison is tired of me doing interviews. Every time a camera crew comes in here it's another chance they'll catch a glimpse of what goes on back here. That makes the officials extremely uneasy, so they decided to teach me a lesson. I guess they want me to lie quietly on my concrete slab while they're trying to kill me. I'm trying to look on the bright side—since I have nothing to read, I have more time to meditate.

I'm very curious to hear all about how the hearing went and what happens next. I hope the court won't take too long to make a decision. Seventeen years is long enough.

I'll write more soon. Right now I'm just tired beyond words.

Twenty-seven

The oral argument, when it finally happened, was a mob scene. I watched on the news, seeing hundreds turn out for the event from nearby and as far away as Australia. I was granted a full evidentiary hearing—after which we would be going back down to circuit court for a new trial with the old evidence and all the new evidence, without a jury, and with a new judge.

OCTOBER 5

The days are passing so quickly. This is the only time of year when I want to slow time down. I spend the entire year trying to get here as fast as I can, then once I'm here I want to slam on the brakes. I'm beginning to have those moments when the feel of autumn is so strong it drowns out everything else. Lately it's been making me think about the perfect sound track for a Halloween party.

The top of any Halloween music list has to be the theme song from the movie Halloween; *right on its heels is "Pet Sematary" by the Ramones. For some reason I've always equated the old Van Morrison song*

"Moondance" with Halloween, too. I love that song. "Bela Lugosi's Dead" by Bauhaus is an October classic, as well as anything by Type O Negative. And Midnight Syndicate. If you've never heard anything by Midnight Syndicate, look them up right this moment. If you distilled the raw essence of every spooky story you ever heard, you would have Midnight Syndicate. I have a friend who swears by them, believing them to be a vital element of any Halloween party. To finish off the list you must have "The Lyre of Orpheus" by Nick Cave and "I Feel Alright" by Steve Earle.

Strangely enough, I've already heard the first Christmas song of the season. It was the one by Paul McCartney—"Wonderful Christmas Time." One of the radio disc jockeys wanted to be the first person to play a Christmas song this year. Shortly afterward the prison forced me to fill out a form indicating who I wanted my remains to be released to.

OCTOBER 12

Rat season is about to start. There are two seasons in here: rat season and cricket season. During the summer the prison is overrun with big black crickets. Once the weather starts turning cold, the rats from the surrounding fields all come into the prison in search of food and warmth. I prefer the rats to the crickets because they're quieter. The crickets can drive you to the breaking point with the chirping and singing. It's not like when you hear them outside. In here everything is concrete, and it echoes. A single cricket in here can make more noise than ten outside. They get into the drains and crawl spaces and scream like banshees for *days at a time. When they start to die, they're everywhere. Once I was taken down the hallway and the whole floor was littered with dead crickets.*

The rats are a millions times more destructive, but at least they do it quietly. You have to be constantly on guard against them because they'll eat holes in everything. They'll gnaw your books, shred your clothes to make nests, and God help you if you're trying to save food. You can't even let your blanket hang off the bed or they'll climb it like a rope. I couldn't begin to count the times rats have woken me up by running across the bed. The guards used to put poison out for them until an inmate put it in someone's coffee.

OCTOBER 14

It's getting cold at night. The temperature has started to drop into the 40s. I woke up shivering, and it felt like the summer had never happened. It suddenly seemed like I'd spent most of my life shivering. I don't mean that in a bad way, although if you hate the cold it's probably horrible. For me it just feels like home.

I miss the snow. I miss looking at it, walking in it, tasting it. I used to love those days when it was so cold everyone else would be tucked away inside trying to stay warm. I would be the only one out walking, so I could look across the fields and see miles of snow without a single footprint in it. It would be completely silent—no cars, no birds singing, no doors slamming. Just silence and snow. God, I miss snow. The stars, the moon, the wind, and blankets of pure, pristine snow.

Have you ever seen that movie Cold Mountain? I've seen it a dozen times and could watch it a dozen more. Not only does the music played by Jack White and company make me cry every time I hear it, but the winter scenes are some of the most beautiful I've ever seen. It's so real it seems like you should be able to see your breath in the air, no matter what time of year you're watching it. Absolutely magickal. I love the stark, bare tree limbs and the ice.

Can you believe it's been over seventeen years since I've touched snow? Since I've heard that soft, comforting sound it makes as it crunches beneath your boots? It won't be much longer. I can feel it in my bones. Soon I'll have snow again. I'll stand in it and look up at the stars until I can no longer feel my feet.

OCTOBER 15

Mannheim Steamroller is coming to Little Rock next month. People have asked me what concerts I'd want to see, and the top two on my list are Mannheim Steamroller and the Trans-Siberian Orchestra. Both put on amazing shows of Christmas music that make my heart ache. The TSO is half symphony and half hair band, with all the magick of Christmas sprinkled on top. Last year the local PBS station played one of their concerts during the holiday season, and I wallowed in every moment of it. It was beautiful. The Trans-Siberian Orchestra is to Christmas what *Midnight Syndicate* is to Halloween. If I could get anything I wanted for my birthday, it would be to see either a TSO or Mannheim Steamroller Christmas show.

P.S. I just watched Dustin McDaniel's debate against the Green Party candidate for attorney general. He claimed during the debate he's not scared of new evidence being heard in my case—that in fact he's helped us by testing even more evidence and giving us the results. Yet the representative sent from his office argued during the September hearing before the Arkansas Supreme Court that the new evidence should not be heard. Is it just me, or does this sound like political double-talk to you? You can't have it both ways, little buddy.

He also said that the past seventeen years of suffering we've been put through are a testament to the fact that the system "works." Otherwise, I'd already be dead. Three innocent people spend almost two decades in a living hell while a child-murderer walks the streets, and the attorney general's office does everything possible to keep evidence from being heard—that's his proof that the system "works"? Perhaps he's helping us all to see the bright side: instead of just torturing me for seventeen years, they could have murdered me.

I will not give in to anger. If I do, then they have won. Pythagoras believed numbers held the secret to enlightenment. He devised a mathematical formula for discovering the number that represents your life's path. Using that formula, my number is eight. In tarot, eight is the "strength" card. It shows a smiling woman gently closing the jaws of a lion while it licks her hand. That lion represents all the harsh, negative aspects of ourselves we must learn to master—our anger, fear, jealousy, greed, et cetera. The woman does not tame the lion with force. She does *it with patience, with gentleness, and with perseverance. Pythagoras said that is the lesson to be learned by those whose birth number is eight. Succeed and the lion carries you to heaven on its back. Fail and it swallows you.*

Please consider voting for Dustin McDaniel's opponent, even if you're usually not a big fan of the Green Party. Every vote McDaniel does not get is a message that you do not approve of what he's doing. Dustin McDaniel is the heart of the problem. He is the driving force behind all that is wrong with this case. He will have the entire local establishment backing him. If there is going to be a difference, then you must make it. Please vote. Please send him a message. Don't let him win. You stopped Fogleman dead in his tracks. Perhaps you can do the same to McDaniel.

OCTOBER 16

It seems like the World Series is being played later and later in the year. I don't mind, for the most part. Baseball is a summer game, played when it's hot and nasty outside—which is why the play-offs have that incredibly "special" feel when you see them in autumn. It gives them a whole different aura because it's cool or cold and late at night—the exact opposite of regular-season baseball games. It causes that fluttery, excited feeling in the pit of your stomach that makes you giddy and happy to be alive. The whole world becomes simple, easy, uncomplicated. It's like you're a child again. I don't want to know statistics or numbers and records. I just like the autumn magick. That said, Novem-

ber games are just wrong. October is perfect; November is too late. Base-ball season should not be nine months long.

Someone recently asked me if there were other innocent people on Death Row in Arkansas. The answer is yes. There are two, besides me. There used to be three, but one was executed.

OCTOBER 25

Halloween is this week, and It's the Great Pumpkin, Charlie Brown *is coming on two nights back to back. They're airing it on both Thursday and Friday. Does time pass as quickly for you out there as it does for me in here? For me it seems like the month of May was just a few weeks ago, and the year went by so fast it's stunning.*

At any rate, the ancient Celtic people called Halloween "Samhain," which means "summer's end." That's because they only recognized two seasons (summer and winter) instead of the four we have today. Halloween was the transition point from summer to winter. It's also the time to honor our family members and ancestors who have died. In fact, that's why it's called Halloween. It's a shortening of "All Hallows' Eve," which is what people call Halloween. November 1 is to honor the saints, and November 2 is to honor departed family members. In Mexican culture they have big "Day of the Dead" celebrations. Catholics walk through cemeteries saying prayers for the dead while priests sprinkle the graves with holy water. The Chinese set aside the entire month of August as "ghost month" to honor their dead.

The archangel who presides over these things is Azrael. He's commonly known as the "Angel of Death," although I think that sounds a little scary to most people. Azrael not only escorts the dead to heaven but also helps the living get through the grieving process. We can also give him the emotions and states of mind we've outgrown, so that we can move forward. Azrael takes away fear, doubt, anger, worry, stress, and resentment. If it stands in the way of your developing a closer relationship with the Divine, Azrael will remove it.

November 4

As you've most likely heard by now, we're going back to court. Jason, Jessie, and I will all be there at once, and a new judge will hear all the evidence. In the opinion handed down by the Arkansas Supreme Court, the judges pretty much slapped down all the absurd jabber that Dustin McDaniel and company offered. Someone described it as a "sweeping victory" for us. Of course, this doesn't mean you'll see any actions of honesty, integrity, or sanity come from the attorney general's office in the near future. They'll continue to do as they've always done. They'll fight to defend a corrupt trial until the state goes bankrupt. The statement they released to the media says it's their constitutional duty to defend the guilty verdict. Perhaps I'm wrong here, but I thought their duty was to defend justice. Their comment was pretty revealing.

At least we no longer have to deal with Burnett. I never thought I'd actually be hoping that Burnett would win a senate seat, but when he did I breathed a sigh of relief. It boggles my mind that a community of people actually chose to have someone like that represent them, but I'm glad they did. By welcoming his poison into their lives, they have removed it from mine. The Lord works in mysterious ways, as my grandmother used to say. Seriously, though—it truly is odd how things work out sometimes, isn't it?

December 4

My thirty-sixth birthday is in one week. This will be my eighteenth birthday in a cage. It's official—exactly half my life has been spent in here. In some ways it seems like I've only been here for a very short period. In other ways it seems like centuries. It doesn't feel like I'm turning thirty-six. It feels more like two hundred thirty-six. Yet at the same time I can still remember being seven years old as if it were last week. Time is an incredibly strange thing. I think all of the most magickal things are probably connected in one way or another to the phenomenon we call time.

I've heard about the Fox News station in Memphis doing a "special report" in which they "analyzed" my body language. They commented on things like how I move my mouth. I wonder how their mouths would move if they'd been repeatedly punched in the face by sadistic prison guards. Or how it would change the way they moved if they were forced to wear chains that cut into their skin for seventeen and a half years. I wonder how they would move if they'd been beaten until they pissed blood, hadn't been exposed to sunlight in

years, and were suddenly being asked invasive questions by rude people
after a decade in solitary confinement. They have no idea how strange
and overwhelming other people's energy can be when you've been
alone for a very, very long time. Ah, well. Perhaps I shouldn't expect
them to understand. Or even be respectful. All I can do is keep moving
forward.

On January 4, 2011, Judge Laser held an open hearing in Jonesboro, and a conference call with my lawyers and with Jason's and Jessie's.

FEBRUARY 6

Today I had one of those brief flashes where I remembered what the
sunset looks and feels like. I completely gave myself over to the memory,
letting it wash through me, losing myself in it. I'm afraid that soon such
memories will be gone because it gets harder and harder to conjure them
up. It's been nearly twenty years since I've actually seen a sunset. I regu-
larly receive letters now from people who had not even been born the last
time I saw a sunset.

Today is Super Bowl Sunday. That doesn't mean much to me, even
though I can feel the energy of it in the air. It almost feels like a really
old holiday, perhaps the not-so-bright child that would result from the
mating of Thanksgiving and the Fourth of July. I'm always amazed at
how such things gradually take on a life of their own. I'm more inter-

*ested in the energy of it than the actual game. If I had to articulate it,
I'd say it's like a happy tension. It's kind of a pleasant feeling, actually.
Kind of nice. And there's not a guard in sight. They're all down the hall
somewhere, watching the game. If you ever decide to escape from prison,
you should do it during the Super Bowl.*

FEBRUARY 10

*Today I received a letter from Senator John Kerry, asking me for a dona-
tion. Much like the one I received last year from Joe Biden, this one also
says that if I don't help the Democrats they won't be able to stop those
evil Republicans from violating my civil rights. After reading it I could
only quote the great Elvis Presley when he said, "What the hell, man?"*

*Lately I've been looking back over the past year at how much I've
learned and improved. My health and strength have improved by tenfold at least. Around this time last year I was worn-out, exhausted, and
in extreme pain. I dedicated nearly all of my time and energy to improving healing techniques and mastering my internal energy flow. When I
reflect on how far I've come in one single year, I'm absolutely amazed.
This year I'm doubling my efforts again, and I'm excited to see what
will come next. I want to push myself beyond all of my previous boundaries. A great deal of esoteric work is like lifting weights—over time you
grow stronger and stronger. You get as much out of it as you put into it.
This past week I've pushed myself harder than ever before, and when I
lie down at night I immediately fall into an exhausted, dreamless sleep.*

It's satisfying, though. It's the kind of satisfaction that comes from knowing you've put all you have into getting something done.

March 21

The hearing has now been pushed back all the way to December. I guess they haven't had enough of my blood yet. And am I the only one who thinks it's strange that the state is fighting so hard to prevent any more DNA testing from taking place? Why wouldn't they want the evidence tested? The whole situation is becoming more insane by the day. In no way does anything happening here fall under the rubric of "justice."

It's officially spring. The wheel is turning again. The sun has entered Aries, and soon it will be April. The year is nearly a quarter over. How can you not be amazed by that? Sometimes I can feel time so vividly that I can almost reach out and touch it, like reading Braille.

July 10

It's been a while since I've written, eh? I just had to take a little time off. I felt worn-out and ragged, angry at those responsible for dragging this situation out for yet another year.

This time of year is always hard. It seems like July and August take longer to pass than the rest of the year combined. I'm longing for those magickal autumn days with every fiber of my being. I ache for the return of October all the way into the core of my bones. I need those short days and long nights when every moment is haunted and beautiful. I want to hear Type O Negative playing "Christian Woman" while I fill the house with candlelight and jack-o'-lanterns. I want to smell cinnamon and dragon's blood incense burning while watching The Great Pumpkin *and eating caramel apples. I want to have a Halloween party sleepover.*

July 24

Did you know that Christopher Columbus saw mermaids? In fact, he saw them so often he treated them as nothing out of the ordinary. They don't teach you that fact in your average public school textbook, but it's easy enough to find. Just research his captain's log for the date of January 9, 1493. On that single day he described sighting three of them. And in 1531 the people of a small village near Germany recorded having captured one. They called it a "bishop fish." It was male and died of starvation after refusing to eat.

My point? The world is full of magick and wonders, most of which are being completely ignored. People like to congratulate themselves for having the world all figured out when nothing is further from the truth. I've been thinking a lot lately about how so many people spend their lives in front of televisions, dismissing any phenomenon that doesn't have its own reality show as "unreal." Think about how many places you've traveled to in your car—like the grocery store. But you've never actually gotten out and explored the spaces between your home and the store. Who knows what you could find in those "familiar" places if you were to explore them?

AUGUST 1

The harvest season has finally arrived. Today marks its opening. Our next stop on the wheel of the year will be the autumn equinox. I've always seen the opening of the harvest as a kind of stairway we walk down to reach the dark and magickal part of the year where all the good things await. The cool, comforting energy that feels more like home than any place can. Today is the landing at the top of the stairs. All we have to do is put one foot before the other, and before you know it, we'll be watching The Great Pumpkin *again. And then . . . the hearing in December. If you come to the hearing, we'll be celebrating my thirty-seventh birthday together. That will be exciting, won't it? It will be my nineteenth birthday in prison.*

Twenty-eight

That's the end of my writing from Death Row. I called Lorri the morning of Saturday, August 6, 2011, and her voice when she picked up the phone was completely different. She said, "I need to talk to you about something very important." My immediate thought was that I'd done something wrong, but in fact it was quite the opposite: Lorri told me that my lawyer Steve Braga had e-mailed her the night before, requesting to talk to her before she and I spoke. Braga and Patrick Benca (the Arkansas state attorney we were working with) had made contact with the attorney general, Dustin McDaniel, and after some negotiation, McDaniel and Scott Ellington (the county prosecutor) offered to release all three of us if we pleaded guilty. Braga refused the offer, which called for my admission of complete and total guilt, period. Braga had countered immediately with the Alford plea: all three of us would plead guilty yet we would maintain our innocence. We would be released but not exonerated by the state.

I thought I was going to have a heart attack. My first reaction was to think: *Tell them anything. Tell them I'll say I've done anything if they'll let me out.* I had reached a breaking point—my soul was

damaged, and my physical health was even worse. Freedom was ter-
rifyingly within reach.

We got off the phone and a week of sheer hell began—I often
think it was worse than the previous eighteen years combined. It
didn't help matters that I hadn't really slept or eaten in days. By the
time the offer was made, I knew I didn't have much time left. I was
dying. Every day that passed made me a little weaker, a little sicker.
And I was losing my eyesight as well. If I didn't jump on this deal,
then the prosecutors would drag the case out for years—going to
trial would be a terrible gamble to take. I would never live to see
outside these walls again. I was willing to do whatever the courts
and lawyers wanted by that point, just to avoid a miserable death in
a filthy prison cell.

When Benca and Jason's and Jessie's attorneys arrived at the Little Rock office of the attorney general on Monday the eighth, they
were surprised to find a conference table lined with state prosecutors, all wearing their best suits and ties. It seems McDaniel and
company meant business. They wanted to avoid the upcoming hearing, which would inevitably have led to a new trial for us. They
wanted to put this case to rest, out of their lives for good—at one
point, McDaniel said to Braga, "Is this going to get rid of Lorri
Davis?" So everyone had turned out to make sure the deal went
down, that day. As McDaniel asked each of our lawyers, starting
with mine, for a vocal acknowledgment and agreement of the plea
deal, things began to fall apart. Benca agreed, Jessie's lawyer agreed,
but when they got to Jason's lawyer, he said they were not prepared
to accept the deal—they hadn't yet discussed it with their client.

McDaniel went berserk, I hear. He said he'd get Jason on the phone from prison immediately. Jason's lawyer said that wouldn't do, he wanted to discuss the plea in person with his client. McDaniel said he'd get the lawyer into the prison in a matter of hours that day. Still, Jason's lawyer refused, saying he had a brief at home he needed to work on. He'd get into the prison to see Jason within a few weeks. We could have been released the next day. Even McDaniel was shocked. He said, "Do you mean to tell me you're going to allow your client to sit in prison for weeks when he could be out tomorrow?"

So that was it for the day. At that point, everyone from our lawyers, Lorri, our friend Jacob Pitts, and more were camped out at the Capital Hotel, and all efforts became focused on getting word to Jason. By the night of the twelfth, as far as everyone knew he still had not responded or perhaps even heard from his lawyers. If word got out to the media, the state had made it clear the deal was off, so secrecy was a must. On that night, Lorri called Holly, the woman Jason had been corresponding with most often in recent years, and discovered that Jason had in fact heard about the deal, and he had said no.

The prosecutor wanted all three of us—Jessie, Jason, and me—to take the deal or there would be no deal. Over the years Jason had grown to love prison. His circumstances were not the same as mine. He had a job, he had befriended the guards, and was actually looking forward to the next year in prison school. Jason had also said previously that he wasn't willing to concede *anything* to the prosecutors. I understood that with all my heart, and I also knew he still believed he would be exonerated one day and walk freely through the prison gates. But his attorneys weren't nearly good enough, and the state was too corrupt to ever let that happen. In many ways Jason was still the sixteen-year-old boy he'd been when we first went in. I was trapped in a nightmare, chained to someone I couldn't even communicate with.

And Holly's response to Lorri was cavalier—she and Jason both felt morally superior to the terms, despite the fact that there were no guarantees in our future. Lorri got off the phone and called Eddie Vedder to update him. He in turn called Holly and begged her to talk some sense into Jason when he called her from prison the next morning, as he did every Saturday.

I paced back and forth in my prison cell, two steps to the door then two steps back. Over and over and over I paced, at all hours of the day and night. I couldn't sleep, couldn't eat, couldn't read, couldn't even sit still. I wept. I cursed. I raged. To see home so close and yet still beyond my reach was pain beyond articulation.

By Monday night, August 16, still no word. Lorri was frantically making preparations for my release anyway: figuring out how to get me an ID, what to do about travel outside the state, not to mention the imminent upheaval of her own life. We had talked often about what would happen if I were freed—she would have to walk away from everything she'd built for herself in Little Rock, because there was no way I could stay for any period of time in the state of Arkansas.

On the night of the seventeenth, word came through to Lorri that Jason had finally agreed. He had finally realized that I was in danger, and that we were all at the end of our rope. He also realized he was going to be left behind if he didn't come along with us on the deal. My own case had garnered much of the WM3 publicity, and if we managed to be freed without him, there would be very little interest left in his case. The funds were nearly gone as it was. During all this time, I called Lorri constantly throughout the day for updates. I couldn't eat or sleep and my nerves were raw. There was nothing that could hold my attention—if we didn't pull this off, Lorri and I both knew this would be it. We were out of energy, out of options. I found out that night, too, that Jason had said yes—and for the first time in days, I sat down on my bed.

We had no idea when we'd be getting out—only the warden and head guard knew what was happening within Varner, and any information leaked would put the media into a frenzy. On the afternoon of the eighteenth, after being seated alone in a prison office for a while, I was shackled and led outside to a van. Jessie was sitting inside and started talking immediately, as though not a day had gone by since we were arrested. He talked about the girlfriend he'd had at age seventeen and going back home to West Memphis. It was overwhelming. We drove to Tucker to pick up Jason. As he got in the van, he looked over at me and I said, "We're going home." He replied, "Yep," and after a few minutes we started talking. There were two guards up front and they wouldn't stop talking, either. They stopped at a gas station and bought us candy bars and Mountain Dews, and we sat in the backseat in shackles, drinking through straws. It was the strangest celebration I've ever been to.

We got to the jail in Jonesboro in the late afternoon. As we pulled up, one of the guards said, "Shit, they're already here." Someone had leaked to the media and there was a crowd. We were told to get down as we drove into the garage, where we were unloaded and taken into the jail. We were put in separate cells overnight, no phone calls allowed. Steve Braga, Patrick Benca, and a couple others came to visit that night and dropped off clothes for the hearing. They told me that the word was spreading now, and that Lorri, friends, and supporters from all over were making their way to Memphis that night. They told me to expect a fairly quick hearing—I'd be entering my plea, and the judge would formally accept it. I sat on the edge of the bed all night, waiting for morning.

The hearing started at about eleven on the nineteenth. I was roused by one of the guards, given my clothes and a shaving razor, and after I dressed I sat on a bench waiting for Jason and Jessie. I watched a guard knotting Jessie's tie for him. We were shackled for what would be the last time, and before we got into a van, a security guard informed us that if he said the word, we were to drop to the ground without thinking. A convoy of vehicles drove to the court-house. We were taken into the jury deliberation room, and sat, still shackled, for about a half-hour. Lawyers for all of us came in finally, as well as Lorri—neither of us has much recollection, it was so crazed. There was a separate room for family members, and Patrick Benca kept texting photos of us to various people next door—as far as I've been told it was emotional pandemonium. My mother and sister were there, though my mother sat in the courtroom throughout, giving interviews and talking to the press. My father didn't come. He sent an e-mail through the WM3 website with his phone number, in case I wanted to be in touch.

We rehearsed our statements. Originally our lawyers were going to enter our pleas for us, but at the last minute Ellington threw a fit, demanding that we accept the plea ourselves, out loud, in front of the family members of the victims, who were nearly all in attendance. Over the years, I'd corresponded with John Mark Byers, and with Pam Hobbs's daughter, Amanda. I was so tired that I hardly registered individual presences. The crowd and the noise from reporters was overwhelming as we were walked, finally unshackled, into the courtroom. It was over with very quickly. Everything went off just as we had rehearsed. I remember seeing Lorri and Eddie sitting right behind me, and then I was declared free.

Judge Laser allowed the three of us to be escorted from the courtroom, and then he spoke to the remaining audience. He said that the plea deal was a tragedy on many counts. It wouldn't bring the children back, and it wouldn't replace a minute of the time we'd spent in prison. He thanked outside forces—supporters, celebrities, and friends—for getting involved and for their enduring loyalty. When I watched the speech on tape afterward, it was the first time I believed the justice system was anything other than corrupt to the core.

Twenty-nine

I n three days I will have been out of prison for six months. It's passed in the blink of an eye. Part of that sensation is due to the shock I felt upon my release, and for weeks afterward. It's taken a great deal of time for me to begin coming back to myself. It's still not complete. Anytime I become exhausted or deeply stressed, the shock begins to creep into the periphery of my psyche like a fog rolling in. I have no idea how long it will take before I'm acclimated to the outside world again. Perhaps never.

People keep asking me what I was thinking the day I walked out of prison. The answer to that is nothing. I wasn't thinking anything at all, much like the day I walked into prison. The trauma was just too great. I had been in the solitary confinement of that concrete cell for nearly a decade, with few visitors. To be suddenly thrust into a courtroom packed with people, reporters, cameras, and action was overwhelming. Each and every person had their own specific scent and energy. It was pleasant and cloying at the same time, but it was sensory overload. Just wearing real clothes for the first time was disorienting in itself, but then you add in everything else and it felt like someone had set off a grenade in my head. Activity swirled all around me, but it all also seemed very far away.

The moment it was over and the chains were gone, Jason and I were taken straight to the Department of Motor Vehicles in a small town called Marked Tree and issued ID cards. From there we drove to the Madison Hotel in Memphis. Eddie Vedder met us there, and an aide-de-camp had set up a hotel suite for us. The first thing I saw when I walked in was a buffet table. Cheeseburgers, fries, sandwiches, salad, soup, just about anything you can imagine. My first meal out of prison was a Black Angus burger, a turkey sandwich, fries, and a glass of Merlot. I felt sick immediately afterward, but it was worth it. Eddie sat on a couch, laughing the entire time. It was just a few of us, but there was a huge party going on in the main dining room downstairs—everyone was celebrating. When we went down to say hello, I tasted champagne for the first time in my life.

That day, Jessie Misskelley returned to his father's home in a small trailer park in West Memphis. Jason and I were given a rooftop party at the Madison in the evening. Eddie and Natalie Maines sang. It was surreal. For the first time in eighteen years I stood outdoors in the dusk, looking at the Mississippi River and watching the sunset. My heart exploded, over and over. I stared at the bridge between Memphis and West Memphis for a long time. And then the night fell. I was drunk on it.

The next morning we boarded a plane (my first) with Eddie Vedder, who flew us up to his place in Seattle. It was heaven. I rested, and just spent time with Lorri. My nerves were frayed and raw. Still are, to a certain degree. And Lorri is still my only comfort.

And then I came to New York. When I walked the city streets for the first time, I was dazed. I walked out in front of cars. I stumbled over my own feet because I hadn't walked any great distance without chains on them in eighteen years. Again, it was Lorri who helped me, saved me. I couldn't truly appreciate the wonders of the city that first time because the surroundings were so unbelievably different from what I'd ever known. Only after a couple of months had passed and I returned to the city could I begin to take it all in. People still recognize me on the street. They shake hands, they hug me, some want to take pictures. I thank them all. And I'm grateful to them. After all, it was the fact that they care that saved my life.

I did speak to my mother on the phone once after my release. It was a difficult conversation to say the least. I've asked my mother and my sister not to talk to the press about me and my life, though they haven't respected my wishes. They've given false information and salacious interviews, and they appear to enjoy the attention it brings them. I haven't had contact with them because every conversation I've had becomes public knowledge immediately.

Jason came to visit me in New York a couple of times in the fall. It's hard to describe our friendship—it's a struggle to find the connection and the common ground now. We are navigating the world in very different ways, and I think of him as I always have: he is a good kid. There is a moment at the end of *Paradise Lost* when Jason's lawyer asks him if he thinks I'm guilty. Jason responds that he doesn't know—maybe. I haven't seen the film for myself and I didn't think of it over the years, but I think of it more often now. It's a moment that is emblematic of the betrayal, pain, and deceit we were all subjected to—everyone involved in the case.

Sundance, late January 2012. Even I had heard of it, inside the prison walls. Now I would see it for myself. Our documentary, *West of Memphis*, would be premiering there. Lorri and I had both been producers on it, and we would see people's reactions firsthand. We would also be meeting some members of two of the victims' families.

When we arrived we were met by Peter Jackson and Fran Walsh, both producers of the film. Lorri and I hadn't seen them in over a month and had missed them a great deal. As soon as I heard those New Zealand accents, the feel of "home" washed over me again. They have been with me every step of the way since my release, helping me. Thinking of them now makes my heart feel like it's about to burst with love.

To say that Sundance was overwhelming would be a huge understatement. It's not something I can write about, even now. I just haven't had enough time to digest the experience. I'm still turning it over and over, examining it from every angle.

I met members of two of the victims' families—John Mark Byers and Pam Hobbs and some of her family. They were there to promote the film alongside the rest of us. It was indescribable, sitting down to dinner with them all. The Hobbs family gave me a black pocket watch and chain, engraved with the words "Time starts now" and the date of my release from prison.

My son, Seth, came to Sundance. He was eighteen when we sat down together to talk outside a courtroom or prison. We're slowly, tentatively, trying to create a bond. We don't know each other, but we're learning. When we talk on the phone, I have the entirely new and foreign feeling of being a father. It's something I'm gradually becoming accustomed to, though I can't say I know what I'm doing when Domini calls to tell me about some new parenting problem and asks me to get involved. There will be more to tell, I'm sure, as time passes. I want to have a relationship with him.

Our film was one of nine chosen to be shown in other parts of the country. In January, I also went to Nashville as part of the Sundance tour. Returning was an unexpected hell for me. I hadn't been back to the South since my release. I had severe panic attacks; the fear that I would never get out of there made it hard to breathe and impossible to sleep. My temperature rose to above 103 degrees, and Lorri nearly called an ambulance. I don't like looking back at it.

The memory from Sundance that I hold dearest is a snowball fight. One night I went outside with Lorri, Peter Jackson, and Fran Walsh. It was the first time I'd touched snow in almost twenty years. It was perfect. It was pure and unblemished, and as white as the moon. And then we went into a frenzy, running wild and throwing snowballs at each other. Peter was laughing like a child, and Fran squealed in delight as she was pelted. I'll see it in my head until the day I die.

These days, I try to look forward. I'm tired of looking back. I'm tired of the case. And I'm sick to death of the "WM3." I am not the West Memphis Three, and it's a title I'd prefer never to hear again. It does nothing but remind me of hell. Sometimes it seems as if I live in a world where I have no identity outside the case. That I am the case and the case is me.

Ultimately, I know that freedom isn't enough. I'm a young man, and the only way all three of us will be able to live the rest of our lives is by being exonerated. I need the person or persons who murdered those three children, and who put me on Death Row for eighteen years, found and brought to justice. WM3.org continues to be a vital source of information about all three of us and the case. *West of Memphis* I hope will shed even more light on our struggle for freedom. My legal team and several others are working constantly on new leads, DNA testing, and investigative work, and we'll continue to do so for as long as it takes.

I want to make the world a more magickal place. To give magick a form that people appreciate, and that changes their lives. To create art that will make people want to forever reject the mundane and mediocre world they've been surrounded by. Whether my tools are the tarot, group energy work, or photography, I want to share with people all the wonder and beauty I discovered while trapped in a cell for nearly twenty years.

EPILOGUE

A person can starve to death in prison, and not through lack of food. What I'm talking about is the withering and death of the human spirit from lack of decency or love for fellow human beings. The talking heads on television project the image of prisoners as animals, and it's true. It's true because the spirit that once made them human has been starved to death, and they become a black hole in human form.

Prison is designed to separate, isolate, and alienate you from everyone and everything. You're not allowed to so much as touch your spouse, your parents, your children. The system does everything within its power to sever any physical or emotional links you have to anyone in the outside world. They want your children to grow up without ever knowing you. They want your spouse to forget your face and start a new life. They want you to sit alone, grieving, in a concrete box, unable even to say your last farewell at a parent's funeral. It's not just that things work out this way—they are designed that way.

I believe there are only two unstoppable forces in the universe. One is love, the other is intelligence. I also believe that a person's capacity to love is directly related to their intelligence level, just as hate corresponds to a person's level of ignorance. The only thing that makes it impossible for the system to destroy you and grind your spirit into nothing is to be more intelligent than it is.

In certain tribal cultures, spirit guides are represented by animals. The animal guides usher people into the next realm of development in their lives. In plain language, they make each of us grow as a person. My guide to growth is a beautiful monkey.

My wife is the single most erotic and intelligent creature that has ever existed. She can have all the poise and grace of a feline, but shining from her eyes is pure monkey mischief. She is my strength and my heart. Without her to keep me going, I would have died long ago. I have no reason to keep breathing, outside of her. She is my life.

In some ways maintaining a relationship while entombed behind these walls is like trying to overcome brain damage. When one area of the brain is damaged, the other areas have to find ways to compensate by evolving and developing new neural pathways that would never have come about under normal circumstances. In here, the normal ways of expressing, giving, and receiving love aren't possible. If you don't evolve, your relationship will die very quickly. You can't kiss your wife good-bye every morning before heading off to work. You can't hold her when she cries, or sneak up from behind with a surprise hug. There is no going out for dinner, or heading to a hotel for a weekend getaway. It creates tremendous stress fractures on a relationship that eventually cause the entire thing to crumble. When you have an argument you can't even hold hands and talk sweetly to each other when making up. You're limited to whatever emotion you can express in a ten-minute conversation on a telephone that other people are listening to and recording every word. The vast majority of people in prison find themselves alone, left behind by people who have moved on.

One of our—Lorri's and mine—greatest inventions was moon water. Another prisoner once discovered me making moon water and said it was so illogical it nearly drove him insane. For months afterward he would stomp his feet in frustration and bellow, "This shit is crazy! It makes no sense! That shit is making my head hurt!" For some reason the thought of it seemed to hurt his mind. Then again, he was a little unbalanced to begin with.

Moon water can be made only once a month, on the night of the full moon. After the sun goes down and the moon rides high, you fill a container with water and set it on a window ledge so that the moon casts a reflection in it. You must leave it there all night, so that it catches as much of the moon's light as possible. You have to remove it right before morning so that the sun's light never touches it. It must then be kept in a dark place. My wife and I did this every full moon for years, and we would take a single sip of the water at the same time each night while thinking of each other. In that moment we were united, no matter how far apart we might be. You take a single sip each night so that you have enough to last the entire month.

For every way the system attempts to separate us, we can't help but seek out new ways to pull ourselves together. In the end, hatefulness and ignorance always fail in the face of intelligence and love. The proof is in the moon water.

Hope

Immortality
And glorious nonsense
A sunburst in my brain
And plans of things to come

—Damien Echols, Varner Unit

An appendix of the Robin Hood Hills murder case and the trials of Damien Echols, Jason Baldwin, and Jessie Misskelley, Jr., can be found at damienechols.com or theblueriderpress.com. Additional information can be found at wm3.org.

ACKNOWLEDGMENTS

Without the following people, this book would have never seen the light of day. I offer them my deepest appreciation.

First and foremost, my wife, Lorri Davis. You are the reason I am still alive. Without you, there is nothing.

Thanks to Johnny Depp, who has proven himself time and again to be my brother in all but blood.

To Eddie Vedder, who has been my friend and safety net for nearly two decades now. We love you.

To Peter Jackson and Fran Walsh, the two most intelligent people I've ever encountered. What I owe you can never be repaid. When I hear your voices, it feels like home.

To Philippa Boyens and Seth Mills, you were and are always there.

To Jacob Pitts, for being what you are and doing what you do. The third leg of our tripod. Thank you.

To our songbird, Natalie Maines. We love you.

To Henry Rollins, god of punk. You never tired, never failed, and never once let us down. You were always there, and I aspire to be more like you.

To my legal team, Steve Braga, Patrick Benca, Lonnie Soury, Dennis Riordan, and Don Horgan. Thank you so much for all you've done.

To my editor, Sarah Hochman, at Blue Rider Press, who worked tirelessly to make this book a reality. Without your energy and guidance this book would not exist.

Also to David Jauss, for planting the seed and tending it in the early days.

A special thanks to Michele Anthony; Ken Kamins; my agent, Henry Dunow; and to David Rosenthal, Aileen Boyle, and Brian Ulicky at Blue Rider Press. To Gregg Kulick and Claire Vaccaro at Penguin for art direction and design, and Shepard Fairey for a beautiful book jacket. You did for me what I couldn't do for myself. Thank you dearly.

Thank you, Nicole Vandenberg, Christi Dembrowski, Josie Leckie, and Matt Dravitzki, for your ever-present work behind the scenes.

Without the following people, I wouldn't be here today: Burk Sauls, Lisa Fancher, Kathy Bakken, Grove Pashley, Chad Robertson, Joe Berlinger, Bruce Sinofsky, Anna Cox, Shodo Harada Roshi, Chisan, Kobutsu, Father Charles Thessing, Father Jack Harris, Cally Salzman, Kate Tippet, Stephanie Shearer, Chris Bacorn, Terry Reed,

Theresa Reed, Jen DeNike, Danny Forester, Danny Bland and Kelly Canary, Jene O'Keefe Trigg and Aaron Trigg, Steve Mark, Brent Peterson, Sam and Young Chico, Cotton and Ladybug Davis, Rachel Geiser, Amy Berg, Mara Leveritt, Betsey Wright, Don Davis, Marcel Williams, Tim Howard, Jason McGehee, Elliot Groffman, Kelly Curtis, Jill Vedder, Stephen Deuters, Nathan Holmes, and Ruth and Bill Carter. Thank you all so, so much.

All my love and appreciation go to Capi Peck, for taking care of Lorri and me when we needed it most. Otter Firk. Also to the whole Arkansas Take Action group. Thank you.

And love and thanks to Margaret Cho, the first person to ever take a chance on my writing.

Damien Echols was born in 1974 and grew up in Mississippi, Tennessee, Maryland, Oregon, and Arkansas. At age eighteen, he was arrested along with Jason Baldwin and Jessie Misskelley and charged with the deaths of three boys, now known as the Robin Hood Hills murders, in West Memphis, Arkansas. Echols received a death sentence and spent almost eighteen years on Death Row, until he, Baldwin and Misskelley were released in 2011. Echols is the author of a self-published memoir titled *Almost Home*. He and his wife, Lorri Davis, live in New York City.

Passing the
Professional
Skills Tests
for Trainee
Teachers
& getting into ITT

SAGE was founded in 1965 by Sara Miller McCune to support the dissemination of usable knowledge by publishing innovative and high-quality research and teaching content. Today, we publish more than 750 journals, including those of more than 300 learned societies, more than 800 new books per year, and a growing range of library products including archives, data, case studies, reports, conference highlights, and video. SAGE remains majority-owned by our founder, and after Sara's lifetime will become owned by a charitable trust that secures our continued independence.

Los Angeles | London | Washington DC | New Delhi | Singapore

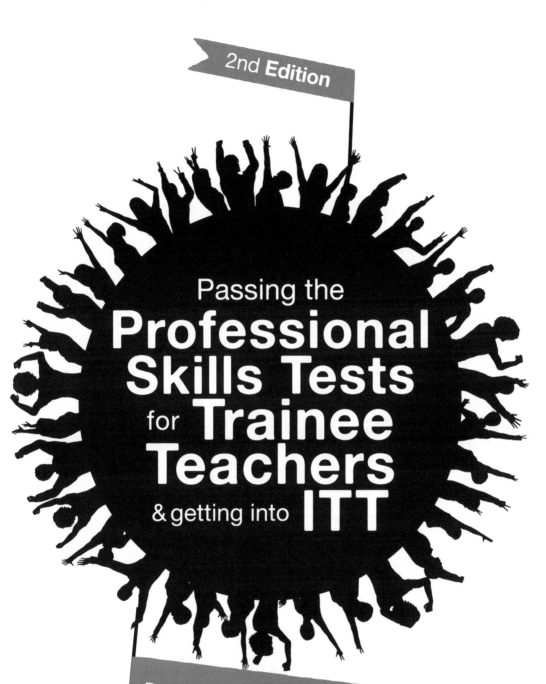

2nd **Edition**

Passing the
**Professional
Skills Tests**
for **Trainee
Teachers**
& getting into **ITT**

Bruce **Bond**, Jim **Johnson**,
Mark **Patmore** & Nina **Weiss**

SAGE | LearningMatters

Los Angeles | London | New Delhi
Singapore | Washington DC

Learning Matters
An imprint of SAGE Publications Ltd
1 Oliver's Yard
55 City Road
London EC1Y 1SP

SAGE Publications Inc.
2455 Teller Road
Thousand Oaks, California 91320

SAGE Publications India Pvt Ltd
B 1/I 1 Mohan Cooperative Industrial Area
Mathura Road
New Delhi 110 044

SAGE Publications Asia-Pacific Pte Ltd
3 Church Street
#10-04 Samsung Hub
Singapore 049483

Editor: Amy Thornton
Development editor: Geoff Barker
Production controller: Chris Marke
Marketing manager: Catherine Slinn
Cover design: Wendy Scott
Typeset by: C&M Digitals (P) Ltd, Chennai, India
Printed and bound in Great Britain by: Henry Ling
Limited at The Dorset Press, Dorchester, DT1 1HD

Library of Congress Control Number: 2015930291

British Library Cataloguing in Publication data

A catalogue record for this book is available from the
British Library.

ISBN 978-1-4739-1345-5 (pbk)
ISBN 978-1-4739-1344-8

Contents

Acknowledgements

We would like to thank the following contributors who responded to questions on applications and interviews to ITT, and shared their thoughts and comments, for the final chapter.

Doreen Challen, *Primary PGCE Tutor, Southampton Education School*
Jean Conteh, *Senior Lecturer in Primary Education, University of Leeds*
Richard English, *Programme Director for the Primary PGCE Course, University of Hull*
Suzanne Horton, *Senior Lecturer in Primary Initial Teacher Education, University of Worcester*
Angela Major, *Principal Lecturer in Education, University of Roehampton*
Ceri Roscoe, *Assistant Head of Primary Programmes with particular responsibility for the BA Primary Education, Manchester Metropolitan University*
Debbie Simpson, *Interim PGCE Primary Programme Leader, University of Cumbria*

We would also like to thank Sam Curran, a recent PGCE student, for his comments informing the student piece in chapter 5.

The numeracy glossary is reproduced courtesy of the TA © Teaching Agency for Schools. Permission to reproduce TA copyright material does not extend to any material which is indentified as being the copyright of a third party or any photographs. Authorisation to reproduce such material would need to be obtained from the copyright holders.

The publishers would like to thank the TA for permission to use the audio icon. This has been taken from the practice Literacy Skills Test on the TA website **www.education.gov.uk** and is the copyright of the Teaching Agency.

About the authors

Jim Johnson is an Honorary Fellow of Nottingham Trent University where, until his retirement, he led the English team in the Department of Education.

Working as a member of the AlphaPlus Consultancy team, **Bruce Bond** has been authoring and editing the QTS Literacy Skills Tests for over 10 years. He was also associated with the development and evaluation of the Initial Teacher Training Pilot. He has taught English in the primary, secondary and further education sectors for over 30 years.

Mark Patmore is a former senior lecturer in mathematical education at the School of Education at Nottingham Trent University. He is currently working in teacher education with other universities and training providers and also provides CPD for teachers of mathematics. After some years as a numeracy consultant for the Teacher Training Agency, Mark was for several years one of the writers for the numeracy skills tests. Mark is now a member of the Test Review Group managed by AlphaPlus Consultancy which monitors the writing of the tests.

Mark is a principal assessor for the Functional Skills Tests for a leading examination board and is involved with assessing and verifying a range of educational qualifications. He is the author or co-author of a number of publications for GCSE and Key Stage 3.

Nina Weiss has worked in the secondary, further education and university sectors for 35 years, delivering teacher training programmes and teaching English language and literature courses ranging from basic skills to advanced level. Since 2008 she has also been authoring and editing the QTS Literacy Skills Tests. Her extensive teacher training experience includes external examining for ITT courses at the University of Greenwich and the UCL Institute of Education, London as well as course leadership of the Post-Compulsory PGCE programme at the Cass School of Education, University of East London. Nina currently teaches English and adult literacy at City and Islington College.

Contributor

Geoff Barker is a full-time writer and Royal Literary Fund Fellow. He contributed Chapter 4 on *Teacher training, applications and interviews* for the first edition of this title, and has now added Chapter 5 on *What is teacher training really like?* for the second edition.

Introduction

Who is this book for?

If you are reading this book it is very likely that you are interested in a teaching career and want to know more about the content of the Professional Skills Tests for trainee teachers and how to pass them. You might currently be a sixth-form or college student considering a Bachelor of Education (BEd) degree, a university student about to finish your subject degree with a view to starting a Postgraduate Certificate in Education (PGCE), or seeking to train as a teacher through the School Direct programme. Or perhaps you are already working and looking for a change of career. What binds together all readers of this book is the desire to share your expertise with others and to inspire young people with your own enthusiasm for learning.

The good news, whatever your circumstances may be, is that you already have expertise which will stand you in good stead when approaching the skills tests. First and foremost, you will have had active experience, as a pupil or student, of an education system either in the UK or overseas. You already know what it is like to be taught and what it feels like to learn. More on this later in Chapter 1.

You will probably have read a lot – whether it's fiction, newspapers, business documents or academic papers – and will also have written clearly and accurately on many occasions when studying or at work. All of this will have developed your literacy skills. At this very moment, you will have life experience of budgeting, shopping, balancing your finances or managing a loan. All of these activities call on the numeracy skills assessed in the Professional Skills Tests.

What are the Professional Skills Tests for trainee teachers?

All new entrants to the teaching profession in England, including those on initial teacher training (ITT) and School Direct Programmes, have to pass the skills tests to be eligible for the award of Qualified Teacher Status (QTS).

Following the Department for Education (DfE) publication, *Training our next generation of outstanding teachers: Implementation plan* (November 2011), the requirements for trainees starting courses in the 2015 academic year remain unchanged: candidates are required to pass the skills tests in their final year of study (with the current exceptions for those on flexible routes into teaching). The tests cover skills in:

- numeracy, and
- literacy.

Trainees are now required to pass pre-entry skills tests in numeracy and literacy before starting their course. The pass mark for these tests has been raised to 63% and the number of resits allowed is now limited to just two.

The tests will assess whether you can apply these important skills to the degree necessary for their use in your day-to-day work in a school, rather than the subject knowledge required for teaching. The tests are taken online by booking a time at a specified centre, are marked instantly and your result – along with feedback on that result – will be given to you before you leave the centre.

You will find more information about the skills tests and the specified centres on the Get Into Teaching website: **www.education.gov.uk/get-into-teaching**

How to use this book

The first chapter in this book will help you understand the context of the skills tests and direct you to useful sources where you can conduct your own research into schools and education. Having a familiarity with key terms and issues in education will prove useful both when approaching the skills tests and also at a later date when you apply for a training place. Subsequent chapters will outline the content and structure of the literacy and numeracy skills tests and offer you practice questions. Then there is a chapter designed to support your application to teacher training courses and provide suggestions and advice for the interview process. Finally, for this second edition a new chapter 'What is teacher training really like?' offers you real insight into initial teacher training from the point of view of the student and the tutor.

1 | It's all about teaching and schools

The importance of literacy and numeracy skills

The professional skills tests... for prospective teachers assess the core skills that teachers need to fulfil their professional role in schools, rather than the subject knowledge needed for teaching. This is to ensure all teachers are competent in numeracy and literacy, regardless of their specialism.

(Department for Education, 2015)

In other words, while all teachers need to be confident in the subject matter they are teaching, they also need to be highly proficient users of English and mathematics. As professionals, teachers work not only with their own pupils but also with other members of the school community including teacher colleagues, classroom assistants, parents and governors. In addition, a teacher's role often requires liaising with external individuals and organisations such as inspectors, health workers, charities, social services, education advisors and visiting speakers, all of whom will look for professional competence. And this 'professional competence' includes the ability to communicate effectively and to work successfully with numbers.

In 2010/11 just 59.5 per cent of pupils achieved English and mathematics GCSEs or iGCSEs at grades A* to C (2012, DfE: BIS). While this figure is improving year on year, teachers across all levels and subjects share the responsibility to equip themselves with the necessary skills to help support their pupils. Teachers should encourage them to take a positive approach to acquiring what are, after all, essential life skills.

How will these skills help me in my teaching career?

As a primary school teacher your timetable will include 'stand-alone' lessons in English and maths where you will be helping to develop the knowledge and confidence of your pupils. Your training course will provide plenty of input to help you understand how children learn, as well as the fundamentals of 'best practice' when teaching these subjects. However, the responsibility for your pupils' literacy and numeracy does not lie solely within these timetabled lessons. As a prospective secondary school teacher whose specialism is not English or maths, the classroom application of these skills may not seem immediately obvious. So for both primary and secondary teachers, here are just a few examples of occasions when awareness of both maths and English are essential across all aspects of a professional teacher's working life:

Classroom teaching:
- creating worksheets and handouts for your pupils;
- labelling displays for classrooms or corridors;
- writing directly onto the board during a lesson;
- providing clear and precise explanations;
- calculating timing in order to maintain pace and cover a topic in a lesson;

- marking pupils' work and homework and providing written feedback or numerical totals;
- calculating proportions for mixing paints or materials, or for allocating resources for creative activities;
- explaining to pupils the breakdown of grading elements in public exams;
- presenting background or historical information chronologically.

Administration:
- constructing clear, timed lesson plans;
- sending clear and succinct emails;
- writing notices or leaflets for notice boards;
- producing internal reports on the outcome of curriculum initiatives;
- researching and filling in 'risk assessment' forms for trips;
- using management information systems;
- budgeting e.g. for consumable resources or trips;
- target setting, using statistics based on pupils' prior achievement;
- compiling, using and analysing statistics such as attendance figures or exam results.

External liaison:
- writing letters or notices for parents/carers;
- composing progress reports for pupils and their parents/carers;
- compiling information and liaising with other professionals such as health workers or educational psychologists;
- working with the Parent Teacher Association on planning and funding events;
- liaising by phone or email with outside speakers;
- devising a schedule and handling money for trips.

Continuing professional development (CPD) and scholarly activity
- sharing best practice with colleagues – using evidence from your own teaching;
- communicating clearly, taking notes and feeding back effectively when attending CPD at school or elsewhere;
- conducting *practitioner research* on both your own and your colleagues' classroom practice;
- writing articles for a wider audience e.g. teaching magazines, educational journals;
- pursuing a Masters or PhD programme.

Doing your homework

What do I need to know about teaching?

> *The skills tests... are set in the context of the professional role of a teacher [and] assess the use of real data and information which teachers are likely to encounter...*
>
> (Department for Education, 2015)

Depending on your experiences to date, the Department for Education information above may come as a pleasant confirmation of your expectations. Or it may provoke a sense of uncertainty and unease. Whichever applies to you, the next section of this book is designed to provide a guide to easily accessible sources which will help you familiarise yourself with typical educational contexts and 'education-specific' language. Of course you can usefully draw on your general knowledge, everyday reading and common sense, but the sources below will also introduce you to topical issues and debates in education, explored from a variety of perspectives. Not only will this research support your preparation for the skills tests, but it will also help you get ready for your teacher training applications and interviews.

As you are researching, it may be useful to create a glossary of *key terms* and their meanings. If you cannot work out the meaning of a word from its context, look at the *Talking to teachers* section below for suggestions of how to find out first-hand. Alternatively, you could use one of the glossaries available online e.g. **www.educationuk.org/global/articles/glossary**, but watch out for the non-UK glossaries which have an entirely different lexicon!

In the meantime, here are some terms which you might find useful.

Term	Definition
Assessment	An activity (e.g. a test, quiz, game, question and answer, piece of writing) which seeks to measure a pupil's knowledge, progress or attainment.
Assignment	A piece of work which a trainee teacher or pupil must complete – usually within a given time-frame and for the purpose of assessment.
Benchmark	An existing point of reference against which attainment (e.g. pupil test scores, school exam results) can be measured.
Curriculum	The set of 'courses of study' offered by a school. In primary and secondary schools this is largely determined by the National Curriculum – see below.
Dyslexia	A disorder (sometimes called a 'specific learning difficulty') which affects the ability to learn to read but does not affect general intelligence.
E-learning	A term which describes any learning which makes use of new technologies such as email, internet, online discussion forums, mobile devices, etc.
Interactive whiteboard	A display board connected to a computer and a projector, and used as a classroom teaching tool.
Key Stages	The stages of school pupils' education to which elements of the National Curriculum (see below) apply: • Key Stage 1 (KS1) Years 1–2 age 5–7 • Key Stage 2 (KS2) Years 3–6 age 7–11 • Key Stage 3 (KS3) Years 7–9 age 11–14 • Key Stage 4 (KS4) Years 10–11 age 14–16
National Curriculum	A programme of study, set by the government, which outlines what pupils need to study at each Key Stage and sets attainment targets.
Phonics	A strategy for teaching reading, based on letter-sound relationships.
Pupil-teacher ratio	The number of pupils in a school divided by the number of full-time teachers.
Reading age	A pupil's level of reading ability as compared to the average age at which a comparable ability is found.

Term	Definition
SATs	Standard Assessment Tasks. These are tests taken by pupils at the end of each Key Stage in order to assess progress against the National Curriculum.
Safeguarding	Actions or policies adopted by an institution in order to promote the welfare of, prevent harm to, and protect children or vulnerable adults.
Special educational needs	Physical disabilities or learning difficulties which make it harder for children to access education and/or learn.
Supply teacher	A teacher who is employed to cover for an absent teacher or a temporary vacancy in a school.
Syllabus	An outline of the contents of a course of study.
Target setting	The practice of setting a level of performance expected of a pupil, department or school.
Year group	The grouping of students by age – see 'National Curriculum' above.

Another thing you might notice while conducting preparatory research into schools is the frequent use of acronyms. Here are some common and useful ones to learn and explore further.

Acronym	Meaning
BME	Black and Minority Ethnic
CPD	Continuing Professional Development
DBS	Disclosure and Barring Service
DDA	Disability Discrimination Act
E&D	Equality and Diversity
EAL	English as an Additional Language
ECM	Every Child Matters
EO	Equal Opportunities
ESOL	English for Speakers of Other Languages
EWO	Education Welfare Officer
EYFS	Early Years Foundation Stage
FE	Further Education
G&T	Gifted and Talented
GCSE	General Certificate of Secondary Education
H&S	Health and Safety
HMI	Her Majesty's Inspector(ate)
HoD	Head of Department
HoY	Head of Year
ICT	Information and Communication Technology
INSET	In-Service Training

Acronym	Meaning
ITE	Initial Teacher Education
ITT	Initial Teacher Training
KS	Key Stage
LA	Local Authority
LSA	Learning Support Assistant
MIS	Management Information System
NQT	Newly Qualified Teacher
NRA	National Record of Achievement
OfSTED	Office for Standards in Education
PSHE	Personal, Social, Health and Economic Education
PTA	Parent Teacher Association
QTS	Qualified Teacher Status
SATs	Standard Assessment Tasks
SENCO	Special Educational Needs Co-ordinator
SENDA	Special Educational Needs Discrimination Act
SLDD	Specific Learning Difficulties and/or Disabilities
SMT	Senior Management Team
TA	Teaching Assistant
UCAS	Universities and Colleges Admissions Service
Y1, Y2 etc.	Year 1, Year 2

Online information sources

There are numerous places online where you can start your research into schools and teaching. These range from the more formal and 'official' websites outlining government regulations and legislation, to less formal sites which encourage question and debate on educational issues. There are also websites which offer teaching tips and resources or provide a forum for teachers to share ideas and experiences. Below is a list of sites worth browsing, but as you explore these you may well come across others to bookmark for future use.

National and local government
- *Direct.gov – direct.gov.uk/en/educationandlearning*
  This government website is designed for the education 'consumer' (pupils and parents) so it uses straightforward language to explain educational options and qualifications. It provides a good basic introduction to the UK educational system.
- **Department for Education (DfE)** – *www.education.gov.uk*
  This is the 'official' website where you can access information on government policy and strategy. The site is fairly complex and primarily aimed at those who already have a stake and interest in the delivery of educational services. There are links to articles and data, and you can find a useful A-Z of terms accessible from the home page. There is also a link from the home page to the Teaching Agency *Get Into Teaching* pages.

- **Get Into Teaching** – *www.education.gov.uk/get-into-teaching*
  Here you will find all the important information about getting into teaching, including applications, bursaries, salaries and Professional Skills Tests. A very useful resource!
- **Local Authority/Council websites**
  Each local authority, city or county council has its own website. Here you will find a link from the home page to information on local education provision, designed for residents within the local area. This is generally factual information, presented in a form which the general public can understand.
- **Legislation.gov.uk** – *www.legislation.gov.uk*
  On this government website you will be able to search under 'education' to find current and past legislation. As you would expect, this is written in fairly complex and legalistic language.

Newspapers and magazines

- **The *Times Educational Supplement* (TES)**
  The TES is a well-regarded weekly publication (in magazine format) specifically designed for teachers and those interested in education. It includes articles and features on UK and international education as well as reviews and lesson ideas. There is also free online access to the TES website *www.tes.co.uk* where you can find teaching resources, teaching forums and a comprehensive jobs section.
- **The *Guardian***
  The *Guardian* newspaper has an education section every Tuesday covering all stages of education from Early Years to Higher Education. Articles are accessible and include personal opinions from educationalists as well as journalists. These articles can also be accessed by going to the *Guardian* online at *www.guardian.co.uk/education*. In addition, there is a connected *Guardian* 'Teacher Network' site *http://teachers.guardian.co.uk* where teachers can share resources and participate in discussions on the Teacher Network blog. There is plenty here of interest to non- or beginning-teachers.

Subject associations

If you are teaching a particular subject e.g. English or maths, there is likely to be a national organisation to promote teaching excellence in your field. This will offer a space where you can share ideas, views and resources with colleagues. Here are a few, but you can try searching for others by using the search phrase 'association for *[your subject]*'.

- **National Association for the Teaching of English (NATE)** – *www.nate.org.uk*
- **Association of Teachers of Mathematics (ATM)** – *www.atm.org.uk*
- **Association for Science Education** – *www.ase.org.uk/home*
- **Association for Language Learning** – *www.all-languages.org.uk*
- **Association for Citizenship Teaching (ACT)** – *www.teachingcitizenship.org.uk*
- **Personal, Social, Health and Economic Education Association** – *www.pshe-association.org.uk*

Unions and teaching associations

The major teaching unions all have members' websites which offer information on legislation, campaigns, pay and conditions, benefits and training. They also have magazines which are available in hard copy and/or online to their members who are encouraged to participate in discussions via Facebook or Twitter.

- National Union of Teachers (NUT) – *www.teachers.org.uk*
  Magazine – *The Teacher*
- National Association of Schoolmasters Union of Women Teachers (NASUWT) – *www.nasuwt.org.uk*
  Magazine – *Teaching Today*
- Association of Teachers and Lecturers (ATL) – *www.atl.org.uk*
  Magazine – *Report*

Other websites

In addition to the above websites, there are several which offer an insight into different aspects of education. Here are a few of the most useful ones:

- BBC News: Education and Family – *www.bbc.co.uk/news/education/*
  News stories, videos, feature articles and analysis.
- BBC Learning – *www.bbc.co.uk/learning/*
  A well laid-out and accessible site with information and resources designed for students, parents and teachers.
- BBC iwonder - *www.bbc.co.uk/iwonder*
  An attractive and accessible website with information on 'big questions' in different curricular areas.
- Oxfam Education – *www.oxfam.org.uk/education/*
  A readable site which focuses on 'global citizenship' information, resources and activities for schools.

There are many teaching resources websites on the internet, both general and subject-specific, and browsing these will give you an idea of the types of materials used by many teachers. Some require you to register before using the site but most have free access to lesson plans and materials. Practising teachers make use of these sites to upload and share their own materials and to benefit from the good practice of others. Examples include:

- www.teachingideas.co.uk
- www.primaryresources.co.uk
- www.teachit.co.uk
- www.teachitprimary.co.uk
- www.teach-ict.com
- Teachers TV
  Despite its name, this bank of resources for teachers (previously viewed on the Teachers TV channel) is now available only online. It comprises a huge collection of broadcast-quality videos covering all aspects of schools and teaching, including CPD, whole school issues, job roles in schools and the teaching of a wide range of curriculum levels and subjects. The materials can be accessed via several websites but are helpfully listed and categorised on *www.proteachersvideo.com*

Talking to teachers

Using real teachers as a resource

If you want to find out more about schools and teaching, who could be better placed to provide this information than someone who is already a teacher? Classroom teachers are an excellent resource. They are on-the-job and will be able to answer your questions using their experience, with illustrative examples and anecdotes. They can also provide valuable tips for skills tests, applications and interviews.

Think about the opportunities to ask questions which draw out the type of information that might be harder to find in more formal settings:

- What made you choose this career?
- What is the best thing about your job?
- What is the hardest thing about teaching?
- Have you got any good techniques for preparing for the skills tests?
- How can I prepare for my teacher-training course interview?
- What is most useful to know before I start my training course?
- What is your number-one piece of advice to a prospective trainee teacher?

Teacher friends and family

Do you know anyone personally who has recently qualified as a teacher? Would they be prepared to spend some time with you to work through some of your questions and give you the benefit of their experience?

School visits and placements

Many teacher training institutions insist that all trainees spend time in a school before they start their course. They may give you guidance on how to find a placement. However, even where this is not compulsory, it is strongly recommended. There is no substitute for spending a period of time observing what goes on in the classroom and, if possible, 'behind the scenes' in the staff-room and at staff meetings. If you get this opportunity, try to speak to as many people as possible. Bear in mind that everyone in a school will have timetables to observe and deadlines to meet, so pick the right time to approach them. Head teachers, deputies, senior managers, classroom teachers, teaching assistants, classroom technicians (e.g. in science, technology or art) and mid-day supervisors can all provide an important perspective on the part education plays in the lives of the pupils in the school.

Although visiting a school may seem daunting at first, you will soon find that you pick up the jargon and begin to get a feel for how the institution is organised. If you are making a one-day visit, you will probably just observe what is going on and make a mental note of any questions you would like to ask should you get the chance. If you are fortunate enough to spend longer in the school then you could try to gain a more comprehensive picture of the institution and the work of the staff. Below are some suggested questions designed to help you gain a deeper understanding of what you are observing.

Questions for school managers

- How is the school day organised? Why?
- How does the school ensure health and safety for pupils and staff?
- How does the school promote equality of opportunity for all pupils?
- What kind of special educational needs do pupils in this school have? How are these catered for?
- What qualities do you look for in beginner-teachers?

Can you think of any other important questions you'd like to ask a school manager?

Questions for classroom teachers

Try to sit in on some lessons and then ask the teacher about how they planned for that lesson.

- Why is the classroom laid out in this way?
- What did you want the pupils to learn by the end of the lesson?
- Why did you choose certain activities and organise them in that particular order?
- What decisions did you have to make during the lesson? Why?
- Why did you choose the resources you used today?
- How did you check that all the pupils were learning?

Again, what would you really like to know about teaching? Think of three more questions to ask a classroom teacher.

Arranging a school visit

While schools are extremely busy places, many institutions welcome people who are interested in becoming a teacher and will do their best to accommodate you and answer your questions. Depending on your circumstances, visits can be arranged in a variety of ways, but do check the regulations regarding Disclosure and Barring Service (DBS) checks before you visit.

Your own school

Try getting in touch with teachers from your old primary or secondary school. They may be able to make a formal arrangement for you to come and spend some time shadowing them. If you are still attending secondary school, and thinking about applying for a teaching degree, you could ask to sit in on lessons with some of the younger pupils. See if you can help out in the classroom.

Your child's school

If you have a child in school, particularly in a primary school, the head teacher may be pleased to invite you in as a volunteer to assist on a regular basis with reading or other classroom activities.

A local school

If you are an undergraduate or graduate hoping to teach in a secondary school, you can apply to join the School Experience Programme (SEP) for up to 10 days. Find out more on the Get Into Teaching website at **www.education.gov.uk/get-into-teaching/school-experience/sep**

If you want to arrange your own school experience, you can use your local authority website (see above) or search via the EduBase portal **www.education.gov.uk/edubase** to find a list of schools in your area. Ring up to find out who is the most suitable person to speak to (for example the person in charge of Teaching and Learning) and then send an email directly to that person explaining your position. Do try to be flexible with visiting dates though, as there are certain times of year when schools are particularly busy. Even better, if you are able to offer your services as a volunteer, your visit will benefit not just you but the school as well.

Making the most of your own experience

What experiences do I already have?

If you are thinking about becoming a teacher, you may well already have taken part in activities which have inspired your decision. These may have helped you to focus on a particular age group. Teaching and learning doesn't just happen in formal classrooms and any experience of motivating pupils is good preparation for your future career.

Here are some typical ways in which prospective trainee teachers work with children, young people or peers before applying for their training course. If you have not yet had an opportunity to teach, some of the activities suggested below may be accessible to you:

- volunteering on youth projects or summer play schemes;
- helping younger pupils in your school with their reading or maths;
- helping out in your own child's school e.g. with classroom activities, school events or trips;
- becoming a mentor or 'study buddy' to local school pupils while doing your degree;
- leading study groups or seminars at university;
- informally tutoring family and friends;
- childminding, babysitting or looking after children;
- gap-year activities such as volunteering overseas or teaching English as a Foreign Language (EFL);
- community volunteering e.g. through Community Service Volunteers (CSV);
- volunteering to work with children in a local community group or in a religious organisation such as a church or mosque;
- employment as a classroom assistant;
- working as a youth leader in an organisation such as Scouts, Guides or Woodcraft Folk;
- supporting school students on work experience in your own workplace;
- mentoring new colleagues or running training sessions in your place of employment.

How can I use my experience?

Experience in teaching contexts will certainly help to develop your familiarity with the skills tests scenarios, but that is not the only benefit. The ability to discuss your thoughts on what makes a good learning experience will also give you more confidence in interviews and impress your interviewer. If you have not yet been a 'teacher' then you will certainly have been a student or 'learner' at several points in your life. This experience will provide you with answers to some of the crucial questions you will need to ask yourself as you become an educator. Whatever the age of their pupils or the subject they are teaching, a teacher's single most important question is always: 'Are my pupils learning?'

A useful exercise

Now – get out a pen and large piece of paper, or open up a blank document on your computer. Give yourself up to half an hour to complete all the questions below. Answer the questions as fully and honestly as possible. Perhaps answer in note form at first and, if you have the time, write it up in full. It's a good literacy exercise, too.

- How would you define 'teaching'?
- How would you define 'learning'?
- What was your best experience as a learner?
- What was your worst experience as a learner?
- What did the teacher do to make the experience good or bad?
- What do good teachers do to help their students learn?
- What attitudes do you think these good teachers have towards their learners?
- What lessons or conclusions about teaching can you draw from the answers to the questions above?

What's the point?

By answering the above questions, did you feel you started to think more critically about your own unique experiences as a student or learner? Did you consider the very nature of teaching and learning? How important is teaching to you personally? Are you motivated to pursue a career in teaching?

References

Department for Education, November 2011. *Training our next generation of outstanding teachers: Implementation plan.* Available at: **www.gov.uk/government/publications/training-our-next-generation-of-outstanding-teachers-implementation-plan** [Accessed 5 February 2015]

Department for Education, July 2012. *Introduction to Professional Skills Tests.* Available at: **http://sta.education.gov.uk** [Accessed 5 February 2015]

Department for Education: The Department for Business Innovation and Skills, January 2012. *GCSE and Equivalent Results in England, 2010/11 (Revised).* Available at: **www.education.gov.uk/rsgateway/DB/SFR/s001056/index.shtml)** [Accessed 5 February 2015]

2 | The Literacy Skills Test

Practice questions are included in all sections and can be found on the following pages:

The Revision checklist for the Literacy test is on pages 20–21

2.1 | Introduction

You need to pass a test of your own literacy skills before you can be admitted to a course of teacher education. This applies to all candidates, whether you see yourselves as having an English specialism or not. This book is designed to help you to pass that test. The necessary knowledge is explained, examples of questions are provided and answers to those questions are supplied, along with *Key points* to indicate the main things that need attention.

The areas covered in the book – spelling, punctuation, grammar and comprehension – are the ones that appear in the test. The particular aspects of spelling, etc., are also the ones that are in the test. The actual form of the questions is also similar. Everything you will be tested on is explained; examples are given and the questions give you plenty of practice for the test. The questions in the test will be a selection from the types of question shown here in each section.

Why is the knowledge of English of intending teachers being tested?

Teachers need to have a confident knowledge of English. A teacher who has a sound idea of how the English language is organised can help children to use it well. Some approaches – especially guided writing – can only be successful if the teacher knows, for example, what it is about a child's writing that makes it good and also knows how it could be improved.

Teachers receive a great deal of written information and have to be able to understand it and act on it with assurance. They often have to write, or collaborate in writing, documents such as school policies, reports on their children, information for parents, etc.

Teachers and their use of English are very much in the public eye. Parents, governors, inspectors and others see them in their professional role and, inevitably, make judgements. Teachers need to know enough and be competent enough to deal confidently with the world they move in.

Finally, the right of children to be taught by somebody who knows enough about English to be able to help them is the basis of the test and of this book.

What is the test like?

The test will be carried out online. For the spelling test, you will use headphones (multiple-choice spelling options will be available for candidates with hearing impairment). The test has four sections: Spelling, Punctuation, Grammar and Comprehension.

You will be asked to:

- type in or select your answers for Spelling;
- type in or delete and amend characters for Punctuation;

- drag and drop multiple choice options into text for Grammar;
- drag and drop options in order to: match statements to categories; complete a list; sequence information; identify points; match text to summaries; identify meaning of words/phrases; evaluate statements; select headings; and identify readership for Comprehension.

You will not be tested on the National Curriculum nor on how to teach English. You will be tested on four main sections of knowledge about literacy: spelling, punctuation, grammar and comprehension.

The spelling section of the test *has* to be attempted first. Once the spelling section is done, you must go on to the other sections and cannot return to spelling. There is no restriction on how you go about the other three sections. You can do them in any order; tackle questions within each section in any order; and move about within each section as much as you like. It may make more sense to do the grammar test last but that is up to you.

In the literacy skills test, each test has a unique pass mark, dependent on the questions that are included. The total number of marks available for each test varies from 45 to 49, again dependent on the questions that are included. Spelling has a total of 10 marks, Punctuation 15, Grammar 10–12 and Comprehension 10–12. If, as is likely, the test has 48 questions, 31 correct answers can gain you a pass.

This is what the four sections cover and how they are approached in the test:

Spelling

Teachers are expected to spell correctly. That includes the words that are likely to appear in their professional work. The emphasis on correct spelling is justified because it avoids ambiguity (for example, advise/advice; affect/effect) and is easier to read than incorrect spelling. In the test, you are expected to use British English spelling but either *-ize* or *-ise* verb endings will be allowed.

You will need to wear headphones for this part of the real test. You will see ten sentences on the screen. One word has been deleted from each sentence. Where a word has been deleted, there appears an icon for *Audio* . When you reach that word in your reading, click the icon and listen through your headphones. You will hear the deleted word. Decide how you think it is spelled and type your decision directly into the box provided in the deletion space. If you need to have the word repeated, click the audio icon again. You can do this as many times as you want, even if you are only part of the way through spelling the word, or have finished and just want to check. You may also make several attempts to spell a word but you should keep in mind that the whole test allows only about 45 minutes.

A multiple-choice spelling option is available for candidates with hearing impairment. As this is a book, not a computer, the practice questions follow the same rubric and format as the hearing impaired multiple-choice questions in the Literacy Skills Test:

Select the correctly spelled word from the box of alternatives. Write your answer in the space in the sentence.

1   As I had used the school's petty cash to buy some materials, I kept all the _____ to give to the head.

> receipts
> receits
> reciepts
> reciets

2   Teachers used their _____ judgement when selecting topics for discussion.

> professional
> proffesional
> profesional
> professionel

Punctuation

Teachers are expected to be able to read and use punctuation correctly, especially in those texts that they are likely to encounter or to produce as part of their professional work. Punctuation that is consistent and that follows the conventions makes a text easy to read. Errors in punctuation not only give a reader more work to do but can also change the meaning or create ambiguity in the text. They can also create a bad impression, especially if the error is caused through obvious carelessness. Knowing what punctuation is needed, and where it should go, reveals both an awareness of the reader's needs and, fundamentally, a high degree of literacy.

Unlike spelling, there is a personal element in punctuation. By the time you have finished the book, you might have noticed that we use more semicolons than most people. Many writers never use semicolons at all. The point is that, if they are used, they should be used consistently.

The point about consistency is such a key one that it is worth considering it here. Suppose you have written this sentence:

My early experience with the class has led me to modify my medium-term plans.

Now suppose that you want to add something to that sentence to express, however mildly, your feelings about having to make the changes. You decide to add the word *unfortunately.* That word can go at the beginning of the sentence (with a comma immediately after it) or at the end (with a comma immediately before it) or in the middle, between *me* and *to.* That is an interruption in the grammatical structure of the sentence and such interruptions are marked by commas. A common failing is to put just one comma, either before or after the interruption, but you actually need two, one before and one after the interruption, like this:

My early experience with the class has led me, unfortunately, to modify my medium-term plans.

Consistency means that you do not put just one comma in this case but that you use both. They are partners.

The test is presented online. You will see a text that has some punctuation omitted. Your task is to identify where to place a punctuation mark, change a lower case letter to an upper case one or create a new paragraph. When you have decided what change to make, double click on the word you have chosen to edit – the word before the punctuation mark – and a dialogue box will appear. The word you clicked will appear in a box. Type in your punctuation and click OK. The box will disappear and the word and your punctuation choice will appear in the text but will now be blue. To add a new paragraph, double click on the word before the new paragraph is to begin, click on the letter 'P' which is in the dialogue box and click OK. You can change your answer if you think you should.

Sometimes, although it is possible to insert a punctuation mark, it may not be necessary or even appropriate. You have to decide. What is very important is that you create a text whose punctuation is wholly consistent. Your criterion is to ask yourself what would be *consistent with the punctuation in the text*. Remember to add up your changes so that they total 15 and also remember there are only 15 correct amendments. If you insert punctuation where it is correct but not necessary, it will not add to your score nor will any marks be deducted.

This is the sort of question you are likely to meet in the book. As this is a book, not a computer, you cannot type in your chosen punctuation mark; instead, you simply note which punctuation mark or other change in punctuation is necessary at which point to make the whole consistent. There will be passages like this for you to practise your knowledge of punctuation; your job is to make it appropriate and consistent in its use of punctuation:

> *although the literacy framework had been working well some staff wondered how to maintain the good work they had done in other areas of the curriculum could drama and pe be retained at the same level as previously*

Grammar

Teachers need to be able to see whether a piece of writing is, or is not, in Standard English, the variety of English that is required in formal texts and, therefore, in almost all writing. They also need to be able to say if the text makes sense and, if not, what prevents it from making sense. Finally, they need to be aware of the style that is appropriate to a particular type of text and to understand what, if anything, is wrong with the style.

The test is multiple choice. You will see a passage that is not quite complete; bits of language are missing. The decision about what should be inserted to complete the passage is a grammatical choice. You will be shown a range of possible bits of language to insert, only one of which would complete that part of the passage satisfactorily. The choice of that insertion will depend on your reading the whole passage carefully as well as the sentence that has to be completed. You insert your choice simply by dragging it into position.

Below is an example of a sentence that is incomplete. Four possible ways of completing the sentence are offered. Your task is to choose the one that fits grammatically:

> *The assembly focussed on the current playground incidents*

Now choose one of the following to complete the sentence:

a. *that were making life difficult for the infants.*
b. *that was making life difficult for the infants.*
c. *that are making life difficult for the infants.*
d. *that is making life difficult for the infants.*

Comprehension

Teachers receive a good deal of written material that they must understand and to which they must respond. This test puts an emphasis on close, analytical reading of a passage of text. You will need to read the passage with attention to the main ideas, with an awareness of its arguments and, sometimes, with an idea of how it affects your existing ideas. You might need to make judgements about the text and to organise and reorganise its content. Since that is what being a teacher now involves, the test assesses your ability to read in this way.

The comprehension test uses a range of multiple choice style questions. You will be expected to drag and drop selected options in order to:

- match statements to categories;
- complete a list;
- sequence information;
- identify points;
- match text to summaries;
- identify meaning of words/phrases;
- evaluate statements;
- select headings;
- identify readership.

The test will present you with the sorts of text that teachers are likely to see and read as part of their professional lives. You will be expected to identify key points, read between the lines, tell fact from fiction, make judgements, etc. Not every test will examine every aspect!

At its simplest, the test might ask you to identify the meaning of words and phrases. Remember that no one test will test every aspect of every one of the four sections. In the following short passage, for example, you are asked to identify from a given list of options who you think is the intended audience for the text:

> *You will have seen from the local press, where results are published from every school in the Authority, that this school has had a consistently high standard of performance in the annual SATs over several years. This fine record is expected to continue for some years, at least. A consequence of this success is that the school is oversubscribed each year and, regretfully, it is not always possible to offer a place to every child whose parents apply to us.*

How to prepare for the test

- Use this chapter to get a good grasp of what understanding is demanded by the test.
- Go to the DfE website (www.education.gov.uk/sta/professional/b00211208/literacy) to read their advice, familiarise yourself with the test and what it looks like, and try the practice tests.
- From that practice, identify which areas you need to improve on and refer to this book.
- Remember that doing well in spelling and punctuation can take you close to the pass mark.
- Read again the Hints in each section of this chapter.

How to use this chapter

For the purposes of the test, literacy is seen as comprising the four topics detailed above: Spelling, Punctuation, Grammar and Comprehension; each of which has its own section in this chapter. There you will find an explanation of the knowledge required, examples of the features of literacy being tested and explicit direction about what to do in the test. There are practice questions for each section. Answers to the practice questions are provided in section 2.6.

Revision checklist

The following chart shows in detail the coverage of the four main chapters. You can use the checklist in your revision to make sure that you have covered all the key content areas.

SPELLING	Pages
Spelling questions will cover the main spelling rules and include words used by people involved in teaching.	29–34
PUNCTUATION	
Paragraphing	35–36
Full stop	36
Commas	36
Colon	38
Semicolon	39
Question mark	39
Brackets/parentheses	39
Speech marks	40
Quotation marks	40
Hyphens	41
Apostrophes	41
Capital letters	43

2.2 | Spelling

Introduction

10 marks are available for spelling.

If you want to write well, good spelling is not as important as good grammar or even good punctuation but it is still important. Some great writers have been poor spellers; some bad writers can spell any word they need.

Correct spelling is not a mark of intelligence but it is very helpful to a reader because poor spelling interferes with the flow of easy reading. If a text is correctly written, the good spellings will not be noticed because all the reader's attention has gone straight to the meaning. Ideally, when someone reads what you write, they should be able to pay attention to what you want to say, to your meaning, and not be distracted by poor spelling. Bad spelling interferes with the reader's attention just as a fault in glass can interfere with the view through a window.

There are no tricks in the test; you will not have to learn how to spell *phthisis* especially for the occasion. If you can spell the kinds of word that are in common use, especially in the world of education, you will have no problems. British spelling rather than American is expected although either *-ise* or *-ize* at the ends of some verbs is acceptable. However, be consistent in your use of whichever you choose.

The actual form of the test is described in the Introduction. For the practice questions in this section (see pages 29–34), a number of sentences are presented, with one word deleted each time. A box below the sentence contains four alternative spellings of the missing word. Complete the sentence by writing in the correct spelling of the missing word.

Essential knowledge

The commonest spelling problem for adults, even educated and well-read adults, is when to use a **double consonant,** as in:

accommodation	*exaggerate*	*harass*
committee	*success*	*assess*
professional	*apprentice*	*misspell*
disappoint	*innumerable*	

Unfortunately, there is no easy way to remember them. They have to be learned by heart. What does help is simply to write a good deal. If you are in the habit of writing, even brief notes to yourself to help you to think through an issue, all aspects of your writing (with the probable exception of handwriting!) will improve. As with so much in life, use it or lose it.

It does help you if you notice those words that you know give you trouble. Look at the following list of some double-consonant words and copy out any that you suspect have been problems for you in the past. When you have a list, look at each word in turn, remember the *whole word*, its sequences of letters, its prefix and suffix (if any), and try to write it again. Then check it.

abbreviate	immeasurable
acclimatise	(in)efficient
address	millennium
allowed	miscellaneous
apparent	miscellany
appear	necessary
apprentice	occur/occurred
approach	occurrence
appropriate	omit/omission
approve	opportunity
approximate	parallel
assess	passage
challenge	permissible
commensurate	permission
commit/committed	possess
correspondence	proceed (but precede)
correspondent	questionnaire
curriculum	recommend
disappear	recur/recurrence
dissipate	satellite
embarrass	succeed
exaggerate	success
excellent	succinct
grammar	terrible
grip/gripped	truthfully
happily	till (but until)
harass	vacillate

There is a special category of words with double consonants. Some stem words, like *fulfil* in *fulfilling*, end in a single consonant – that is, a vowel and a consonant – but then double the final consonant if either *-ed* or *-ng* is added. Some other words in this category are:

   commit   *begin*

Note: Benefit, benefited *are exceptions.*

Remarkably, since spelling is normally either right or wrong, you are allowed two choices for *bias* and *focus*. Both *biassed* and *biased* and both *focussed* and *focused* are acceptable spellings.

> **HINT**   Some spellings just have to be learned. Make a list of your own 'hard words'.

We spell words in English in the way we do for a variety of reasons, such as trying to represent:

- a difference in meaning, despite a similarity in sound – for example, *there, their, they're*;
- related meanings, despite some variation in sound – for example, *medicine, medical, medicinal*;

- an earlier pronunciation – for example, *knight*;
- a foreign origin – for example, *chalet.*

If the way we sound words was the only guide to their spelling, *phonics* might be spelled *fonnix.* Many English Northerners say *look* to rhyme with *spook;* most Southerners rhyme it with the Northern *luck.* But the main reason for spelling words as we do is that they **represent the sounds we speak**. This often seems unlikely but it does account for more spelling features than any other factor. Therefore, it helps to use this when learning some words that are fairly regular phonically.

Some of the words that can be learned like this are:

> *homophone*   *pronounce*   *pronunciation*   *effect*

It can help to see if a word you find hard to spell can be pronounced in a way that reminds you of its spelling. On the other hand, be careful. Some words have the same sound – in the following examples, *e* – but are written differently:

> *ate*   *jeopardy*   *pleasure*   *said*

A few words are often pronounced wrongly. *Mischievous* is sometimes spoken with an *ee* sound before the *-ous* and the speller needs to beware of that influence.

Although the sound/letter correspondence is so important in English, it still needs to be recognised that there are many **homophones**: words that sound alike but do not look alike or mean the same thing.

Learn by heart words that cannot be learned in any other way. One other way, in some cases, might be to invent a mnemonic. The student who wrote:

> *The children took too my personality.*

might have been helped by something like:

> **Two** *days ago, I went* **to** *work despite feeling* **too** *tired to get up.*

Other homophones include:

allot/a lot	*meet/meat/mete*
aloud/allowed	*pare/pear/pair*
ate/eight	*practise/practice*
doe/dough	*read/red*
due/dew	*sore/saw*
hare/hair	*wait/weight*
lead/led	*wear/where*
lent/leant	*wheel/weal*

Incidentally, although students have asked on three occasions for an 'explanation of the difference between *as* with an *h* and *as* without an *h*', this is not strictly a homophone. It is simply a reminder that the way in which any of us speaks is not always a good guide to how words are written.

Some words seem to be easily confused. Students have written:

people off all ages

instead of:

people of all ages.

Some write:

could of

instead of:

could have.

The main reason for this error is that *could have* is often abbreviated in speech to *could've*. The pronunciation of *could've* is almost identical to that of *could of*, which is a spelling error. The pronunciation of *should've*, *must've*, *would've*, etc. (the abbreviations of *should have, must have, would have,* etc.) accounts for the frequent spelling confusions of *should of*, *must of*, *would of*, etc.

The difference is in meaning in the case of *off* instead of *of* and in grammar in the case of *of* instead of *have*. *Off* is used to mean something like *movement from a position*, as in *jump off*, *take off*, *off with his head*. After a modal verb such as *could*, you need another, main, verb such as *have*, not a preposition like *of*.

Some words are best learned by heart, such as either those that look as if, by analogy, they should be spelled like another word you know or those that simply have no analogy. These include such words as:

awe	*ladle*	*rhythm*
awful	*merit*	*sceptic*
curiosity	*mileage*	*schedule*
curious	*monotonous*	*scheme*
eighth	*naive*	*separate*
fifth	*occasion*	*sixth*
half	*prestige*	*suspicion*
halves	*prevail*	*table*
heroes	*prevalent*	*thorough*
humorous	*psychiatrist*	*tried*
humour	*pursue*	*try*
ideology	*queue*	*twelfth*
judgement	*repertoire*	*unanimous*
label	*rhyme*	*vicious*

Notice that some words have a pattern of letters that is fairly consistent – for example, the four-vowel pattern of a repeated *ue* in *queue,* the *-ous* ending in *humorous*. Some words, like *prevail* and *prevalent*, not only add a morpheme (such as *-ent*) when they become another part of speech but also change the spelling of the stem word (the *i* is dropped from *prevail* as the *u* is dropped from *humour* when it is changed to *humorous*).

Some words are spelled one way when they are nouns and another way when they are verbs:

Noun: *practice*   *advice*   Verb: *practise*   *advise*

If you could say *the* before a word, it is a noun and ends in *-ice*. If you could say *I*, *you*, *we*, *they* before it, it is a verb and ends in *-ise*.

Some long words can be broken down into parts:

miscellany = misc + ell + any

You need to notice the features of each part: the *sc*; the double *ll*; the recognisable word *any*.

Some words can be broken down into smaller words:

weather = w + eat + her   *together = to + get + her*

We confess our indebtedness to a boy aged five for revealing that truth about *together*!

Remember the patterns – the sequences of letters – in words that repeat particular letters:

minimise   *curriculum*   *remember*

Remember is often misspelled, simply because of the crowded repetition of *e* and *m*.

Notice what happens when a **suffix** is added.

Just as *humour* loses its second *u* when it becomes *humorous,* so we find other changes when a word takes a suffix:

To form the plural of a word that ends in *y*, drop the *y* and add *ies*:

fairy   *fairies*   *country*   *countries*

To add *-ed* or *-ing* to a verb that ends in *-e*, drop the *e*:

manage   *managed*   *managing*
create   *created*   *creating*
solve   *solved*   *solving*

To add *-ed* or *-ing* to a verb with a short vowel sound, double the final consonant:

rap   *rapped*

To add *-ed* or *-ing* to a verb with a long vowel sound, keep the final consonant single:

reap   *reaped*

If you can develop a feel for the ways that English words are built, for their **morphology**, it will help you to see where one part ends and another begins. This can help particularly with longer and less common words and with the common affixes:

mis + take   *dis + tinc + tion*   *dis + agree + able*

It is not obvious but the suffix is *-tion,* not *-ion.*

> **HINT**   Note that the prefixes *mis* and *dis* end in one *s* only. That helps when you add *dis* to *appear* to make *disappear*: not *dissappear.*

Some words, connected by meaning – and in these cases, therefore, by spelling – vary a little in the way they sound but that has to be ignored:

photo   *photograph*   *photographer*   *photographic*

The letters *sc* represent the *s* sound if the following letter is *e* or *i*:

discipline   *adolescent*   *descent*

On the other hand, they represent the *sk* sound if the following letter is *r, l, a, o, u*:

discrepancy   *discussion*

When do you write *ie* and when do you write *ei*? This rule works:

For the sound *ee*, put *ie* as in:

believe   *mischief*   *niece*

For the sound *ee*, put *e* before *i* when the preceding letter is *c*:

conceive   *deceive*   *receive*

However, this only applies to words where the sound is *ee* and not to words like:

weight   *forfeit*   *friend*

Many people ignore that last part of the rule.

> **HINT**   *i* before *e*, except after *c*, when the sound is *ee*.

Most words that end with the sound in *rec**ent*** use *-ent*:

confident   *emergent*   *equivalent*   *excellent*
impatient   *independent*   *prevalent*   *reminiscent*

Very few words use *-ant*:

    preponderant   *quadrant*   *redundant*

> **HINT** Since far more words end in *-ent or -ence*, it pays to focus on and learn any that end in *-ant* or *-ance*.

A very common error is to use the wrong letters to represent the vowel sound in *sir*. Words like these just have to be learned by heart:

    pursue   *separate*   **bird**   *word*

The sound *s* is often written with a *c*, especially if the *c* is followed by an *e* or *i*, as in:

    concede   *deficit*   *necessary*

Sometimes, it is written with a *-ce*, especially at the end of a word:

    practice   *prejudice*

Sometimes, it is written with an *s*, even when it is not expected:

    idiosyncrasy   *consensus*   *supersede*

Or with an *-se*:

    practise   *premise*

And even with *-sc*:

    miscellaneous *miscellany*   *scene*

General tips

Keep a dictionary nearby to check problem words and then try to learn them. Look out for commonly used letter-strings, for affixes and other morphological features and simply for anything unusual.

See if you tend to make particular errors, such as not noticing that *separate* has an *a* in the middle or that *develop*, unlike *envelope*, does not end with an *e*.

Try sounding out. On the whole, words that are phonically regular do not cause spelling problems but some writers lose their faith in that regularity. Try it.

Look at the whole of a word, not just its individual letters, and try to remember that whole. If it helps, say the letters to yourself rhythmically.

Look for possible analogies, for example, *eight*, *height* and *weight*.

Pay special attention to the letter-strings in foreign words. Their foreignness includes their combining letters differently from English:

fjord   craic   khaki   macho   *graffiti   Pilsner*   *cha siu*

Do not trust the spell check on a word processor. Any spell check will allow *top* when you meant *to*, *were* when you meant *where* and *feather* when you meant *father.* A spell check will correct non-words, like *teh* when the writer intended *the*, but it is still necessary to read through a late draft to check the spelling yourself.

If you know which words you tend to get wrong when you use a word processor *(have* and *because*, in my case!), go to *Tools*, *Autocorrect* and type in both the way you regularly type them (wrongly) and also the correct way. The processor will then automatically correct your spelling. But remember that this does nothing for your own ability to spell!

Questions

In the Literacy Skills Test you will be asked to spell ten words. These will be examples of words that are most likely to be encountered within the professional context of teaching. They represent the vocabulary, and its correct spelling, that fellow professionals, parents and pupils would expect every teacher to know.

All the words below are in general use; some follow generic spelling rules and some are spellings that just have to be learned by heart.

Select the correctly spelled word from the box of alternatives. Write your answer in the space in the sentence.

1. Annie enjoyed doing so much _____ work on her Charlemagne Extended Project Qualification.

indipendent
indipendant
independent
independant

2. The group had made _____ progress with their task.

demonstrible
demonstratable
demonstrable
demonstreble

3. Some useful _____ resources can be found on the internet.

asessment
assessmant
asesment
assessment

Questions

4. Research shows there is a marked increase in creativity during _____.

adolescence
adolescents
adolesence
adolesensce

5. Pupils were encouraged to _____ their own reading topics.

persue
purrsue
parsue
pursue

6. Most of the class found the _____ in the school's production of *A Midsummer Night's Dream* quite unconvincing.

fairys
faries
fairies
fareys

7. _____ ingredients in Home Economics assessed the pupils' numeracy skills.

Weighting
Wieghing
Weighing
Waying

8. The prospect of visiting the coast _____ the pupils' enthusiasm for the project.

fuelled
feulled
fueled
fuled

9. Some of the pupils were deeply _____ by the contents of the diaries.

effected
afected
efected
affected

Questions

10. Two posts offering greater _____ were being advertised in the school.

   responsability
   responserbility
   responsibility
   responsebilty

11. Most pupils found the _____ tests *very* helpful.

   practise
   practiss
   practisce
   practice

12. The experiment proved that substances do not _____ when they dissolve.

   disapear
   dissappear
   disappear
   disappeare

13. Field trip regulations include strict regulations about the _____ of knives.

   possession
   posession
   possesion
   possessions

14. It proved _____ to move the whiteboard just for one meeting.

   impracticible
   unpracticible
   impracticable
   unpracticable

15. The class responded well to the range of _____ poems their teacher presented.

   humouros
   humorous
   humourous
   hummorous

Questions

16. The small sample shows how percentages can give an _____ impression.

   exagerated
   exaggarated
   exagarated
   exaggerated

17. _____ the heavy snow meant that the school concert had to be postponed.

   Regretably
   Regrettably
   Regrettebly
   Regreatably

18. Some left-handed pupils _____ write across the page from right to left.

   automaticly
   autimatically
   automaticaly
   automatically

19. The conference addressed new approaches to _____ delivery.

   curiculum
   curriculum
   curicullum
   curicculum

20. Some pupils may not admit to problems with mathematics due to _____.

   embarassment
   embarrasment
   embarrassment
   embarasment

21. Teachers need a sound knowledge of their subject areas and related _____.

   pedergogy
   pedogogy
   pedagogy
   pedagogey

Questions

22. Pupils are _____ to attend school in casual clothing on Own Clothes Day.

aloud
allowed
alowed
aloued

23. When he came to _____ art materials among the children he was working with, Joe found that he had miscounted.

alot
a lot
alott
allot

24. The junior school choir sang with a _____ that was beyond their age.

maturity
maturaty
matturity
maturety

25. Support and _____ are key parts of the anti-bullying policy.

counciling
counselling
counsiling
councelling

26. What had once seemed a _____ collection of options now seemed very logical.

miscellanious
miscellaneous
missellanious
miscelanious

27. My answer to the question about death rates in Napoleon's army had to be an _____.

aproximation
approximation
approximacion
approcsimacion

33

Questions

28. It was clearly _____ of me to be late for the exam.

reprehensable
repprehensable
repprehensabel
reprehensible

29. Irina spent weeks discussing whether a degree or an _____ would suit her better.

apprenticeship
aprenticeship
aprentiship
aprentiseship

2.3 | Punctuation

Introduction

15 marks are available for punctuation. That is almost halfway to the pass mark.

Punctuation has often been undervalued yet its importance in conveying your meaning to a reader clearly and unambiguously is great. Poor or missing punctuation can lead to the reader getting a quite false impression, as in:

After we left the pupils, the parents and I went to meet the headteacher.

if what you meant was:

After we left, the pupils, the parents and I went to meet the headteacher.

In the second sentence the comma changes the meaning so that it is clear that the pupils also went to meet the headteacher.

A literate teacher may need to check his or her spelling often but is, by definition, able to use punctuation well.

The aspects of punctuation in the test are concerned with ways in which writers mark off *units of meaning* (such as a sentence), ways in which the actual status of the language being used is clarified and ways in which words themselves are punctuated.

The main ways of marking 'units of meaning'

Any text is made up of parts: the whole text, the paragraphs, the sentences, the clauses and the phrases. These are the units of meaning greater than the individual word. The main ways in which we mark off where one unit ends and another begins are:

- paragraph;
- full stop;
- comma.

None of these is straightforward; all are partly a matter of personal style. Consequently, the key is to be consistent with punctuation within any one text.

Paragraphing

A paragraph is a group of one or more sentences that have enough related meaning, enough similarity in content or topic, to form a group. The writer decides where to begin and end each paragraph, depending on how he or she regards the main groups of meaning. A good text is divided along consistent lines, following the same idea about what makes a chunk of meaning, and one sentence within the paragraph states the main idea. This is the topic sentence; it often comes first.

Good paragraphing also makes considered use of sentence adverbs, those connectives, such as *However*, *Furthermore*, *On the other hand*, *Fortunately*, etc., that link the meaning of the new paragraph to the previous one.

However, the choice of where to start a new paragraph can sometimes be very subjective. The main reason is to show when a writer is:

- switching to a new idea;
- highlighting an important point;
- showing a change in time or place;
- emphasising a contrast; or
- indicating progression toward a summary or conclusion.

The test might show you a text that could have paragraphs but that is printed without any; you might be asked to identify where paragraph boundaries could come.

> **HINT**   If you are uncertain about inserting a paragraph break, check the number of definite punctuation omissions you have already amended. Remember, there are only 15 unequivocally missing pieces of punctuation. If you have made 14 changes and cannot see another obvious omission, apart from the need for a paragraph break, this is probably the fifteenth instance where punctuation is needed.

Full stop

Full stops define a sentence, literally, by showing its limit. You need to develop a sense of what a sentence is to use full stops properly. If the largest unit of meaning is the unbroken, complete text and the next largest is the paragraph, the largest below that is the sentence. As a rule, it is one or more clauses long, has a sense of relative completeness about it and usually has a verb and its subject.

Over 80 per cent of all the punctuation marks used in British English are full stops and commas.

> **HINT**   To help you to get a better grip of sentences and their need for a final full stop, look at *Clause*, *Sentence* and *Verb* in the Glossary. Keep that in mind as you read about commas.

Commas

It is not a simple task to use commas well. The first and simplest guidance is:

if you are not sure whether to use a comma or a full stop, use a full stop and begin a new sentence.

It was just what I had been looking for, from my experience with the previous class I felt a need for children who wanted to learn.

should be:

It was just what I had been looking for. From my experience with the previous class, I felt a need for children who wanted to learn.

Commas help us to separate items in a list. They can, therefore, be used as an alternative to the word *and* but not as well as *and*:

Above all, Zeinab likes to teach maths, geography, art and history.

You do not need a comma after *art* because *and* here does the job of a comma. This could be written using *and* instead of a comma:

Above all, Zeinab likes to teach maths and geography and art and history.

Sometimes, we use a phrase or word at the beginning of a sentence and then start to write what we mean.

The sentence above is an example: it begins with *sometimes* and then continues with the subject of the sentence, *we*. Put a comma after that opening word or phrase before continuing with what you want to say. Apart from that *sometimes*, other common **sentence-openers**, or sentence adverbs, are:

On the other hand,
However,
Suddenly,
Next,
Instead,
Unfortunately,

Sometimes, we want to vary what we say by changing the order in which we say things. This might be because we want to *emphasise* something or other:

My last tutor asked if he could copy my maths plans because he felt that they were a good model.

This could be turned round without changing, adding or omitting any words but by adding a comma at the break:

Because he felt that they were a good model, my last tutor asked if he could copy my maths plans.

This is a rather tricky use of the comma. It can be important because it tells the reader precisely what the meaning is. The use of commas can put an end to *ambiguity*. This comma-free sentence is ambiguous:

The teachers who live in Gotham are all over six feet tall.

As it stands, this seems *very* improbable. But suppose the sentence is just about a group of people over six feet who simply happen to live in Gotham. That is more than probable. The fact that they live in Gotham is almost an afterthought. The essence of the sentence, the main clause, is:

The teachers are all over six feet tall.

Now, an extra, incidental bit of information is given. It is a relative clause:

who live in Gotham

This extra clause can be **embedded** in (set inside) the main clause. To show that it is extra, it is separated from the rest by commas:

The teachers, who live in Gotham, are all over six feet tall.

(This use of the embedded clause is a sophistication that the devisers of the Primary National Strategy wanted to see promoted in schools.)

Not only clauses are embedded. We embed phrases and single words. They may appear at the beginning of a sentence (see the opening sentence adverbs above), in the middle or at the end. Children can be helped by having a discussion about what to embed in a sentence (if anything) and where in the sentence the embedded item might go:

Naturally, the choice of where to apply was rather limited.

or:

The choice of where to apply was rather limited, naturally.

or:

The choice of where to apply was, naturally, rather limited.

The embedded item is bounded by a capital letter and a comma at the beginning of the sentence, by a comma and a full stop at the end and by two, paired commas in the middle.

When we write *dialogue*, a comma ends the text before the quotation marks and the spoken words begin:

Gobinda said, 'Come along with me, children.'

What commas cannot do is end a sentence.

Additional ways of marking 'units of meaning'

These additional ways are the use of:

- colon;
- semicolon;
- question mark;
- brackets.

Colon

The commonest use of the colon is to introduce a list:

The children brought a wealth of evidence from the playground: sweet wrappers, milk straws, cards to swap, crisp packets and some cigarette packets.

Another use is to introduce some reasoning or evidence to support the part of the sentence that comes before the colon:

> *Some of them blamed the secondary school children: they reminded the class that several teenagers regularly took a short cut across their playground.*

Semicolon

The semicolon is rarely used in the writing of many people; not only students and teachers but some of our greatest writers ignore this mark. It is possible to write without using it but it can allow a writer to put two independent clauses together that could stand as individual sentences but that the writer feels are unusually closely related. This book contains examples in its text.

Another use of the semicolon is to mark off items in a list following a colon, especially if the items in the list are each several words long:

> *The school still had some problems: a falling roll; two teachers due to retire within the year; an imminent Ofsted inspection.*

However, commas can also do that job. Be careful: if one of those items has so many words that the phrase itself needs a comma, all the items must be separated by a semicolon.

Question mark

This mark ends a sentence that asks a question:

> *Is your personal statement nearly ready?*

> *Will we need supply cover for next Tuesday?*

It is not necessary at the end of a sentence that implies a question but that has the structure of a statement (that is, the subject comes before the verb):

> *I wonder if there will be any supply teachers available.*

> *I asked him when he would be ready for swimming.*

If the sentence is within quotation marks, the question mark comes before the final quotation mark:

> *'Can we get together about this Performance Management meeting?'*

> *'Could you tell me why your assignment is 3,000 words over the limit?'*

Brackets or parentheses

These marks (the two words really mean the same) begin and end an aside in a sentence. Often, a writer composes a sentence but wants to add something to it that is not strictly part of the sentence; rather, it is almost an afterthought or something that he or she would like to say as well as the sentence:

Not many of us (at least, not those under 60) can remember what it was like to teach in those controversial times.

We have had no child statemented (none that we were successful in having statemented, anyway!) for over five years now.

HINT   Look at *Parenthesis* in the Glossary.

Punctuation which indicates the status of the language being used

The status of the language being used is shown by the use of:

- speech marks;
- quotation marks.

Speech marks (double quotes) and quotation marks (single quotes) can help you to make it clear to the reader that this or that piece of your writing is to be read in a particular way. Both can be, and are, in some published texts, used to mark **direct speech**, such as the dialogue in a story.

A teacher might write a story with a class. Any dialogue, words actually spoken by a character, will need to be put inside **speech marks**:

When Fergus the king asked Nes to be his wife, she replied, "Only if I get something in return."

"What is that?" he asked.

Quotation marks can be used for the same purpose but they are valuable in their own right. They can draw the reader's attention to the way that some word or phrase sits oddly in the text as a whole:

When buying travel insurance for their children, parents and carers are advised to be mindful of the so-called 'get out clause' used by some insurance firms.

They help the reader to see that a part of the text actually comes from some source other than the writer:

Song asked his teacher for help with his exposé but was told to 'just get on with it'.

They tell the reader that some of the text is the name of a film or the title of a book:

Shamila started to read 'Harry Potter and the Goblet of Fire' but the spiders scared her so she stopped.

> **HINT** Parentheses, speech marks and quotation marks all work in pairs. If the test shows just one parenthesis or speech/quotation mark, you know that there has to be another. Look for where it might be.

Punctuation within words

The marks that occur within single words are:

- hyphens;
- apostrophes;
- capital letters.

They give the reader information about that word, rather than showing how larger units of meaning are organised or bounded.

Hyphens

Hyphens link two words that have another meaning when they occur together. Some of the first elements are words in themselves, others are abbreviations or suffixes:

well-stocked, ex-headteacher, post-Ofsted, pro-uniform, U-turn, T-shirt

This sort of hyphenated word is a kind of halfway point between two words and one.

Apostrophes

The apostrophe, a minefield for some writers, has two main uses but is sometimes wrongly used for a third purpose.

Abbreviation or omission

When we write, we sometimes choose to leave letters out of words to get closer to the way we speak English. Because we rarely sound the full value of *we will, we do not, we shall not, we cannot*, we may abbreviate them:

we'll, don't, shan't, can't

One of the trickiest of these abbreviations is the use of *it's*, easily confused with *its*. The solution is simply never to write *it's*. *It's* is always an abbreviation, usually of *it is* but sometimes of *it has*. Abbreviations are normal in informal writing but unknown in formal texts. Only use *it's* when you mean to write an informal text and when you mean either *it is* or *it has*:

It's appropriate to write formally.

means the same as:

It is appropriate to write formally.

It's become obvious that clear writing matters.

means the same as:

It has become obvious that clear writing matters.

You will then write *its* only without an apostrophe and only when it is appropriate: as the direct equivalent of *her* or *his* before a noun:

The new teaching assistant put down her bag, helped Nathan out of his wheelchair and covered its seat with a cushion.

Only use the apostrophe as abbreviation when you feel quite confident and in control as a writer.

> **HINT** Never write *it's*. Write *it is* or *it has* instead and you can forget that apostrophe problem.

Possession

Books have titles. Write down who or what *possesses* the titles:

the book

then put an apostrophe:

the book'

and ask: does this word end with the letter *s*? If not, add one:

the book's

and continue:

the book's title.

If there are several books, you would have the sequence:

the books

then put an apostrophe

the books'

and ask: does this word end with the letter *s*? If it does, leave it alone:

the books'

and continue:

the books' titles.

There is no need to think about singular or plural provided you place the apostrophe before you check if the word ends in *s* or not. Of course, the way this works means that, in most cases, the placing of the apostrophe does say whether the word before is singular or plural but that does not always help. If men have ambitions and you want to write about that affliction, the singular and plural – *man* and *men* – would look like this:

the man	*the men*
the man'	*the men'*
the man's	*the men's*
the man's ambitions	*the men's ambitions*

The wrong use of the apostrophe plus *s* as a plural form

The sight of cards on market stalls saying *Cabbage's* and *Cauliflower's* (and *Ca'fe* in one town) has led to the rather unfair name of *Greengrocers' Apostrophe* for this wrong use of *'s* instead of the simple plural 's'.

There is a special, and wrong, case of the apostrophe-as-plural that goes far beyond the efforts of any greengrocer. We now have quite a few words in English that end with a vowel, especially *o*: *video, studio, radio, data, scampi, criteria*, etc. Some people add *'s* to these words to indicate a plural: *video's*, etc. There is no need. For most of these words, simply add *s* (the commonest way of making plurals in English). In the case of *data* and *media* and *criteria*, these words are already plural; there is no need to add anything to them at all. However, you can only have one criterion and many criteria and one medium being part of the media.

Capital letters

A capital letter is always needed at the beginning of a new sentence:

Only in my wildest dreams could I have succeeded in obtaining a place on such a course.

It is needed for titles and proper nouns: the names of people and places:

The letter from the Headteacher, Mrs Pendlebury, welcomed me to Ordsall.

There is no need to use a capital for *headteacher* if there is no name to follow.

Questions

Like all the tests, this one is computerised. Details of what you do in the test and how you do it are on page 20, but it will also help you a lot to look at the website http://media.education.gov.uk/assets/files/pdf/l/literacy%20skills%20test%20specification.pdf. If you want to change anything, that can be done. You will not need to delete any punctuation.

The test will present you with a text from which much of the punctuation has been deleted. Your task is to create a properly punctuated complete text from this incomplete one. The key thing, again, is consistency: read the text and its existing punctuation as information about how to complete it. Remember, there are only 15 omissions of punctuation in the test.

Questions

The passages below are examples of the kind of test you will have.

Since you are doing this test in a book and not on a computer, read the whole passage and add any punctuation you feel is necessary in pencil or by making a note. Where you want to change a lower case to a capital letter, put a circle round the letter and write *cap* in the margin; where you want a new paragraph, put a forward slash (/) immediately before the first word of the new paragraph and write *np* in the margin.

1. As soon as we speak we reveal a great deal of ourselves to our audience. Suppose you ask someone,

    "shall we have a drink

    Suppose the other person replies

    "Yes, I'd like a whiskey me."

    That tag, *me*, tells you that the speaker probably comes from manchester.

    Sometimes, what people say does tell you something about their origin but it is less definite. A friend asks you and another friend,

    "Now, what would youse two like to drink?"

    The questioner may or may not come from Ireland but will certainly have a background there because that use of youse, unknown in standard English, has its roots in the Irish having one form of 'you' for one person tú and another form of 'you' for two people sibh. However none of this means that any of these speakers could actually speak any Irish!

2. The concern of the head of english was evident after reading the Can do Better' report on literacy. If we look at boys performance in English, we have to agree that there is, generally some cause for concern. Is there anything that can be done to help them improve?

    Among the short term approaches that seemed to help boys are

    enthusiastically encouraged private reading;

    clearly set tasks

    explicit teaching of reading strategies;

    a wide range of outcomes from reading;

    reading preferences that are discussed.

3. What is it about Standard English that makes it standard Like every language, English has gone through many changes. The Saxons and Angles who settled here brought their own languages with them predominantly Saxon, and

after a while the dialects of Anglo-Saxon overcame the Celtic languages that had flourished along with Latin until soon after the Romans left in 410 AD. The languages spoken by the later Scandinavian invaders were probably just about intelligible to some of the Anglo Saxons but changes and borrowings continued: the new invaders legacy to us includes **they, them, their**. Anglo-Saxon, modified by Scandinavian, with dialects that were barely intelligible to other Anglo-Saxon speakers, continued for hundreds of years but, thankfully it became simpler The German word for **big** is **gross** but it has six versions. Our Anglo-Saxon ancestors had eleven versions of adjectives we have just three: **big, bigger, biggest**. Even when we complicate matters by having **good, better best,** that is still easier than Anglo-Saxon.

2.4 | Grammar

Introduction

8–12 marks are available for grammar.

One of the main jobs of a teacher is to work with colleagues in producing documents for a variety of audiences, from known people within the school to outside bodies, and for a range of purposes, from planning teaching to explaining and presenting work that has been done. That collaboration involves drafting, redrafting and proof-reading. This test does not test your writing nor your knowledge of grammatical terms; rather, it will test:

- **your grasp of written Standard English;**
- **your ability to identify and use it unambiguously;**
- **your understanding of which style is appropriate to the text in question.**

How will these three aspects of grammatical knowledge be tested? What, in detail, do those aspects mean you need to know?

The grammar section of the test presents you with two or three short pieces of text. The text is usually an example of the everyday reading or writing material that a teacher might be expected to encounter in the course of their professional duties. Such texts might include:

- notes or letters to parents and carers;
- notes or letters to or from colleagues;
- minutes of meetings;
- information about training and professional development;
- articles for school newsletters or websites.

Within the document there are gaps in the text. At these points there is a question with multiple choices. Four options are provided as possible alternatives to fill the gap; only one is correct. The three remaining distracters contain faults and are incorrect. People who already use English competently and with confidence would not make such faults and would notice them in the writing of other people or, perhaps, in an early draft of their own work.

The items of grammatical knowledge that will be tested are set out and explained below.

Consistency with standard written English

Each test presents you with some examples of English; only one example is acceptable as Standard English. You have to choose and identify that one. To be able to do that, you need to have an awareness of what kinds of error are possible, of the features of non-Standard English and of the appropriate, standard alternative.

This is the list of features of non-standard English that the test covers:

- failure to observe sentence boundaries;
- abandoned or faulty constructions and sentence fragments;
- lack of cohesion;
- lack of agreement between subject and verb;
- should have/of, might have/of;
- inappropriate or incomplete verb forms;
- wrong or missing preposition, e.g. different from/than/to;
- noun/pronoun agreement error;
- determiner/noun agreement error;
- inappropriate or missing determiner;
- problems with comparatives and superlatives;
- problems with relative pronouns in subordinate clauses;
- inappropriate or missing adverbial forms.

Failure to observe sentence boundaries

Perhaps the commonest failing in adults' writing is this problem with deciding where a sentence ends and needs a full stop (see section on punctuation). Be very wary of sentences that go on and on. It is very easy to ignore that length and, worse still, the complexity that falls into the sentence as it develops. It is far better to write more sentences, varying in complexity, with some short, simple, one-clause sentences among them. For example:

It was my great opportunity, from my experience with the previous class I knew how to make the most of the first group's ideas.

Should be:

It was my great opportunity. From my experience with the previous class, I knew how to make the most of the first group's ideas.

Look at 'Comma' in the section on punctuation. Generally, unless you know you can write well, do not be too ambitious as a stylist. Your writing is more likely to be sound standard English if you follow the advice about short sentences. If you are not sure whether it should be a comma or a full stop, put a full stop. In most cases, you will be safe.

HINT Use full stops more often.

Abandoned or faulty constructions and sentence fragments

A sentence should use consistent structures. It is very easy, especially if you write slowly, to lose track of the way you are writing, the structures you are using. The best way to avoid this problem is to reread what you write as you write and, particularly, to look out for any faults that you know you are prone to. Usually, the way that you begin the sentence is the way it should continue.

This is a faulty construction:

Concerned about the falling numbers in the city's schools so the Director of Education proposed that two primary schools should be closed and one re-opened as a junior school.

It should be either:

Concerned about the falling numbers in the city's schools, the Director of Education proposed that two primary schools should be closed and one re-opened as a junior school.

or:

The Director of Education proposed that two primary schools should be closed and one re-opened as a junior school because he was concerned about the falling numbers in the city's schools.

or:

Because he was concerned about the falling numbers in the city's schools, the Director of Education proposed that two primary schools should be closed and one re-opened as a junior school.

This is a sentence fragment:

Although there was still uncertainty about the best choice of software.

This has obviously become separated from the sentence of which it should be a part. In a sense, this is the other side of the previous problem with sentence boundaries: this time, the writer has probably put in an unnecessary full stop that cuts this fragment off from the rest. The whole sentence might have looked like this:

Although there was still uncertainty about the best choice of software, the Governors decided to go ahead with the purchase of new computers.

Here, the full sentence is given and the whole is much easier to grasp. The word 'sentence' is notoriously difficult to define but those criteria of completeness and comprehensibility are central.

An alternative to that whole sentence would be:

The Governors decided to go ahead with the purchase of new computers although there was still uncertainty about the best choice of software.

It is worth noting here, as in some other examples in this book, that there are often at least two ways to structure a sentence, often with little or no change to the words themselves. What has been altered here in the two acceptable alternatives is the sequence of the two clauses and the punctuation: if the minor (subordinate or dependent) clause comes first, separate it from the following main clause with a comma.

> **HINT** Get into the habit, when you read a text, of seeing if some of its sentences can be restructured.

Lack of cohesion

Most of us think of grammar as the way that words are combined to make phrases, clauses and sentences. In recent decades, a lot of attention has been paid to the way that sentences are also linked together so that we know that this series of sentences is one text, not a random collection from different texts. All of us automatically use a variety of ways to make our writing (and our speech) link together as a whole, to give it cohesion.

Lack of cohesion is what happens when the writer has not made the links between sentences – or within them – as clear as they would be if they were cohesive. Cohesion deals with the various ways in which writers create these clear links. The test focuses on one of these ways, the cohesive link that depends on the appropriate use of pronouns (see the section on punctuation, and *Cohesion*, *Connective* and *Pronoun* in the Glossary).

This short passage lacks cohesion:

> A first-year **student** should receive good support from the tutors and from the student union. Nevertheless, **they** have substantial responsibility.

What is wrong here is that the noun *student* is singular but the pronoun that refers to it, *they*, is plural. This is a common error and can only be rectified by rereading as you write, checking each use of a pronoun and making sure that there is no ambiguity about which noun it refers to.

The two sentences above should read:

> First-year **students** should receive good support from the tutors and from the student union. Nevertheless, **they** have substantial responsibility.

Here, both the noun and its pronoun are plural. Sometimes the pronoun needs to be changed and sometimes, as here, it is easier to change the noun. It would be possible to revise the two problem sentences like this:

> A first-year **student** should receive good support from the tutors and from the student union but would, nevertheless, have substantial responsibility.

Here, there would be a problem in choosing a pronoun because English has only *he* or *she*, neither of which is acceptable here. One way to get round this little problem is to leave out the pronoun altogether, as the sentence above shows. That omission of a word that would normally be present is another kind of **cohesive device**: ellipsis.

Lack of agreement between subject and verb

This is another very common error. It can show itself in many ways:

- two nouns (e.g. *maths and English*) with a singular verb (e.g. *is*);
- plural determiner (e.g. *these*) with a singular verb (e.g. *was*);
- singular determiner (e.g. *this*) with a plural verb (e.g. *were*);
- singular verb (e.g. *is*) with some non-English plurals (e.g. *data*).

Here are some examples of those four basic kinds of error.

Two nouns with a singular verb:

> *Underlying the good SAT results **was** the hard **work** of the pupils and a determined staff.*

This should be:

> *Underlying the good SAT results **were** the hard **work** of the pupils and a determined staff.*

The subject of the verb *was* is plural: *work* and *staff*; two nouns make a plural subject. If the subject is plural, the verb should be plural: *were*.

Plural determiner with a singular verb:

> ***Some** teachers who had been trained in ICT **has** made excellent use of word processing.*

Some is a plural determiner – it introduces a plural noun, *teachers* – so it needs a plural verb: *have*, not *has*. That sentence should read:

> ***Some** teachers who had been trained in ICT **have** made excellent use of word processing.*

Singular determiner with a plural verb:

> *Many of us grew up with a very prescriptive view of language without realising that **that** view of grammar **were** inadequate.*

The second use of *that* is a singular determiner so it needs a singular verb: *was*, not *were*.

That sentence should read:

> *Many of us grew up with a very prescriptive view of language without realising that **that** view of grammar **was** inadequate.*

As you probably noticed, most of these determiners can also function as pronouns.

Singular verb with some non-English plurals:

There was some argument about the findings because the research **criteria was** *in dispute.*

The word *criteria* is a plural because it comes from Greek and follows a Greek way of forming plurals. The singular form is *criterion*. Since *criteria* is plural, the verb should be *were*:

There was some argument about the findings because the research **criteria were** *in dispute.*

An equally safe version would be:

There was some argument about the findings because the research **criterion was** *in dispute.*

Of course, the meanings of the two sentences would be different!

English uses many words that still have their original forms of singular and plural. Some people feel that, when they are used in English, those singular and plural forms should still be used. At the moment, for instance, it seems that there is still a useful distinction in English between *criterion* and *criteria* that is worth retaining. On the other hand, some foreign loan-words are known in English in either, predominantly, a plural form (for example, *graffiti*, *agenda*, *data*) or a singular form (for example, *rhododendron*). Few of us talk of *graffito* or *rhododendra* for the simple reason that we do not know the Italian or Greek plurals (and, if we did, who – or whom – would we talk to?).

All language changes and that applies to Standard English as well as to other varieties. It is likely that words like *data* will settle down as singular forms because nobody else uses them as plural. Perhaps *data* itself will become both singular and plural, rather like *sheep*. *Criterion* and *criteria* are easier words to use confidently because both are used quite widely in British English. The point about using standard English is to use the variety of it that is being used and understood currently.

This degree of uncertainty also applies to some other parts of this book. You will find at least as much uncertainty about these and other matters in Bill Bryson's helpful book, *Troublesome Words*.

Of all the words that still use their original, foreign plural forms, *data* and *criteria* are probably the ones most likely to be used by people in education.

Should have/of, might have/of

English makes a lot of use of modal verbs like *would*, *could*, *must*, *need not* and *ought to*, followed by the verb *have*. When we speak, we usually abbreviate *have* to a sound that we write as *'ve*. So we write *might have*, *should have*, etc. The pronunciation of *could've* is almost identical to that of *could of*, which is an error. The pronunciation of *should've*, *must've*, *would've*, etc. (the abbreviations of *should have*, *must have*, *would have*, etc.) accounts for the frequent confusions of *should of*, *must of*, *would of*, etc. It is always wrong to write *of* in these constructions. It is always right to write *have*.

*In the headteacher's view, the school might not **of** been put under Special Measures if the stable staffing the school had benefited from earlier had been maintained.*

This should read:

*In the headteacher's view, the school might not **have** been put under Special Measures if the stable staffing the school had benefited from earlier had been maintained.*

It is always worth bearing in mind that written standard English is different from any spoken English in many ways and that it is not safe to rely too much on the sounds that are spoken as a guide to the way that the words are written. Nobody pronounces the last letter in *comb* but most of us put it in when we write the word.

Inappropriate or incomplete verb forms

One recommendation that is made repeatedly in this book is to reread what you write as you write. Even good writers can make embarrassing mistakes if they do not check what they write (this is being written by someone who consistently typed *the* as *teh* until he persuaded the Tools/Autocorrect facility to sort it out automatically). Whole words can be missed out, especially if the writer's attention is focused on another bit of the content. You need to be aware of this tendency that we all have and to pay particular attention to a fairly common error: the verb form that is either not appropriate or that is missing altogether.

Most of the class had learned use the spell check by half-term.

This should read:

*Most of the class had learned **to** use the spell check by half-term.*

One possible factor affecting this problem is that there are constructions in American English that do omit the word *to*: for example, *That afternoon, the class decided to **go explore** the neighbouring building site.* In British English, the word *to* would be used: *That afternoon, the class decided to **go to explore** the neighbouring building site.* The test is based on British English.

Sometimes, the verb itself gets left out:

Later, most of the children to show their findings to the headteacher.

This should read:

*Later, most of the children **wanted** to show their findings to the headteacher.*

It should be obvious that *wanted* is not the only verb that could fit this space but some verb, in an appropriate tense, is certainly needed.

> **HINT** This is one area where, as a writer, you can rely on the way you use language when speaking.

Wrong or missing preposition, e.g. different from/than/to

Words like *with*, *near*, *to*, *towards*, *through*, *in*, *by*, etc. are prepositions. They are usually found between two nouns (*a cat **on** a mat*), a verb and a noun (*a cat sat **on** a mat*) or some other part of speech and a noun or pronoun (*older **than**.*) Despite what was said above, there are some bits of language that change very slowly, if at all, and prepositions are among them. We still use the same prepositions that our ancestors used centuries ago. Prepositions are a *closed* word class.

The problem with them – and it is a problem; adult users of English probably have more trouble with prepositions than with any other part of speech – is that it is very easy to use an inappropriate one. This can alter what we are trying to say and cause misunderstanding.

There are some prepositions that use more than one word: complex prepositions, such as *different from*. An alternative to this is *different to*. At the moment, the complex preposition *different than* is considered to be non-standard English. In that case, do not use it in formal writing; that is, in most writing.

The performance of this year's Y2 class was quite different than last year's.

should be either:

The performance of this year's Y2 class was quite different from last year's.

or:

The performance of this year's Y2 class was quite different to last year's.

Noun/pronoun agreement error

If you substitute pronouns for nouns in these sentences, you will notice a change in the pronouns but not in the nouns:

The man liked the woman.

becomes:

He liked her.

The woman liked the man.

becomes:

She liked him.

Two nouns have become four pronouns.

Aloysius assaulted the entire staff of the school.

becomes:

He assaulted them.

The entire staff of the school wanted to exclude Aloysius.

becomes:

They wanted to exclude him.

Man, woman, Aloysius, entire staff of the school all remained the same wherever they were in the sentences and whatever job they were doing. Nouns do not change according to position and job (although they can take a plural *s/es* and a possessive *'s or s'*). On the other hand, pronouns change a lot:

I	*me*	*my*	*mine*	*myself*
you	*you*	*your*	*yours*	*yourself*
she	*her*	*her*	*hers*	*herself*
he	*him*	*his*	*his*	*himself*
it	*it*	*its*	*its*	*itself*
we	*us*	*our*	*ours*	*ourselves*
they	*them*	*their*	*theirs*	*themselves*

Some years ago, the Prime Minister of the day rejected criticisms 'about Mr Lamont and I'. That is a very common error that is easy to avoid if you ask yourself what you would put if Mr Lamont were not involved. Would you write or say:

about I

or would you say:

about me

The basic rule is to ignore the use of the pronouns (whether *he and I* or *her and me* or whichever) and to ask yourself: 'Would I use *I* here or would I use *me*?' So, just as you would almost certainly write:

I have an interview in Wythenshawe next week.

You should also write:

My friend and I have interviews in Wythenshawe next week.

As you would almost certainly write:

The head showed me round the school.

You should also write:

The head showed my friend and me round the school.

To write:

The head showed my friend and I round the school.

is an unusual example of non-standard English, unusual because it is not the English of working-class users but that spoken by middle- or aspiring middle-class users of English who believe that the *he and I* form seems more acceptable. It isn't.

Try to remember a simple sentence, such as:

I love my mother.

The word *I* comes before the verb *love* and, because it comes before the verb in this very simple sentence, it is the subject of the verb and of the sentence. If you write:

My mother loves me.

the subject is *My mother.* You do not do the loving, you *are* the loved. You are the object of the verb and of the sentence. *I* is different from *me* because it has a different meaning and does a different job.

Determiner/noun agreement error

In a radio broadcast some years ago, the then Secretary of State for Education referred to:

Those sort of programmes.

This is the error that happens when you get confused about how to link a determiner – words like *all*, *some*, *three*, *many*, *that*, *those*, *my*, *the*, *a/an* – to its noun. Such errors happen most often in brief phrases followed by a verb. This sentence-opening is acceptable English:

Determiner	noun phrase	verb ...
This	*type of error*	*is ...*

It is acceptable because the determiner and the verb are singular and so is the *headword* of the noun phrase, *type.* You need to know which word in the phrase is the headword, the real centre of the phrase. If the headword is singular, the verb and the determiner should also be singular. If the headword is plural, the verb and the determiner should also be plural. It is common to find sentences like this:

Although drafting and redrafting have been requirements since the 1989 National Curriculum in English, these kinds of activity is stumbling blocks for many children.

This should be:

Although drafting and redrafting have been requirements since the 1989 National Curriculum in English, these kinds of activity are stumbling blocks for many children.

This error, which is far more widespread in speech, is easy to understand but it is still not acceptable as standard English. The writer has been trapped into using the singular verb *is* because the nearest word that *looks* like a subject – but is not – is the singular noun *activity.* In noun-phrases like:

sorts of book

kinds of poetry

types of text

the headword in every case is a plural: *sorts*, *kinds*, *types*. That plural headword is followed by a preposition and a singular noun. The next word is likely to be a verb and, in Standard English, the verb has to agree with the headword of the noun phrase; that is, if the headword is plural, the verb should be plural, too.

So should the determiner.

Inappropriate or missing determiner

The singular determiners *this*, *that* and the plural determiners *these*, *those* are also called demonstrative pronouns. We said earlier that many determiners also act as pronouns.

If you were writing about your plans for the next half-term, you might begin:

> *Mike needed to make sure that **the** key points made at **the** university Open Day were reflected in his personal statement.*

You would not – and should not – begin:

> *Mike needed to make sure that **those** key points made at **that** university Open Day were reflected in his personal statement.*

What is wrong about the second usage is that the determiners *those* and *that* refer back to something that has already been said and this is the opening so nothing has been said. *The* is wholly appropriate in this case because it introduces and establishes what you are going to write about.

Problems with comparatives and superlatives

The computer that this is being written on is new but it is not as new as the one my friend recently bought. His computer is *newer*. He says that his son, being something of an expert in these matters, has just bought a computer that is so new that nothing newer exists! That computer is – for the moment – the newest.

We are all used to making comparisons between things and people. In standard English, this is done by using one of the two comparative forms: add *-er* to an adjective, as happened with *new/newer*, or precede it with *more*, as with *more recent*. If we want to state the ultimate in such a series, it is superlative: superlatives are expressed by adding *-est*, as with *newest*, or by preceding the adjective with *most*, as in *most recent*.

In most cases, it makes sense to write sentences that contain comparatives or superlatives but not both.

> *If children are put into groups according to whatever seating arrangements suit the activity best, the result seems to be a class that is **calmest** and **more attentive**.*

This should be:

> *If children are put into groups according to whatever seating arrangements suit the activity best, the result seems to be a class that is **calmer** and **more attentive**.*

It is hard to imagine a situation where it would be appropriate to write *calmer and most attentive*. To avoid this, simply reread it yourself and ask if it feels as though it makes good sense.

Since the comparison between the computers mentioned earlier obviously depended on there being another computer to compare with the first, it was necessary to bring in a third computer to see which was the newest. Superlatives are used when three or more things are being compared and comparatives when two only are being compared. Yet it is common to write or say sentences like:

Pawel is the **tallest** twin.

This should be:

Pawel is the **taller** twin.

There are only two twins so a comparative form of *tall* is all that is needed.

> **HINT** Alice is tall; Lucy is the taller of the *two*; Annie and Joe are the smallest of the four cousins. Compare two, it's *taller*; compare three or more, one will be *tallest*.

Problems with relative pronouns in subordinate clauses

First, we will look at **subordinate clauses**.

Suppose you write a simple sentence, with one clause, a main clause; something like this:

I still need some information about my new class.

You can say something more, perhaps about why you need that information; something like this:

I still need some information about my new class so that I can plan to help them.

What you have added to that main clause is another one, subordinate to it, that is called, reasonably enough, a subordinate clause. It needs the main clause to make full sense. It is a clause because it has a verb – *can plan* – and a subject – *I*.

Next, look at **relative pronouns**. These are pronouns that can introduce a subordinate clause. Most subordinate clauses are introduced by connectives such as **and, so that, because, if, unless, although**. Some, however, are introduced by a pronoun. These relative pronouns refer back to a noun in the main clause. The relative pronouns are:

who, whom, which, that

They appear in sentences like these:

*The headteacher believed that the school needed a teacher **who** could develop ICT work.*

After a lot of discussion, the interviewing panel agreed to appoint the candidate **whom** *the headteacher preferred.*

The Chair of the interviewing panel restated the criteria **which** *they had drawn up.*

The result of the interviews was one **that** *the whole panel was happy with.*

It is also possible to leave out the relative pronoun in many cases. This sentence:

She was the one **whom** *they wanted.*

could also be written as:

She was the one **that** *they wanted.*

but also as:

She was the one they wanted.

The likely error that some fall into is to use a relative pronoun that is not appropriate. **Which** is the pronoun we use when we are dealing with inanimate things. It is appropriate in this sentence:

Over the term, the class had read texts **which** *really extended their range of interests and abilities.*

It is not appropriate in this sentence because teachers are not inanimate:

They had chosen the teacher **which** *the headteacher wanted.*

That should be either:

They had chosen the teacher **whom** *the headteacher wanted.*

or:

They had chosen the teacher the head wanted.

When do you use **who** and when do you use **whom**? Whether you should use **who** or **whom** is the same question as whether to use **he** or **him, she** or **her, I** or **me, we** or **us**. Suppose you are writing a very formal piece and you try the two options in this sentence:

The panel chose the candidate **who/whom** *was best.*

Ask yourself whether you would be more likely to write:

She was best.

or:

Her was best.

Unless you have a very unusual and inadequate grasp of English, you would say *She was best*. That means you would choose *who*. On the other hand, if you wanted to write this sentence:

*The headteacher asked the rest of the panel **who/whom** they liked.*

You could ask yourself whether it would make more sense to write:

They liked she.

or:

They liked her.

You would choose *her* and so you would also choose *whom*.

Although many of us hardly ever use *whom*, especially when speaking, the test is based on formal writing and does expect it to be used.

Inappropriate or missing adverbial forms

Sometimes, we can confuse the use of an adjective and an adverb. We know that we can write:

Mushraf was a fast runner.

where *fast* is an adjective, rather like *quick*. However, we can also write:

Mushraf ran fast.

where *fast* is an adverb, just like *quickly*. We know that many adverbs do not end in *-ly*. This very reliable bit of knowledge might tempt some of us to write sentences like this, where an adjective is used instead of an adverb:

On the whole, student options were intelligent chosen.

This should be:

On the whole, student options were intelligently chosen.

This is not the sort of error that native users of a language tend to make but it is the sort that can easily creep into a written text. That is why we repeatedly advise you to read and reread as you write. Get a feel for the sense and the flow of what you write and for the tone of voice you are using as a writer.

Sense, clarity and freedom from ambiguity

Some fiction and much poetry deliberately make very profitable use of the ambiguities and optional meanings that can be made from language. Most writing, however, has to make clarity a priority. Make your writing as easy to read as possible; change anything that is ambiguous; check it all the time to make sure that it makes sense.

You will be tested on your ability to spot when a piece of writing is clear and when it is not. This means that you need to have a good idea of the place that grammar can play in helping a text to be clear. The test will show you examples of writing and ask you to identify which of several options would make the piece clear.

These are some of the factors that make writing unclear:

Lack of coherence

Some texts are easier to read than others. If it is easy to understand, it must be coherent: it has *coherence*; the bits hold together to make a whole. Writers use a variety of ways to make this happen; for example, that pronoun *this* refers back to the idea of coherence in the previous sentence. Pronouns are crucial in making links *between* sentences in a continuous text.

Writers use other devices to make clauses hold together *within* a sentence. For example, they use *connectives* so that one clause can be linked in meaning to another; in this sentence, *so that* is a connective, linking the main clause *they use connectives* to its subordinate clause.

That use of grammatical devices to create that coherence is called *cohesion*. Those devices are called *cohesive devices*. There are several others that are not discussed here.

In the test, you will be asked to identify when a text lacks coherence because there are problems with:

- tense;
- unrelated participles; or
- an ambiguous use of pronouns.

These are all explained below.

Wrong tense or tense inconsistency

Tense is the aspect of a verb that deals with time. It is possible to use more than one tense in one sentence, as in this:

> My father **was** a sheet-metal worker, I **am** a teacher and my daughter **is going to be** a teacher.

The first verb, *was*, is a form of the past tense; the second, *am*, is a form of the present; the third, *is going to be*, is a form of the future tense.

Other forms of the past include *has been*, *used to be*. Other forms of the present include *am being* (with verbs other than **be**, the present can also use *do*, as in *do like, do care*, etc.). Other forms of the future include *will be*.

There is no problem with the use of different tenses in that simple sentence. That is because the meaning of the sentence really is about different times so it is right to use different tenses. The key to all this is to keep a close eye on what you mean to write, what tense fits what you are trying to say. Keep rereading and checking! If you do, you are less likely to use tenses inconsistently, the commonest failing with this aspect of written grammar.

> **HINT** Over time, you will strengthen your grasp of tense if you read fairly quickly. Slow readers – and writers – easily lose track of what happens when.

*Shahida began his book at half-term and **finishes** it last week.*

should be:

*Shahida began his book at half-term and **finished** it last week.*

Began and *finished* are both verbs in the past tense. That fits the meaning of the sentence and is therefore consistent. It would also be consistent if the truth was this:

Shahida began his book at half-term and will finish it next week.

There, *began* is in the past tense and *will finish* is in the future tense but the sentence is grammatically consistent because it fits the meaning.

A sentence such as:

*The staff will have written their reports by Friday and so **met** the deadline.*

should be:

*The staff will have written their reports by Friday and so **will meet** the deadline.*

In the first sentence, the staff have not yet completed the reports so it is not true to say they have already met a deadline. That does not make sense and so is inconsistent.

Unrelated participles

What are participles and in what ways might they be unrelated? In a sentence such as:

The school had closed for Easter.

the word *closed* follows a subject, the noun *school*, and immediately follows a form of the verb *to have*. A word that could do that is a **participle**, a part of the verb which expresses tense (in this case, a form of the past tense). Past participles often end in *-ed* but may end in *-en* (*written*), *-n* (*shown*), *-d* (*read*) or *-t* (*thought*).

In a sentence such as:

The school is closing for Easter.

the word *closing* follows a subject, the noun *school*, and immediately follows a form of the verb *to be*. Therefore, *closing* is also a participle and it expresses a form of the present tense.

A participle never has a subject, such as the pronouns *I*, *you*, *she*, *he*, *it*, *we*, *they*, immediately before it; the verb *to be* or *to have* has to come between them, as in the examples above.

Participles can be found in some clauses of this type:

Collaborating with someone who has more competence, a learner can be helped to construct new meanings.

In that sentence, the question of who does the *collaborating* is answered by the subject of the next clause: *the learner.* That is an example of a *related participle*; the participle is unambiguously related to a subject. However, the participle is not related to the subject in a sentence like this:

Collaborating with someone who has more competence, the teacher can help the learner to construct new meanings.

Here, the subject of that second clause is the teacher but the person who collaborates with someone who has more competence is the learner. The participle, *collaborating*, is *unrelated* to the subject, *the teacher*.

Unrelated participles are unacceptable because they are confusing and may be ambiguous. They should be avoided.

The sentence:

Being well-managed, the head of Armitage School could afford to employ a 0.5 teaching assistant after Christmas.

is unacceptable because it is the school that is well-managed, not the head. The sentence:

Providing far more than the national average of free dinners, Seddon Junior School might be expected to have considerable problems.

is acceptable because there is no doubt that it is the school that provides many free dinners.

Attachment ambiguities

Always keep an eye on the meaning of what you write or read. This book stresses that again and again but it is clear from what many people write that this advice is easily overlooked.

For example, if you wrote:

The headteacher told me about the exclusion appeal.

you could add to that sentence a phrase about when the appeal was to be held. Where would that phrase appear? If you wrote:

On Monday, *the headteacher told me about the exclusion appeal.*

that states unambiguously that Monday was the day that you were told. If you wrote:

*The headteacher told me about the exclusion appeal **on Monday.***

the change of position now *implies* that the appeal will take place on Monday. The problem is that it still allows the reader to *infer* that Monday was when you heard about the appeal. Does the phrase **on Monday** refer to the verb *told* or to the noun *appeal*? One sentence has two possible meanings although one – the timing of the appeal – is the more likely because *appeal* and *on Monday* appear close to each other.

It is easy to avoid this ambiguity by turning that added two-word phrase into a clause, as in:

*The headteacher told me about the exclusion appeal **that would take place on Monday.***

Vague or ambiguous pronoun reference

This kind of ambiguity is very common. In children's writing, it is very common indeed. One of the best activities that teachers can demonstrate, model and encourage is how to redraft a piece of writing by checking that there is no ambiguity about which nouns the pronouns refer to. Unless children (and other writers!) write quickly enough to be able to keep in mind what they are writing as they write, and unless they check what they write, it is very likely that they will use pronouns such as *he*, *she*, *it*, *they* (and the other forms of the pronoun, such as *him*, *her*, *them*, etc.) in ways that do not refer clearly to their nouns.

*All the new computers and most of the stationery materials have been stored in the old stock cupboards. Nothing more can be done with **them** until the electrician arrives.*

should be:

All the new computers and most of the stationery materials have been stored in the old stock cupboards. Nothing more can be done with the computers until the electrician arrives.

Unless the computers are specified – and that means using the noun, not the pronoun – it seems as if the electrician has to do something with the stationery as well. This would be, at least, confusing.

Clarity matters and, therefore, so does explicitness: that means using nouns instead of pronouns if it would be confusing to do otherwise.

*Liam and Aloysius took Ryan and Nathan to see if **their** food was ready.*

should be:

Liam and Aloysius took Ryan and Nathan to see if all their food was ready.

or:

Liam and Aloysius took Ryan and Nathan to see if Liam's and Aloysius' food was ready.

or:

> *Liam and Aloysius took Ryan and Nathan to see if Ryan's and Nathan's food was ready.*

Which you use depends on your meaning. Some of these seem clumsy but even clumsiness is better than confusion. This particular confusion is very common in children's writing.

Confusion of words, e.g. imply/infer

All varieties of all languages change all the time. That is the single most obvious fact about language. Using standard English does not mean using the language of a century or two ago if it is very different from usage today. On the other hand, many older usages are still widespread among literate users of English so you are advised still to follow that variety of standard English.

One usage that seems to be common can cause real problems with understanding. English has many words that look and sound rather alike and so are sometimes used interchangeably but their meanings are quite different. If you say to a fairly educated person that you are *disinterested* about the children you teach, you should get some approval because it means that you are impartial, not that you are uninterested. So:

> *Just because I said I didn't mind teaching either Y3 or Y4, the headteacher thinks I'm* **disinterested***.*

should be:

> *Just because I said I didn't mind teaching either Y3 or Y4, the head thinks I'm* **uninterested***.*

If you have no great preference, you really are *disinterested*!

The words *infer* and *imply* are more often misused than not. *Infer* is used far more often than *imply* and often it is used wrongly.

> *He* **inferred** *that I'm not bothered who I teach.*

should be:

> *He* **implied** *that I'm not bothered who [to be formal, whom] I teach.*

The odd thing about this particular confusion is that the words are almost opposite. If you imply something to a friend, your friend should infer the same message from you. *Infer* means *conclude*, as in:

> *From the way he was talking about falling numbers, I* **inferred** *that there could be a redundancy soon.*

Imply means to *suggest something without directly saying so*, as in:

> *I know she didn't say definitely but she* **implied** *that she might have a job for me next term.*

Here are some other words that are often confused:

Except in uncommon usages such as: *The staff room had been burgled when someone effected an entry from the playground side*, the word effect is used as a noun:

*Unexpectedly, the music had a calming **effect** on a usually unruly class.*

Affect is almost always a verb, as in:

*Yes, the music definitely **affected** them strongly.*

Rebut, *refute* and *deny* are sometimes used as though they were interchangeable. Their meanings are related but distinct:

*When I implied that the deputy had forgotten about the Theatre in Education visit, she **refuted** what I had said by showing me the letter she had written to book the visit.*

Here, the deputy head proved that the implied accusation was wrong by providing evidence; she *refuted* it.

*She was angry and **rebutted** the accusation, calling me a nasty-minded trouble-maker who should think about a suitable job, such as pig-farming.*

The deputy is more emotional and does not bother with the evidence.

*All she needed to do was to **deny** it.*

The accuser now wishes that the deputy had restricted herself to a mere denial, without proving the point and without the anger. *Deny* can be an angry verb and it can involve proof but something else has to be added to make those points: *denied angrily, denied the accusation and showed the proof.*

Here are some other words that may get confused:

Discrete means separate, individually distinct, discontinuous (OED) not continuous; *discreet* means able to avoid embarrassing others – or yourself:

*Some of his sentences were a list of **discrete** words, unconnected by any grammatical device.*

but:

*There was so much rumour in the air that we all appreciated having such a **discreet** colleague.*

Accept means to receive something, particularly without fuss; *except* means that somebody or something is not part of a general situation:

*The head **accepted** my apology and carried on conducting the assembly himself.*

but:

*After the staff meeting, the head dismissed everybody **except** me.*

Contemptuous means that the subject feels contempt for somebody or something; *contemptible* is what that somebody or something is:

*My tutor was quite **contemptuous** of my efforts.*

but:

*Privately, even I had to agree that they really were **contemptible**.*

Militate means to have an influence against some evidence; *mitigate* means to reduce an effect, to soften or to appease:

*The latest SAT results **militate** against the last inspection report.*

but:

*The clarity and liveliness of Jeannie's story **mitigated** her general performance in school.*

Continuous means that something is without a break; *continual* means that something happens regularly:

*On their way to the swimming baths, the class walked in a **continuous** line.*

but:

*There is a **continual** outburst of delight every Friday.*

Different means that *this* is not like *that*; *differing* means that opinions or evidence clash:

*This year's Y6 class is quite **different** from last year's.*

but:

*The staff sat in silence as the **differing** views of the headteacher and her deputy thickened the air of the tiny staff room.*

Allusion means a rather indirect reference to something that you probably know about; *illusion* means an idea that does not fit reality:

*Without mentioning any names or any events, the head made an **allusion** to the incident at the outdoor pursuits centre that lost the school its best speller.*

but:

*The miscalculated test results caused us to live in a happy **illusion** until the SATs brought in reality.*

Stationary means without movement; *stationery* means paper, pens, etc.:

*Luckily, the class knew they had to be quite **stationary** before crossing a busy road.*

but:

*We were distraught by the lack of paper until the **stationery** supplies arrived.*

It helps to use a dictionary often, for spellings, for meanings – especially shades of meaning – and simply to get into the habit of using a valuable source of information. Other books, such as Bill Bryson's *Troublesome Words*, may also help.

Professional suitability and style

All native users of a language learn, from their earliest experiences of it, to match their style to their audience, to their own purpose in speaking or writing and to the topic being discussed. This test is about your ability to tell the difference between appropriate and inappropriate style. In particular, try to avoid these stylistic usages:

Non-parallelism in lists

When you write a list, look at the words you use to introduce the list. Each item in the list should follow grammatically from that introduction:

In future planning, I should remember to:

a. *to plan who should be in each group;*
b. *friendship groups.*

should be:

In future planning, I should remember to:

a. *plan who should be in each group;*
b. *consider friendship groups.*

No native user of English would say or write:

In future planning, I should remember to to plan who should be in each group.

or:

In future planning, I should remember to friendship groups.

Inconsistent register and tone

We can make a mistake with the tone of what we write. This is usually because we use a tone that is too formal or one that is too informal. Most writing is formal so a formal style is more appropriate in most cases.

An inconsistent style can show itself in the use of colloquialisms:

*It was reported last night that the Secretary of State was **doing her nut** over the slow progress of her latest initiative for small rural schools.*

The opening phrase, *'It was reported'*, implies that the speaker was a newsreader and the intended audience the general public. *'Doing her nut'* is inappropriate in a news report. The tone and style should be appropriate to the audience.

This would be more consistent in tone if it was written like this:

> *It was reported last night that the Secretary of State was **concerned** over the slow pro-gress of her latest initiative for small rural schools.*

An inconsistency of tone can also be created by mixing the use of active and passive con-structions in the same sentence:

> *Some of the children **opened** [active] the letters for home, **read** [active] them and **were torn up** [passive].*

should be either:

> *Some of the children **opened** [active] the letters for home, **read** [active] them and **tore them up** [active].*

or:

> *Some of the letters for home **were opened** [passive] by the children, **read** [passive] and **torn up** [passive].*

In this last example, the auxiliary verb *were* has been left out from *were read* and *were torn up*. That is another case of *ellipsis*, what Dan Slobin calls *optional deletion*.

Finally, an inconsistent tone can also be created by mixing the use of the informal *you* and the more formal *one* in the same sentence. *You* is almost universal in speech, in sen-tences such as:

> *You never can tell.*

You is also appropriate in writing, especially informal writing; it is also appropriate in fairly formal writing. What is inappropriate is to mix the two styles:

> *Since **you** played such an active role in last year's Easter Fair, **one** should take up the challenge again this year.*

should be:

> *Since **you** played such an active role in last year's Easter Fair, **you** should take up the challenge again this year.*

On the other hand:

> *Although **you** always found that the middle term used to be the most productive, **one** finds the level of production more evenly spread over the year now.*

should be:

> *Although **one** always found that the middle term used to be the most productive, **one** finds the level of production more evenly spread over the year now.*

or:

> *Although I always found that the middle term used to be the most productive, I find the level of production more evenly spread over the year now.*

Both *one* and *you* can mean *people in general* or *people like us* or *me*. *You* can sometimes be confusing if it both carries that very general meaning and also means the other person. In other words, *you* is usually a second person pronoun, coming between *I* and *she/he/it*, and it can be confusing if it is used as a third person pronoun like *one*.

Be consistent.

Shift in person within sentences or across sentences

This is related to the last point above. Like that, it is related to what happens when formal and informal styles or register get mixed. It is also related to *cohesion* and the use of pronouns. If you mean the same people, do not confuse things by referring to them as *you* when you really mean *they*:

> *Too many **people** are leaving doors open when **you** shouldn't.*

should be:

> *Too many **people** are leaving doors open when **they** shouldn't.*

or:

> *Too many **of you** are leaving doors open when **you** shouldn't.*
>
> ***One** hopes that the new community room will be ready before next term begins so that **we** can make full use of it.*

should be:

> ***We** hope that the new community room will be ready before next term begins so that **we** can make full use of it.*

Many problems with writing can be reduced greatly if you get into and keep the habit of reading what you write as you write it, rereading chunks and checking it at the end. Keep an eye on what you mean to say.

Excessive length and rambling sentences

This issue is related to earlier ones about abandoned constructions and failures to observe sentence boundaries. The key point is to see if very long sentences can be rewritten as more than one sentence. Long sentences are more than acceptable but only if the writer can control them:

> *Charlie is obviously a child that although has developed a high level of phonic understanding and is capable of breaking down unknown words is still with my regards to the definition of a reader not successful.*

should be:

> *Charlie obviously has a high level of phonic understanding. He is able to break down unknown words. However, he is still not a successful reader in my view.*

The uncorrected sentence above is a genuine product of a trainee teacher. So is the following sentence:

> *With certain aspects of literacy I agree with Yetta Goodman (1980) whose research indicated that literacy is a naturally occurring and developing process in 'our literate society', however, this development is minimal in comparison with the expected requirements, for example children may naturally occur certain literacy skills.*

should be:

> *Concerning certain aspects of literacy, I agree with Yetta Goodman (1980) whose research indicated that literacy is a naturally occurring and developing process in our literate society. This development is minimal in comparison with the expected requirements. For example, children may naturally acquire certain literacy skills.*

You might have noticed that the uncorrected version has other problems, unconnected with sentence length or boundary. Problems rarely come singly.

Redundancy/tautology

If an expression means what you want to say, there is no need to add to it. It would make no sense to refer to the *STA Agency* because the acronym means *Standards and Testing Agency*.

> *The headteacher reported that the governing body had **definitely** excluded Aloysius.*

should be:

> *The headteacher reported that the governing body had excluded Aloysius.*

Exclusion is itself a word with no limits so there is no point in saying that it is *definite*.

Some kinds of apparent redundancy are more problematic. One change in standard English over recent decades is that the verb *check* has almost been replaced by *check out*. They mean the same but it could be argued that the apparently redundant *out* is now part of a developing standard English.

Inappropriate conjunctions (also known as connectives)

Look at what was said above about relative pronouns and relative clauses in 'Problems with relative pronouns in subordinate clauses'. Clauses that begin with *who*, *whom*, *which*, *that* are in a different category from those that begin with one of the long list of connectives such as *if, because, unless, so that, in case, although*, etc. All these words can begin a subordinate clause but the relationship with the main clause is different.

*The trouble with Roy is **because** he will not buckle down to hard work.*

should be:

*The trouble with Roy is **that** he will not buckle down to hard work.*

or:

*There is trouble with Roy **because** he will not buckle down to hard work.*

Some problems occur because the main clause has been completed and there seems to be a break in the writer's thinking before continuing with the subordinate clause:

*Roy's improvement has been **so** dramatic **so that** he could be quite near the top this year.*

should be:

*Roy's improvement has been dramatic **so** he could be quite near the top this year.*

or:

*Roy's improvement has been **so** dramatic **that** he could be quite near the top this year.*

Some conjunctions occur not only between clauses but also between phrases and even between single words. The problem is that sometimes these necessary words get left out:

The headteacher received a long silence at the staff meeting when he announced his intention to sing dance at the interval during the Christmas play.

should be:

*The headteacher received a long silence at the staff meeting when he announced his intention to sing **and** dance at the interval during the Christmas play.*

Remember that you will not be tested on all the items in this section nor is this list a syllabus. A glance at the sheer bulk of any grammar text should remind you that this is not exhaustive.

If you get stuck at any point, reread what you have done, ask if it makes clear sense and see if it is as consistent with the rest of the sentence, paragraph or text as you can make it.

Questions

The actual test is computerised. You will be shown part of a sentence and then presented with a range of optional clauses or phrases that might complete the sentence. Decide which would be the best option to complete the sentence grammatically and drag it into the space provided. The test in this book involves you in precisely the same kind of thinking as the computerised test.

Questions

The grammar section of the test asks you to complete some sentences. That tests your ability to detect when something is wrong. You will see the first part of a sentence and then four optional ways to complete it. Three of these options are wrong or unsatisfactory in some way. Your task is to choose the best way to complete the sentence.

There are three tests of grammar:

- of your ability to detect unrelated participles;
- of your ability to detect the wrong tense or tense inconsistency;
- of your ability to detect any lack of agreement between subject and verb.

Unrelated participles

In the following tests, underline the one sentence that seems to you to be **appropriate in its use of a related participle rather than an unrelated one.**

TEST A

1. Realising the role that speech plays in helping children to solve practical tasks, it follows that children should be given tasks that require talk.

2. Realising the role that speech plays in helping children to solve practical tasks, Vygotsky placed language at the centre of all learning.

3. Realising the role that speech plays in helping children to solve practical tasks, language was seen by Vygotsky as central to learning.

4. Realising the role that speech plays in helping children to solve practical tasks, children's unassisted work is stressed by many teachers.

TEST B

1. Persuaded by her staff that afternoon playtimes were increasingly disruptive, the head decided to have no playtimes in the afternoon but to end school ten minutes early.

2. Persuaded by her staff that afternoon playtimes were increasingly disruptive, afternoon play was abandoned by the head and replaced with an earlier hometime.

3. Persuaded by her staff that afternoon playtimes were increasingly disruptive, the school exchanged its afternoon play for a shorter afternoon session.

4. Persuaded by her staff that afternoon playtimes were increasingly disruptive, the children had no play but could leave school ten minutes earlier.

Questions

TEST C

1. The curriculum, according to Peters, is not wholly an end in itself, conceding that even history can be viewed in an instrumental way.

2. Peters believes that the curriculum is not wholly an end in itself, conceding that even history can be viewed in an instrumental way.

3. Conceding that even history can be viewed in an instrumental way, the view that the curriculum is an end in itself is not fully supported by Peters.

4. Conceding that even history can be viewed in an instrumental way, Peters' view of the curriculum is not wholly in favour of education as an end in itself.

TEST D

1. Thought to be the easiest class in the school to teach, the head was surprised by the mayhem they caused during silent reading.

2. Thought to be the easiest class in the school to teach, it was surprising to the head that they could cause so much mayhem during silent reading.

3. Thought to be the easiest class in the school to teach, the mayhem they caused during silent reading was a surprise for the head.

4. Thought to be the easiest class in the school to teach, the children caused mayhem during silent reading.

Wrong tense or tense inconsistency

In the following tests, underline the one sentence that seems to you to be **appropriate in its use of the right and most consistent tense**.

TEST A

1. Although I wish now that I had worked harder, my A level results were very pleasing and it has meant being able to be more ambitious in the applications I made.

2. Although I wish now that I had worked harder, my A level results were very pleasing and it has meant that I have been able to be more ambitious in the applications I made.

3. Although I wish now that I had worked harder, my A level results were very pleasing and it has meant that I was able to be more ambitious in the applications I made.

4. Although I wish now that I had worked harder, my A level results were very pleasing and it has meant that I am able to be more ambitious in the applications I made.

Questions

TEST B

1. I don't consider myself a very gifted person, although I did well enough, but my headteacher father believes I'll make a good teacher and that, although I have always been a little naïve, life was good.

2. I don't consider myself a very gifted person, although I did well enough, but my headteacher father believes I'll make a good teacher and that, although I have always been a little naïve, life being good.

3. I don't consider myself a very gifted person, although I did well enough, but my headteacher father believes I'll make a good teacher and that, although I have always been a little naïve, life is good.

4. I don't consider myself a very gifted person, although I did well enough, but my headteacher father believes I'll make a good teacher and that, although I have always been a little naïve, life will be good.

TEST C

1. Whatever I do, my mind fills with thoughts of what could happen if I chose a course where I can't fit in, the other students don't respond, the staff are cold and unhelpful and my tutor is bad-tempered.

2. Whatever I do, my mind fills with thoughts of what could happen if I chose a course where I can't fit in, the other students don't respond, the staff are cold and unhelpful and my tutor was bad-tempered.

3. Whatever I do, my mind fills with thoughts of what could happen if I chose a course where I can't fit in, the other students don't respond, the staff are cold and unhelpful and my tutor has been bad-tempered.

4. Whatever I do, my mind fills with thoughts of what could happen if I chose a course where I can't fit in, the other students don't respond, the staff are cold and unhelpful and my tutor being bad-tempered.

TEST D

1. Perhaps the best action for me to take is to talk with friends, at least once I have examined what different areas offer, compared facilities, accommodation and opportunities and growing a little more sure of myself.

2. Perhaps the best action for me to take is to talk with friends, at least once I have examined what different areas offer, compared facilities, accommodation and opportunities and grow a little more sure of myself.

3. Perhaps the best action for me to take is to talk with friends, at least once I have examined what different areas offer, compared facilities, accommodation and opportunities and grew a little more sure of myself.

Questions

4. Perhaps the best action for me to take is to talk with friends, at least once I have examined what different areas offer, compared facilities, accommodation and opportunities and grown a little more sure of myself.

Lack of agreement between subject and verb

In the following tests, underline the one sentence that seems to you to be **appropriate in its agreement between subject and verb**.

TEST A

1. The trouble with both the way I talk and the way I write are that for much of the time I cannot trust myself to remember what I started with.

2. The trouble with both the way I talk and the way I write were that for much of the time I cannot trust myself to remember what I started with.

3. The trouble with both the way I talk and the way I write was that for much of the time I cannot trust myself to remember what I started with.

4. The trouble with both the way I talk and the way I write is that for much of the time I cannot trust myself to remember what I started with.

TEST B

1. A friend told me that the likeliest cause of this problem is that the unrelentingly abusive attitudes shown by my first English teacher is quite traumatic for me.

2. A friend told me that the likeliest cause of this problem is that the unrelentingly abusive attitudes shown by my first English teacher were quite traumatic for me.

3. A friend told me that the likeliest cause of this problem is that the unrelentingly abusive attitudes shown by my first English teacher was quite traumatic for me.

4. A friend told me that the likeliest cause of this problem is that the unrelentingly abusive attitudes shown by my first English teacher being quite traumatic for me.

TEST C

1. I wish it were that simple. In fact, are it that teacher, the one who helped me somehow to qualify for university, the sicknesses I had as a child or my supportive but rather stern parents?

2. I wish it were that simple. In fact, were it that teacher, the one who helped me somehow to qualify for university, the sicknesses I had as a child or my supportive but rather stern parents?

Questions

3. I wish it were that simple. In fact, was it that teacher, the one who helped me somehow to qualify for university, the sicknesses I had as a child or my supportive but rather stern parents?

4. I wish it were that simple. In fact, is it that teacher, the one who helped me somehow to qualify for university, the sicknesses I had as a child or my supportive but rather stern parents?

TEST D

1. As I look ahead, I know that the future, whether I am lucky or not or leave teaching or stay with it, and whatever anyone else does or says, was mine to make.

2. As I look ahead, I know that the future, whether I am lucky or not or leave teaching or stay with it, and whatever anyone else does or says, has been mine to make.

3. As I look ahead, I know that the future, whether I am lucky or not or leave teaching or stay with it, and whatever anyone else does or says, will be mine to make.

4. As I look ahead, I know that the future, whether I am lucky or not or leave teaching or stay with it, and whatever anyone else does or says, will have been mine to make.

2.5 | Comprehension

Introduction

8–12 marks are available for comprehension.

Most of the test is about writing. This section is about reading.

Teachers now have to read a great deal of written material about their professional lives and work. This material can be government documents (for example, on the law concerning exclusion from school), the educational press and very frequent information about the local educational scene. Because every teacher now has to do so much professionally demanding reading, there is a greater stress than there was previously on their being able to:

- identify the key points in a text;
- 'read between the lines' in order to make inferences and deductions;
- differentiate between fact and fiction in a written text;
- understand which points are more significant than others and how this relative importance affects a text;
- comprehend a text well enough to be able to re-present the meaning in a different way from the original;
- retrieve factual information and/or specific ideas from a text;
- judge whether specific comments made about a text are actually supported, implied, implicitly or explicitly contradicted, or simply not present in that text;
- summarise information from a section, or about a topic, in a text;
- identify or adapt suitable information from a text for a specific audience.

The test will expect you to be sufficiently proficient in these skills in order to complete the following tasks:

- attribute statements to categories;
- complete a bulleted list;
- sequence information;
- present main points;
- match texts to summaries;
- identify the meanings of words and phrases;
- evaluate statements about the text;
- select headings and subheadings;
- identify possible readership or audience for a text.

These are the nine possible comprehension question types.

The test you take will test only a selection of these aspects of literacy.

The comprehension test presents candidates with a short text and a series of questions on it. Read the whole text first. Good reading means paying almost simultaneous attention to the word or phrase you are concentrating on at the time and also to as much of the whole text as you have read and can keep in mind. To do this test well, you will need to focus on what is significant in the whole text so that you are able to select those bits and ignore the rest. Some questions ask you to see how this bit of the text relates to that bit, to notice how parts of the text are organised, to sequence ideas and to check what some phrases or words mean in the context. None of this is extraordinary and an attentive and reasonably experienced reader should not have difficulties.

Questions

There are nine possible comprehension question types; each Literacy Skills Test will test a selection of these. However, for the sake of this exercise, tasks have been set using all nine comprehension question types.

Read this extract from an Ofsted document and complete the following tasks.

Ofsted to revise the framework for initial teacher education (ITE)

Ofsted is proposing to raise expectations of providers of teacher training to help ensure that more trainees are better prepared with the practical skills that teachers need most, such as the ability to manage behaviour and teach reading effectively.

Feedback on the current inspection arrangements has been positive but also suggests the need to continue to raise expectations. This means drawing up clearer, more challenging criteria with fewer, more streamlined judgements and one overarching judgement for overall effectiveness. Ofsted is also seeking views on reducing the eight-week notice period for an inspection to three weeks.

Her Majesty's Chief Inspector (HMCI) of Education said, 'The quality of teaching is an essential element in any school so the selection and training of the next generation of teachers is crucial. We hope that changes to the way we inspect initial teacher education will enable inspectors to focus even more on the things that are important: teaching pupils to read, behaviour management and trainees' ability to teach a range of learners, including those with special educational needs and/or disabilities.

'Inspection helps to raise standards and ensure the best training is provided. We want more trainees to become good or outstanding teachers and gain employment in schools. This is why, in the new arrangements, we want to focus inspection afresh on observing current and former trainees in the classroom. I'd like to encourage anyone with an interest in initial teacher education, in particular those who provide training, are currently in training, or thinking of joining a teacher training programme, to tell us their views.'

Building on the strengths of the current arrangements, it is proposed that inspection will look more closely at the selection of trainees and the quality of partnerships ITE providers have with settings, schools and colleges. It will focus even more on the quality of training and trainees' subject knowledge and their

Questions

understanding and competence in developing pupils' literacy skills, including using systematic phonics to teach reading. Ofsted is also considering incorporating a thematic element into inspections, on a rolling programme, in order to gain more evidence on the effectiveness of training to teach specific subjects and aspects such as managing behaviour.

The proposals include a more proportionate approach to inspection that is informed by a robust risk assessment process so inspections can be targeted where improvement is needed most. Partnerships previously judged to be satisfactory will be inspected at an early stage in the new cycle and those that continue to be satisfactory will be subject to a monitoring inspection, which will take place 12–18 months after the inspection. Finally, a full inspection is likely to take place within three years of the previous inspection.

Ofsted proposes that initial teacher education inspections will also:

- *retain the focus on trainees' outcomes at the heart of the inspection*
- *be underpinned by clear and more challenging criteria for judging partnerships to be outstanding or good*
- *take account of the views of users, trainees and former trainees, including newly qualified and recently qualified teachers*
- *use an on-line questionnaire to gather the views of trainees*
- *integrate judgements on equality and diversity throughout the report, including reporting on the performance of different groups of trainees*
- *introduce a focused monitoring inspection; for example, to look at the provision of phonics training where newly qualified teacher feedback raises concerns*
- *continue to involve leaders, managers, tutors, mentors, trainees and former trainees in discussions during an inspection*
- *continue to take account of a partnership's self-evaluation, and*
- *continue to drive improvement in the sector by providing an external evaluation of strengths and weaknesses.*

The proposals take into account feedback from providers, inspectors and other stakeholders with an interest in ITE.

Attributing statements to categories

Read the statements below and decide which refer to:

ITEP   Initial Teacher Education Providers

TT   Trainee Teachers

O   Ofsted

HMCI   Her Majesty's Chief Inspector

Questions

Put the correct code in the box to the left of each statement.

(*In the computerised test, you will be asked to drag the code to the box.*)

They are going to require more from teacher training courses.

They regard the training of the next cohort of teachers as very significant.

They are going to be expected to know how to develop literacy skills.

They are going to have to look more closely at placements.

Completing a bulleted list

Look at the phrases below. Put a tick next to the three that most accurately complete the stem. The final one has been done for you.

(*In the computerised test you will be asked to drag a number of phrases one at a time to the bulleted list.*)

It is anticipated that all future ITE inspections will:

-
-
-
- **continue to take account of a partnership's self-evaluation.**

target inspections only where improvement is most needed

focus entirely on specific themes such as behaviour management

be strengthened by tougher criteria for judging outstanding or good trainees

be preceded by a notice period of only three weeks

improve ITE by providing an external evaluation of strengths and weaknesses

gauge the diversity of partnerships ITE providers have established

be reinforced by a more demanding measure of outstanding or good partnerships

take account of the views of newly or recently qualified teachers

Sequencing information

From the seven statements below select the three that most accurately reflect the order of the steps to be taken in the new cycle of inspection of the partnerships ITE providers have with their settings, schools and colleges.

Questions

Write FIRST, SECOND OR THIRD in the box to the left of your choice of statement.

(In the computerised test you will be asked to click on the labels FIRST, SECOND or THIRD, one at a time, and drag them to the boxes beside your chosen answer.)

	All partnerships will undergo an initial risk assessment.
	Partnerships previously judged to be satisfactory will be inspected.
	Those showing most need for improvement will be inspected first.
	All partnerships will be inspected within three years of this revision.
	Those that continue to be satisfactory will be inspected within 12 to 18 months.
	Partnerships will have a full inspection within three years of a previous inspection.
	Partnerships' chances of being inspected will be proportionate to their quality.

Presenting main points

From the list below, select the four points that most accurately describe Ofsted's main objectives in revising the inspection framework for ITE. Tick the box to the left of the point to indicate your four choices.

(In the computerised test you will be asked to click on your four choices, one at a time, and drag them to four empty bullet points in the adjacent box.)

	Gauge the effectiveness of the teaching of phonics by newly qualified teachers.
	Look more closely at how trainees are evaluated and selected for ITE.
	Scrutinise the inspection criteria used to assess teachers in schools.
	Encourage teachers working in schools to tell them their views on ITE.
	Upgrade the quality of training given by ITE providers.
	Ensure practical teaching skills are top of the agenda for trainees.
	Introduce a thematic approach into the inspection of behaviour management.
	Introduce one comprehensive criterion for the general effectiveness of ITE provision.
	Reduce the notice period given prior to inspection of ITE provision.

Questions

Matching texts to summaries

Reread paragraphs 1, 3 and 5. From the list of statements below, select the one that most accurately summarises the content of these three paragraphs. Tick the box next to your choice.

(In the computerised test you will be asked to drag a tick symbol to the box beside your choice.)

☐ It is vital to build on the strengths of the current arrangements and raise the expectations of the next generation of trainee teachers.

☐ It is time for a complete overhaul of the inspection process for ITE so that schools can focus even more on the things that are important.

☐ The most important attributes of the trainee teacher emerging from ITE are the abilities to control and manage behaviour and to teach literacy effectively.

☐ Teaching can be improved by raising expectations, introducing a more rigorous selection of trainees and improving the quality of settings, schools and colleges.

Identifying the meanings of words and phrases

Select the most suitable alternative for the phrase as it appears in the context of the passage. Tick the box next to your choice.

(In the computerised test you will be asked to drag a tick symbol to the box beside your choice.)

'... raise expectations of providers of teacher training' (paragraph 1) is closest in meaning to:

☐ investigate the endeavours of providers of teacher training

☐ lift the requirements of providers of teacher training

☐ boost the hopes of providers of teacher training

☐ increase the demands on providers of teacher training

'... a more proportionate approach to' (paragraph 6) is closest in meaning to:

☐ a more commensurate method of

☐ a more detached pathway to

☐ a more competitive move towards

☐ a more rigorous course of

Questions

Evaluating statements about the text

Read each of the statements below about the Ofsted revision of the framework for initial teacher education and decide which of them:

is supported by the text	**S**
is implied to be the case, or implicitly supported, by the text	**I**
states something for which there is no evidence or support in the text	**NE**
is implicitly contradicted or implicitly refuted in the text	**IC**
is explicitly contradicted or refuted in the text.	**EC**

Put the appropriate code in the box alongside each statement.

(In the computerised test you will be asked to drag the code to the appropriate answer.)

☐ The views of trainee teachers are not being sought at this stage.

☐ Many trainee teachers feel they have not been fully prepared with the essential practical skills for teaching.

☐ Inspection helps to raise standards and ensure that the best training is given.

☐ Some new teachers are not as good at managing behaviour as they should be.

☐ The present system for the selection of trainees is satisfactory.

Selecting headings and subheadings

From the four options below, choose the most suitable subheading for the second half of the text to be inserted at the top of paragraph 5. Tick the box next to your choice of subheading.

(In the computerised test you will be asked to drag a tick to your choice of answer.)

☐ Selecting for quality

☐ Going from strength to strength

☐ Need for a fresh focus

☐ Calling all teachers

Identifying possible readership or audience for a text

From the list of possible audiences for this document, select the audience that you think it would be most relevant to, and put an **M** in the box alongside; and the one you think it would be least relevant to, and put an **L** in the box alongside.

Questions

*(In the computerised test you will be asked to drag an **M** for the most relevant audience, or an **L** for the least relevant audience, into the appropriate boxes.)*

☐ Headteachers in primary schools

☐ Teaching staff in a university school of education

☐ Teachers of English in primary schools

☐ Qualified teachers working in schools

Remember: only three of these nine aspects of literacy will appear in the actual test.

2.6 | Answers and key points

Spelling

1. *independent*

> **Key points**
> Most words that end with that sound end in *-ent.*

2. *demonstrable*

> **Key points**
> Some words, like *demonstrate, educate,* lose an element when they gain a suffix.

3. *assessment*

> **Key points**
> Words vary in the way that they spell the *s* sound. This word has two pairs of doubles.

4. *adolescence*

> **Key points**
> Words vary in the way they spell the *s* sound. This word uses *sc.*

5. *pursue*

> **Key points**
> The sound represented here by *ur* is represented by different letter-strings in other words. They simply have to be learned by heart.

6. *fairies*

> **Key points**
> Luckily, this is one of the most reliable rules. Nouns that end in a consonant and *-y,* such as *fairy, party,* etc., drop the *y* and add *-ies* in the plural form.

Answers

7. *weighing*

> **Key points**
> This is clear but complex. If the sound is *ee*, the rule for using *i* and *e* together really is '*ie* except after *c*'. If the sound is not *ee*, the *e* comes first.

8. *fuelled*

> **Key points**
> Verbs that end in a single *-l*, like *instil*, take a second *l* when either *-ed* or *-ing* is added.

9. *affected*

> **Key points**
> The distinction between *affect* and *effect* baffles many educated adults. If you *affect* something, you have an *effect* on it. Try that as a mnemonic, with the *a* of *affect* coming first, as in the alphabet.

10. *responsibility*

> **Key points**
> Another case of having to learn by heart. There are just two ways to spell the suffixes we find in *capable* and *terrible*. Of *-able/ible* and *ability/ibility*, *able/ability* is the more common.

11. *practice*

> **Key points**
> *Practice/practise* and *advice/advise* confuse a lot of us. The words ending in *-ice* are nouns and could have the word *the* before them; the words ending in *-ise* are verbs and could have the word *I* in front of them.

12. *disappear*

> **Key points**
> Morphology, the way that words are built up from their parts, helps here. The prefixes *mis-* and *dis-* end in a single *-s*. What follows is a stem word, like *-take* or *-appear*. Those who write *dissappear* have imagined a non-existent prefix *diss-*.

Answers

13. *possession*

> **Key points**
> Here, the sound *s* is represented twice by *ss*. The double *ss* is very likely in the middle of a word and quite likely at the end.

14. *impracticable*

> **Key points**
> This is a mixture of morphology and the need to learn by heart whether a word uses *-able* or *-ible*. The morphology involved is a series of prefix + stem + suffix: *im + practice + able*. *Practice* loses *e*; *able* changes.

15. *humorous*

> **Key points**
> The stem word, the abstract noun *humour*, drops the *u* when it adds the adjective suffix *-ous*. This happens in other words, such as *labour, laborious* (but notice the added *i* in *laborious*).

16. *exaggerated*

> **Key points**
> Remember that the commonest type of misspelling is the use or non-use of the double consonant (incidentally, notice that word *misspelling*). This is one of the hardest to remember because there are no analogies.

17. *regrettably*

> **Key points**
> This is not about *able/ible* but about the way that a verb that ends in a consonant such as t is likely to double that consonant when an adverb suffix, such as *-ably*, is added. There are also analogies with *forget, forgettably*.

18. *automatically*

> **Key points**
> Apart from the use of a Greek suffix, *auto-*, meaning *self*, it is also a case of a fairly long and complex word whose spelling is close to the way it is said.

Answers

19. *curriculum*

> **Key points**
> Another example of the double consonant; these words are best learned by heart.

20. *embarrassment*

> **Key points**
> A useful mnemonic with this word might be: He went **R**eally **R**ed and **S**miled **S**hyly with embaRRaSSment.

21. *pedagogy*

> **Key points**
> Meaning 'the science of teaching'. The origin is Greek: 'paidagagos' – the slave who took children to and from school. This is a spelling best learned by heart.

22. *allowed*

> **Key points**
> Confusion between such homophones as *allowed, a loud* and *aloud* is serious because it shows that the writer does very little reading and that the simple grammatical and meaning distinctions between the participle *allowed* and the adverb *aloud* have been overlooked.

23. *allot*

> **Key points**
> The words *allot* and *a lot* are also homophones; they sound the same as each other but have different meanings. We *allot* when we distribute something among recipients. There may be *a lot* of recipients.

24. *maturity*

> **Key points**
> It is another example of the way that an adjective, *mature*, drops the final *e* when the noun suffix *-ity* is added but it is also quite regular phonically.

Answers

25. *counselling*

Key points
The usual UK spelling is 'counselling'. While the US version, 'counseling', is acceptable, the misspellings in the question (counciling, counsiling, councelling) are incorrect. Most errors arise from the confusion of the words 'council' and 'counsel'.

26. *miscellaneous*

Key points
Notice the use of *sc* for the *s* sound, the double *ll* and the *e* in the final syllable. Also, its parts are *misc + ell + an + eous*.

27. *approximation*

Key points
The use of a double consonant is a frequent problem; the use of *x* is infrequent.

28. *reprehensible*

Key points
There are no double consonants but the use of *i* in the final consonant is fairly rare.

29. *apprenticeship*

Key points
Here, there is a double consonant; the *s* sound is represented by *ce*.

Punctuation

1. As soon as we speak, (1) we reveal a great deal of ourselves to our audience. Suppose you ask someone,

    (2) "Shall we have a drink? (3)" (4)

    Suppose the other person replies, (5)

    "Yes, I'd like a whiskey, (6) me."

    That tag, *me*, tells you that the speaker probably comes from (7) Manchester.

Answers

Sometimes, what people say does tell you something about their origin but it is less definite. A friend asks you and another friend,

"Now, what would youse two like to drink?"

The questioner may or may not come from Ireland but will certainly have a background there because that use of (8) 'youse', unknown in standard English, has its roots in the Irish having one form of 'you' for one person (9) (tú) and another form of 'you' for two people (9) (sibh). However, (10) none of this means that any of these speakers could actually speak any Irish!

Key points
(1) The subordinate clause appears first so it should be separated from the main clause by a comma.

(2) The first letter in the sentence needs a capital letter.

(3) A question requires a question mark.

(4) Direct speech needs speech marks both at the beginning and at the end. The two marks, paired, form a consistency.

(5) The mark before a direct quotation is usually a comma.

(6) A comma is needed to separate the tag 'me' from the rest.

(7) The city of Manchester requires a capital letter.

(8) This is a bit of language that differs from the rest of the text and needs quotation marks to identify it.

(9) The Irish words tú and sibh break into the rest and are best placed within brackets.

(10) A comma is needed after 'However'. This is important because 'however' can have two different meanings:

– nevertheless; yet; on the other hand; in spite of that

– to whatever extent or degree; no matter how

The comma indicates the intended meaning. Consider the two sets of sentences below:

However the scripts were analysed, the marks remained the same.

However, the scripts were analysed; the marks remained the same.

Or

The marks remained the same however the scripts were analysed.

The marks remained the same; however, the scripts were analysed.

Answers

2. The concern of the (11) Head of (12) English was evident after reading the (13) 'Can do Better' report on literacy. If we look at (14) boys' performance in English, we have to agree that there is, generally (15), some cause for concern. Is there anything that can be done to help them improve?

Among the (16) short-term approaches that seemed to help boys are (17):

enthusiastically encouraged private reading;

clearly set tasks (18);

explicit teaching of reading strategies;

a wide range of outcomes from reading;

reading preferences that are discussed.

Key points

(11) and (12) As proper nouns, the head of english needs capital letters: 'Head of English'.

(13) The title of a document should be in single quotation marks.

(14) The performance belongs to the boys so an apostrophe is needed after the **s**.

(15) The interruption of the flow of the sentence by the word 'generally' should be marked by twinned commas, one before and one after the word.

(16) A hyphen should be used to link the two words to show they are one unit of meaning. Without a hyphen 'short term' could mean a school term of only a few weeks.

(17) A list is being introduced so a colon is necessary.

(18) Each item on the list is more than one word long and needs separating with a semicolon.

---

3. What is it about (19) Standard English that makes it standard? (20)

(21)

Like every language, English has gone through many changes. The Saxons and Angles who settled here brought their own languages with them, (22) predominantly Saxon, and after a while the dialects of Anglo-Saxon overcame the Celtic languages that had flourished along with Latin until soon after the Romans left in 410AD. The languages spoken by the later Scandinavian invaders were probably just about intelligible to some of the Anglo-(23)Saxons but changes and borrowings continued: the new invaders' (24) legacy to us includes **they, them, their**. Anglo-Saxon, modified by Scandinavian, with dialects that were barely intelligible to

Answers

other Anglo-Saxon speakers, continued for hundreds of years but, thankfully, (25) it became simpler. (26) The German word for *big* is *gross* but it has six versions. Our Anglo-Saxon ancestors had eleven versions of adjectives; (27) we have just three: *big, bigger, biggest*. Even when we complicate matters by having *good, better,* (28) **best**, that is still easier than Anglo-Saxon! (29)

Key points

(19) There is no need for a capital for **standard**; the lower case version is now the accepted convention.

(20) A question requires a question mark.

(21) After the first sentence, comes the beginning of an answer. A new paragraph is needed.

(22) **predominantly Saxon** breaks into the sentence and needs a pair of commas, one before and one after.

(23) A hyphen is needed for Anglo-Saxon (as for Irish-American).

(24) The noun is **invaders** so they need an apostrophe before **legacy**.

(25) **Thankfully** is also an interruption and a pair of commas is needed.

(26) A sentence ends with a full stop.

(27) There are two sentences but their meanings are so closely related that they need a semicolon to link them.

(28) The series of three items in a list without an **and** requires a series of commas.

(29) This is an exclamation but that shows how personal punctuation is.

Grammar

Unrelated participles

A   2   *Vygotsky* is the one who did the *realising*; who *realised*.

B   1   The *headteacher* was the one who was *persuaded*.

C   2   It was *Peters* who *conceded*, who did the *conceding*, not his views.

D   4   The *children were thought*, nobody and nothing else.

Key points

This relates to the issue of agreement between subject and verb. You clarify the matter by asking **who did** it.

Answers

Wrong tense or tense consistency

A   2

> **Key points**
> *have been* makes most sense because it matches or agrees with the other verbs: the series of *wish* and *had worked* followed by *was* and *has meant*. *Made* confirms the choice of *have been* because it makes *was* impossible.

B   4

> **Key points**
> When there are several verbs in a sentence, some in different tenses, the question is to decide what other verb this one should be like. This verb is part of a series beginning *I'll make* and so is in the future tense.

C   1

> **Key points**
> There is a series of short clauses beginning with *I can't* and all have to use the same verb form.

D   4

> **Key points**
> *grown* makes most sense because it is the only option that fits the use of the verb form *have examined*: *compared* parallels *grown* because the two verbs make use of the *have* of *have examined*.

Lack of agreement between subject and verb

A   4

> **Key points**
> The subject of the sentence is *trouble,* a singular noun, so the verb has to be singular also: *is*. There can often be a problem with subjects whose headwords are a long way from the verb; it is very easy to be trapped into picking up the nearest noun and thinking that that is the subject (in this sentence, the trap is *way*). This question does also ask you to be careful about the tense: the present.

Answers

B   2

> **Key points**
> The subject is *attitudes* so the verb has to be in the plural: *were*. Again, there is always a problem with a sentence with several nouns: out of *friend, cause, problem, attitudes, teacher*, which is the subject of this verb? The correct tense confirms the answer.

C   3

> **Key points**
> This seems quite easy but the issue is that there are, apparently, several subjects: *teacher, sicknesses, parents*. The clue is the word *or* which tells you, logically, that only one thing is the subject, not everything listed. This is confirmed by the singular *it*.

D   3

> **Key points**
> This time, the tense not only fits the grammar but also the obvious sense of *the future*.

Comprehension

Attributing statements to categories

| 0 | They are going to require more from teacher training courses. |

> **Key points**
> Para 1 says that Ofsted is proposing to raise expectations of providers of teacher training.

| HMCI | They regard the training of the next cohort of teachers as very significant. |

> **Key points**
> Para 3 reports the HMCI saying that the training of the next generation of teachers is crucial.

Answers

| TT | They are going to be expected to know how to develop literacy skills. |

Key points
Para 5 says that inspections will focus even more on the quality of training and trainees' subject knowledge and their understanding and competence in developing pupils' literacy skills.

| ITEP | They are going to have to look more closely at placements. |

Key points
Para 5 says that inspection will concentrate on the quality of partnerships ITE providers have with settings, schools and colleges.

Completing a bulleted list

It is anticipated that all future ITE inspections will:

take account of the views of newly or recently qualified teachers

Key points
Bullet point 3 says Ofsted proposes to take account of the views of users, trainees and former trainees, including newly qualified and recently qualified teachers

target inspections only where improvement is most needed

Key points
Para 6 says Ofsted proposes that future inspections will be informed by a robust risk assessment process so they can be targeted where improvement is needed most.

improve ITE by providing an external evaluation of strengths and weaknesses

Key points
Bullet point 9 says that Ofsted proposes to drive improvement in the sector by providing an external evaluation of strengths and weaknesses.

Answers

Sequencing information

FIRST Partnerships previously judged to be satisfactory will be inspected.

> **Key points**
> This is the first part of the new proportionate process described in paragraph 6.

SECOND Those that continue to be satisfactory will be inspected within 12 to 18 months.

> **Key points**
> This is the next step in the process.

THIRD Partnerships will have a full inspection within three years of a previous inspection.

> **Key points**
> This is the final stage of the new process.

Presenting main points

Upgrade the quality of training given by ITE providers.

> **Key points**
> Para 1 says that Ofsted is proposing to raise expectations of providers of teacher training.

Look more closely at how trainees are evaluated and selected for ITE.

> **Key points**
> Para 5 says that Ofsted proposes that inspection will look more closely at the selection of trainees.

Ensure practical teaching skills are top of the agenda for trainees.

> **Key points**
> Para 1 says that Ofsted is proposing to ensure that more trainees are better prepared with the practical skills that teachers need most. The point (about behaviour management) is then repeated three times elsewhere in the text.

Answers

Introduce one comprehensive criterion for the general effectiveness of ITE provision.

> *Key points*
> Para 2 says that clearer, more challenging criteria with fewer, more streamlined judgements and one overarching judgement for overall effectiveness are to be drawn up.

These points should **not** be included:

Encourage teachers working in schools to tell them their views on ITE.

> *Key points*
> Para 4 says HMCI would like 'in particular those who provide training, are currently in training, or thinking of joining a teacher training programme, to tell us their views'. This list does not include practising teachers.

Gauge the effectiveness of the teaching of phonics by newly qualified teachers.

> *Key points*
> Bullet point 6 suggests that inspections will look at the provision of phonics training received by trainees where their feedback raises concerns.

Introduce a thematic approach into the inspection of behaviour management.

> *Key points*
> Para 5 talks about a thematic element to inspection; not just about the inspection of behaviour management.

Scrutinise the inspection criteria used to assess teachers in schools.

> *Key points*
> The document concerns the scrutiny of teaching in ITE, not the teaching in schools.

Reduce the notice period given prior to inspection of ITE provision.

> *Key points*
> This is not a main objective; it is a topic on which Ofsted is seeking views.

Answers

Matching texts to summaries

Reread paragraphs 1, 3 and 5. From the list of statements below, select the one that most accurately summarises the content of these three paragraphs. Tick the box next to your choice. (*In the computerised test you will be asked to drag a tick symbol to the box beside your choice.*)

The most important attributes of the trainee teacher emerging from ITE are the abilities to control and manage behaviour and to teach literacy effectively.

Key points
When summarising the three paragraphs look for the key points they share. All three stress the importance of being able to manage behaviour and to teach literacy.

While the other statements are significant, they are not common to all three paragraphs and should not be chosen.

Identifying the meanings of words and phrases

'... **raise expectations of providers of teacher training**' (paragraph 1) is closest in meaning to:

investigate the endeavours of providers of teacher training

Key points
This is only a part of raising expectations. **Do not** choose this option.

lift the requirements of providers of teacher training

Key points
In this context 'requirements' and 'expectations' are very close in meaning. **This option should be selected.**

boost the hopes of providers of teacher training

Key points
In this context, 'boosting hopes' is not the same thing as 'raising expectations'. **Do not** choose this option.

Answers

increase the demands on providers of teacher training

> **Key points**
> Increasing demands is not the same thing as raising expectations; it is the result of raising expectations. **Do not** choose this option.

'... **a more proportionate approach to'** (paragraph 6) is closest in meaning to:

a more commensurate method of

> **Key points**
> The words 'commensurate' and 'proportionate' have a very similar meaning, i.e. that of 'balance' or 'equality' or 'levelness'. **This option should be selected.**

a more detached pathway to

> **Key points**
> The words 'detached' and 'proportionate' do not have the same meaning. **Do not** choose this option.

a more competitive move towards

> **Key points**
> In this context there is no defined competitor for inspection and this option should not be chosen. **Do not** choose this option.

a more rigorous course of

> **Key points**
> This means a tougher course of inspection; this does not have the same meaning as 'balanced' or 'in proportion'. **Do not** choose this option.

Evaluating statements about the text

EC	The views of trainee teachers are not being sought at this stage.

> **Key points**
> Paragraph 4 states: 'I'd like to encourage anyone ... in particular ... those who are currently in training, ... to tell us their views.'

Answers

| NE | Many trainee teachers feel they have not been fully prepared with the essential practical skills for teaching. |

Key points
This does not appear in the text.

| S | Inspection helps to raise standards and ensure that the best training is given. |

Key points
Paragraph 4 says that inspection helps to raise standards and ensure the best training is provided.

| I | Some new teachers are not as good at managing behaviour as they should be. |

Key points
In four places the document states that classroom behaviour and management are issues that need to be addressed with a view to improvement. This implies that in some newly qualified teachers, these skills are lacking.

| IC | The present system for the selection of trainees is satisfactory. |

Key points
Paragraph 5 opening sentence 'it is proposed that inspection will look more closely at the selection of trainees ...' Without actually saying as much, this contradicts the idea that the current system is satisfactory.

Selecting headings and subheadings

Selecting for quality

Key points
This is one of a number of important points in this section of the text. **Do not** choose it.

Answers

Going from strength to strength

> *Key points*
> This covers 'building on the strengths' (paragraph 5); 'retain the focus on trainees' outcomes'; continue to involve leaders et al. in inspections; and continue to drive improvement (bullet points). **This option should be selected.**

Need for a fresh focus

> *Key points*
> This is one of a number of proposals in the document; further, the need to 'focus afresh' is mentioned in the first half of the document (paragraph 4). **Do not** choose it.

Calling all teachers

> *Key points*
> This is a fairly minor point in the document first mentioned in paragraph 4. **Do not** choose it.

Identifying possible readership or audience for a text

Headteachers in primary schools

> *Key points*
> These headteachers might be interested but only if they were partnership schools or offering ITE training. **Do not** choose this option.

Institutions providing initial teacher education

> *Key points*
> These institutions are likely to be very interested as they are the subject of inspection. **Choose this audience as the 'most relevant' (M).**

Teachers of English in primary schools

> *Key points*
> These teachers might be interested especially in the references to literacy and phonics. However, they would not be directly affected by many of the other details. **Do not** choose this option.

Answers

Qualified teachers working in schools

Key points

These teachers are only very marginally affected by this review. The HMCI does not include them on the list of people involved in ITE from whom it would be interesting to hear and they are not directly mentioned in the text. **Choose this audience as the 'least relevant' (L).**

3 | The Numeracy Skills Test

Practice questions are included in all sections and can be found on the following pages:

Mental arithmetic page 116
Using and applying general arithmetic page 122
Interpreting and using statistical information page 144
The Revision checklists for the Numeracy test are on pages 109–111

3.1 | Introduction

Introduction to the test

The numeracy skills test is a computerised test, which is divided into two sections:

- section 1 for the mental arithmetic questions;
- section 2 for the written questions known as 'on-screen' questions.

The **mental arithmetic** section is an audio test heard through headphones. Calculators are not allowed, but noting numbers and jotting down working will be permitted. (You will be issued with a wipe-clean board and a pen to help with this.) There are 12 questions in this section. Note: this section must be answered first; each question has a fixed time in which you must answer (18 seconds); you cannot return to a question if you later wish to change your answer. Questions will be asked to test your ability to carry out mental calculations using fractions, percentages, measurement, conversions and time (see the detailed content list on page 109).

The **'on-screen'** questions: there are 16 written questions in this section. Seven questions are focused on *interpreting* and using written data and nine are focused on *solving* written arithmetic problems. Questions and answers will be in one of the following forms:

- multiple-choice questions where you will choose the single correct response from a fixed number of alternative answers;
- multiple-response questions where you choose single or multiple correct statements from a fixed number of given statements;
- questions that require a single answer;
- questions where you will select the answer by pointing and clicking on the correct point in a table, chart or graph (to change an answer click on an alternative point);
- questions where you will select your answer from a number of alternative answers and place the answer into the answer box provide (to change an answer drag it back to its original position and choose another).

In this part of the test you can use the 'on-screen' calculator. You answer questions using the mouse and the keyboard and you can move between questions by using the 'next' and 'previous' buttons. You can return to questions either by using the 'flag' button and then the 'review' button or by waiting until the end of the test when you will have the option of reviewing all the questions – provided there is time!

Section 3.4 provides guidance, examples and questions on *solving* written arithmetic problems. Your ability to use general everyday arithmetic is assessed. For example in working correctly with: time; money; ratio and proportion; fractions; decimals and percentages; distance and area; conversions between currencies; and simple formulae and averages, including mean, median, mode and range.

Section 3.5 provides guidance, examples and questions on *interpreting* and using written data. Your ability to identify trends correctly, to make comparisons and draw conclusions, and interpret charts and tables correctly is assessed.

Time for the test

The time limit for the whole test is approximately 48 minutes – at the end of which the test will shut down automatically.

The contexts for the questions

One of the aims of the numeracy skills test is to ensure that teachers have the skills and understanding necessary to analyse the sort of data that is now in schools. Consequently most questions will be set within contexts such as:

- national test data;
- target setting and school improvement data;
- pupil progress and attainment over time;
- special educational needs (SEN);
- GCSE subject choices and results.

Hints and advice

The mental arithmetic, audio section

Each mental arithmetic question is heard twice. After the first reading an answer box appears on the screen. You will have a short time – 18 seconds – to work out the answer and type it into the answer box, after which the next question will automatically appear. As mentioned earlier, you cannot move forwards or backwards between questions. At the start of the test you will hear a practice question.

- Concentrate the first time the question is read, and note down the key numbers. For example, a question could be: 'In a class of 30 pupils, 24 are boys. What fraction are girls?'. You should jot down 30 and 24. The second time the question is heard, concentrate on what to do with those numbers (for example, $30 - 24 = 6$ (so there are 6 girls) then $\frac{6}{30} = \frac{1}{5}$).
- Start to work out the answer as soon as you have the information. You may be able to do this while you hear the second reading of the question.
- If you cannot answer a question don't worry or panic – enter a likely answer, then forget it. Remember, you don't need to get every single question right.
- Note that you don't have to worry about units, i.e. £ or € or cm, for example. The units will appear in the answer box.
- Listen carefully to what the question requires in the answer. For example, a question could ask for a time 'using the 24-hour clock', or an answer 'to the nearest whole number', or 'to two decimal places'. (There are notes on this in Section 3.4)
- Fractions need to be entered in the lowest terms. For example, 6/8 should be entered as 3/4 and 7/28 should be entered as 1/4.
- Practise using mental strategies. For example, purchasing five books that cost £5.99 can be worked out by multiplying 5 x £6 (£30) and subtracting 5 x lp (5p) to give the answer of £29.95.
- Remember the link between fractions and percentages – see page 108.

The on-screen questions

- Try not to spend more than two minutes on any one question and keep an eye on the time remaining. If you think you are exceeding the time then move on – you can always return to any you still need to complete at the end of the test and insert an answer. Try not to leave any answers blank at the end of the test.
- Read each question carefully. For example, a question may ask for the percentage of pupils who achieved level 4 and above. Don't just look at those who gained level 4; the question included the words 'and above', so you need to include those who achieved 'above', i.e. achieved level 5, level 6, and so on.
- Check that you are giving the correct information in the answer. A table may give you details of the number of marks a pupil achieved but the question may be asking for a percentage score.

The on-screen calculator

When the mental arithmetic section of the test is finished, a basic four-function calculator will be available on the screen for you to use for the rest of the test. No other calculators can be used. You can move the calculator around the screen using the mouse. The on-screen calculator works through the mouse and through the number pad on the keyboard. If you wish to use the number pad you must ensure that the number lock key 'Num Lock' is activated.

Notes on using the on-screen calculator

- To cancel an operation, press $\boxed{\text{CE}}$.
- Always use the 'clear' button $\boxed{\text{C}}$ on the calculator before beginning a new calculation.
- Always check the display of the calculator to make sure that the number shown is what you wanted.
- Check calculations and make sure that your final answer makes sense in the context of the question. For example, the number of pupils gaining level 5 in a test will not be greater than the size of the cohort or group.

Other hints

1. Rounding up and down

- Make sure that any instructions to round an answer up or down are followed – or the answer will be marked as incorrect.
- Use the context to make sure whether a decimal answer should be rounded up or down. For example, an answer of 16.4 lessons for a particular activity is clearly not appropriate and the answer would need to be rounded up to 17 lessons.
- Questions may specify that the answer should be rounded to the nearest whole number or be rounded to two decimal places. See the notes at the start of Section 3.4.
- When carrying out calculations relating to money, the answer shown on the calculator display will need to be rounded to the nearest penny (unless otherwise indicated). Hence, if calculating in pounds, round to two decimal places to show the number of pence. If 10.173 is the answer in pounds on the calculator display, rounding to the nearest penny gives £10.17.

2. Answering multi-stage questions

The calculator provided is not a scientific calculator and therefore care needs to be taken with 'mixed operations' (i.e. calculations using several function keys). It is important that the function keys are pressed in the appropriate order for the calculation. It may also be useful to note down answers to particular stages of the calculation.

It is important to remember to carry out the calculation required by the question in the following order: any calculation within brackets followed by division/multiplication followed by addition and/or subtraction. Thus, the answer to the calculation $2 + 3 \times 4$ is 14 and not 20; the answer to $\frac{18}{3+6}$ is $\frac{18}{9} = 2$; and the answer to $\frac{18}{3} + 6 = 6 + 6 = 12$. See the notes at the start of Section 3.4.

3. Dealing with fractions

Although fractions will appear in the usual format within a question (for example, $\frac{3}{4}$), to enter a fraction in an answer, use the 'forward slash' key (for example, 'one-half' would be entered as 1/2). To use the on-screen calculator to calculate with fractions then it is probably easier to deal with the fraction first, converting it into a decimal, and then multiply by this decimal. For example, to calculate $\frac{5}{8}$ of 320, first enter $5/8 = 0.625$. Multiply 0.625 by 320, obtaining 200 as the answer.

How to use this section

This chapter is divided into five sections, following this introduction.

Section 3.2: this very short section has been included to remind you of the basic arithmetic processes. The majority of you will be able to miss this unit out, but some may welcome a chance to revise fractions, decimals, percentages, etc.

Sections 3.3 to 3.5: these cover the three 'content' areas (see above), one area per section.

Section 3.6: this contains answers and key points for all the questions in the main section.

In each section, the additional required knowledge, language and vocabulary are explained, and worked examples of the type of questions to be faced are provided, together with the practice questions. The answers for these questions are given in Section 3.6, together with further advice and guidance on solutions.

Revision checklists

The following charts show in detail the coverage of the three main chapters and the practice tests. You can use the checklists in your revision to make sure that you have covered all the key content areas.

Revision checklist for Section 3.3: Mental arithmetic

Syllabus Reference	Content	Question
1a	Time – varied contexts	1, 7, 18, 21, 34, 39, 44
1b	Amounts of money – varied contexts	12, 38, 41, 43
1c/d/e	1c Proportion – answer as a fraction 1d Proportion – answer as a percentage 1e Proportion – answer as a decimal	37 27 22
1f	Fractions	16, 29, 45
1g	Decimals	32
1h	Percentages – varied contexts	2, 11, 19, 20, 24, 26, 30, 35, 42
1i/j/k	1i Measurements – distance 1j Measurements – area 1k Measurements – other	23, 36 25, 40
1l/m/n/o/p/q	1l Conversions – from one currency to another	
	1m Conversions – from fractions to decimals	15
	1n Conversions – from decimals to fractions	
	1o Conversions – from percentages to fractions	31
	1p Conversions – from fractions to percentages	4, 9, 13, 28, 33
	1q Conversions – other	6
1r	Combination of one or more of: addition, subtraction, multiplication, division (may involve amounts of money or whole numbers)	3, 5, 8, 10, 14, 17

Revision checklist for Section 3.4: Solving written arithmetic problems

(Note: Only the main references are used; many questions will cover more than one reference.)

Syllabus Reference	Content	Question
3a	Time – varied contexts	7, 17, 23, 29, 31, 33
3b	Amounts of money	2, 57, 60(a)
3c, d, e, f	3c Proportion – answer as a fraction	14
	3d Proportion – answer as a percentage	14
	3e Proportion – answer as a decimal	14, 62(b)
	3f Ratios	3, 59, 60(b)
3g	Percentages – varied contexts	4, 5, 6, 8, 9, 10, 11, 12, 13, 18, 27, 39, 42, 47, 56(a), 62(a)
3h	Fractions	19, 24, 54
3i	Decimals	41
3j, k, l, m, n	3j Measurements – distance	21, 26, 28, 30, 36
	3k Measurements – area	22
	3l Conversions – from one currency to another	2
	3m Conversions – from fractions to decimals or vice versa	14
	3n Conversions – other	15, 16, 20, 24, 38, 48, 61
3o, p, q, r, s	3o Averages – mean 3p Averages – median 3q Averages – mode	45, 58
	3r Range	35, 56(b)
	3s Averages – combination	1, 34, 44
3t	Given formulae	32, 40, 43, 46, 49, 50, 5 1, 52, 53, 55

Revision checklist for Section 3.5: Interpreting and using written data

(Note: Only the main references are used; many questions will cover more than one reference.)

Syllabus Reference	Content	Question
2a	Identify trends over time	9, 13, 17, 19, 21
2b	Make comparisons in order to draw conclusions	2, 5, 10, 11, 12, 14, 23, 24
2c	Interpret and use information	1, 3, 4, 6, 7, 8, 15, 16, 18, 20
3o	Averages	9

3.2 | Key knowledge

Fractions, decimals and percentages

You must remember decimals and place value:

hundreds	tens	ones	.	tenths	hundredths
4	3	5	•	2	7

4 hundreds + 3 tens + 5 ones + 2 tenths + 7 hundredths

$$= 400 + 30 + 5 + \frac{2}{10} + \frac{7}{100}$$

$$= 435.27$$

Take care when adding or subtracting decimals to line up the decimal points. Remember, too, when multiplying decimals by 10 that all the digits move one place to the left, so 435.27 × 10 becomes 4352.7 (the rule you will probably remember is 'move the decimal point one place to the right'); and when dividing by 100, the digits move two places to the right, so 4352.7 ÷ 100 becomes 43.527 (similarly the rule you may remember is 'move the decimal point two places to the left').

When multiplying two decimals the method you may remember is to *ignore* the decimal points, do the multiplication and then count up the number of decimal figures in the question numbers. The total will give the number of decimal figures in the answer number, so that 0.4 × 0.5 is calculated as 4 × 5 = 20; there are 2 decimal figures in the question numbers (0.4 and 0.5) so there are 2 in the answer. Therefore, the answer is 0.20. It would be better to think of this calculation as follows:

$$0.4 \times 0.5 = \frac{4}{10} \times \frac{5}{10} = \frac{20}{100} = 0.2$$

You must remember how to work with fractions. There are several ways of 'looking' at a fraction, for example: $\frac{3}{4}$ = 3 parts out of 4; or 3 divided by 4 or 3 shared by 4 = 3 ÷ 4 = 0.75; or three lots of a quarter = $3 \times \frac{1}{4}$; or a quarter of 3 = $\frac{1}{4} \times 3$.

One way to calculate, say, of $\frac{2}{5}$ of £ 20 is: find a fifth, £20 ÷ 5 = £4 then multiply this by 2 = £8. Another way is to change the fraction into a decimal:

$$\frac{2}{5} = 2 \div 5 = 0.4, \text{ then multiply } 0.4 \times £20 = £8.$$

You will need to know how to simplify a fraction by dividing both the numerator and the denominator by the same factor.

Example

$\frac{12}{28} = \frac{3}{7}$ dividing the numerator and the denominator by 4

or $\frac{54}{72} = \frac{27}{36} = \frac{9}{12} = \frac{3}{4}$ dividing top and bottom by 2 then by 3 and then by 3 again.

You must remember that percentages are fractions with denominators of 100 (per cent means per 100). For example, 5% represents $\frac{5}{100}$, 75% represents $\frac{75}{100}$. You can convert percentages to decimals by dividing by 100, so 5% = $\frac{5}{100}$ = 0.05, and 75% = $\frac{75}{100}$ = 0.75.

To change a fraction into a percentage, first change it into a decimal and then multiply by 100.

Example

$\frac{3}{8}$ as a percentage us 3 ÷ 8 = 0.375, 0.375 × 100 = 37.5%

To find the percentage of a quantity, change the % into a decimal and then multiply the result by the quantity.

Example

To find 30% of 50 first change 30% into a decimal (= 0.3) and then multiply by 50 giving 0.3 × 50 = 15

or find 10% of 50 = $\frac{1}{10}$ × 50 = 5 so 30% = 3 × 10% = 3 × 5 = 15

You need to be able to calculate percentages in problems such as 'what is 14 marks out of 25 marks as a percentage?'

Example

Either find 14 out of 25 as a fraction and then multiply by 100 giving us $\frac{14}{25}$ = $\frac{14}{25}$ × 100 = 14 × 4 = 56%

or use equivalent fractions: $\frac{14}{25}$ = $\frac{56}{100}$ (multiplying numerator and denominator by 4 to get a denominator of 100)

= 56%

Example

Percentages are useful for comparisons:

In a test Richard got 40 right out of 80, Sarah got 45% and Paul managed to get $\frac{5}{8}$ correct. Who did best and who did worst in the test?

Richard got 50%; Paul got $\frac{5}{8}$ × $\frac{100}{1}$ = 62.5%: so Sarah did the worst and Paul did the best.

Here are some common fractions, decimals and percentages.

You should learn these.

1%	$\frac{1}{100}$	0.01	(divide by 100)
5%	$\frac{1}{20}$	0.05	(divide by 20)
10%	$\frac{1}{10}$	0.1	(divide by 10)
$12\frac{1}{2}$%	$\frac{1}{8}$	0.125	(divide by 8)
20%	$\frac{1}{5}$	0.2	(divide by 5)
25%	$\frac{1}{4}$	0.25	(divide by 4)
50%	$\frac{1}{2}$	0.5	(divide by 2)
75%	$\frac{3}{4}$	0.75	(divide by 4, multiply by 3)

Questions

1. Calculate these totals without using a calculator:

   (a) 1.8 + 2.0 + 0.5   (b) 0.4 + 0.04 + 4   (c) 2.1 + 0.09 + 7 + 0.9

   (d) 2.8 + 3.2 – 0.6   (e) 0.04 + 1.04 + 0.4   (f) 2.01 + 0.09 + 7 + 0.09

2. Calculate these without using a calculator:

   (a) 1.4 x 30   (b) 0.5 x 0.7   (c) 0.4 x 5

3. Write these percentages as fractions in their simplest form:

   (a) 2%   (b) 25%   (c) 85%   (d) 12.5%   (e) 47%

4. Write these fractions as percentages:

   (a) $\frac{3}{8}$ (b) $\frac{13}{25}$ (c) $\frac{12}{40}$ (d) $\frac{36}{60}$

5. Work these out:

   (a) 25% of £40   (b) 75% of £20   (c) 12% of 50   (d) 20% of 45

6. Simplify these fractions, writing them in their lowest terms:

   (a) $\dfrac{24}{36}$ (b) $\dfrac{18}{30}$ (c) $\dfrac{30}{75}$ (d) $\dfrac{75}{100}$

7. Which is largest?

   $\dfrac{90}{150}$ $\dfrac{39}{60}$ $\dfrac{61}{100}$

Mean, median, mode and range

The *mean* is the average most people give if asked for an average – the mean is found by adding up all the values in the list and dividing this total by the number of values.

The *median* is the middle value when all the values in the list are put in size order. If there are two 'middle' values the median is the mean of these two.

The *mode* is the most common value.

The *range* is the difference between the highest value and the lowest value.

Example

This example should illustrate each of the four calculations.

The children in Class 6 gained the following marks in a test:

Boys	45	46	48	60	42	53	47	51
	54	54	49	48	47	53	48	45
Girls	45	47	47	55	46	53	54	63
	48	50	46	51	48	48		

Work out the mean, median, mode and range for the boys and girls and compare the distributions of the marks.

The calculation for the boys:

$$\text{Mean}: \frac{42+45+45+46+47+47+48+48+48+49+51+53+53+54+54+60}{16}$$

$$= 49 \text{ (to the nearest whole number)}$$

Median: there are 16 values, so the median is midway between the 8th and 9th values

$$= \frac{48 + 48}{2} = 48$$

The *mode* is 48.

The *range* is $60 - 42 = 18$.

8. Now work out the values for the girls. Then compare the distributions.

3.3 | Mental arithmetic

Notes

The mathematics required in this part of the test should usually be straightforward. The content and skills likely to be tested are listed in the Introduction (see page 105). Look back at this to remind yourself.

> *Key point*
> When you are taking the test, listen for, and jot down, numbers that may give short-cuts or ease the calculations, such as those that allow doubling and halving. For example, multiply by 100 then divide by 2 if you need to multiply by 50, or multiply by 100 and divide by 4 if you are multiplying by 25. To calculate percentages, first find 10% by dividing by 10 then double for 20% or divide by 2 for 5% and so on. Look back at the hints in the Introduction.

Remember

- Calculators are not allowed.
- Questions will be read out twice. When answering the questions in this section, ask someone to read each question out to you and then, without a pause, read out the question again.
- There should then be a pause to allow you to record the answer before the next question is read out. The pause should be 18 seconds long.

Hint

You might find it helpful to ask someone to read out these practice questions. They will need to read them out at a sensible speed, as if they were reading a story to children. Remind them that each question should be read out twice and that they should then pause for 18 seconds, before reading out the next question. Numbers in these questions are in words, rather than using digits, to emphasise that they are spoken.

Questions

1. As part of a two and a quarter hour tennis training session, pupils received specialist coaching for one hour and twenty minutes. How many minutes of the training session remained?

2. A test has forty questions, each worth one mark. The pass mark was seventy per cent. How many questions had to be answered correctly to pass the test?

3. Dining tables seat six children. How many tables are needed to seat one hundred children?

4. Three classes of twenty-eight pupils took the end of Key Stage two mathematics test. Sixty-three pupils gained a level five result. What percentage is this?

Questions

5. A coach holds fifty-two passengers. How many coaches will be needed for a school party of four hundred and fifty people?

6. Eight kilometres is about five miles. About how many kilometres is thirty miles?

7. The journey from school to a sports centre took thirty-five minutes each way. The pupils spent two hours at the sports centre. They left school at oh-nine-thirty. At what time did they return?

8. It is possible to seat forty people in a row across the hall. How many rows are needed to seat four hundred and thirty-two people?

9. Pupils spent twenty-five hours in lessons each week. Four hours per week were allocated to science. What percentage of the lesson time per week was spent on the other subjects?

10. A science practical assessment contained two tasks. In the first task all fifteen members of a class scored four marks each. In the second task nine members scored five marks each and the other six members scored three marks each. What was the total number of marks scored by the class?

11. In a test, eighty per cent of the pupils in class A achieved level four and above. In class B twenty-two out of twenty-five pupils reached the same standard. What was the difference between the two classes in the percentage of pupils reaching level four and above?

12. Two hundred pupils correctly completed a sponsored spell of fifty words. Each pupil was sponsored at five pence per word. How much money did the pupils raise in total?

13. A pupil scores forty-two marks out of a possible seventy in a class test. What percentage score is this?

14. There are one hundred and twenty pupils in a year group. Each has to take home two notices. Paper costs three pence per copy. How much will the notices cost?

15. What is seven and a half per cent as a decimal?

16. In a class of thirty-five pupils, four out of seven are boys. How many girls are there in the class?

17. In a school there are five classes of twenty-five pupils and five classes of twenty-eight pupils. How many pupils are there in the school?

18. A school has four hours and twenty-five minutes class contact time per day. What is the weekly contact time (assume a five-day week)?

19. In part one of an examination, a pupil scored eighteen marks out of a possible twenty-five marks. In part two he scored sixteen marks out of twenty-five. What was his final score for the examination? Give your answer as a percentage.

Questions

20. In a year group of one hundred and twenty pupils, eighty per cent achieved a level four or a level five in Key Stage two English. Sixty pupils achieved a level five. How many pupils achieved a level four?

21. A teacher wants to record a film on a three-hour video tape which starts at eleven fifty-five p.m. and ends at one forty-five a.m. the following day. How much time will there be left on the tape?

22. In a year group of one hundred and forty-four pupils fifty-four pupils travel to school on school buses. What proportion of the year group does not travel on school buses? Give your answer as a decimal.

23. A space two point five metres by two point five metres is to be used for a flower bed. What is this area in square metres?

24. In a class of thirty pupils, sixty per cent of the pupils are girls. How many boys are there in the class?

25. A teacher takes pupils in the school minibus forty miles to the regional hockey trials. He estimates travelling at an average speed of twenty-five miles per hour. How many minutes will the journey take?

26. Twenty per cent of the pupils in a school with three hundred and fifteen pupils have free school meals. How many pupils is this?

27. In a practical assessment lasting one hour and twenty minutes a teacher allocated twenty minutes for setting up apparatus. What proportion of the lesson time was available for the actual assessment?

28. A pupil scores fourteen out of a possible twenty-five in a test. What is this as a percentage?

29. Three-fifths of a class of thirty-five pupils are boys. How many are girls?

30. A school's end of key stage mathematics test results for a class of twenty-five pupils showed that nineteen pupils achieved level five or above. What percentage was this?

31. What is twelve and one half per cent as a decimal?

32. What is four point zero five six multiplied by one hundred?

33. Two-fifths of pupils starting secondary school in September did not speak English as their first language. What percentage of the pupils did speak English as their first language?

34. A bus journey starts at eight fifty-five. It lasts for forty minutes. At what time does it finish?

Questions

35. Twenty per cent of the pupils in Year Ten play hockey. Twenty-five per cent play basketball. The rest play football. There are two hundred pupils in Year Ten. How many play football?

36. For a charity swim twenty-five pupils each swam ten lengths of a twenty-five metre swimming pool. What was the total distance they swam? Give your answer in kilometres.

37. Out of one hundred and forty-four pupils in Year Eleven, forty-eight do not continue in full-time education. What proportion of Year Eleven pupils does continue in full-time education. Give your answer as a fraction in its lowest terms.

38. A teacher travels from school to a training course. After the course is over she returns to school. The distance to the training venue is twenty-four miles and expenses are paid at a rate of forty pence per mile. How much will she receive?

39. A teacher plans to show a twenty-minute video to a group of pupils. The video will be followed by a discussion and then the pupils will take a fifteen-minute test. The lesson will last for fifty minutes. How long can the discussion last?

40. For a practical task a science teacher needs twenty-five millilitres of liquid for each pupil. There are twenty pupils in the class. How many millilitres of liquid are needed?

41. A teacher travelled by train to a GCSE meeting. The return ticket cost twenty-four pounds seventy. She took a taxi ride from the station to the meeting venue which cost five pounds forty pence each way. What was the total cost of the journey?

42. In a test a pupil achieved a mark of forty-nine out of seventy. What is this mark as a percentage?

43. To make a small bookcase in Design, fifteen pupils each needed two point five metres of wood. The wood costs four pounds per metre. What was the total cost of providing the wood for the pupils?

44. A school trip to a lecture and discussion on one of Shakespeare's plays was planned to leave the school at oh-nine-fifteen. The trip was expected to take one and a half hours each way. The lecture and discussion were advertised as lasting two and a half hours. At what time would the coach be expected to arrive back at school? Give your answer using the twenty-four hour clock.

45. In a school's language GCSE course, pupils had to choose one language. One half chose French, one third chose German and the rest chose Chinese. What fraction of the pupils chose to study Chinese?

3.4 | Solving written arithmetic problems

Notes

Many of the questions in the skills test will require you to be able to interpret charts, tables and graphs. These are usually straightforward but do make sure that you read the questions carefully and read the tables or graphs carefully so that you will be able to identify the correct information. These questions are so varied that it is difficult to give examples for all of them – practice makes perfect, though.

There are some questions for which you may wish to revise the mathematics.

Fractions and percentages

See the brief notes in Section 3.2 for the essential knowledge. If you have to calculate percentage increases (or decreases), the simplest method is: find the actual difference, divide by the original amount and then multiply by 100 to convert this fraction to a percentage.

Example

Last year 30 pupils gained a level 3 in the National Tests. This year 44 gained a level 3. Calculate the percentage increase.

Actual increase = 14.
Percentage increase = $\frac{14}{30}$ x 100 = 46.667%.

(But note the comment below on rounding.)

Rounding

Clearly this answer, 46.667%, is too accurate. It would be better written as 46.7% (written to one decimal place) or as 47% (to the nearest whole number). You need to be able to round answers to a given number of decimal places or to the nearest whole number (depending on what the question is demanding). The simple rule is that if the first digit that you wish to remove is 5 or more, then you add 1 to the last remaining digit in the answer. If the first digit is less than 5 then the digits are just removed.

Examples:
46.3 = 46 to the nearest whole number
0.345 = 0.35 to two decimal places
34.3478 = 34.348 to three decimal places
34.3478 = 34.35 to two decimal places
34.3478 = 34.3 to one decimal place
34.3478 = 34 to the nearest whole number

Ratio and proportion

These sorts of questions are best illustrated with examples:

> ### *Example*
>
> (a)   Divide £60 between 3 people in the ratio 1:2:3.
>
>   The total number of 'parts' is 1 + 2 + 3 = 6.
>
>   Therefore 1 part = £60 ÷ 6 = £10.
>
>   Therefore the money is shared as £10; £20; £30.
>
> (b)   Four times as many children in a class have school dinners as do not. If there are 30 children, how many have school dinners?
>
>   The ratio is 4:1 giving 4 + 1 = 5 parts. Therefore 1 'part' = 30 ÷ 5 = 6. Therefore 4 x 6 = 24 children have school dinners.

Don't confuse ratio and proportion. Ratio is 'part to part' while proportion is 'part to whole' and is usually given as a fraction. If the question asked 'What proportion of children have school dinners?' the answer would be $\frac{24}{30} = \frac{4}{5}$.

Notes on measures

You need to know and be able to change between the main metric units of measurement. For example:

Length   1 kilometre = 1000 metres
           1 metre = 100 centimetres or 1000 millimetres
           1 centimetre = 10 millimetres

Mass   1 kilogram = 1000 grams
           1 tonne = 1000 kilograms

Capacity   1 litre = 1000 millilitres = 100 centilitres

Notes on algebra

Generally a formula will be given to you, either in words or letters, and you will need to substitute numbers into that formula and arrive at an answer through what will be essentially an arithmetic rather than algebraic process. Remember the rules that tell you the order in which you should work through calculations.

- **Brackets should be evaluated first.**
- **Then work out the multiplications and divisions.**
- **Finally work out the additions and subtractions.**

Thus: (i) 2 x 3 + 4 = 6 + 4 = 10, but 2 + 3 x 4 = 14 (i.e. 2 + 12) not 20

(ii) $\dfrac{6+4}{2} = \dfrac{10}{2} = 5$ not 3 + 4 = 7

Here do not divide the 6 by 2 which would give 3 + 4 = 7 or the 4 by 2 which would give 6 + 2 = 8.

(iii) 2(3 + 6) = 2 x 9 = 18

Note that some of the questions that follow have several parts. In the actual test each 'part' would be a separate question, for example question 1 could be split into three different questions (one for the mean, one for the mode and one for the median).

Questions

1. There were 30 pupils in a class. Their results in a test are summarised in the table below.

Mark out of 40	Number of pupils achieving mark
19	2
24	8
27	1
29	5
33	2
34	5
36	7

What are the mean, mode and range for these results?

In the test this question could be a 'select and place' question worded as follows: Place the correct values in the summary table below.

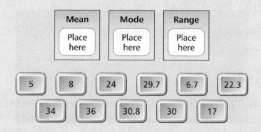

2. A teacher was planning a school trip to Germany. Each pupil was to be allowed €100 spending money. At the time she planned the trip £1 was equivalent to €1.43. When the pupils went to Germany the exchange rate was £1 = €1.38. How much more **English** money did each pupil need to exchange to receive €100?

Questions

3. Five times as many pupils in a school obtained level 3 in the Key Stage 2 mathematics test as obtained level 4. If a total of 32 pupils took the test, and just 2 pupils obtained level 5, how many obtained level 3?

4. Teachers in a mathematics department analysed the Key Stage 2 National Test results for mathematics from three feeder schools.

Level	School A Number of pupils	School B Number of pupils	School C Number of pupils	Totals
2	5	3	4	12
3	6	8	8	22
4	16	18	15	49
5	6	3	8	17
Totals	33	32	35	

Which school had the greatest percentage of pupils working at level 4 and above?

5. The national percentage of pupils with SEN (including statements) is about 18%. A school of 250 pupils has 35 children on the SEN register. How many children is this below the national average?

6. A small primary school analysed its end of Key Stage 2 results for mathematics for the period 2011–14. The table shows the number of pupils at each level.

Mathematics	Level 5	Level 4	Level 3	Level 2	N
2014	19	15	7		1
2013	14	18	3		
2012	23	21	4		
2011	21	16	5	5	1

Which of the following statements is correct?

A   The percentage of pupils gaining level 4 or level 5 in 2011 was greater than in 2014.

B   The percentage of pupils who failed to gain a level 5 was greater in 2013 than in 2012.

C   The number of pupils gaining level 5 in 2014 was 5 percentage points higher than in 2013.

7. An end of year assessment for a class of 27 Year 10 pupils was planned to take 6 hours. As part of the assessment each pupil required access to a computer for 25% of the time. The school's ICT suite contained 30 computers and could be booked for a number of 40-minute sessions.

How many computer sessions needed to be booked for the class?

Questions

8. A pupil achieved a mark of 58 out of 75 for practical work and 65 out of 125 on the written paper. The practical mark was worth 60% of the final mark and the written paper 40% of the final mark. The minimum mark required for each grade is shown below.

Grade	Minimum mark
A*	80%
A	65%
B	55%
C	45%
D	35%

What was the grade achieved by this pupil?

9. A pupil obtained the following marks in three tests.

In which test did the pupil do best?

Test 1	Test 2	Test 3
$\dfrac{45}{60}$	$\dfrac{28}{40}$	$\dfrac{23}{30}$

10. The bar chart below shows the marks for a Year 7 test.

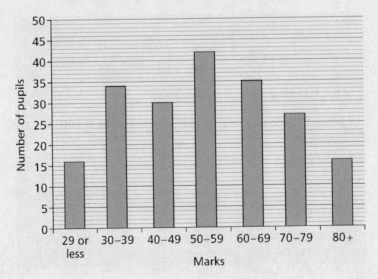

The pass mark for the test was 60 marks. What percentage of pupils passed the test?

11. This table shows the national benchmarks for level 4 and above at Key Stage 2.

Percentile	95th	Upper quartile	60th	40th	Lower quartile	5th
English	97	87	82	73	66	46
Mathematics	98	86	80	72	64	45
Science	100	96	93	87	81	63

Schools' results are placed into categories:

A*   within the top 5%;

A   above the upper quartile and below the 95th percentile;

B   above the 60th percentile and below the upper quartile;

C   between the 40th and the 60th percentiles;

D   below the 40th percentile and above the lower quartile;

E   below the lower quartile and above the 5th percentile;

E*   below the 5th percentile.

What grades would be given for the core subjects in a school whose results were:

English   98%
Mathematics   85%
Science   83%

12. A teacher analysed the number of pupils in a school achieving level 4 and above in the end of Key Stage 2 English tests for 2011–14.

	Year			
	2011	2012	2013	2014
Pupils achieving level 4 and above	70	74	82	84
Pupils in year group	94	98	104	110

In each year the school was set a target of 75% of pupils to achieve a level 4 or above in the end of Key Stage 2 English tests.

(a) By how many percentage points did the school exceed its target in 2014? Give your answer to the nearest whole number.

(b) In which year was the target exceeded by the greatest margin?

Questions

13. The levels gained in mathematics by the Year 6 pupils in a school in the National Tests are shown below. The results are given for Classes 6A and 6B.

Level	Class 6A	Class 6B
N	1	3
2	2	3
3	11	7
4	11	14
5	5	1
6	0	0

(a) What percentage of the year group gained level 4 or above?

(b) Which class had the greater percentage gaining level 4 or above?

14. Four schools had the following proportion of pupils with SEN.

School	Proportion
P	$\frac{2}{9}$
Q	0.17
R	57 out of 300
S	18%

Which school had the lowest proportion of pupils with SEN?

A School P   B School Q   C School R   D School S

15. This table shows the marks gained by a group of pupils in Year 3 in a mathematics test.

Pupil	Marks	Pupil	Marks
A	23	K	47
B	62	L	38
C	58	M	22
D	35	N	24
E	42	O	81
F	49	P	39
G	76	Q	65
H	80	R	71
I	23	S	73
J	62	T	25

Questions

The school will use the results to predict their levels for mathematics at the end of Year 6, and will target those pupils who, it is predicted, will miss level 4 by one level.

This is the conversion chart the school uses to change marks to expected levels.

Mark range	20–24	25–51	52–79	80 and over
Expected level	2	3	4	5

How many pupils will be targeted?

16. A school has analysed the results of its students at GCSE and A level for several years and from these produced a graph which it uses to predict the average A level points score for a given average points score at GCSE.

    Use the graph below to predict the points score at A level if the GCSE points score were 6.

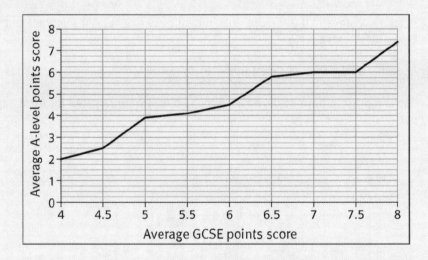

17. A junior school has a weekly lesson time of 23.5 hours. Curriculum analysis gives the following amount of time to the core subjects:

English:	6 hours 30 mins
Mathematics:	5 hours
Science:	1 hour 30 mins

    Calculate the percentage of curriculum time given to English. Give your answer to the nearest per cent.

Questions

18. A support teacher assessed the reading ages of a group of 10 Year 8 pupils with SEN.

Pupil	Actual age		Reading age	
	Years	Months	Years	Months
A	12	07	10	08
B	12	01	11	09
C	12	03	9	07
D	12	03	13	06
E	12	01	10	02
F	12	11	12	00
G	12	06	8	04
H	12	07	10	00
I	12	06	11	08
J	12	02	10	10

What percentage of the 10 pupils had a reading age of at least 1 year 6 months below the actual age?

19. A teacher analysed pupils' performance at the end of Year 5.

Pupils judged to have achieved level 3 and below were targeted for extra support.

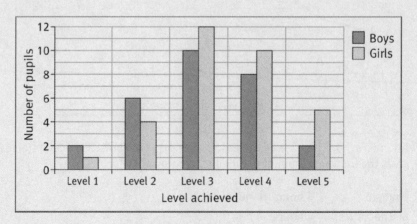

What fraction of the pupils needed extra support?

20. A plastic drinking cup has a capacity of 100ml.

How many cups could be filled from a 1.5 litre carton of juice?

Questions

21. A teacher recorded the number of laps of a rectangular field walked by pupils in Years 5 and 6 in a school's annual walk for charity.

Year group	Number of pupils	Number of laps
5	65	8
6	94	10

The rectangular field measured 200 metres by 150 metres.

The teacher calculated the total distance covered.

Which of the following shows the total distance in kilometres?

A 1022   B 1460   C 10220   D 111.3

22. A primary teacher required each pupil to have a piece of card measuring 20cm by 45cm for a lesson. Large sheets of card measured 60cm by 50cm. What was the minimum number of large sheets of card required for a class of 28 pupils?

23. For a GCSE German oral examination 28 pupils had individual oral assessments with a language teacher.

Each individual assessment took 5 minutes. There was a changeover time of 2 minutes between each assessment.

A day was set aside for the assessments to take place with sessions that ran from 09:00 to 10:10, 10:45 to 11:55 and 13:15 to 15:00.

At what time did the last pupil finish?

A 14:09   B 14:00   C 13:43   D 13:45

24. A teacher produced this table for pupils in Year 5 showing their predicted levels in English, mathematics and science in the end of Key Stage 2 tests in Year 6.

Pupil	English	Mathematics	Science
A	2	3	3
B	5	5	5
C	5	3	5
D	5	3	4
E	4	3	3
F	4	4	4
G	4	3	5
H	4	4	3

Questions

What proportion of the pupils were predicted to gain level 4 or above in all three subjects in the tests?

Give your answer as a fraction in its lowest terms.

25. Using the relationship 5 miles = 8km, convert:

(a) 120 miles into kilometres;

(b) 50km into miles.

(Give your answers to the nearest whole number in each case.)

26. A ream of photocopier paper (500 sheets) is approximately 5cm thick. What is the approximate thickness of 1 sheet of paper? Give your answer in millimetres.

27. A teacher organised revision classes for pupils who achieved grades C and D in mock examinations and used the following table to assess the number of pupils who might benefit from attending the classes.

Grade	Boys	Girls	Total
A*	3	5	8
A	4	3	7
B	6	8	14
C	7	4	11
D	4	5	9
E	3	3	6
F	2	2	4
G	1	0	1

What percentage of the pupils would benefit from attending the classes?

Give your answer to the nearest whole number.

28. A piece of fabric measuring 32cm by 15cm was required for each pupil in a Year 8 design and technology lesson. What was the minimum length of 120cm wide fabric required for 29 pupils?

29. A school trip is organised from Derby to London – approximately 120 miles. A teacher makes the following assumptions.

(a) The pupils will need a 30-minute break during the journey.

(b) The coach will be able to average 40 miles an hour, allowing for roadworks and traffic.

(c) The coach is due in London at 9 a.m.

What would be the latest time for the coach to leave Derby?

30. A teacher organised a hike for a group of pupils during a school's activity week. The route was measured on a 1:50 000 scale map and the distances on the map for each stage of the hike were listed on the chart below.

Stage of hike	Distance on map (cm)
1. Start to Stop A	14.3
2. Stop A to Stop B	8.7
3. Stop B to Stop C	9.3

What was the total distance travelled on the hike?

Give your answer to the nearest kilometre.

31. The following table shows the time for 4 children swimming in a relay race.

1st length	John	95.6 seconds
2nd length	Karen	87.3 seconds
3rd length	Julie	91.3 seconds
4th length	Robert	89.4 seconds

What was the total time, in minutes and seconds, that they took?

32. A teacher completed the following expenses claim form after attending a training course.

Travelling From	To	Miles	Expenses
School and return	Training centre to school	238	Place here
Other expenses	Car parking		£7.50
	Evening meal		£10.50
		Total claim	Place here

The mileage rates were:

30p per mile for the first 100 miles

26p per mile for the remainder.

Complete the claim form by placing the correct values in the expenses column.

£40.88	£65.88	£71.38	£73.88	£83.88	£87.00	£89.40

33. A classroom assistant works from 9:00 a.m. until 12 noon for 4 days per week in a primary school and has a 15 minute break from 10:30 until 10:45. She provides learning support for pupils – each pupil receiving a continuous 20 minute session. How many pupils can she support each week?

34. The mean height of 20 girls in Year 7 is 1.51m. Another girl who is 1.6m joins the class. Calculate the new mean height.

Questions

35. A primary school teacher produces a table showing the differences between the reading age and the actual age for two tests for a group of 16 pupils.

Reading age minus actual age (months)

Test 1	Test 2
−10	−9
−9	−8
−7	−7
−7	−6
−5	−2
−2	0
0	0
0	2
3	4
3	3
3	6
6	7
7	8
9	9
9	10
10	10

(a) Which test had the greatest range in the values of 'reading age – actual age'?

(b) What proportion of pupils made no progress? Give your answer to one decimal place.

36. Equipment for a school is delivered in boxes 15cm deep. The boxes are to be stacked in a cupboard which is 1.24m high. How many layers of boxes will fit into the cupboard?

37. To inform planning a head of science produced a pie chart showing the subject choices made by 150 pupils entering the sixth form. How many more pupils chose to study maths than chose to study chemistry?

Sixth Form Choices

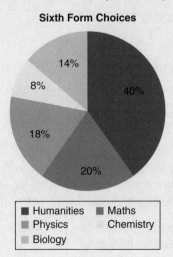

14%

8%

40%

18%

20%

■ Humanities ■ Maths
■ Physics   Chemistry
■ Biology

Questions

38. A teacher planned a school trip from Calais to a study centre. The distance from Calais to the centre is 400km. The coach is expected to travel at an average speed of 50 miles per hour, including time for breaks. The coach is due to leave Calais at 06:20. What time should it arrive at the study centre?

Use the conversion rate of 1km = $\frac{5}{8}$mile.

Give your answer using the 24-hour clock.

39. A newly qualified teacher in his first year of teaching was given a Year 11 class of 20 pupils. As part of his preparation for a parents' evening he studied a table of end-of-term test results for the class.

	Class Y11 – End-of-term test marks (%)				
	Year 10			Year 11	
Name	Test 1	Test 2	Test 3	Test 4	Test 5
A	39	40	41	47	
B	42	44	47	50	
C	42	45	46	50	
D	47	49	48	51	
E	46	48	53	52	
F	50	52	53	57	
G	59	57	58	57	
H	53	55	55	57	
I	55	57	57	61	
J	66	63	65	64	
K	61	60	63	66	
L	56	61	66	68	
M	56	61	66	68	
N	64	66	67	69	
O	51	57	63	69	
P	74	67	69	73	
Q	60	65	71	74	
R	71	73	76	79	
S	75	76	78	81	
T	73	77	82	85	

(a) Indicate all the true statements.

    A   All pupils showed an improvement in achievement between test 1 and test 4.

    B   The median percentage mark for test 4 was 65%.

    C   The range of percentage marks for test 3 was greater than for test 4.

(b) The teacher expects the trend of improvement shown by pupil O will continue in the same way for test 5.

Questions

Write down the correct value for the improvement for pupil O.

Note: In the actual test this question would be worded: 'Select and place the correct value for the improvement for pupil O in the test 5 column in the spreadsheet'.

69	73	75	78

40. Moderators sample the coursework marked by teachers in school. A moderator will select a sample from a school according to the guidelines and rules. One rule that fixes the size of the sample to be selected is:

Size $(s) = 10 + \dfrac{n}{10}$ where n is the number of candidates in a school.

What would be the sample size if there were 150 candidates?

41. The SEN co-ordinator for a school explains to the local authority that the proportion of pupils in the school who receive SEN provision is 0.35. The proportion of pupils receiving SEN provision who also have an SEN statement is 0.12.

What percentage, correct to one decimal place, of pupils in the school has an SEN statement?

A   0.5%

B   4.2%

C   4.7%

D   2.3%

42. As part of a target-setting programme a teacher compared the marks for 10 pupils in each of 2 tests.

Pupils' marks out of 120

Pupil	Test 1	Test 2
A	70	66
B	61	68
C	64	63
D	56	41
E	70	78
F	60	59
G	64	77
H	72	80
I	39	44
J	62	57

Write down the letters for those pupils who scored at least 5 percentage points more in test 2 than test 1.

Questions

Note: In the actual test this question would be expressed as 'Indicate by clicking anywhere on the rows which pupils scored at least 5 percentage points more in test 2 than test 1'.

43. A pupil achieved the following scores in Tests A, B and C.

Test	A	B	C
Actual mark	70	60	7

The pupil's weighted score was calculated using the following formula:

$$\text{Weighted score} = \frac{(A \times 60)}{100} + \frac{(B \times 30)}{80} + C$$

What was the pupil's weighted score?

Give your answer to the nearest whole number.

44. A teacher used a spreadsheet to calculate pupils' marks in a mock GCSE exam made up of two papers. Paper 1 was worth 25% of the total achieved and Paper 2 was worth 75% of the total achieved.

This table shows the first four entries in the spreadsheet.

	Paper 1 Mark out of 30	(25%) Weighted mark	Paper 2 Mark out of 120	(75%) Weighted mark	Final weighted mark
Pupil A	24	20	80	50	70
Pupil B	20	16.7	68	42.5	59.2
Pupil C	8	6.7	59	36.9	43.6
Pupil D	20	16.7	74	46.3	63

Pupil E scored 18 on Paper 1 and 64 on Paper 2.

What was the final weighted mark for Pupil E?

45. The table below shows the percentage test results for a group of pupils.

Pupil	Test 1	Test 2	Test 3	Test 4	Test 5	Test 6	Test 7	Test 8
A	92	85	87	82	78	26	92	95
B	53	70	72	38	15	27	83	73
C	61	77	69	68	60	30	90	77
D	95	100	93	30	92	30	100	70
E	72	49	47	42	46	82	72	92
F	58	78	38	46	34	58	98	78

Questions

Indicate all the true statements.

A   The greatest range of % marks achieved was in test 2.

B   Pupil C achieved a mean mark of 66.5%.

C   The median mark for test 6 was 30.

46. A single mark for a GCSE examination is calculated from three components using the following formula:

Final mark = Component A × 0.6 + Component B × 0.3 + Component C × 0.1

A candidate obtained the following marks.

Component A   64
Component B   36
Component C   40

What was this candidate's final mark? Give your answer to the nearest whole number.

47. A pupil submitted two GCSE coursework tasks, Task A and Task B. Task A carried a weighting of 60% and Task B a weighting of 40%. Each task was marked out of 100.

The pupil scored 80 marks in Task A.

What would be the minimum mark score required by the pupil in Task B to achieve an overall mark across the two tasks of 60%?

48. A reading test consists of 4 parts. The scores are added together to provide a raw score. The table below converts raw scores into an age-standardised reading score.

	Age in years and months							
	6.05	6.06	6.07	6.08	6.09	6.10	6.11	7.00
Raw score	Age-standardised reading score							
16	97	97	96	96	96	96	96	96
17	98	98	98	98	97	97	97	97
18	99	99	99	99	99	98	98	98
19	101	100	100	100	100	100	99	99
20	102	102	101	101	101	101	101	101

A pupil whose age is 6 years and 10 months obtained scores of 2, 5, 4 and 7 from the four parts of the test.

What was the pupil's age standardised reading score?

Questions

49. A teacher calculated the speed in kilometres per hour of a pupil who completed a 6km cross-country race.

    Use the formula: Distance = speed x time.

    The pupil took 48 minutes.

    What was the pupil's speed in kilometres per hour?

50. A readability test for worksheets, structured examination questions, etc. uses the formula:

$$\text{Reading level} = 5 + \left\{ 20 - \frac{x}{15} \right\}$$

    where x = the average number of monosyllabic words per 150 words of writing.

    Calculate the reading level for a paper where x = 20. Give your answer correct to two decimal places.

51. To help pupils set individual targets a teacher calculated predicted A-level points scores using the following formula:

$$\text{Predicted A-level points score} = \left(\frac{\text{total GCSE points score}}{\text{number of GCSEs}} \times 3.9 \right) - 17.5$$

    GCSE grades were awarded the following points.

GCSE grade	A*	A	B	C
Points	8	7	6	5

    Calculate the predicted A-level points score for a pupil who at GCSE gained 4 passes at grade C, 4 at grade B, 1 at grade A and 1 at grade A*.

52. A candidate's final mark in a GCSE examination is calculated from two components as follows:

    Final mark = mark in component 1 x 0.6 + mark in component 2 x 0.4

    A candidate needs a mark of 80 or more to be awarded a grade A*. If the mark awarded in component 2 was 70, what would be the lowest mark needed in component 1 to gain a grade A*?

53. Over a period of years a school has compared performance at GCSE with performance at Key Stage 3 and established rules for the core subjects which they use to predict GCSE grades. In order to do this they converted GCSE grades to points using the following table.

Questions

Grade	A*	A	B	C	D	E	F	G
Points	8	7	6	5	4	3	2	1

For double science the school uses the rule:

GCSE points = Key Stage 3 level – 1

What would be the expected grade for a candidate who gained a level 5 in double science at Key Stage 3?

54. In the annual sports day at a school, pupils took part in a running race or in a field event or both. Pupils who took part in both were given an award. In Years 5 and 6 all 72 pupils took part in a running race or in a field event or both.

    $\frac{1}{2}$ took part in a running race and $\frac{3}{4}$ took part in a field event. How many pupils were given an award?

55. A school used the ALIS formula relating predicted A-level points scores to mean GCSE points scores for A-level mathematics pupils. The formula used was:

    Predicted A-level points score = (mean GCSE points score x 2.24) – 7.35

    What was the predicted A-level points score for a pupil with a mean GCSE points score of 7.55? Give your answer correct to one decimal place.

56. The head teacher in a primary school collects information about the reading ages of a year group. There are 80 pupils in the year group.

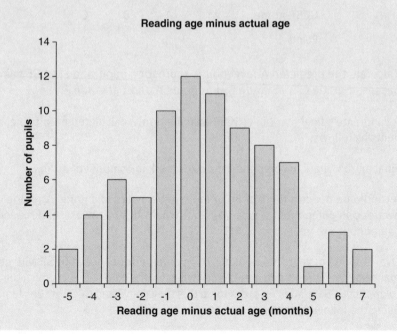

Reading age minus actual age

Questions

(a) What percentage of pupils has a reading age equal to their actual age?

(b) Indicate all the true statements.

A More pupils have reading ages below their actual age than above.

B Six pupils have reading ages of 5 months or more above their actual age.

C The range of reading ages in the group is 12 months.

57. An art teacher has £55 in her budget to buy coloured pencils. One supplier is offering a 25% reduction in their catalogue price of coloured pencils. The catalogue price is £20 per box.

How many boxes of coloured pencils can she buy?

58. There were 27 pupils in a Year 8 history class.

One pupil was absent when there was a mid-term test. The mean score for the group was 56.

On returning to school the pupil who had been absent took the test and scored 86.

What was the revised mean test score?

Give your answer correct to one decimal place.

59. Teachers in a primary school studied the achievement of pupils over a four-year period. End of Key Stage 2 test results of pupils at the school are given in the table below.

	Number of pupils		
Year	Level 3	Level 4	Level 5
2011	10	60	18
2012	45	60	25
2013	54	48	26
2014	38	58	24

In what year was the ratio of the combined level 3 and level 4 results to the level 5 results exactly 4:1?

60. An art teacher plans to take a group of 66 GCSE pupils together with a number of accompanying adults to an art gallery and museum.

The admission charges are as follows.

	Adults	Students
Art gallery	£8.50	£4.50
Museum	£5.50	£3.50
Combined ticket	£12.00	£6.00

Questions

One adult is admitted free when accompanying 30 students.

The group visits both the art gallery and the museum.

(a) How much is saved on the total student admission costs by buying combined tickets?

The school requires a ratio of at least 1 adult for every 20 students on educational visits.

(b) What is the cost of the combined tickets for the adults taking into account the free places they will get?

61. A teacher is planning a visit to an activity centre with a group of students. They will use the school minibus.

The round trip is approximately 200 miles. The fuel consumption for the minibus is 32 miles per gallon. The minibus uses diesel fuel which costs £1.34 per litre.

1 gallon = 4.546 litres

What is the estimated fuel cost for the visit? Give your answer to the nearest pound.

62. To inform a staff meeting a teacher prepared a table comparing pupils' results at level 5 and above in maths and science following end of Year 9 tests.

There were 120 boys and 112 girls in Year 9.

Number of pupils achieving at each level

Subject		Level 5	Level 6	Level 7
English	Boys	20	48	32
	Girls	10	48	40
Mathematics	Boys	20	56	32
	Girls	12	52	32
Science	Boys	20	56	36
	Girls	16	52	32

(a) In which subject was the percentage of boys achieving level 6 and above greater than the percentage of girls achieving level 6 and above?

(b) What proportion of pupils did not achieve a level 5 or above in English in the tests? Give your answer as a decimal to two decimal places.

3.5 | Interpreting and using written data

Notes

Some terms, concepts and forms of representation which are used in statistics may be unfamiliar. The following notes are intended to give a brief summary of some of the unfamiliar aspects.

Some of the information received by schools, for example analyses of pupil performance, uses 'cumulative frequencies' or 'cumulative percentages'. One way to illustrate cumulative frequencies is through an example. The table shows the marks gained in a test by the 60 pupils in a year group.

22	13	33	31	51	24	37	83	39	28
31	64	23	35	9	34	42	26	68	38
63	34	44	77	37	15	38	54	34	22
47	25	48	38	53	52	35	45	32	31
37	43	37	49	24	17	48	29	57	33
30	36	42	36	43	38	39	48	39	59

We could complete a tally chart and a frequency table.

Mark, m	Tally	Frequency
9	1	1
10	0	0
11	0	0
12	0	0
13	1	1
and so on		

But 60 results are a lot to analyse and we could group the results together in intervals. A sensible interval in this case would be a band of 10 marks. This is a bit like putting the results into 'bins'.

	13	22	33		
		24	31, 37		
		28	39		
$0 \leq m < 10$	$10 \leq m < 20$	$20 \leq m < 30$	$30 \leq m < 40$	$40 \leq m < 50$	etc.

Note that ≤ means 'less than or equal to' and < means 'less than', so $30 \leq m < 40$ means all the marks between 30 and 40 including 30 but excluding 40.

Here are the marks grouped into a frequency table.

Mark, m	Frequency	Cumulative frequency
$0 \leq m < 10$	1	1
$10 \leq m < 20$	3	4
$20 \leq m < 30$	9	13
$30 \leq m < 40$	25	38
$40 \leq m < 50$	11	49
$50 \leq m < 60$	6	55
$60 \leq m < 70$	3	58
$70 \leq m < 80$	1	59
$80 \leq m < 90$	1	60

Note how the cumulative frequency is calculated:

← $4 = 1 + 3$

← $13 = 1 + 3 + 9$, i.e. $4 + 9$

← $38 = 1 + 3 + 9 + 25$, i.e. $13 + 25$

The last column 'Cumulative frequency' gives the 'running total' – in this case the number of pupils with less than a certain mark. For example, there are 38 pupils who gained less than 40 marks.

The values for cumulative frequency can be plotted to give a cumulative frequency curve as shown below.

Note that the cumulative frequency values are plotted at the right-hand end of each interval, i.e. at 10, 20, 30 and so on.

You can use a cumulative frequency curve to estimate the median mark: the median for any particular assessment is the score or level which half the relevant pupils exceed and half do not achieve.

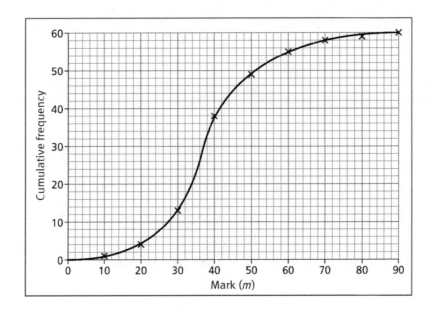

There are 60 pupils, so the median mark will be the 30th mark. (Find 30 on the vertical scale and go across the graph until you reach the curve and read off the value on the horizontal scale.) The median mark is about 37 – check that you agree.

It is also possible to find the quartiles. These are described in the Glossary on page 206.

The lower quartile will be at 25% of 60, that is the 15th value, giving a mark of about 31; the upper quartile is at 75% of 60, thus the 45th value, giving a mark of about 45.

The diagram below should further help to explain these terms. It also helps to introduce the idea of a 'box and whisker' plot.

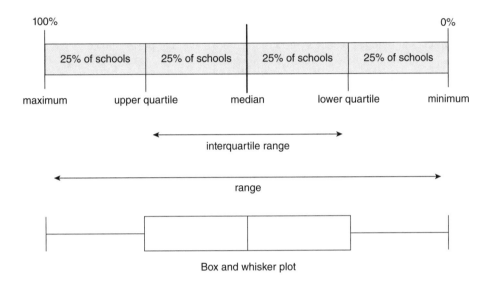

Box and whisker plot

The 'whiskers' indicate the maximum and minimum values, the ends of the 'box' the upper quartile and the lower quartile, and the median is shown by the line drawn across the box.

The 'middle 50%' of the values lie within the box and only the top 25% and the bottom 25% are outside the box. If the ends of the box are close together, then:

- the upper and lower quartiles are close, i.e. the interquartile range (that is the difference between them) is small;
- the slope of the cumulative frequency curve (or line) will be steep.

If the ends of the box are not close, then:

- the interquartile range is greater;
- the data is more 'spread out';
- the slope of the curve is less steep.

You need to interpret 'percentile' correctly: the 95th percentile does not mean the mark that 95% of the pupils scored but that 95% of the pupils gained that mark or lower – it is better perhaps to think that only 5% achieved a higher mark.

The use of percentiles is shown in this table:

Example

Comparing a school's performance with national benchmarks, average NC levels

Percentile	95th	Upper quartile		6oth	4oth		Lower quartile		5th
English	4.26	4.1	**3.89**	3.89	3.78		3.56		3.36
Mathematics	4.25	3.92		3.85	3.63	**3.63**	3.59		3.24
Science	4.38	4.16		3.91	3.93		3.70	**3.54**	3.49

The figures in bold represent a particular school's average performance.

This table shows, for example, that 5% of pupils nationally gained higher than an average level of 4.26 in the English tests and that 40% of pupils nationally gained an average level of 3.63 or less in mathematics. In other words 60% gained a level higher than 3.63.

The table also shows that the school's performance in English was above average (the 50th percentile) and in line with the 60th percentile, below average in mathematics and well below in science.

Questions

1. A secondary school has compared performance in the Key Stage 2 National Tests with performance at GCSE. The comparison is shown on the graph below.

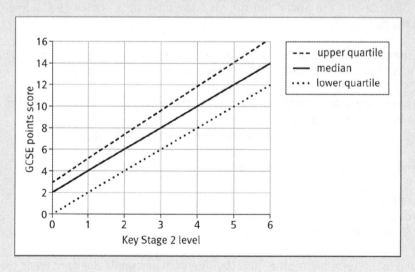

Questions

(a) What is the median GCSE points score of those pupils scoring a 2 at Key Stage 2?

(b) A pupil had a Key Stage 2 score of 5 and a GCSE points score of 11. Is it true to say that he was likely to be within the bottom 25% of all pupils?

(c) Is it true that 50% of the pupils who gained level 4 at Key Stage 2 gained GCSE points scores within the range 8 to 12?

2. A teacher produced the following graph to compare performance between an end of Year 9 test and the 2013 GCSE examinations.

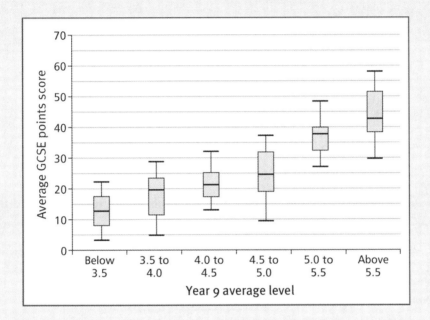

Indicate all the true statements.

A The median GCSE points score for pupils whose average Year 9 level was 5.0–5.5 was 48.

B 50% of pupils whose average Year 9 level was 4.0–4.5 achieved average GCSE points scores of between 17 and 25.

C The range of average GCSE points scores achieved by pupils whose average Year 9 level was above 5.5 was about 28.

3. A German language teacher compared the results of a German oral test and a German written test given to a group of 16 pupils.

Questions

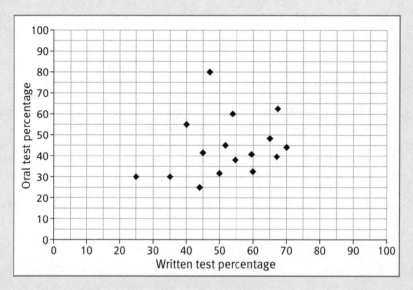

Indicate all the true statements.

A The range of marks for the oral test is greater than for the written test.

B $\frac{1}{4}$ of pupils achieved a higher mark on the oral test than on the written test.

C The two pupils with the lowest marks on the written test also gained the lowest marks on the oral test.

4. A teacher compared the result of an English test taken by all Year 8 pupils.

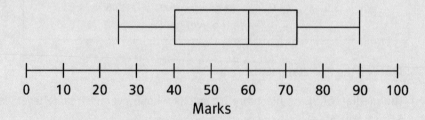

Indicate all the true statements.

A $\frac{1}{4}$ of all pupils scored more than 70 marks.

B $\frac{1}{2}$ of all pupils scored less than 60 marks.

C The range of marks was 65.

5. In 2013 a survey was made of the nightly TV viewing habits of 10-year-old children in town A and town B. The findings are shown in the pie charts below:

Questions

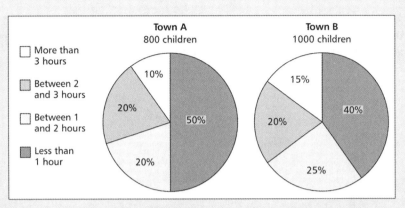

Use these pie charts to identify which of the following statements is true.

A More children in town A watched TV for less than 1 hour than in town B.

B More children in town B watched for between 2 and 3 hours than in town A.

C 100 children watched more than 3 hours in town A.

6. A teacher kept a box and whisker diagram to profile the progress of her class in practice tests. There are 16 pupils in the class.

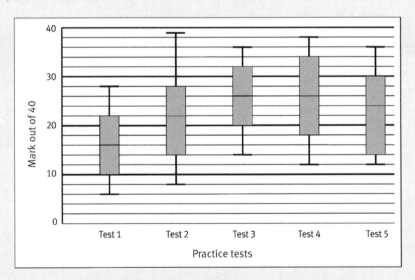

(a) In which test did 12 students achieve 20 or more marks?

(b) Indicate all the true statements.

A The highest mark was achieved in test 2.

B The median mark increased with each test.

C The range of marks in test 3 and test 4 was the same.

Questions

7. At the beginning of Year 11 pupils at a school took an internal test which was used to predict GCSE grades in mathematics. From the results the predicted grades were plotted on a cumulative frequency graph.

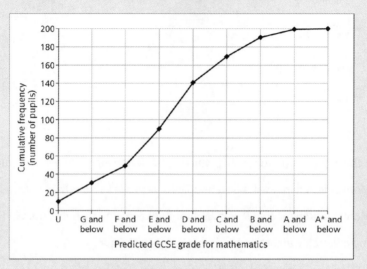

Indicate the true statement.

A 30% of the pupils were predicted to achieve grade C.

B 85% of the pupils were predicted to achieve grade C.

C 15% of the pupils were predicted to achieve grade C.

8. This bar chart shows the amount of pocket money children in Year 7 receive.

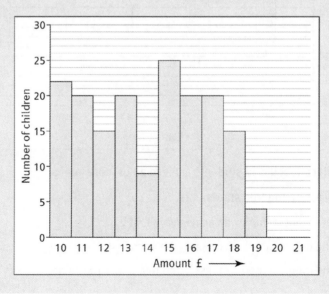

Questions

(a) How many children were surveyed?

(b) What is the modal amount of pocket money received?

9. A teacher recorded the marks given to five pupils in a series of mental arithmetic tests. Each test was based on 25 questions with 1 mark awarded for each correct answer.

Pupil	Test 1	Test 2	Test 3	Test 4
V	16	16	17	18
W	15	17	16	19
X	14	16	18	18
Y	16	17	18	18
Z	11	13	15	17

Indicate all the true statements.

A The marks for all the pupils increased steadily

B Pupil Z could be expected to gain a mark of 19 in the next test.

C The mean, the median and the mode have the same value for test 4.

10. A Year 7 teacher was given information from feeder primary schools about pupils in the tutor group.

The two box plots below show the reading scores for two feeder schools A and B.

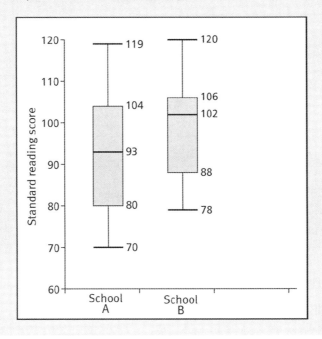

Questions

A standard reading score of 100 shows that a pupil's reading score was exactly on the national average for pupils of the same age. Standard scores of more than 100 show above average reading scores and below 100 show below average reading scores for pupils of the same age.

Indicate all the true statements.

A The difference in the median scores for the two feeder schools was 9.

B The interquartile range of the scores for school B was 18.

C The range of scores was 9 less for school B than for school A.

11. Use the box plots and the information from question 10 to indicate the true statements.

A 50% of the pupils in school A had a reading score of 93 or more.

B 25% of pupils in school B scored 88 or less.

C The interquartile range for the two schools was the same.

12. A mathematics teacher prepared a scatter graph to compare the results of pupils' performance in two tests. There were 24 pupils in the class.

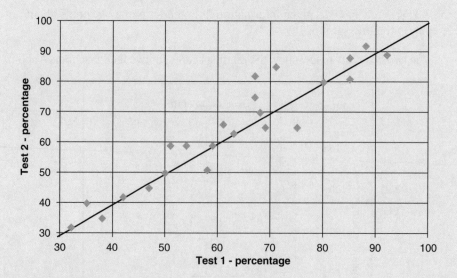

Indicate all the true statements.

A 6 pupils showed no improvement between the two tests.

B A pupil who scored 71 in test 1 showed the greatest improvement in test 2.

C 9 pupils gained a lower percentage in test 2 than in test 1.

Questions

13. A teacher compared the results of pupils in a school's end of Key Stage 2 mathematics tests.

Mean points scored per pupil

Results in mathematics	2011	2012	2013
Boys	22.5	23.2	24.5
Girls	24.3	24.8	25.6

Difference between boys' and girls' mean mathematics points scores			Mean difference for three-year period 2011–2013
2011	2012	2013	
1.8		1.1	

Write down:

(a) the difference between the boys' and girls' mean mathematics points scores for 2012;

(b) the mean difference for the three-year period 2011–2013.

Note: In the actual test this question could be worded: 'Place the correct values in the shaded boxes for:

- *the difference between the boys' and girls' mean mathematics points scores for 2012; and*

- *the mean difference for the three-year period 2011–2013.*

14. This box and whisker diagram shows the GCSE results in four subjects for a school in 2013.

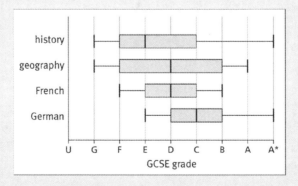

Indicate all the true statements.

A 50% of the pupils who took history gained grades F to C.

B French had the lowest median grade.

C 50% of the pupils who took German gained grades C to A*.

Questions

15. The marks of ten students in the two papers of a German examination were plotted on this scatter graph:

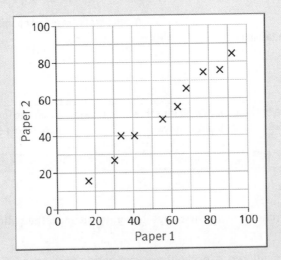

A student scored 53 marks on Paper 1 but missed Paper 2. What would you estimate her mark to be on Paper 2?

16. The straight line shows the mean levels scored in Year 9 assessments for a school plotted against the total GCSE points scores. The points A, B, C, D show the achievement of four pupils.

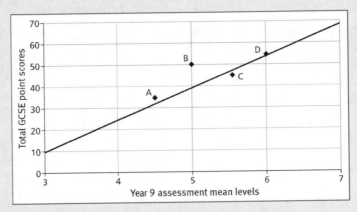

Indicate all the true statements.

A Pupil D achieved as well as might have been predicted at GCSE.

B Pupil C achieved a higher level in the Year 9 assessments than Pupil B but scored fewer points at GCSE than Pupil B.

C At GCSE Pupil B achieved better than might have been predicted but Pupil A achieved less well than might have been predicted.

Questions

17. A teacher compared pupil performance in reading in the Key Stage 2 National Tests.

Level achieved	Sex	Year	Percentage of Pupils School	National
3 and above	All	2003	81.8	79.5
3 and above	All	2004	82.3	79.0
3 and above	All	2005	83.4	81.1
3 and above	All	2006	83.6	81.1
3 and above	Boys	2007	78.4	73.9
3 and above	Boys	2008	77.6	74.2
3 and above	Boys	2009	79.0	76.7
3 and above	Boys	2010	79.0	76.4
3 and above	Girls	2011	85.3	84.3
3 and above	Girls	2012	87.1	84.0
3 and above	Girls	2013	88.2	85.7
3 and above	Girls	2014	88.4	85.8

Indicate all the true statements.

A The performance for the school is consistently above the national average.

B Girls outperform boys in the reading tests in the school.

C The percentage of boys achieving level 3 and above increased annually in the school.

18. 20 pupils in a class took Test A at the beginning of a term and Test B at the end of the term.

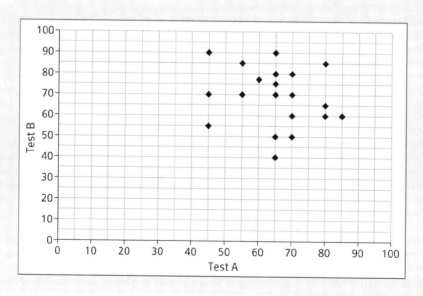

Questions

Indicate all the true statements.

A The range of marks was wider for Test A than for Test B.

B The lowest mark in Test A was lower than the lowest mark in Test B.

C 40% of the pupils scored the same mark or lower in Test B than in Test A.

D More pupils scored over 60% in Test A than in Test B.

19. A teacher analysed the reading test standardised scores of a group of pupils.

Pupil	Gender	Age 8+ test standardised score	Age 10+ test standardised score
A	F	100	108
B	M	78	89
C	M	88	92
D	M	110	102
E	F	102	110
F	F	88	84
G	M	119	128
H	F	80	84

Indicate all the true statements.

A All the girls improved their standardised scores between the Age 8+ and the Age 10+ tests.

B The greatest improvement between the Age 8+ and the Age 10+ tests was achieved by a boy.

C $\frac{1}{4}$ of all the pupils had lower standardised scores in the Age 10+ tests than in the Age 8+ tests.

20. The graph shows the predicted achievements of pupils in English at the end of Year 9, based on the results of tests taken at the beginning of Year 9.

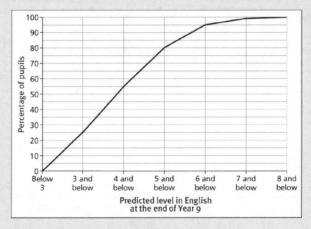

What percentage of pupils was predicted to achieve level 4 and above?

Questions

21. Schools in a federation analysed the percentages of pupils gaining 5 A*–C grades in their GCSE examinations over a six-year period. The results are shown in this table.

Percentage of pupils gaining 5 A*–C grades

School	2009	2010	2011	2012	2013	2014
A	47.9	48.6	54.7	54.6	55.8	58.4
B	64.5	64.8	65.0	65.2	65.4	65.6
C	66.1	65.3	64.3	63.7	63.5	63.0
D	49.7	54.7	57.0	63.6	63.7	63.8
E	58.3	59.1	58.5	59.3	58.7	59.5

Which schools improved each year over the six-year period?

22. A research project compared the performance of Year 9 pupils taught mathematics, science and English in mixed classes or in single-sex classes.

This table shows the results.

		Median level achieved	
Subject	Boys only classes	Girls only classes	Mixed classes
English	7	8	8
Mathematics	7	8	7
Science	7	7	6

Indicate all the true statements.

A The single-sex groups produced better results in science.

B The mixed classes produced better results in English.

C In mathematics girls achieved higher scores than in mixed classes.

23. At a staff meeting teachers were shown a table showing the proportion of pupils achieving level 6 and above in the end of Year 9 tests.

Proportion of pupils achieving level 6 and above in:	Year			
	2011 (%)	2012 (%)	2013 (%)	2014 (%)
English	75.8	76.3	75.8	76.5
Mathematics	69.6	70.2	70.8	71.4
Science	59.0	61.2	62.8	64.0

Questions

Indicate all the true statements.

A The greatest year-on-year improvement was for science between 2011 and 2012.

B All subjects achieved a year-on-year improvement over the four-year period.

C The smallest improvement over the four-year period was for English.

24. For a department meeting a head of mathematics produced a box and whisker graph comparing the performance in the end of year tests of four classes in Year 7.

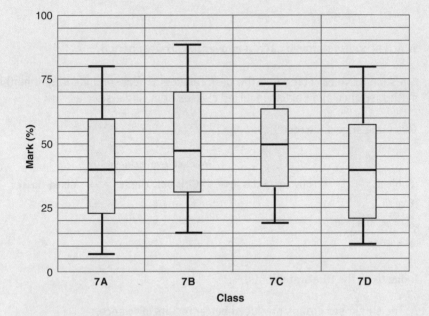

Indicate all the true statements.

A The lowest mark was scored by a pupil in class 7D.

B The median mark in class 7C was 10 marks higher than the median mark in class 7A.

C In class 7B one quarter of the pupils achieved a mark of 70% or more.

3.6 | Answers and key points

3.2 Key knowledge

Answers

1. (a) 4.3   (b) 4.44   (c) 10.09   (d) 5.4   (e) 1.48   (f) 9.19

Key point
Remember to line up the decimal points.

2. (a) 42   (b) 0.35   (c) 2

3. (a) $\dfrac{1}{50}$ (b) $\dfrac{1}{4}$ (c) $\dfrac{17}{20}$ (d) $\dfrac{1}{8}$ (e) $\dfrac{47}{100}$

Key point
Cancel down by dividing both numerator and denominator by the same factor.

4. (a) $\dfrac{3}{8} \times \dfrac{100\%}{1} = 3 \times 12.5\% = 37.5\%$ (b) $\dfrac{13}{25} \times \dfrac{100\%}{1} = 52\%$

(c) $\dfrac{12}{40} \times \dfrac{100\%}{1} = \dfrac{3}{10} \times \dfrac{100\%}{1} = 30\%$ (d) $\dfrac{36}{60} \times \dfrac{100\%}{1} = \dfrac{6}{10} \times \dfrac{100\%}{1} = 60\%$

Key point
There are different ways of simplifying – which way is best depends on the numbers in the question, but if the denominator is a multiple of 10, it is probably easier to try to cancel down to get 10, as in (c) and (d), unless you are using a calculator in which case change the fraction into a decimal then multiply by 100.

5. (a) $0.25 \times £40 = £10$ (b) $0.75 \times £20 = £15$ (c) $0.12 \times 50 = 6$ (d) $0.2 \times 45 = 9$

Key point
Change each percentage into a decimal.

6. (a) $\dfrac{2}{3}$ divided by 12, or by 2, then 2 then 3   (b) $\dfrac{3}{5}$ divided by 6

(c) $\dfrac{2}{5}$ divided by 15, or by 3, then 5   (d) $\dfrac{3}{4}$ divided by 25

Answers

7. $\dfrac{39}{60}$

> **Key point**
> Change each fraction to a decimal.

8. Girls:

        mean   = 50 (to the nearest whole number)
        median = 48
        mode   = 48
        range   = 63 − 45 = 18

For both boys and girls the median, mode and range are the same but the mean for the girls is slightly higher so one could deduce that the girls are slightly better than the boys, but the difference is not significant.

> **Key point**
> Make sure you put the values in order before finding the median. See the working out for the boys if you have any difficulties.

3.3 Mental arithmetic

1. 55 minutes

> **Key point**
> Count on from 1 hour 20 minutes.

2. 28

> **Key point**
> 70% of 40 = 0.7 x 40 or $\dfrac{7}{10} \times 40$

3. 17

> **Key point**
> Note: 100 ÷ 6 = 16.666 therefore 17

Answers

4. 75%

Key point
The calculation is 3 x 28 = 84, then (63 ÷ 84) × 100. Note: in a mental arithmetic test the fractions will cancel easily, as here to $\frac{3}{4}$.

5. 9

Key point
Note: 450 ÷ 52 = 8.65, therefore 9

6. 48

Key point
Calculate as 30 ÷ 5 = 6, then 6 x 8 = 48 or 8 ÷ 5 = 1.6 so 30 x 1.6 = 3 x 16 = 48

7. 12:40

Key point
Count on 1 hour 10 minutes + 2 hours.

8. 11

Key point
10 rows for 400 people, so one more row needed for the remaining 32

9. 84%

Key point
21 hours remaining = $\frac{21}{25}$ = 84%

10. 123

Key point
The calculation is: 15 x 4 + 9 x 5 + 6 x 3 = 60 + 45 + 18 = 123

Answers

11. 8%

> **Key point**
> Remember: to convert fractions with denominators of 25 to a percentage, multiply the numerator by 4: $\frac{22}{25} = 88\%$, therefore 8% difference.

12. £500

> **Key point**
> Simplify quickly by changing into £: 200 x 50 x 5p = £2 x 50 x 5

13. 60%

> **Key point**
> Common factor is 7, therefore $\frac{1}{20}$

14. 720p or £7.20

> **Key point**
> Work out as 120 x 2 x 3 = 120 x 6

15. 0.075

> **Key point**
> Think of $7\frac{1}{2}\%$ as 7.5% then divide by 100.

16. 15

> **Key point**
> Work out as $\frac{3}{7} \times 35$

17. 265

> **Key point**
> (5 x 25) + (5 x 28)

Answers

18. 22 hours and 5 minutes

Key point

5 x (4hr 25 mins) = (5 x 4hr) + (5 x 25 min) = 20hr + 125mins =20hr + 2hr 5 mins

19. 68%

Key point

18 + 16 = 34 then double

20. 36

Key point

First calculate 80% of 120 which is 0.8 x 120 = 96 (so 96 pupils achieved level 4 or level 5). Then subtract the pupils who achieved level 5, that is 60 pupils, leaving 36.

21. 1 hour 10 minutes

Key point

The calculation is 3hr – 1hr 50 mins

22. 0.625

Key point

The fraction is $\frac{54}{144}$. You now need to simplify this. You might recognise that 18 is a common factor, but if not then divide by 2 giving $\frac{27}{72}$ and then by 9 giving $\frac{3}{8}$. This then is the fraction who travel by bus. Therefore the fraction who don't travel by bus is $\frac{5}{8}$ and you should recognise this as 0.625 Alternatively you could first find the number who don't travel by bus, 144 – 54 = 90. Then express that as a fraction, $\frac{90}{144}$, divide by 16 or keep dividing by 2, and get $\frac{5}{8}$ which is 0.625.

23. 6.25m^2

Key point

The calculation is 2.5 x 2.5. You should know that 25^2 is 625.

Answers

24. 12

> **Key point**
> Quicker to find 40% or 0.4 x 30 = 12

25. 96

> **Key point**
> The calculation is, using the formula: Time = distance ÷ speed, $\frac{40}{25}$ x 60 (the x 60 is to change the answer into minutes) which simplifies to $\frac{8}{5}$ x 60 and then to 8 x 12.

26. 63

> **Key point**
> The calculation is 0.2 x 315 = 63.

27. 75%

> **Key point**
> The lesson is 80 minutes long. There are 60 minutes left for the assessment and as a fraction this is $\frac{60}{80}$ = 75%.

28. 56%

> **Key point**
> With 25 as the denominator you should know that you multiply the numerator by 4.

29. 14

> **Key point**
> Find $\frac{1}{5}$ and double to give $\frac{2}{5}$ x 35 = 14

30. 76%

> **Key point**
> $\frac{19}{25}$, multiply 19 by 4 to get the %

Answers

31. 0.125

> **Key point**
> Write it as 12.5 and divide by 100.

32. 405.6

> **Key point**
> Simple to multiply by 100 but be careful!

33. 60%

> **Key point**
> Either start with the fraction $\frac{2}{5}$ who don't speak English. This is equivalent to 40% so 60% speak English, or work with $\frac{3}{5}$ who do speak English and this is 60%.

34. 9:35

> **Key point**
> Treat 40 minutes as 30 minutes + 10 minutes, i.e. 8:55 $\longrightarrow$ 9:25 $\longrightarrow$ 9:35

35. 110

> **Key point**
> 20% + 25% = 45% so 55% play football

36. 6.25

> **Key point**
> The calculation is 25 x 10 x 25 = 6250 metres, then divide by 1000 to change into kilometres giving 6.25.

37. $\frac{2}{3}$

> **Key point**
> Either find the number who do stay in full-time education. This is 144 − 48 = 96. Then express this as a fraction and simplify it: $\frac{96}{144} = \frac{8}{12} = \frac{2}{3}$. Or express those who do not stay in full-time education as a fraction and subtract. Thus $\frac{48}{144} = \frac{1}{3}$ so $\frac{2}{3}$ stay.

Answers

38. £19.20

Key point
The calculation is 2 x 24 x 0.4

39. 15 minutes

Key point
20 + 15 = 35 minutes

40. 500

Key point
The calculation is 20 x 25 = 500

41. £35.50

Key point
The calculation is £24.70 + 2 x £5.40

42. 70%

Key point
The calculation is $\dfrac{49}{70} = \dfrac{7}{10}$

43. £150

Key point
The calculation is 15 x 2.5 x 4

44. 14:45

Key point
The calculation is start at 09:15, add 3 hours for travelling time and then add 2 hours 30 minutes for the lecture and discussion time.

45. $\dfrac{1}{6}$

Key point
You need to add $\dfrac{1}{2}$ and $\dfrac{1}{3}$. $\dfrac{1}{2} + \dfrac{1}{3} = \dfrac{3}{6} + \dfrac{2}{6} = \dfrac{5}{6}$ so $\dfrac{1}{6}$ study Chinese.

3.4 Solving written arithmetic problems

1. Mean = 29.7; mode = 24; range = 17

Key point

$$\text{Mean} = \frac{19\times2+24\times8+27\times1+29\times5+33\times2+34\times5+36\times7}{30} = \frac{890}{30} = 29.7$$

Mode = most frequent mark, not the number of times it occurs.

2. £2.53

Key point

100 euros = £$\frac{100}{1.43}$ = £69.93 and 100 euros = £$\frac{100}{1.38}$ = £72.46

3. 25 gained level 3

Key point

If 2 gained level 5 then 30 gained either level 3 or level 4. The ratio of level 3 numbers to level 4 numbers is 5 to 1. Divide 30 by (5 + 1), i.e. into 6 equal groups so each group has 5 pupils so 25 pupils gained level 3 and 5 gained level 4.

4. School A

Key point

Percentages are: school A = 66.7%; school B = 65.6%; school C = 65.7%

5. 10 below

Key point

Find 18% of 250 = 0.18 x 250 = 45, so 10 below

6. B and C are correct

Key point

Looking at actual pupil numbers can be misleading since the totals vary each year. So, in 2011, for statement A, the fraction is $\frac{37}{48}$ and in 2014 it is $\frac{34}{42}$, but the percentages are 77% and 81% respectively.

Answers

7. 3

> **Key point**
> 25% of 6 hours is 1 hour 30 minutes so 2 sessions (80 minutes) is too short.

8. A

> **Key point**
> The calculation is $(\frac{58}{75} \times 0.6) + (\frac{65}{125} \times 0.4) = 0.464 + 0.208 = 0.672$, i.e. 67.2%

9. Test 3

> **Key point**
> Convert to percentages.

10. 39%

> **Key point**
> Total number of pupils = 16 + 34 + 30 + 42 + 35 + 27 + 16 = 200
> Pupils with 60 marks or more = 35 + 27 + 16 = 78

11. English A* Mathematics B Science D

> **Key point**
> You need to read both question and table carefully.

12. (a) 1%   (b) 2013

> **Key point**
> (a) in 2014 $\frac{84}{110}$ = 76% (b) you will have to work out and compare the percentages
> for the years 2011–14 – you have already worked out the value for 2014.

13. (a) 53.4% (b) class 6B

> **Key point**
> Easy to make mistakes by confusing 'year group' and 'class'.
> Total for each class: class A = 30 pupils, class B = 28 pupils

Answers

Total for year = 58 pupils

(a) Total pupils gaining level 4 or better = 11 + 5 + 14 + 1= 31

As a percentage = $\frac{31}{58}$ x 100 = 53.4%

(b) In class A the percentage = $\frac{16}{30}$ x 100 = 53.3%

in class B the percentage = $\frac{15}{28}$ x 100 = 53.6%, therefore answer is class 6B

14. School Q

Key point

Change each figure into decimals:

$\frac{2}{9}$ = 0.222   57 out of 300 = 0.19   18% = 0.18

15. 7

Key point

Look at table 2. To miss level 4 by 1 level thus gaining level 3 means you need to identify pupils scoring marks between 25 and 51.

16. 4.5

Key point

Use a ruler to help – find 6 on the horizontal axis and read off the corresponding value on the vertical axis.

17. 28%

Key point

Because the times both involve half hours, it is simply working out $\frac{6.5}{23.5}$ x 100 = 27.66% = 28% to the nearest per cent.

18. 50%

Key point

Subtract, remembering 12 months in a year. Pupils A, C, E, G, H fit the criterion.

Answers

19. $\dfrac{35}{60} = \dfrac{7}{12}$

Key point
Count pupil numbers carefully – jot down totals.

20. 15

Key point
1500 ÷ 100 = 15

21. A

Key point
Number of 'pupil laps' = (65 x 8 + 94 x 10) = 1460

Total distance = 1460 x 700 = 1022 000 metres = 1 022km

22. 10

Key point
Use a sketch – 3 small sheets per width of large sheet.

23. A 14:09

Key point
Remember the last pupil doesn't need 2 minutes' changeover time.

24. $\dfrac{1}{4}$

Key point
The question says 'level 4 or above'. Remember to simplify the fraction.

25. (a) 192km (b) 31 miles (actually 31.25)

Key point
The calculations are: (a) $120 \times \dfrac{8}{5}$ (b) $50 \times \dfrac{5}{8}$

Answers

26. 0.1mm

> **Key point**
> Take care with the units – work in millimetres, i.e. 50 ÷ 500.

27. 33%

> **Key point**
> The fraction is $\frac{20}{60}$ so as a percentage this is 33.3333%, i.e. 33% to the nearest whole number.

28. 128cm

> **Key point**
> You can fit 8 lots of 15cm across the 120cm width.

29. 5:30 a.m.

> **Key point**
> Remember time = distance ÷ speed. The travel time = 120 ÷ 40 = 3 hours. Add 0.5 hour, therefore total time = 3.5 hours.

30. 16km

> **Key point**
> Total map distance = 32.3cm = 32.3 x 50 000cm on the ground = 16.15km

31. 363.6 seconds = 6 minutes 3.6 seconds

> **Key point**
> Add up the time in seconds and decimals of seconds giving 363.6 seconds then convert.

32. £65.88; £83.88

> **Key point**
> Remember to work in £ on the mileage rate.

Answers

33. 28 pupils

> **Key point**
> From 9:00 to 10:30 is 90 minutes ⟶ she can see 4 pupils.
> From 10:45 to 12:00 is 75 minutes ⟶ she can see 3 pupils.
> Total for the day = 7 pupils, total over 4 days = 28 pupils.
> If the calculations were done using the total figures:
> >   her working week = 4 x 3 hours less 4 x 15 minutes = 11 hours
> >   11 hours = 660 minutes ÷ 20, giving 33 pupils
>
> This would be incorrect because it ignores the 'structure' of the school morning.

34. 1.514m

> **Key point**
> The total height for the 20 girls = 20 x 1.51 = 30.2m
> The new total height = 30.2 + 1.6 = 31.8 m but this is for 21 girls
> The new mean height = 31.8 ÷ 21= 1.514m

35. (a) Test 1   (b) 0.3

> **Key point**
> (a) The range for test 1 is −10 to 10 which is 20.
> >   The range for test 2 is −9 to 10 which is 19.
> >   So test 1.
> (b) 5 pupils made no progress so as a fraction this is $\frac{5}{16}$ which equals 0.3125. This rounds to 0.3.

36. 8 layers

> **Key point**
> The calculation, working in centimetres, is 124 ÷ 15 = 8.266, so round down.

37. 18

> **Key point**
> There are two ways of solving this: The first way would be to (a) find the number studying maths. This is 20% of 150 = 30. (b) Find the number studying chemistry – 8% of 150 = 12, and then find the difference: 30 – 12 = 18.

Answers

The second way would be to find the difference in the percentages: 20% – 8% = 12%. Then find 12% of 150 = 18.

38. 11:20

Key point
400km = 250 miles

39. (a) B and C are true.

(b) 75

Key point
The test scores for test 4 are in order so the median is midway between the 10th and 11th pupils' scores. The range is the difference between the highest and lowest scores. In (b) the scores increase by 6 each time.

40. 25

Key point
Sample size = 10 + 150 ÷ 10 = 25

41. B is correct.

Key point
35% (0.35) receive SEN provision. Of these 12% (0.12) have a statement, so the calculation is 0.12 x 0.35 = 0.042, i.e. 4.2%.

42. B, E, G, H

Key point
Find 5% of 120 = 6 so look for marks in test 2 that are 6 marks higher than in test 1.

43. 72

Key point
Remember to work out brackets first and to round up.

Answers

44. 55

> **Key point**
> You can check the method by working through the data for Pupil A.
> The calculation for Pupil E is $\frac{18}{30} \times 0.25 + \frac{64}{120} \times 0.75 = 0.15 + 0.4 = 0.55 = 55\%$

45. B and C are true

> **Key point**
> Greatest range is test 5 $(92 - 15 = 77)$

46. 53

> **Key point**
> The calculation is $64 \times 0.6 + 36 \times 0.3 + 40 \times 0.1 = 53.2$, i.e. 53

47. 30

> **Key point**
> The calculation is $80 \times 0.6 + M \times 0.4 = 60$ so $M \times 0.4 = 60 - 48 = 12$ Therefore
> $M = \frac{12}{0.4} = 30$

48. 98

> **Key point**
> Total of the scores is $2 + 5 + 4 + 7 = 18$. Read across the table along the row with 18 and the score in the column headed 6.10 is 98.

49. 7.5km/h

> **Key point**
> Speed = distance ÷ time = $6 \div 0.8$ (NB work in hours, 48 mins = $\frac{4}{5}$hr = 0.8 hr)

Answers

50. 23.67

> **Key point**
> You must work out 20 ÷ 15 first, not 25 x 20 then divide by 15.
>
> Therefore reading level = 5 + (20 − 1.33) = 5 + 18.67 = 23.67

51. 5.51

> **Key point**
> The total points are given by (4 x 5) + (4 x 6) + (1 x 7) + (1 x 8) = 59
>
> The calculation is then $(\frac{59}{10}$ x 3.9) − 17.5 = 5.51

52. 87

> **Key point**
> The calculation is 80 = A x 0.6 + 70 x 0.4
>
> $\qquad\qquad$ 80 = A x 0.6 + 28
>
> Therefore $\quad$ A x 0.6 = 52
>
> $\qquad\qquad$ A = 52 ÷ 0.6 = 86.67, i.e. 87

53. Grade D

> **Key point**
> The calculation is: GCSE points = 5 − 1= 4. Therefore grade = D.

54. 18

> **Key point**
> $\frac{3}{4} - \frac{1}{2} = \frac{1}{4}$ so $\frac{1}{4}$ receive an award.

55. 9.6

> **Key point**
> Work out brackets first.

Answers

56. (a) 15%   (b) B and C are true.

> **Key point**
> (a)   There are 12 pupils so the percentage is $\frac{12}{80}$ which is 15%.
>
> (b)
>
>   A. There are 27 pupils with reading ages below their actual age (i.e. to the left of zero) and there are 41 pupils with reading ages above their actual ages – so not true.
>
>   B. 1 + 3 + 2 pupils have reading ages of 5 months, 6 months and 7 months above their actual age – so true.
>
>   C. The range of reading age – actual age is from −5 to +7 – so true.

57. 3 boxes

> **Key point**
> The catalogue price of a box is £20. A 25% reduction gives a price of £15. (Remember the calculation is: 20 − 0.25 x 20.) £55 ÷ £15 = 3.67. So she can buy only 3 boxes.

58. 57.1

> **Key point**
> Total for 26 pupils = 26 x 56 = 1456. New total = 1456 + 86 = 1542
> New mean = 1542 ÷ 27

59. 2014

> **Key point**
> Multiplying each level 5 score by 4 should help identify the year.

60. (a) £132   (b) £24

> **Key point**
> (a) The cost of separate tickets for 1 student is £4.50 + £3.50 = £8.00. So for 66 students the cost = 66 x £8.00 = £528. The cost of 66 combined tickets is 66 x £6 = £396. The saving is £528 − £396 = £132.
>
> (b) 66 students will require 4 adults (note: 3 adults will only 'cover' 60 students). 2 adults will be free – since 66 is greater than 60. So only 2 adults will have to pay. Cost = 2 x £12.00 = £24.00.

Answers

61. £38

Key point

The calculation can be broken down into stages:

- the number of gallons used = $\dfrac{200}{32}$ = 6.25;
- the number of litres = 6.25 x 4.546 = 28.4125;
- the cost = 28.4125 x £1.34 = £38.07 which rounds to £38.

If you do these sorts of calculations try to avoid rounding any intermediate answers and round when you get the final answer.

62. (a) Science   (b) 0.15

Key point

(a)   Maths:

Number of boys @ levels 6 and 7 = 56 + 32 = 88

Number of girls @ levels 6 and 7 = 52 + 32 = 84

Total number of boys = 120; total number of girls = 112

Therefore % boys = $\dfrac{88}{120} \times 100 = 73\%$

% girls = $\dfrac{84}{112} \times 100 = 75\%$

Science:

Number of boys @ levels 6 and 7 = 56 + 36 = 92

Number of girls @ levels 6 and 7 = 52 + 32 = 84

Total number of boys = 120; total number of girls = 112

Therefore % boys = $\dfrac{92}{120} \times 100 = 77\%$

% girls = $\dfrac{84}{112} \times 100 = 75\%$

Thus in science the percentage of boys achieving level 6 and above was greater than the percentage of girls.

(b)   Total number of boys achieving levels 5, 6 and 7 = 20 + 48 + 32 = 100

Therefore 120 −100 = 20 did not.

Total number of girls achieving levels 5, 6, and 7 = 10 + 48 + 40 = 98

Therefore 112 − 98 = 14 did not.

Total who did not achieve levels 5, 6 and 7 = 34

Total pupils = 120 + 112 = 232

$\dfrac{34}{232}$ = 0.14655 so 0.15

Answers

Chapter 3.5 Interpreting and using written data

1. (a) 6   (b) No   (c) Yes

> **Key point**
> (a) Find 2 on the Key Stage 2 axis and move up the graph until you reach the median line. Read off the value on the GCSE axis.
>
> (b) Find 11 on the GCSE axis and 5 on the Key Stage 2 axis. The lines through these values intersect in the space between the lower quartile line and the median line so it is not true – remember that 25% of the pupils are below the lower quartile.
>
> (c) Find 4 on the Key Stage 2 axis, 50% lie between 8 (the lower quartile) and 12 (the upper quartile).

2. B and C are true.

> **Key point**
> A. The median is the line inside the 'box'.
> B. 50% is represented by the box.
> C. Range = highest – lowest = 58 – 30 = 28

3. A and B are true.

> **Key point**
> A. Oral range = 80 – 25 = 55; written range = 70 – 25 = 45.
> B. Imagine a line drawn from (0, 0) to (100, 100). This is the line where scores on both tests were the same. There are 4 points above this line, $\dfrac{4}{16} = \dfrac{1}{4}$
> C. Lowest written marks are 25 and 35, both pupils scoring 30 in the oral, but another pupil scored 25 in the oral.

4. B and C are true.

> **Key point**
> A. This is false. The upper quartile is at 73, so 1/4 of all the pupils scored more than 73 marks, not 70.
> B. Median is at 60 so true.
> C. Range = 90 – 25 = 65 so true.

Answers

5.   B is true.

> **Key point**
> It is important to realise that, although the pie charts appear to be the same size, they represent different 'quantities' – 800 children and 1000 children.
>
> Statement A is not true. 50% of 800 = 40% of 1000
>
> $$(0.5 \times 800 = 400 \text{ and } 0.4 \times 1000 = 400)$$
>
> Statement B is true. 20% of 1000 is more than 20% of 800
>
> $$(0.2 \times 1000 = 200, 0.2 \times 800 = 160)$$
>
> Statement C is not true. 10% of 800 = 80

6.   (a) Test 3   (b) Only A is true.

> **Key point**
> Remember that each 'part' of a box and whisker plot represents 25%.

7.   Only C is true.

> **Key point**
> 140 pupils get D and below, 170 get C and below so 30 get grade C.

8.   (a) 170   (b) £15

> **Key point**
> (a)   Add up the values given by the tops of each bar:
>
> 22 + 20 + 15 + 20 + 9 + 25 + 20 + 20 + 15 + 4
>
> (b)   The modal amount is that received by the most children, i.e. £15 received by 25 children.

9.   B and C are true.

> **Key point**
> A is not true. Pupils V, X and Y have 2 years with the same mark.
>
> B is true – while it is unlikely the indications are that pupil Z's marks go up by 2 each test.
>
> C is true – the mean is 18 – add the marks (=90) divide by 5. The median is 18 – the middle value when the marks are put in order – and the mode is 18.

Answers

10. A and B are true.

> **Key point**
> A. Medians are 102 and 93.
> B. Interquartile range for B = 106 – 88
> C. School A range = 119 – 70, school B range = 120 – 78

11. A and B are true.

> **Key point**
> A. 50% lie above the median line.
> B. 25% lie below the lower quartile.
> C. IQ range for A = 24 and for B = 18.

12. A and B are true.

> **Key point**
> A. 6 pupils on the line of equal scores – so true.
> B. True – gained 85 and is the greatest distance above the line.
> C. Not true – 8 pupils below the line.

13. (a) 1.6   (b) 1.5

> **Key point**
> (a) Simple subtraction   (b) Simple calculation of the mean

14. A and C are true.

> **Key point**
> A. History 'box' extends from F to C.
> B. History has a lower median grade.
> C. German median is at grade C so 50% gained C to A*.

Answers

15. About 45–49 marks

> **Key point**
> You need to draw in the line of best fit through the points.

16. A and B are true.

> **Key point**
> A.   D lies on the line.
> B.   C is to the right of but below B.
> C.   A is above the line so A also achieved better than might have been predicted.

17. A and B are true.

> **Key point**
> A.   Check the school numbers are always greater than the national figures.
> B.   Check the girls' numbers are always greater than the boys'.
> C.   Decreased in 2008.

18. C and D are true.

> **Key point**
> A.   Range for A = 85 − 45 = 40, range for B = 90 − 40 = 50
> B.   Lowest value for A = 45 and for B = 40
> C.   Imagine a line drawn from (0, 0) to (100, 100), 8 pupils on or below the line and $\frac{8}{20}$ = 40%
> D.   14 scored over 60% in Test A and 13 scored over 60% in Test B

19. B and C are true.

> **Key point**
> A.   Pupil F score decreased.
> B.   Pupil B score increased by 11.
> C.   Two pupils (D, F) had lower scores.

Answers

20. 75%

> **Key point**
> 25% were predicted to gain level 3 and below so 75% were predicted to gain more than level 3, i.e. level 4 and above.

21. Schools B and D

> **Key point**
> B and D are the only two schools with values increasing each year.

22. A and C are true.

> **Key point**
> A. is true – level 7 in science for single-sex classes and 6 for the mixed classes.
> B. is not true – the level achieved for the girls only classes were the same as the mixed classes.
> C. is true – the girls only classes achieved level 8 compared with level 7 for the mixed and the boys only classes.

23. A and C are true.

> **Key point**
> A. is true – the actual increase is $61.2 - 59.0 = 2.2$
> B. is not true – the English performance decreased in 2013
> C. is true – for English the calculation is $76.5 - 75.8 = 0.7$
> For mathematics it is $71.4 - 69.6 = 1.8$
> For science it is $64.0 - 59.0 = 5.0$

24. B and C are true.

> **Key point**
> A. is not true – the lowest mark is for class 7A at about 6.
> B. is true – the median mark in class 7C is 50, in class 7A it is 40.
> C. is true – the 'upper' whisker starts at 70.

4 | Teacher training, applications and interviews

This chapter about teacher training, applications and interviews is divided into the following sections:

4.1   Is teacher training really for me?
4.2   What makes a good ITT application?
4.3   What makes a good ITT interview candidate?

For ease of reference, the chapter poses the sort of questions you may well be asking right now, followed by the typical responses that ITT providers might give.

4.1 Is teacher training really for me?

Think carefully about applying for ITT. Ask yourself the question now: 'Is this really for me?' Consider what it is going to cost you in fees for the course. How will you manage to cope with the studying? This is obviously going to be a pretty big commitment on your part. Are you ready for it? Be honest with yourself – you've got to be certain that this is the right course for you.

We all have memories of teachers at school. Some teachers may even have inspired you in your choice of future profession. Others may have been terrible, scary or indifferent. What sort of teacher do you want to be? Do you want to be remembered by your pupils as successful, passionate, inspirational and fun?

Teaching is not an easy choice, but it can be extremely rewarding. Remember that being a good teacher doesn't happen overnight – you will need to be patient as you will have to work hard at it. Try to identify and improve your weaknesses, and continue to reinforce your strengths.

How much do my A level subjects count?

Your A-level subjects may give an indication of some of your strengths. However, not everyone comes via the A-level road. Some people enter BEds (or other degrees, than PGCEs) from college Access courses.

However, the current official minimum admission requirements for ITT are not A levels or GCSEs. They are either a level 3 qualification for BEds or a first degree for PGCE. Your A level subjects do not matter – it is the subject of your degree which is important. You do, however, need GCSEs (or equivalencies) in English and maths, and, if training for primary education, science.

How much does my degree subject count?

This varies across institutions. Many will look for a match between degree and the curriculum, so applicants should be ready to explain the relevance of their degree study to becoming a teacher. If you have a psychology degree, for example, you should emphasise that the skills you have developed are a good basis for teaching curriculum subjects such as maths and science. Provide clear examples.

Do I need to have experience in a school before applying?

The simple answer is 'yes'. And generally, the more experience the better. How can you really know that you want to become a teacher if you haven't been into a school? Gaining experience in a school is becoming essential as the government increases the role of schools in training. But it's not just about clocking up *experience*: it's about what you make of that time and what you take from it. There are several good reasons:

- **You are about to invest a year of your life and a lot of money in your ITT course. So you want to be *certain* that teaching is really what you want to do. You need to see close up what classroom life is like and what teachers actually have to do during, and out of, class time.**
- **You have to become *familiar* with the curriculum and the way in which schools work. School experience will give you an up-to-date basis of experience to build on by the time you start your course. Make sure you can discuss what you have done, observed and learned from your experiences.**
- **You need to know that you are able to function in a classroom. You will have to be *comfortable* taking on the mantle of 'teacher'. Some people, however strong their commitment to teaching, find it terribly difficult to step into that role. Early experience may help you to consider whether you are actually cut out for teaching. You need to be confident that you have made the right choice of career.**

Many teacher education programmes will expect at least ten days as an observer/helper prior to starting your course. Be prepared to answer questions about your time in school:

- **How do teachers manage their classrooms?**
- **How do teachers interest and engage pupils in learning?**

Think of other possible questions to do with your experiences in school and prepare suitable answers. You might want to practise answers aloud to ensure that you are clear, fluent and sound natural.

Do I have to be super confident and outgoing?

No. All types of personalities can be successful teachers. However, a school's personnel will be reassured if you appear reasonably confident and assertive. You do not need to be the most outgoing person in the world, but it will certainly help if you feel confident in your own abilities as a beginning trainee teacher. If you can develop the ability to engage learners – making learning fun – and are able to connect with the pupils in your class, they are much more likely to trust and respect you. Listening carefully to questions and responding to them sincerely and honestly are more impressive than super-abundant confidence. The ability to inspire pupils is a key requirement, but remember that you will develop plenty of skills as you yourself learn.

Should I be thick-skinned and able to take criticism?

If you are extremely thick-skinned, you probably won't listen to all the little things that you should be heeding. This means that you won't learn as much as you should – and you will certainly annoy people around you. However, if you are so sensitive that you see criticism almost everywhere, and if you mistakenly begin to translate that into 'people not liking you', then you will sink into self-doubt and anxiety. In such a tough environment it therefore stands to reason that you will need to find a happy middle ground.

Sift out what actually matters in what others say – acting on anything immediately if you need to – and then bounce back. That's resilience. The number one quality prized by those who supervise trainee teachers is for them to take on board what is said to them, and then to act on it *immediately*. Work hard, think positive and always be on time – in school placements these qualities can go a long way to avoiding unnecessary criticism.

Trainee teachers will have to be able to reflect critically on their own practice. They should also be willing to accept constructive criticism from others. Criticism from tutors and school-based mentors will be offered constructively with the sole intention of helping you to be the best teacher you can possibly be.

What qualities do I really need to succeed on an initial teacher training course?

Here are 12 important qualities in a trainee teacher or NQT:

- *Desire:* you will need to really want to teach children or young people.
- *Commitment:* you must be willing to work extremely hard – the training period is very intensive and demanding (but, for your own sanity, try to remember to maintain a healthy work-to-life balance!).
- *Resilience:* take the rough with the smooth, and bounce back.
- *Enthusiasm:* be an energetic learner yourself and pass on your own enthusiasm to your pupils.
- *Humility:* try to relate to your pupils and learn from them, rather than thinking that you're the one with all the knowledge.
- *Self-motivation:* constantly reflect on the quality and effectiveness of what you offer your pupils – see yourself as a perpetual learner and learn from all that you do.
- *Organisation:* manage your time well and keep well organised – you may need to juggle several balls at the same time during a teaching degree.
- *Awareness:* be aware of the reasons why you are required to do what you have to do.
- *Teamwork:* learn to work with others – be flexible in outlook and willing to change your ideas based on evidence.
- *Responsibility:* don't be afraid of taking risks and seeking responsibility – you won't learn by holding back or hiding behind others.
- *Initiative:* be an active, resourceful learner – it's not all handed to you on a plate.
- *Sense of humour:* stay cheerful and good humoured – make an effort to engage with your peers and tutors.

Time to reflect

The ideal trainee teacher and NQT is someone who is enthusiastic, knowledgeable, reflective – and is able to communicate effectively. You'll also need to be creative in your thinking. Have the confidence to believe in yourself and the flexibility to adapt your thoughts, ideas and teaching.

Be passionate about what you believe in and about your subject. This will always shine through. It's probably a good idea to look through the Teachers' Standards in order to gain an insight into what is expected as a trainee and as a teacher. High levels of academic competence are also required. Good teachers love working with children and young people in their care. Think about the positive effect you can have on your pupils future lives – you can make a huge difference in your new role.

4.2 What makes a good ITT application?

When you are applying for a course it makes obvious sense that you need to present yourself in the best possible light. Distinguish yourself from other applicants by coming across as an outstanding candidate in your written application. Don't spoil your own chances of success with poor content or untidy presentation.

Spelling, punctuation and grammar don't matter that much, do they?

Yes they do. They are essential. Why? Because teachers are the models for pupils. If you are going to teach children how to spell and how to use punctuation and grammar correctly, it stands to reason that you will be proficient in these areas yourself.

Some ITT providers automatically discard applications that show that prospective students cannot be bothered to proof-read them. If someone cannot put in the effort at this stage, they certainly won't put in the necessary effort as a trainee or teacher. It is therefore important for you to make the right first impression, especially in such a competitive market. Work through your application carefully, using a dictionary to avoid spelling mistakes. Ask a friend or relative with strong literacy skills to check it for you.

If you are dyslexic you may make a very good teacher. Many dyslexic teachers manage to equip themselves with a range of effective strategies to make sure that they provide a good model for children in their care. Indeed, they are often at an advantage because they understand from first-hand experience many of the difficulties that pupils may have with literacy.

How much does the presentation of my application matter?

Presentation is every bit as important as spelling, punctuation and grammar. Your application must be well written, concise and it needs to address the important issues. Nowadays most applications are online, so it is important that font size and style is readable and appropriate. Dispense with smiley faces and emoticons!

What sort of thing should I include in my personal statement?

The content of the personal statement is very important. Keep it relevant and concise. Make sure that it:

- **shows your commitment to education;**
- **demonstrates your lively interest in how you as a teacher can help pupils to learn and develop;**

- **summarises some of your various talents and skills, showing clearly how these are relevant to teaching; and**
- **provides a flavour of you as a person.**

Ask yourself, why should anyone invite you to interview on the basis of this letter? Structure your application so that it doesn't become a long list of 'I did this, then I did that'. It is far better to have focused paragraphs which include select examples.

And remember not to fall into the trap of over-emphasising your wish to 'work with children', which in itself is not sufficient when applying for a *teaching* course. It's important to show an interest in children, but just make sure that you don't overdo it.

Do you want to know all about my bachelor's degree and what I have studied?

No, it's not really necessary to go through details of your bachelor's degree in your letter of application. You can include the important information on the form. In your personal statement, simply identify how you think your degree study has prepared you to enter the teaching profession. How has the experience developed you as a person, socially and intellectually? How does this relate to the skills and qualities that you believe are important in a teacher?

Do you need to know all about my previous studies?

Your previous studies will be listed in the appropriate sections of the application form, so there will be little value in restating this in your personal statement – unless it relates directly to teaching or working with children.

What about all the extra-curricular activities I have done?

Importantly, what do your extra-curricular activities say about you? Include these only if you can answer questions about how these have matured your outlook or will enhance your teaching ability. If you have been a sports coach, a summer school tutor, or been involved in musical activities, for example, these may have direct relevance to your curriculum knowledge, your teaching skills and your management of young people. This demonstrates that you can manage time successfully, prioritise and contribute to wider teams – all key skills for teachers. A history of working with children will strengthen your application and can show your suitability for the course. If, however, you state that your main interests are shopping or meeting up with friends, how will you be able to expand upon this convincingly at interview?

Are you interested in any travelling I may have done?

Yes, but think about what your travelling says about you as a person. Voluntary work overseas will count for more than a two-week package holiday in Ibiza. As always, pull out the most relevant features and explain exactly how they support your application. Keep it brief unless this was relevant work with children, such as Camp America or teaching EFL abroad.

Are you interested in any part-time jobs I have had?

Yes, if they have involved working with children or are of direct relevance to teaching. If not, you may still have transferable skills and qualities that will be beneficial as a student and class teacher. Emphasise skills you have developed dealing with the public, working as a member of a team, or taking responsibility for completing a task to high standards. You can mention good timekeeping and give examples of your ability to demonstrate a professional manner in the workplace.

Are you interested in my work history?

Interviewers will want to find out about your past career, if you are coming to ITT after working full time. Also, why are you ready to take a different pathway now? Do not leave big gaps in your cv – although interviewers may not necessarily probe areas like this, they may still be wary. If you are making a major career change, you should explain your motivation, and identify transferable skills or knowledge from your previous work. It is extremely important to have classroom experience to underpin a career change – you need to show that you are clear what the change involves, as teaching is never an easy option. For some applicants, it may be difficult to gain that classroom experience while working. Using annual leave to gain that experience can be a worthwhile sacrifice (and demonstrates a true commitment to teaching as your future career).

Do you want to know all about my political views and/or my views on the current controversies in education?

No, but an awareness of topical issues within education is important. Are you aware of government initiatives, policy and practice with regard to education? An understanding of education illustrates your commitment to a future teaching career. Useful sources of information include the BBC education website and the *Times Educational Supplement*. *In* addition, refer back to Chapter 1 for lots of information on how to update yourself on current issues in education. Some teacher education programmes will ask you to choose an educational topic and read up about it before the interview. Look at it in depth so you are able to express your point of view clearly – political outlook is unimportant.

How much knowledge do I need about the subject I am applying to teach?

This depends on the course for which you have applied, but the prospectus and entry criteria will give you an idea of this. You should have good starter knowledge at the level you will be teaching – and you will develop this during your course. If applying for primary education, the more knowledge you have about national curriculum areas the better, but no-one is expected to have an in-depth knowledge across the board. Show solid understanding of at least one of the following: mental maths, grammar, spelling and phonics. Good subject knowledge for secondary teaching can be impressive, but this is of course only part of the picture – you need to be able to teach the subject to others.

What type of references do I need?

The most useful references are, for example, from a school or organisation where the applicant has worked recently, or from a university tutor or work manager (full-time/ part-time employment).

4.3 What makes a good ITT interview candidate?

If you have prepared a strong ITT application, you will be well on the way to appearing a strong interview candidate – even *before* you arrive at your interview. Keep up the good work on the day of the interview.

To prepare thoroughly for interview, practise making positive statements about yourself, as this will really help to make you fluent with your replies by the time of your interview. Practise answering the type of questions you are likely to be asked at interview. Saying it out loud really will help get you interview-fit.

What should I wear?

Wear what you'd expect a professional attending an interview to wear – better to be overdressed than underdressed. Most institutions will expect *smart* (rather than *smart casual*). And definitely not jeans and a T-shirt – you'll want to be remembered for what you have said in your interview, not what you have worn.

Is it a good idea to bring anything else with me to the interview (apart from what I have been told to bring along with me)?

Interviews are tightly scheduled, so time is going to be limited. It's unlikely that you'll have the chance to discuss items you've not been instructed to bring. But it does make sense to bring pens and pencils if you know you are going to be doing a test or written task.

Who will interview me?

You will probably be interviewed by a combination of course staff and senior staff from their partner schools. The school staff's views will be at least as important as those representing the teacher training institution.

Do I need to know all about schools and education?

No, you can't know everything. But demonstrate that you can reflect intelligently on the experience and knowledge that you do have. Do some homework on the web as well (see Chapter 1), as some background knowledge of current issues in education shows interest and commitment.

How much do I need to know about the subject I am applying to teach – will I be quizzed on this?

That depends on the institution and your chosen course. For secondary education courses (and primary education courses offering a specialism) you may be quizzed on your subject knowledge. For other primary courses, institutions will expect students to be honest about what they consider their strengths and weaknesses across primary subjects.

Do I need to be able to provide specific examples of what I have done in the past?

You will need to be able to talk about and reflect on your own school experiences. Institutions may ask you to illustrate your experience with a specific example. Be ready to speak in depth about what you have seen in the classroom – and what you have learnt from that experience. The interviewers will gain an insight into your ability to work with children and how you reflect on these situations. Ideally you will also show how you successfully foster positive relationships with pupils and staff in schools.

Do I need to be prepared to work with the other candidates – or will the interview be individual?

This will vary, but many institutions expect you to interact through group activities. Be prepared, as some interviews may start as a group interview to see how well you work with others. In such a group context, you should aim to engage actively, taking part without forcing your opinions onto others. Observers will be looking for several things:

- **the ability to get involved (without dominating the group);**
- **playing a full part in the task/discussion;**
- **building constructively on the work or ideas of others;**
- **negotiating while not always just agreeing;**
- **listening to others' points of view.**

TIP: A good tactic is to ask a question that encourages someone to expand on their point. Make eye contact with the person who is speaking and remember to smile.

How much will I be expected to know about the course?

Do your homework and find out what you can about the course from the website and course handbook. Attend open days to find out how the course is structured. Be ready to answer the following questions:

- **Why do you want to study at this institution?**
- **Why have you applied for this particular course?**

Do I need to have wanted to be a teacher for a long time?

No. It is more important to show that you have been into schools to find out what teaching entails – and that you are keen to be a teacher right now. Relevant recent experience will show commitment and suitability for teaching. Enthusiasm, passion and the ability to help pupils develop and grow in their learning is more important than simply stating 'I've always wanted to be a teacher'. Ideally you should be sure what age group you want to teach. Think of your own *angle* or *story* – this is your application. Be honest and be yourself.

Is it OK to say that although I want to teach now, I don't plan to teach until I retire?

This may not be the wisest move. Training costs money, time and effort – and no institution will want to invest in someone who may teach for only a year or two. Although you may even end up changing career at a later date, this will be the earliest stage of your career as a teacher – and you should always present yourself in a positive light at interview.

Will I have to teach pupils during my interview?

Yes, you might. Increasingly, interviewers are looking for evidence of applicants' suitability to teach, and what better way could there be than to ask you to interact with a group of unknown pupils! This could involve reading or telling a story, or leading a simple activity, while you are being observed. Those watching will of course be considering your potential, and will not expect you to function as a qualified teacher. Your pre-existing classroom experience should prepare you well for this.

Don't worry – you've prepared thoroughly for this interview. Now go and show everyone what a good ITT interview candidate you really are!

5 | What is teacher training really like?

This chapter on teacher training is divided into two sections:

5.1 One student's perspective
5.2 ITT tutors' perspective

5.1 One student explains what it's really like as a trainee teacher

From an early age, I always had an interest in education. In fact, it sometimes feels like it is the only thing that I have been any good at in my life – bringing me immense pleasure and enjoyment. This was the main reason for me entering ITT and pursuing a career as a secondary mathematics teacher. I decided that I wanted to inspire children to see the benefits of education.

I found the process of applying to my course fairly straightforward and not particularly daunting. The interview was a different matter, although this may have been because I was only 17 at the time. I did not really know what to expect from the whole process and had not really been given any guidance about the interview. I would have liked to have had a rough outline of what they were going to ask me so that I could have prepared some stronger responses. I accept there has to be an element of unpredictability with interviews, but some general guidance would have really benefited me and allayed some of my worries (see chapter 4).

Having said that, the interview was not too surprising. I answered the usual questions on my background and why I wanted to pursue a career in teaching, and what I thought the job would entail. However, a couple of the questions really threw me.

How I would teach this topic? What's the point of this subject in real life?

I found this sort of questioning difficult: tough questions which forced me to answer on the spot – and think outside the box.

My chosen university was relatively supportive in providing me with information, such as required reading for the course. Looking back on my three years at university though, I feel that initially I was not fully prepared for the course. For someone embarking on ITT, I would advise them to get some proper teaching experience *before* they start the course so that they can get a taste of what the real thing is like – and so that it will not be a shock to them when they start teaching. Before beginning my course, I got some work experience as a Teaching Assistant in a school for two weeks. Although I enjoyed the experience, I now feel that I should have aimed to get more out of my time in the classroom and really tried to experience what teaching is like. This would have given me a more realistic idea of what to expect later. I was to find the placements on my course particularly challenging. I think if I had experienced more teaching practice *before* the course started, I would have been much better prepared to cope with the demands of my placement. I think perhaps my lack of genuine teaching practice somewhat hindered my development into a confident teacher who had the respect of the class.

I have always cared a lot about what I have achieved in my own education, and for the majority of my course this aspect concerned me the most. Generally, I thought the assignments and academic work were OK. Although for some students it may be quite exciting to write an essay the night before it is due in, for me it made sense to start on essays as early as possible. Before starting the course, I imagined that I would learn more about how to teach particular topics on my ITT course. Instead, I seemed to pick this up as the course progressed and I also learned through experience on placement. As expected, we studied theory in depth, and this proved useful as I began to see the link between theory and practice.

There is no doubt about the importance of academic qualifications. During the first two years of my degree, academic attainment occupied my thoughts a great deal, while in my final year I worried about obtaining Qualified Teacher Status (QTS). At times, I thought that I was never going to do it. I have never been particularly confident and I sometimes wondered whether I was capable of achieving QTS. I built it up in my mind to be always just out of reach. I often doubted my ability to complete the training and, at some points, thought I was never going to get my degree. It became everything to me and dominated my life. In the end, I managed to get a first in my degree, get my dissertation published, and also obtain a 2 (good) in my teaching. I have frequently doubted my teaching ability, but to be graded a good teacher allowed me to break free from those doubts. I do not believe that I necessarily studied any harder than my peers; I would say we were all a hard-working bunch. At the time of training, however, it was frustrating to observe that teaching often seemed more natural to others than it did to me.

The skills tests are hard to quantify in terms of difficulty, although you could possibly say that they are approximately grade C GCSE Maths and English. Some people found them quite easy, others really struggled. I believe that getting used to the format of the tests is the main thing, as there is a certain technique required to pass them. The tests online provided by the government are useful, but I would definitely advise buying a book or workbook to supplement your study. Prepare for the tests as you would for any other exam. Become familiar with all the course content, do some revision and make sure you try out a few practice tests (see chapters 2 and 3). You may also want to consider getting a tutor. I have witnessed the benefits of this, as I have since tutored many people for the skills tests. It is always good to have someone else to work with: if this is not a tutor, then you may want to find an amenable friend or family member. My university offered free support sessions for this, which is another option.

While my course panned out pretty much as I had expected, I could not have predicted how placements worked. I guess the hardest aspect of the whole course was the teaching in school placements. There was never a dull moment and you certainly had to think on your feet. As a kid I was fairly well behaved at school, but I did see bad behaviour in some pupils. However, I think what surprised me most on placement was the sheer volume of tasks which a trainee teacher has to undertake – planning lessons, admin, teaching, as well as marking. It was certainly a very full-on experience, but I also derived some satisfaction from all the work. One thing is for sure: working in a school is never boring – and it is often a thrilling job.

You cannot change how unpredictable the placements are going to be, because there is always going to be an element of volatility. If you study hard, you can do well in the academic work, but placements are more complex. At first, my placement was quite tough. But the unpredictability also makes the placement exciting. Over time I found my feet and eventually achieved some sort of competency, although as a teacher I am still a long way off being the finished article. The trickiest part of the course was teaching lessons on my placement, but this all got easier with time and practice. You are learning something new every day.

It was really weird to go into a school as a teacher and have pupils call me 'Sir'. It was a good feeling though! I was just surprised at how different this was from attending school as a pupil, and I really gained an insight into what being a teacher is like. Some of my family work in education, so I always had a rough idea, but going into a school and being expected to take charge of a class suddenly made it real. On my placements, though, I felt similar to how I did on work experience: I did not really feel like I quite belonged. This appears to be something which many student teachers experience.

The quality and personality of the teachers varied in each school that I worked in, and this variety makes working in a school much more interesting. Most of the teachers were helpful and supportive and, over the course of my three years' training, no one really caused me any problems. However, teachers tend to be busy, so often I simply had to learn things for myself, which helped me develop essential skills of independence and problem-solving. Teachers tend to be very close in their departments, which makes for a productive working environment.

Managing a class of children was difficult, irrespective of the class size. At first, standing at the front of the class was nerve-wracking. I have always had problems with my confidence, and here I was thrown out of my comfort zone. I had always been a follower in life, while secretly I craved to be a leader. Becoming a teacher gave me the chance to be in charge for once, rather than being told what to do! This was a very liberating experience and something which I came to enjoy.

Planning a lesson was quite simple, although I think that there is an unnecessary amount of paperwork in schools. It was pretty time-consuming having to prepare for every lesson. However, this was also a valuable learning experience for me, as was marking. I soon discovered the best times to do marking and lesson planning – straight after school so that I could try to have some time to myself in the evenings. Remembering to find time for yourself is very important when you are training to be a teacher.

I enjoyed explaining concepts and ideas to the pupils the most, as well as going around and helping them while they were doing their work. I also liked talking to them during form time and extra-curricular activities – this helped me to get to know them on a different level (while not having to discipline them all the time). Knowing the pupils better made teaching them much easier. I am an extrovert who likes talking to people, and as I expected, these were the parts of the placement that I enjoyed the most.

The personality and teaching style that you develop as a teacher is important. I would advise students not to be scared to become their own type of teacher: it helps to have a vision of the teacher you want to be, and not to let anyone change that. All too often teachers are encouraged to be too similar. It is important to develop your own style and identity. Some people might say that certain types of people cannot be a teacher, but I would disagree: anyone can be a teacher if they put their mind to it. The reality is that it takes some people longer than others. There were a few people who dropped out of my course but quite a few of them transferred to a primary teaching course. What helps people succeed is determination. You are going to have to show resilience at some stage.

I believe the ITT course provides a wonderful learning experience. It certainly makes you ready to become a teacher, particularly if you prepare well from the start for placement. The course can also give you so much more: I think I have definitely grown as a person as a result. Plenty of people thought that I would never get through teacher training. But I did, and I have more confidence now than ever before. I can pursue new goals in my life. Having qualified as a teacher, I am finally starting to get rid of my own doubts. If I had not gone on teacher training, none of this would have been possible.

5.2 Some insight from a conversation with a group of ITT tutors at the University of Exeter

This is not an exhaustive description of teacher training. The conversation was based on a series of questions designed to get some insight into what training is really like.

The role of the teacher

Classroom persona is really important. A trainee teacher should assume the role of a teacher – and begin to embody it, really. The change of viewpoint can challenge those who have previously worked in schools in a different role, such as teaching assistants (TAs). They not only have to take on a new teacher persona, but they must step away from the TA persona too.

Prospective trainees should make the most of any pre-course school experiences: both the time in school that they organise themselves before they apply, and the time that they spend in school before they start the course. Learn from early teaching experiences. Really think about what you observe in the classroom and consider what you want and need to get out of it. The real 'work' of teacher training starts here: listen, watch and keep alert and curious. Try to see the learning that is happening and ask how you can tell that learning is taking place. Did the children learn from the lesson? Ensure you are open-minded. Are you ready for the experience to change your view of teaching? Make sure that when you go into the classroom you are prepared to look at the teaching, specifically. Be prepared to look at the learning first and then evaluate the teaching (the teaching can only be good if the learning is good).

When you teach, there is an element of acting, or performing. Act and look like a teacher – dress like a teacher, too. You should, of course, maintain a 'difference' between yourself and the class. You are there as a teacher, not a friend. Remain professional throughout and always have your teacher's hat on.

Do not repeat the past

While it may seem quite tempting to some prospective trainees to go back to their old school to do pre-course experience, you should think twice about this. ITT providers will be much more impressed if you go somewhere new. You will also learn more. You will have a clearer view of who you are in the new school – and not be treated as an ex-pupil. You will be able to consider schools and education with a fresh perspective.

Behaviour

Managing behaviour at school should not be seen in isolation, because it is all inter-twined with planning good lessons and delivering well-paced learning. Behaviour in the classroom tends to be more of an anxiety than a huge problem to tackle. Trainees often worry about it, perhaps after reading articles in the press about really bad behaviour in some schools. You will need to learn quickly that a 'well-behaved' class is not a silent, obedient one. Everything is a little more complicated than that. Good learning behaviour includes a lot of oral interaction; often between groups of learners.

You are accountable, first and foremost, for the pupils' learning. A teacher is accountable for the overall learning of all pupils, not just the behaviour and day-to-day work of one or two individuals, which might be what the TA is responsible for. In this way, the difference between a TA and a teacher is clear. Classroom teaching is different from one-on-one: it is about realising the needs of the individual and the class as a group all the time. Try to see the bigger picture – you are helping with the learning of the whole class over a whole year – and not just a single lesson.

In reality, there is no big secret to managing behaviour. If you plan good lessons, and have a clear structure and a strong positive presence, the behaviour will often fall into place. The majority of trainees 'crack' behaviour in the first few weeks of the course – or are clearly en route towards 'cracking it' at that early stage.

Trying to maintain good behaviour in class is one worry, but trainees soon realise that the bigger challenge is to keep the children's attention and focus on lessons. The world today is full of swift, slick information and entertainment delivery – children are used to, and expect, that now. There will frequently be one or two students with behaviour issues that trainees (and teachers, for that matter) cannot resolve with a 'quick fix'. 'Behaviour' is not really about them alone – it is about the whole class, and the context (environment, content, teaching and learning resources, teaching and learning activities, support).

Reflective practice

All teachers have bad lessons that just do not go right. This can happen, and always will. You need to pick yourself up, reflect on what went wrong – and move on, quickly. The key is to look back on lessons and really try to pin down why something went wrong (if it did) so that you can fix the problem for the next time. In the end, teaching is a learning expe-rience, both for the learners, and for you as a trainee teacher.

Perfection is just not possible. Some trainees will be high achievers who find it difficult to cope with this idea. A perfectionist streak does not really help in teacher training. You must learn and improve as a teacher, but be realistic about what you can achieve in your lessons. Often students who are too concerned with perfection become derailed when some problems arise – or they find it really difficult to be the 'teacher' in the room. If you *are* a perfectionist, learn from your experiences and mistakes. Embrace them. Use them as handy indicators to improve your teaching. You are at the beginning of a process. Do not worry: it all takes time and you will need to stick at it.

Teaching practice *will* feel uncomfortable at times. And you will learn things about your-self that you may not like. You need to be ready and willing to take this on. Teaching may feel like holding up a mirror to yourself. The vast majority of trainees appear to be really self-critical. Do not make the mistake of looking outside yourself for fault. Try to keep a sense of proportion when thinking about things that may have gone wrong. No one will go through teaching practice without 'a bad day', but if you do experience one, be prepared to learn from it as much as you can. And move on.

Trainees often need reassurance that they will get plenty of help and support while they are still learning. Some 'deep end' models of teacher training exist, but most trainees receive good support so they can work through all the challenges. Trainees should think hard about how much support they would like or need. Look carefully at what different courses offer. You can ask more questions to find this out. There are a number of routes available into teaching, but the structure of courses can vary from place to place – and this includes how much support you get, too. Sometimes, prospective trainees can struggle to understand how their courses will work, so it really does pay to take time to find this out. Proper research into the courses you apply to will help you make the right choice for *you*.

Applicants need to prepare well, but they should also realise that tutors are constantly assessing them. Some trainees may even have to teach as part of their interviews. If this is the case, keep in mind that perfection is not a realistic goal. If all trainees could teach fabulously from the start, they would have no need for training!

Always be realistic

When applying, find out how many places each provider has to offer. If the provider has only one place for your particular subject, an impressive second place means that you still will not be offered a place. If, however, a provider has ten places to offer, your chances should improve dramatically. Be aware of your own value. Look at your choices, and see the whole 'market' of teacher training – and how ITT providers and trainees fit into this. A thoughtful and intelligent approach will work best.

Academic assignments

All courses (including School Direct) will have an academic element. If you have not written an academic piece like an essay for a long time, you will have to prepare for this, because you will need to write two long social science essays for most courses. Do not worry, you are not alone: many trainees who have written essays more recently than you may also fear their academic assignments. Trainees should not, however, become overwrought about 'academic' work. It does not have to be daunting at all. Preparation is key and, often, the hardest part is making a start with the writing. Remember you should not be stuffing your essay with as many difficult words as possible to impress your tutors. Think clearly, write clearly. And, when you are editing your essay, read your work out loud.

Specialisms

Your subject or specialism is important (some primary trainees have this too). You should embrace this and get the most you can from it. A specific focus on a subject can really add an extra string to your bow when you enter the world of teaching. Always try to use it to your advantage.

Working with others

The vast majority of the time, working with other teachers in schools is really positive. Mentors and other members of staff will be keen to help. Mentors can be pushed for time, however, so trainees should always be sensitive to this. You always need to be professional about your relationship with your mentor too. Being over-friendly can sometimes be as detrimental as not really getting on with a mentor at all. A trainee is there to learn and that should be the focus, first and foremost.

State schools in England have their own unique 'culture'. If you have no first-hand experience of this – for example, you were educated privately or in another country – you should take time to find out more about it. The British Council has some information on the UK state education system that might be of use to trainees or candidates for whom this applies.

Getting the most out of training

Trainee teachers say they enjoy teaching and get a huge amount out of working with pupils. They enjoy having a peer group during training. Everyone benefits from the friendships they build during training – sharing ideas and learning from their own and each other's successes and mistakes.

Teacher training is a journey. You will really gain from the experience if you are ready to learn new things. Be prepared to open your mind to what you see and do. You will probably find that you change as a person, too. By the end of the course, most trainees are very different people. Group photographs before and after training show that the students hold themselves in a different way. It is not helpful for tutors to think of it as throwing trainees in at the deep end and seeing if they survive. The process is more about supporting you and gradually giving you more and more responsibility as you go. As a trainee teacher, always be open-minded. Be prepared to learn new things that you never even considered about schools, education, children – and yourself.

Dropping out

There is no single reason why trainees drop out. Generally speaking, though, it is a case of life getting in the way. Drop outs are perhaps not as high as is believed. Although the following article is not current, you may find it of interest as part of the bigger picture.

www.tes.co.uk/article.aspx?storycode=2444282

Challenges

The most challenging part of the course is often the workload – and the sheer range of skills trainees are developing *at the same time*. Becoming a teacher is an identity shift for many and you are sure to change during the course of the year, especially if you have recently graduated. Prepare yourself for the pastoral role of teachers: you may soon be exposed to issues that you have just never had to think about before. Although you may start your course with a very clear focus on teaching your subject, it is so much more than that. You may be surprised by the pupils, their variety, their needs and all the things that you will need to discover about yourself, too.

Literacy Glossary

*Abbreviation A shortened form of a word or phrase; usually, but not always, consisting of a letter or group of letters taken from the word or phrase. For example, the word *approximately* can be replaced by the abbreviation 'approx'.

Accent An accent is the distinctive system of pronunciation that listeners identify as being used by a regional or social group. Accents are neither easy nor hard to follow, merely familiar or unfamiliar.

*Acronym An abbreviation made from the initial letters of a group of words and often pronounced as a single word, for example, RAM (random access memory).

Adjective An adjective is a word, phrase or clause that tells us about a noun: *clever child*, *tense student*, *concerned teacher*; *a lesson about Spain*; *the teacher who had done supply work there previously*. The clause comes after the noun whereas the phrase may come before (*the predictably over-anxious child from Ashton*) as well as more typically, afterwards.

Adverb Adverbs tell us when, where or how something took place. They usually modify verbs but can also modify adjectives, other adverbs or sentences: *Joe sang happily*; *Annie is a very engaged reader*; *Alice danced very gracefully*; *Lucy had, fortunately, brought her trumpet with her*.

Not all adverbs end in *ly*. *Fast* is usually used as an adverb. *Very*, used above, is an adverb that appears only as an intensifier of some other word.

Adverbial clause An adverbial clause does the work of an adverb: it tells us when, where or how something took place: *The head came into the hall when all the children were there*; *Ann did her print-making where she usually worked*; *Pam ran down the corridor as if she was being chased*.

Adverbial phrase An adverbial phrase also does the work of an adverb. It is a group of words based on an adverb but coming before or after it or both: *very quickly*, *talked as volubly as the deputy*. An adverb can be substituted for an adverbial phrase.

Agree/agreement If one person does something, the verb should be in its singular form: *Annie sings*. If more than one does something, the verb should be in its plural form: *Joe and Sally are painting*.

*Analogy Drawing a comparison to show a similarity; for example, if you were describing the flow of electricity, you might choose to use the flow of water as an analogy.

*Apostrophe A **punctuation mark** used for two purposes:

- to show that something belongs to someone (the *possessive* form); for example, *the pupil's work*, or
- to show that letters have been missed out (a *contraction*); for example, *you've* is the shortened form of *you have*.

Attachment ambiguity Ambiguity may arise when it is unclear if a phrase should be attached to this or that other phrase. In *The teacher told the class what had happened to the caretaker on the stairs*, it is possible to understand that *on the stairs* was where something happened to the caretaker but also that it was *on the stairs* that the teacher told the class.

*Audio Of, or relating to, sound.

Brackets: see **punctuation: parentheses**.

British English This term is normally used to describe the features common to English English, Welsh English, Scottish English, and Hiberno-English.

Bullet points Bullets should only be used to aid comprehension by highlighting key points and breaking up long passages of text. Overuse can be distracting and make text harder to digest. Ideally bullet points should lead out from a 'platform' or 'stem' statement and complete a grammatically correct sentence. However, there are no hard and fast rules on this. Often what is acceptable is governed by a preferred 'house-style'.

Capital letters: see **punctuation**. Use capitals for proper nouns, acronyms and the beginning of sentences. Note that upper case in an acronym does not necessarily denote upper case in the full description, e.g. EPQ/extended project qualification; PGCE/post-graduate certificate in education.

Clause A group of words with a finite verb (it would be a phrase if it did not have a finite verb). As it is finite, the verb typically has a subject. A clause may be a sentence: *Alice laughed.* A sentence may contain several clauses: *Alice laughed and Lucy giggled* links two clauses of equal significance with the conjunction *and*; this is a co-ordinate sentence. *Alice laughed because Lucy giggled* links two clauses that differ in significance; this is a complex sentence in which a main clause – *Alice laughed* – is linked to a subordinate clause that is not independent of other clauses but exists to explain the main clause on which it depends.

Coherence/cohesion A well-made text feels coherent. What holds it together is the writer's use of cohesion: cohesive devices that relate parts of the text to each other. Adverbs between sentences are such devices: *The IT suite was heavily used. **However,** rising numbers were putting pressure on its use.*

Repetition of a word or some reference to it is another device. Perhaps the one we are most aware of is the use of a pronoun to refer to its noun. A noun may refer back to its noun: *The Ofsted report was scrutinised by the Governors before **it** was presented to parents. Although **some** were apprehensive, most of the class looked forward to the cliff-walk.*

*Colloquial A colloquialism is a term used in everyday language rather than in formal speech or writing; for example, the use of the word *kids* rather than *children* in the following sentence:
The kids in Years 4 and 5 are having a swimming gala next week.

*Colon: see **punctuation**.

*Comma: see **punctuation**.

*Compound word A word made when two words are joined to form a new word; for example, *foot/ball*, *foot/fall*. Sometimes, a hyphen is used between the two parts of the word, as in *over-anxious*.

*Conjunctions (see also connectives) These are words such as *and*, *but* and *or*, that are used to join words, phrases or clauses. There are two kinds of conjunction:

- **Co-ordinating conjunctions** (*and*, *but*, *or* and so).These link items that have equal status grammatically, for example:

  *We could fly to Paris **or** we could take the train.*
  *He plans to fly to Dublin **but** he will arrive there very early.*

- **Subordinating conjunctions** (*when, while, before, after, since, until, if, because, although, that*). If the two items do not have equal status, a subordinating conjunction is used. Most commonly, this happens when a main clause is joined to a subordinate clause, for example:
- *I was late for the meeting **because** the train was delayed.*

Connective Connectives connect words, phrases, clauses and sentences. Those that operate *within* the sentence, that connect words, phrases and clauses, are called conjunctions: *and, but, if, or, because, although, etc.* Those that connect sentences (*Pam and Tom worked very hard all term. **Luckily, their efforts paid off**) include some conjunctions but also adverbs such as: *On the other hand, Later, While we were singing, etc.*

Consistency A good style is, among other things, consistent. The writer will always spell *judgement* with that first *e* or always without it. Punctuation demands a very consistent style, as when adverbs such as *however* always appear between commas if they occur in the middle of a sentence.

*Consonant Consonants are letters and speech sounds that are not vowels. See **vowel**.

Contraction If we try to write down informal speech, we will sometimes need contractions. These help us to write some contracted combinations of words: *do not* becomes *don't*, *will not* becomes *won't*. The words are contracted by omitting some letters and inserting an apostrophe into the space that is left. Occasionally, as with *won't*, there is also a change in spelling.

*Contradict, contradicted, contradiction To contradict is to state that something is the opposite of what has been said; a contradiction is a statement that contradicts.

Convention While the rules of grammar, like the laws of gravity, get their authority by describing how things are, there are some practices that are matters of social convention and have no other explanation. The conventions governing spelling and punctuation, for example, have changed over time.

*Dash Use a dash, rather than a hyphen, to represent ranges of numbers, e.g. 11–16 years.

A pair of dashes can be used to separate an interruption within a sentence, e.g. 'Most pupils – especially in extended schools – enjoy after school activities'. If the interruption comes at the end of the sentence, only one dash is used.

*Definite article The; see **determiner**.

*Department for Education In full at first mention, then the DfE.

*Determiner These are words used with nouns to help define them, for example, *this computer*, *a pencil*, *the book*, and limit, i.e. determine the reference of the noun in some way. Determiners include:

- articles (*a*/*an*, *the*)
- demonstratives (*this*/*that*, *these*/*those*)
- possessives (*my*/*your*/*his*/*her*/*its*/*our*/*their*)
- quantifiers (*some*, *any*, *no*, *many*, *few*, *all*, *either*, *each*, etc.)
- numbers (*one*, *two*, *three*, etc.), and
- some question words (*which*, *what*, *whose*).

Words that are used as determiners are followed by a noun (though not necessarily immediately). For example, *this* book is yours; *this* black book is yours; *which* book is yours?

Many determiners can also be used as **pronouns**. These include demonstrative pronouns, question words, numbers and most quantifiers. When used as pronouns, determiners are not followed by a noun; they refer to the noun: *this* is for you (where *this* refers to *this school*, *this book*, etc.).

Dialect A variety of a language that is spoken by a specific group or in a specific area of the country and whose words and grammar show some differences from those used in other dialects of English. The prestige of a dialect derives from the prestige of its speakers, not from its linguistic features. *Accent* is usually taken to be related but different because it focuses on the *substance* of the language: in the case of an accent, that substance is the sound of speech.

*Dialogue A conversation between two or more people.

Digraph Two letters that represent one sound: *ch* and *ck* in *check*; *sh* in *show*; *ph* in *phonically*.

*Discourse marker A word or phrase (such as *however, nevertheless, well, OK,* or *right!*) that is used to signal a pause or change of direction in conversation.

Ellipsis If a sentence can be understood when a word or a group of words is removed, the parts deleted have been ellipted. One of the commonest examples of ellipsis is the dropping of the relative pronoun *that*: *The school [that] I like best.* A more sophisticated usage is: *My class, if lively, is still well behaved. If lively* here is an ellipted version of something like *even if it is lively.*

*Evaluate To assess; when asked to evaluate whether a statement is supported or implied by a text, you are being asked to judge how clearly the text does or does not spell out the information given in the statement.

*Fewer/less Use 'fewer' for things you can count (e.g. books, pupils) and 'less' for things you can't count (e.g. space, scope).

Grammar Grammar, or syntax, is usually used to mean how sentences are organised. It can, however, also refer to the organisation of larger units: the text level. *Cohesion* is the study of the grammar of these larger units. *Morphology* is the branch of grammar that deals with word-formation.

*Hyphens Use hyphens for compound adjectives, e.g. the up-to-date situation but keep the directory up to date, a long-term plan but in the long term. Do not use a hyphen between an adverb and the adjective or the verb it modifies, e.g. a hotly disputed penalty, a constantly evolving policy.

*Imply, implied, implicit Something implied is hinted at without being stated explicitly. It is implicit.

*Indefinite article *A* or *an*; see **determiner.**

Infinitive The (non-finite) form of a verb that opens with *to*: *to learn, to study, to think.*

Morpheme The smallest bit of language that has meaning. A morpheme may be a whole word (*cabbage*) or a word may have several morphemes (*un + help + ful, govern + or, head + teach + er*). **Suffixes** and **prefixes** are all morphemes.

Morphology see **grammar.**

Noun Nouns refer to objects, ideas, things, places. They take a plural form (usually, add *s*).

Some nouns, however, do not normally take a plural form: *happiness.* They have a possessive form (add *'s* or *s'*). They can be substituted by a pronoun, take a word like *the, this, a* before them and take a verb after them.

- **Noun phrase:** a group of words that works as a noun. A pronoun could be substituted for it: *The first person to have been Chair of the Education Committee.*
- **Noun clause:** a group of words that has a finite verb and that acts as a noun. Here, the clause acts as the subject: ***That I was late with my reports yet again*** was hard to swallow. Here, it acts as the object: *The class was desperate to know **if the school trip was still on.***
- **Collective nouns** refer to a group of things or people: *collection, family, group, class, set.* It is usually safest to treat collective nouns as singular unless the meaning is that they should be read as plural.
- **Proper nouns** refer to specific people, places, organisations, etc., and have a capital initial letter: *Dot, Mike; Salford, Canterbury; Training and Development Agency.*

Paragraph One or more sentences grouped together because they are about the same topic or because they form one utterance in a dialogue. It is separated from the adjacent paragraphs by beginning on a new line.

Parenthesis A word or phrase that interrupts the sentence is marked at both boundaries by parentheses: brackets, commas or dashes:

The Irwell (which flows through Salford) was the focus of their local studies.
The Irwell – which flows through Salford – was the focus of their local studies.
The Irwell, which flows through Salford, was the focus of their local studies.

Participle The present participle is a form of the verb that ends in *ing*: *learning, reading, writing*; the past participle is a form of the verb that ends, normally, in *ed*: *talked, walked, displayed*. However, there are irregular verbs that have other endings: *bought, written, sung*, etc.

The present participle is used to construct continuous tenses: *she **was teaching**, she **is teaching**, she **will be teaching***. It sometimes works as a noun (it can then be called a gerund): *learning is good*.

The past participle follows an auxiliary verb to form the perfect past tense: *I **have taught**, they **have learned***. The passive voice uses an auxiliary with a past participle: *the class **was cheated out** of their expected success, the in-service day **was cancelled***.

Both participles can be used as adjectives: *broken, breaking, entangled*.

Phoneme A single speech sound. We use 44–48 different phonemes when we speak English, depending on the accent we use. Spelling tries to represent phonemes but tries to do other things as well that may conflict with that attempt. The letters *th* in *this* represent one phoneme but in *thing* they represent a different phoneme.

Phonetics Phonetics is a way of describing the sounds we use in speech. It has nothing to do with phonics.

Phrase A group of words without a verb (it would be a clause if it had a finite verb). Phrases can be **nouns**: *the twentieth position in the class*; **adjectives**: *very clever*; **adverbs**: *too early*; or **verbs**: *was practising*.

Plural The plural form of a noun shows that more than one thing is being referred to. Plural nouns typically end in *s* (*book + s = books; girl + s = girls*), *es* (*box + es = boxes, circus + es = circuses*) or *ies* (*fairy* becomes *fairies, story* becomes *stories*). There are also some irregular plurals, such as *children, women, men, geese, sheep*.

Possessive Possessive pronouns – *my/mine*, etc. – show who or what owns what: *my whiteboard, its cursor*. In writing, nouns show possession by adding an apostrophe and, as appropriate, the letter *s*.

Predicate The part of a sentence that is not the subject; it is about the subject: *The headteacher **arrived too early.***

Prefix A **morpheme** that is added at the beginning of a word: *a* in *atheist, un* in *unhelpful.*

Preposition Prepositions usually link a noun or noun phrase with another one or with a verb. Prepositions such as *at, on, in, over, by, with, near, through* are used to introduce adjective phrases in *The display **over** the radiator* or *That boy **by** the boundary fence* and to introduce adverb phrases in *Joe is **on** the go as usual* and *Annie's balloon rose **into** the sky.*

Pronoun A word used instead of a noun, a noun phrase or a group of nouns. It may be a **personal pronoun**: *I/me, you/you, he/him, she/her, it/it, we/us, they/them*; a **possessive pronoun**: *my/mine, your/yours, his/his, her/hers, our/ours, their/theirs, its/its*; a **reflexive pronoun**: *myself, herself, themselves*; or an **interrogative pronoun** (used in questions): *who/whom, whose, which, what.*

Punctuation The standard set of marks used in written and printed texts to clarify meaning and to separate sentences, words and parts of words. The most commonly used punctuation marks in English are:

- **apostrophe** (')
- **colon** (:)
- **comma** (,)
- **exclamation mark** (!)
- **full stop** (.)
- **hyphen** (-)
- **inverted commas** (see *speech marks*)
- **parentheses** (singular: *parenthesis,* also known as brackets or ellipses (singular, ellipsis) (( ))
- **semi-colon** (;)
- **speech marks,** also known as quotation marks or inverted commas (" " or ' ')
- **question mark** (?).

    Also included are special signals such as:

- the use of a space before and after a block or words to indicate the start of a new **paragraph**
- the convention of using an upper case (or capital) letter to begin a proper name or a new sentence.

*Redundancy Redundancy is the use of duplicative, unnecessary or useless wording, also known as **tautology.**

Relative clause Relative clauses come after nouns and function as adjectives. Typically, they open with a relative pronoun: *who, whom, that, which, whose*: *The teacher **that we hoped to appoint** was not as experienced as two other candidates.* Note that, in this case, the relative pronoun, *that,* can be deleted without losing the meaning.

Sentence A sentence is a clause or a group of clauses. Each clause needs to have a finite verb.

- **Finite verbs** are ones that tell us about tense; they almost invariably have a subject: *Ann and Tony both found maths easy.*
- **Non-finite verb** forms are the infinitive – *to teach* – and the participles that end in *-ed* or *-ing*.
- Sentences can be declarative: *The class rushed into the hall*; **interrogative**: *Can't your class do anything quietly?*; **imperative**: *Slow Down!* or **exclamative**: *That's great!*

*Sentence stem In the test items, this is the first part of a sentence that requires completion by choosing from several possible endings, for example:
There were four kinds of meetings that day: ... followed by a list.

Singular Nouns can be singular or plural: *book* or *books*; *woman* or *women*. Verbs can also show singularity – *I teach*, *she teaches* – or plurality – *we teach, they teach*.

STA The Standards and Testing Agency is an executive agency of the Department for Education. The STA is responsible for the development and delivery of all statutory assessments from Early Years to the end of Key Stage 3. This work was previously carried out by the Qualifications and Curriculum Development Agency.

*Standard English The variety of English used in public communication, particularly in writing.

*Statement A sentence that contains a fact or proposition, for example, *this is a glossary.*

Subject A sentence has a subject (a noun or a pronoun) that does something (the verb):
She *taught sentence structure very clearly.*

Suffix A **morpheme** that is added at the end of a word: *ed* in *walked, ful* in *helpful.*

Syntax Grammar: how sentences are organised.

Tautology The unnecessary repetition of the same idea in different words: in *The Governors met together*, the last word is unnecessary.

*Unit of meaning An identifiably discrete idea.

Verb Words that say what we do or are: *The teacher **stopped** the class because one child **was being** silly.*

- **Active verbs** (verbs in the active voice) tell us what someone did: *Lucy **thanked** the teacher.* **Passive verbs** (verbs in the passive voice) tell us what was done to somebody: *The teacher was **thanked** by Lucy.*
- **Auxiliary verbs** – the main ones are *be, have, do* – accompany main verbs to show tense: *They **have** painted, they **do** run.* Some, called **modal verbs**, express possibility or obligation: *can, could, may, might, will, would, shall, should, must, ought to.*

- **Tense** is the way that a verb tells us when something happened. This is shown in the different forms of the verb, from the past – *learned, has learned, had learned* – to the present – *learns, is learning, does learn* – to the future – *will learn, will have learned*, etc.
- **Number** is the way that a verb shows if one or more than one **subject** did something: *Alice sings, Annie and Joe sing*.

*Vowel The letters a, e, i, o, u; see also **consonant**.

Note

Entries marked with * have been reproduced by courtesy of the TA © Teaching Agency. Permission to reproduce TA copyright material does not extend to any material that is identified as being the copyright of a third party nor to any photographs.

Numeracy Glossary

Accuracy The degree of precision given in the question or required in the answer. For example, a length might be measured to the nearest centimetre. A pupil's reading age is usually given to the nearest month, whilst an average (mean) test result might be rounded to one decimal place.

Bar chart A chart where the number associated with each item is shown either as a horizontal or a vertical bar and where the length of the bar is proportional to the number it represents. The length of the bar is used to show the number of times the item occurs, or the value of the item being measured.

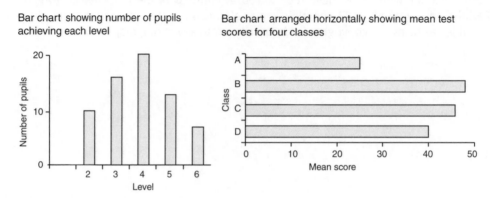

Bar chart showing number of pupils achieving each level

Bar chart arranged horizontally showing mean test scores for four classes

Box and whisker diagram Diagram showing the range and quartile values for a set of data.

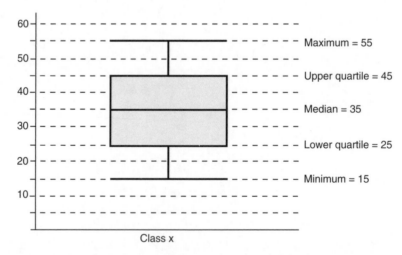

Cohort A group having a common quality or characteristic. For example, 'pupils studying GCSE German this year have achieved higher grades than last year's cohort' (pupils studying GCSE German last year).

Consistent Following the same pattern or style over time with little change. For example, a pupil achieved marks of 84%, 82%, 88% and 85% in a series of mock GCSE tests; her performance was judged to be consistently at the level needed to obtain GCSE grade A*.

Conversion The process of exchanging one set of units for another. Measurement and currency, for example, can be converted from one unit to another, e.g. centimetres to metres, pounds to euros. Conversion of one unit to the other is usually done by using a rule (e.g. 'multiply by $\frac{5}{8}$ to change kilometres into miles'), a formula (e.g. $F = \frac{9}{5} C + 32$, for converting degrees Celsius to degrees Fahrenheit), or a conversion graph.

Correlation The extent to which two quantities are related. For example, there is a positive correlation between two tests, A and B, if a person with a high mark in test A is likely to have a high mark in test B and a person with a low mark in test A is likely to get a low mark in test B. A scatter graph of the two variables may help when considering whether a correlation exists between the two variables.

Cumulative frequency graph A graph in which the frequency of an event is added to the frequency of those that have preceded it. This type of graph is often used to answer a question such as, 'How many pupils are under nine years of age in a local education authority (LA)?' or 'What percentage of pupils gained at least the pass mark of 65 on a test?'.

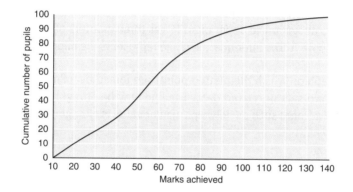

The graph shows the marks pupils achieved. Two pupils scored 10 marks or less, 30 pupils scored 42 marks or less, 60 pupils scored 60 marks or less and 90 pupils scored 95 marks or less. If these were results from a test with a pass mark of 65 marks, then from the graph we can see that 63% of pupils gained 64 marks or less, and so failed the test.

Decimal Numbers based on or counted in a place value system of tens. Normally we talk about decimals when dealing with tenths, hundredths and other decimal fractions less than 1. A decimal point is placed after the units digit in writing a decimal number, e.g. 1.25 The number of digits to the right of the decimal point up to and including the final nonzero digit is expressed as the number of decimal places. In the example above there are two digits after the decimal point, and the number is said to have two decimal places, sometimes expressed as 2 dp. Many simple fractions cannot be expressed exactly as a decimal. For example, the fraction $\frac{1}{3}$ as a decimal is 0.3333... which is usually represented as 0.3 recurring. Decimals are usually rounded to a specified degree of accuracy, e.g. 0.6778 is 0.68 when rounded to 2 dp. 0.5 is always rounded up, so 0.5 to the nearest whole number is 1.

Distribution The spread of a set of statistical information. For example, the number of absentees on a given day in a school is distributed as follows: Monday – 5, Tuesday –17, Wednesday – 23, Thursday – 12 and Friday – 3. A distribution can also be displayed graphically.

Formula A relationship between numbers or quantities expressed using a rule or an equation. For example, final mark = (0.6 x mark 1) + (0.4 x mark 2).

Fraction Fractions are used to express parts of a whole, e.g. $\frac{3}{4}$. The number below the division line, the denominator, records the number of equal parts into which the number above the division line, the numerator, has been divided.

Frequency The number of times an event or quantity occurs.

Greater than A comparison between two quantities. The symbol > is used to represent 'greater than', e.g. 7>2, or >5%.

Interquartile range The numerical difference between the upper quartile and the lower quartile. The lower quartile of a set of data has one quarter of the data below it and three-quarters above it. The upper quartile has three quarters of the data below it and one quarter above it. The inter-quartile range represents the middle 50% of the data.

Line graphs A graph on which the plotted points are joined by a line. It is a visual representation of two sets of related data. The line may be straight or curved. It is often used to show a trend, such as how a particular value is changing over time.

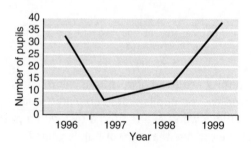

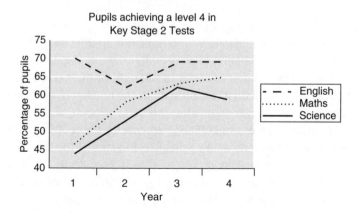

Mean One measure of the 'average' of a set of data. The 'mean' average is usually used when the data involved is fairly evenly spread. For example, the individual costs of four textbooks are £9.95, £8.34, £11.65 and £10.50. The mean cost of a textbook is found by totalling the four amounts, giving £40.44, and then dividing by 4, which gives £10.11. The word average is frequently used in place of the mean, but this can be confusing as both median and mode are also ways of expressing an average.

Median Another measure of the 'average' of a set of data. It is the middle number of a series of numbers or quantities when arranged in order, e.g. from smallest to largest. For example, in the following series of number: 2, 4, 5, 7, 8, 15 and 18, the median is 7. When there is an even number of numbers, the median is found by adding the two middle numbers and then halving the total. For example, in the following series of numbers, 12, 15, 23, 30, 31 and 45, the median is (23 + 30) ÷ 2 = 26.5.

Median and quartile lines Quartiles can be found by taking a set of data that has been arranged in increasing order and dividing it into four equal parts. The first quartile is the value of the data at the end of the first quarter. The median quartile is the value of the data at the end of the second quarter. The third quartile is the value of the data at the end of the third quarter.

    Quartile lines can be used to show pupils' progression from one key stage to another, when compared with national or local data:

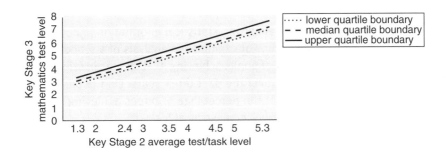

Mode Another measure of the 'average' of a set of data. It is the most frequently occurring result in any group of data. For example, in the following set of exam results: 30%, 34%, 36% 31%, 31%, 30%, 34%, 33%, 31% and 32%, the mode is 31% because this value appears most frequently in the set of results.

Operations The means of combining two numbers or sets of numbers. For example, addition, subtraction, multiplication and division.

Percentage A fraction with a denominator of 100, but written as the numerator followed by '%', e.g. $\frac{30}{100}$ or 30%. A fraction that is not in hundredths can be converted so that the denominator is 100, e.g. $\frac{650}{1000} = \frac{65}{100} = 65\%$. Percentages can be used to compare different fractional quantities. For example, in class A, 10 pupils out of 25 are studying French; in class B, 12 out of 30 pupils are studying French. However, both $\frac{10}{25}$ and $\frac{12}{30}$ are equivalent to $\frac{4}{10}$, or 40%. The same percentage of pupils, therefore, study French in both these classes.

Percentage points The difference between two values, given as percentages. For example, a school has 80% attendance one year and 83% the next year. There has been an increase of 3 percentage points in attendance.

Percentile The values of a set of data that has been arranged in order and divided into 100 equal parts. For example, a year group took a test and the 60th percentile was at a mark of 71. This means that 60% of the cohort scored 71 marks or less. The 25th percentile is the value of the data such that 25% or one quarter of the data is below it and so is the same as the lower quartile. Similarly, the 75th percentile is the same as the upper quartile and the median is the same as the 50th percentile.

Pie chart A pie chart represents the 360° of a circle and is divided into sectors by straight lines from its centre to its circumference. Each sector angle represents a specific proportion of the whole. Pie charts are used to display the relationship of each type or class of data within a whole set of data in a visual form.

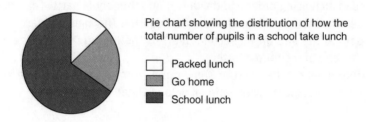

Pie chart showing the distribution of how the total number of pupils in a school take lunch

☐ Packed lunch
▨ Go home
■ School lunch

Prediction A statement based on analysing statistical information about the likelihood that a particular event will occur. For example, an analysis of a school's examination results shows that the number of pupils achieving A*–C grades in science at a school has increased by 3% per year over the past three years. On the basis of this information the school predicts that the percentage of pupils achieving A*–C grades in science at the school next year will increase by at least 2%.

Proportion A relationship between two values or measures. These two values or measures represent the relationship between some part of a whole and the whole itself. For example, a year group of 100 pupils contains 60 boys and 40 girls, so the proportion of boys in the school is 60 out of 100 or 3 out of 5. This is usually expressed as a fraction, in this case, $\frac{3}{5}$.

Quartile (lower) The value of a set of data at the first quarter, 25%, when all the data has been arranged in ascending order. It is the median value of the lower half of all the values in the data set. For example, the results of a test were: 1, 3, 5, 6, 7, 9, 11, 15, 18, 21, 23 and 25. The median is 10. The values in the lower half are 1, 3, 5, 6, 7 and 9. The lower quartile is 5.5. This means that one quarter of the cohort scored 5.5 or less. The lower quartile is also the 25th percentile.

Quartile (upper) The value of a set of data at the third quarter, 75%, when that data has been arranged in ascending order. It is the median value of the upper half of all the values in the data set. In the lower quartile example, the upper quartile is 19.5, the median value of the upper half of the data set. Three quarters of the marks lie below it. The upper quartile is also the 75th percentile.

Range The difference between the lowest and the highest values in a set of data. For example, for the set of data 12, 15, 23, 30, 31 and 45, the range is the difference between 12 and 45. 12 is subtracted from 45 to give a range of 33.

Ratio A comparison between two numbers or quantities. A ratio is usually expressed in whole numbers. For example, a class consists of 12 boys and 14 girls. The ratio of boys to girls is 12:14. This ratio may be described more simply as 6:7 by dividing both numbers by 2. The ratio of girls to boys is 14:12 or 7:6.

Rounding Expressing a number to a degree of accuracy. This is often done in contexts where absolute accuracy is not required, or not possible. For example, it may be acceptable in a report to give outcomes to the nearest hundred or ten. So the number 674 could be rounded up to 700 to the nearest hundred, or down to 670 to the nearest ten. If a number is half way or more between rounding points, it is conventional to round it up, e.g. 55 is rounded up to 60 to the nearest ten and 3.7 is rounded up to 4 to the nearest whole number. If the number is less than half way, it is conventional to round down, e.g. 16.43 is rounded down to 16.4 to one decimal place.

Scatter graph A graph on which data relating to two variables is plotted as points, each axis representing one of the variables. The resulting pattern of points indicates how the two variables are related to each other. This type of graph is often used to demonstrate or confirm the presence or absence of a correlation between the two variables, and to judge the strength of that correlation.

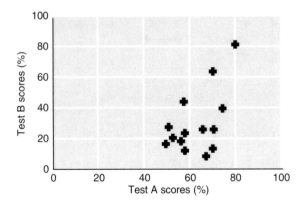

Sector The part or area of a circle which is formed between two radii and the circumference. Each piece of a pie chart is a sector.

Standardised scores Standardised scores are used to enable comparisons on tests between different groups of pupils. Tests are standardised so that the average national standardised scores automatically appear as 100, so it is easy to see whether a pupil is above or below the national average.

Trend The tendency of data to follow a pattern or direction. For example, the trend of the sequence of numbers 4, 7, 11, 13 and 16 is described as 'increasing'.

Value added The relationship between a pupil's previous attainment and their current attainment gives a measure of their progress. Comparing this with the progress made by other pupils gives an impression of the value added by a school. Below is a scatter graph showing progress made by a group of pupils between the end of Key Stage 1 and the end of Key Stage 2:

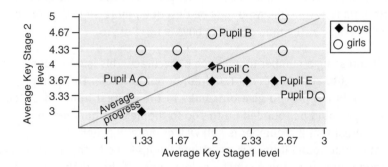

The 'trend line' shows the average performance. Pupils above the line, such as A and B, made better progress than expected; those below the line, such as pupils E and D made less progress than that expected.

How Key Stage 2 relates to Key Stage 1:

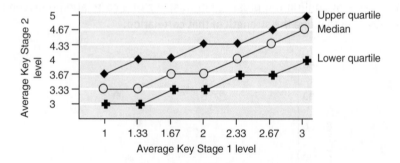

Here the median line shows the national average progress.

Variables The name given to a quantity which can take any one of a given set of values. For example, on a line graph showing distance against time, both distance and time are variables. A variable can also be a symbol which stands for an unknown number, and that can take on different values. For example, the final mark in a test is obtained by a formula using the variables A and B as follows: final mark= (Topic 1 mark x A) + (Topic 2 mark x B).

Weighting A means of attributing relative importance to one or more of a set of results. Each item of data is multiplied by a pre-determined amount to give extra weight to one or more components. For example, marks gained in year 3 of a course may be weighted twice as heavily as those gained in the first two years, in which case those marks would be multiplied by two before finding the total mark for the course.

Whole number A positive integer, e.g. 1, 2, 3, 4, 5.